Richmond Times-Dispatch

THE STORY OF A NEWSPAPER

by Earle Dunford

Cadmus
Publishing

Library of Congress Cataloging-in-Publication Data

Dunford, Earle, 1926

Richmond Times-Dispatch: The Story of a Newspaper

Index

ISBN 0-9629648-9-1

Library of Congress Number 95-071517

Author: Earle Dunford

Managing Editor: Don J. Beville

Editors: Omar Mardan, Forrest Anne Hill, Reyn Kinzey

Text and Cover Designers: Linda B. Berry, Diane L. Butler

Production Supervisor: Laurie Andersen

Printed in the United States of America

10 9 8 7 6 5 4 3 2 1

Distributed by:

The Cadmus Publishing Group

Don J. Beville, Publisher

1974 E. Parham Rd.

Richmond, VA 23228

804/266-0140

To JANE CARROLL DUNFORD,
who never complained about my working long hours
or nights or weekends or holidays.

FOREWORD

Try as he might, no one could write disinterestedly about a newspaper where he was treated well for 36 years. I did not try.

Anyone who completes this work will probably feel I have a favorable opinion, overall, about *The Richmond Times-Dispatch* and the old *Richmond News Leader*. That is correct.

Yet, I felt no inhibition about expressing occasional negative opinions on some aspect or another of both papers. I have followed the advice of Stewart Bryan, the publisher, who told me in 1989 that he wanted a book showing "warts and all." They are here, especially some feuds.

Bryan and Executive Editor Alf Goodykoontz conceived the idea of this newspaper history. (Neither has seen the text prior to publication.) For one thing, D. Tennant Bryan, the former publisher, and Virginius Dabney, the former editor of *The Times-Dispatch,* were already in their 80s; the younger men wanted to get the older men's reminiscences while both were alert. Also, the 150th anniversary of *The Richmond Dispatch,* to which today's *Times-Dispatch* traces its origin, was coming in the year 2000.

Virtually every newsroom employee, past or present, who was interviewed for this work was asked if he or she ever felt "Fourth-Floor pressure" to slant a story or withhold embarrassing facts. (Executive offices are on the fourth floor.) The answer was always a resounding NO.

The style in this work is primarily that of The Associated Press and *The Times-Dispatch*. If there are variances—such as "T-D" instead of *"Times-Dispatch,"* it is because I am quoting directly. If Vietnam sometimes is spelled "Viet Nam," it is because I am quoting directly. Likewise, if some strange usage different from today's appears, it is because I am quoting an article from another era.

There are two canards that newspaper veterans in Richmond have never been able to put down. One is the above-mentioned "Fourth-Floor pressure." The second is that reporters on *The Times-Dispatch* and *The News Leader* were not competitive. Yet, I know that as a reporter I was mortified to be beaten by *The News Leader;* as an editor, I raised hell with reporters who lost stories they should have gotten first.

I worked for four managing editors and two publishers. Each had his foibles, but all treated me fairly. I had serious disagreements at times with all of the ME's, and I argued with three of them. Although I admired the competence of John H. Colburn, the first of the four, I was too intimidated by him to argue. As for publishers, there was no need to argue with Tennant Bryan or his son Stewart, even if arguing with the publisher is considered politic.

The reason is that both let the news departments decide what was news and how to play it. Tennant Bryan rarely set foot in the newsroom and rarely suggested stories, unless some member of "Old Richmond" society had died and Bryan thought a brief obituary was called for. Stewart Bryan was more likely to show up in the newsroom, where, unlike his father, he was greeted by first name. Still, his suggestions for news stories were usually just that. "There may be a story. . . " If reporters and editors checked the situation and were convinced there was no story there, that was it.

I have put together this history by interviewing 65 past and present members of the newspapers' staffs and by doing research. The latter job involved considerable reading of microfilm of old papers and picking through yellowed clippings—some about 140 years old. Most interviews were taped and transcripts were made. A few were done by telephone. At least one interview involved only note-taking because the subject's muttering was too much for the transcriber. I have also read other newspaper histories.

Finally, a very personal observation: Executives will say that combining two newspapers means that a better paper results. Maybe so, but the resulting paper is not as good as the two papers operating separately and competitively. The death of any good paper is a tragedy. *The News Leader* was a good paper.

MY SPECIAL THANKS GO TO OMAR MARDAN—a friend from college days 50 years ago. He made suggestions and edited the manuscript—as he did for many years when he was a news department editor and I was a reporter or junior editor. My thanks go also to the library staff at Richmond Newspapers Inc.—especially Kathleen Albers—and to the staffs at the Virginia Historical Society, the Virginia State Library and the libraries of the University of Virginia and the University of Richmond.

CONTENTS

PROLOGUE

In the early 1950s, a tall, slim, aristocratic, impeccably attired visitor told a monthly staff meeting of *The Richmond Times-Dispatch:*

"I hope you are here because you like it here. I'm here," he continued almost diffidently, "because old Maj. Lewis Ginter wanted to unload *The Richmond Times* on my grandfather."

As one of a dwindling number of the old school of true Southern gentlemen, D. (for David) Tennant Bryan always spoke the truth. That, in fact, was how the Bryan family came to own the Richmond newspaper. Joseph Bryan, Tennant's grandfather, an industrialist concerned mainly with railroads, had been given *The Times* by Ginter, an industrialist concerned mainly with tobacco.

Today, a representative of the fourth generation, J. (for John) Stewart Bryan III, Tennant Bryan's son, is publisher of *The Richmond Times-Dispatch,* the survivor of *The Richmond Times.*

SECTION A

• Publishers

Top: Joseph Bryan, Middle: John Stewart Bryan, Bottom: D. Tennant Bryan (left), and J. Stewart Bryan III.

JOSEPH BRYAN

To trace the history of Richmond's newspapers, one must look foremost at the Bryan family, in particular at Joseph Bryan.

He was the executor of the estates of both his father-in-law, John Stewart, and John's brother Daniel. Both men had achieved considerable wealth. Joseph Bryan was convinced, unlike many other men of property, that the future of the South lay in industrialization. He and Major Lewis Ginter took over a bankrupt firm, Tanner & Delany Engine Co., and transformed it into the Richmond Locomotive Works, which by 1893 had about 800 employees and made 200 locomotives a year.[1]

His industrial interests were steadily aimed southward. He and his associates were key figures in the development of the Georgia Pacific Railway Company, which, they hoped, would link the Deep South with the West Coast. Joseph Bryan was also prominent in the affairs of the Danville and Terminal railroad systems and of the Sloss-Sheffield Steel and Iron Company, the most important industry in Birmingham.[2]

His goal of a vibrant, industrial South—adhering to traditional capitalistic principles but independent of the North—was not achieved for various reasons, mostly the depression of the 1890s.[3]

Joseph Bryan considered himself "first and foremost a Virginian," but when he died November 20, 1908, the Birmingham *Age-Herald* called him "one of Birmingham's most ardent prophets." Both papers of that city carried his obituary on Page One.[4]

Joseph Bryan was born in 1845 on his father's plantation in Gloucester County, Virginia. His father took him 11 years later to Episcopal High School in Alexandria, which was "the beginning of five years of almost unbroken unhappiness," Joseph's son, John Stewart Bryan, wrote in an adoring biography of his father.[5] Whippings, cold weather and beatings by fellow students were much of the cause of Joseph Bryan's unhappiness.

In October 1862, he entered the University of Virginia, where enrollment was down to 46 from 604 the previous year.[6] Turning 18, he left the university and served the Confederacy with the Richmond Howitzers and Mosby's Rangers.[7]

After the war, he returned to Charlottesville and received his law degree in 1868. He met his wife-to-be, Isobel Lamont Stewart, daughter of John Stewart, a client, at their home Brook Hill just north of Richmond, and they married in 1871.

"Establishing residence there," wrote W. David Lewis, a historian, "Bryan moved his law practice to Richmond and earned a reputation representing various railroad and canal companies. Within a decade his abilities, family connections, and ceaseless devotion to work had set him firmly on the road to wealth and power."[8]

John Stewart Bryan, recounting the postwar adversity of his ancestors, wrote, "The Bryans were too much committed to the Confederate cause to escape their share of the universal ruin of patriots. The younger sons of John Randolph Bryan were among the fortunate few who procured a college education in the years after the war, but of the four sons who emerged from that dark era, Joseph Bryan was the only one able in his lifetime to regain the economic place that all would have held as a matter of course if the war had not destroyed the fortunes of their father."[9]

A historian at the State University of New York at Plattsburgh, James M. Lindgren, phrased it more succinctly. "Bryan lamented that Virginia's traditions—economic orthodoxy, elite rule, lower-class deference and black subservience—had eroded with the defeat of 1865 and the ensuing hard times."[10]

Lindgren stresses Bryan's reliance on "Christian stewardship that would give Virginia an enlightened hegemony by a refined capitalist elite." He added, "Joseph Bryan's ancestry and cultural upbringing established the context for his devotion to the traditional ideals of elite rule, social hierarchy, and political order."[11]

Tradition also meant good manners. John Stewart Bryan recalled a letter he received from his father after a Christmas party. It read, "The fact that you were born a gentleman doesn't even give you a prima facie presumption that you will die one. You have got blood in your veins that can carry you to Hell on so many different routes that you will be lucky if you escape at all. To be a gentleman is an all-day job every day."[12]

When Joseph Bryan took over Major Ginter's *Richmond Times,* he inherited a money-loser that also had union printers. Bryan brought in Mergenthaler Linotype machines—the first publisher in the South to do so. *The Dispatch* did the same, and the union struck both papers.

Members of the union were allowed "to work in their offices, and the union declared both papers 'fair and open.' No contract was again entered into by the union until 1917," wrote John Stewart Bryan.[13] Another first for Bryan in Richmond was the publication of a two-color Confederate flag on the front page of *The Evening Leader* on Memorial Day 1899. (Bryan had secretly been printing that paper for three years.)

Like most publishers, the Bryans over the years have had their differences with unions. The first Bryan, Joseph, met his initial problem head-on. When pressmen demanded higher wages in 1896, he told them, "I have had this paper since 1889[14], and I have paid good wages every week; you neither knew nor cared what it cost me to meet those charges, yet now, because you think you can extort money from me, you threaten a strike. Before I will yield to any such coercion, I will take an ax and break that press to pieces and throw it into the James River. And let me tell you one thing. After the battle of Spottsylvania I had no food for two days, and I found a dead Yankee who had some rotten pork in his hand; I took a ramrod and fished it out and ate it, and can do it again. And if you can't do it, don't go to war with me."[15] They didn't.

Bryan found no inconsistency in publishing newspapers and holding political office. He ran three times in the 1870s for a seat in the General Assembly and lost each time. But he did become a member of the State Democratic Committee. There he found himself in opposition to much of what other Democrats favored in 1896: populism, the presidential candidacy of William Jennings Bryan and the candidate's "free silver" position.

That position during the 1896 election led Carter Glass of the *Lynchburg News* to call Bryan "the ring-master of the McKinley side show in Virginia" and *The Richmond Times* "the organ of the bond sharks and money jobbers."[16]

Bryan's determined position on maintenance of the gold standard and his feuding with Virginia Democrats who did not entertain elitist ideas cost the *Times* in circulation. It was in 1896 that Bryan quietly began printing the *Manchester Leader.* John Stewart Bryan says that it "deliberately set out to be a friendly journal and not an organ of economic and political purity [but it] achieved a startling success for those days."[17] *The Leader's* circulation grew from 13,000 in 1896 to 22,000 by the time of the Spanish-American War two years later.

"The colorless *Leader,*" says John Stewart Bryan, "was really intended to hold readers which the crusading *Times* had lost, and it did. *The Times,* however, never abated its opinions nor qualified its expression."

Joseph Bryan's feuds with Virginia Democrats in no way meant he was a Republican. That party, says James M. Lindgren, "stood for principles and programs that Bryan thought repugnant, including black civil rights, a protective tariff, national banks, and centralized government."[16]

Developments beyond the borders of the United States forced Bryan to change his ideas on several fronts. He initially opposed war with Spain but later endorsed the effort. Having earlier opposed American imperialism, he also conceded that markets as far away as Asia were important to Richmond merchants and manufacturers; so a "civilizing mission" for America and for business was a necessity. "What brought about the reversal in editorial policy at *The Times,*" says Lindgren, "was Bryan's recognition that social stability depended on economic expansion."[19]

He was not for black equality with whites, although he became ambivalent on increased rights for blacks. Realizing that economic prosperity depended on a better deal for both races, he campaigned for a secret ballot open to blacks and whites. "Exclusionary constitutional revisions, he said, "would be acceptable only 'as a last extremity.'"

Yet, in 1898, he went back to the white supremacy position in a new state constitution. He said Virginia faced "threats of discord and blood-shed" and "cannot carry this black burden any longer and maintain our political integrity'."[20]

As vehement as Bryan was in support of traditional capitalism and as involved as he was in railroading, he thought all things had their limits. When railroad interests tried to get their lobbyist, Thomas Staples Martin, elected to the United States Senate, Bryan's *Times* called for a government investigation of railroads' policies. Bryan wrote a businessman in Lynchburg, "We are for RRs, but in their place—& not ruling in matters of State. The condition of things in which we find ourselves is horrible to contemplate. Two or three RR officials practically dictating the policy & naming all the officers of the State."[21]

In 1904, in a letter to John Stewart Bryan, then vice president of *The Times-Dispatch,* Joseph seemed to stress principle above profit. The question was whether to print an anti-union advertisement of the Kellogg Postum Cereal Co. Critics might reason that the advice was in line with his antipathy to unions.

His advice: "I think you will do the spirit of the paper and its corps more harm by refusing to publish this ad, than any benefit (real or supposed) derived from its non-publication would offset. You will lose your own grip from the consciousness that the refusal has been from harm to yourself rather than a fear of harm to justice. There has been a distinct inclination by *The Times-Dispatch* to court the labor unions, and it has gone far enough. I have no fight with them, but I shall be impartial and treat both sides with justice."[22]

In an earlier letter to his son, Joseph Bryan laid out his philosophy about newspapermen. "I have been a soldier, a mule trader, a lawyer, a railroad president and builder, and still am a director; I have mined coal and iron, operated pig iron smelters, built locomotives, developed real estate, run streetcar lines; I have had intimate association with bankers, brokers,

Home Edition

THE NEWS LEADER

28,116

VOLUME XII. NO. 94. RICHMOND AND MANCHESTER, VA., WEDNESDAY AFTERNOON, APRIL 18, 1906. ONE CENT.

ROARING FLAMES FAST BURNING SAN FRANCISCO

Wrecking Earthquake Is Followed by Raging Flames That Are Rapidly Consuming Whole Business Section of City.

ROM WATER FRONT FIRE PUSHES UNCHECKED TOWARD PALACE HOTEL

ITY HALL, COSTING SEVEN MILLION, AMONG GREAT BUILDINGS RUINED

21 BODIES HAVE BEEN TAKEN TO CITY MORGUE

UNION SQUARE, SHOWING ST. FRANCIS' HOTEL.

LATER DETAILS OF EARTHQUAKE AND FIRE IN SAN FRANCISCO

PALACE HOTEL CATCHES FIRE

Destruction of Business Part of City Seems Now Inevitable. Spreckels, Phelan and O'Farrell Buildings Prey to Flames.

400 BODIES AT 11 A. M.

POSTAL MEN DRIVEN OUT

LOOKING TOWARDS MARKET ST. DOWN KEARNEY

MR. AND MRS. LOWENBERG HAVE LEFT STRICKEN CITY

CALL BUILDING IS DESTROYED

WIRES NOW SAFE IN FERRY HOUSE

TALL DOMED BUILDING IS CALL BUILDING

SAN FRANCISCO CITY HALL

MANCHESTER - Page 2
PETERSBURG - Page 4

The News Leader *of 1906, with a circulation of only 28,116, went all out in its coverage of the San Francisco earthquake and fires.*

doctors, lawyers and newspapermen, and have taken an active part in the work of the Episcopal Church. So I think I have sufficient background to form an opinion, and I unhesitatingly put lawyers at the top and newspapermen at the bottom of all the men that I have ever known, and preachers next to newspapermen." The son, a lawyer, wanted to know, therefore, why his father wanted him to take over the family newspapers and not practice law.

"Because, my son," he replied, "you have a weak stomach, and it takes a powerful digestion to stand the strain of battle in court all day and writing briefs all night."[23]

JOHN STEWART BRYAN

If Joseph Bryan was known as an industrialist and publisher, his son, John Stewart Bryan, who took control of Richmond's daily newspapers in 1908 at the death of his father, was known as much for his endeavors in education as in publishing.

Four generations of Bryans have published Richmond papers, and John Stewart Bryan surely was the most intellectual of the group. He was rector of the University of Virginia for two years and president of the College of William and Mary for eight.

Editorialists noted at his death that he was intimate with the Greek and Latin masters[24] and that at the Yorktown sesquicentennial in 1931, he delivered an entire address in French.[25]

In 1936, he wrote nine articles for *The News Leader* on a tour of Latin America. He was appalled that there was virtually no "evidence of what we are trained to understand as freedom."

"The appalling situation in South America," he wrote, "is primarily due to the fact that the people have turned over to selfish interests the duty that should have been performed by an aroused citizenship."[26]

Bryan plunged headfirst into civic affairs—local and national. He had been a delegate to the Democratic National Convention in Baltimore that nominated Woodrow Wilson in 1912.

Although his papers supported Franklin D. Roosevelt for president each of the four times he ran, Bryan could be caustic about what he didn't like in Washington. In 1935, he called on his fellow newspaper publishers to crusade against the "powerful and insidious mechanism" of government propaganda.

There were 53 publicity agents in federal departments, he said, adding: "Wherein does it differ one bit whether it is done by Stalin or by Mussolini or by Hitler and Goering, as long as it is done."[27]

Newsroom of The News Leader *in 1924 on Eighth Street, just before the paper moved to Fourth Street.*

At his death nine years later, however, tributes came from President Roosevelt and Labor Secretary Frances Perkins, as well as from John D. Rockefeller Jr., Walter Lippmann and David Lawrence.

John Stewart Bryan may not have been the industrialist that his father was, but he was not averse to building a newspaper empire. He and S. Emory Thomason of Chicago gained control in the late 1920s of the *Chicago Journal,* the *Greensboro* (N.C.) *Record* and the *Tampa Tribune.*

When questions arose about the financing of those purchases and their relationship to International Paper and Power Co., the Federal Trade Commission started investigating. *The Times-Dispatch* then jumped into the fray and carried a lead story on May 10, 1929, that equaled almost anything written in the "new journalism" style 40 years later.

Bryan was so incensed by the story in the paper that his family had sold in 1914 that he sued *The Times-Dispatch* for $500,000.

The story that upset Bryan had the byline of Basil Manly, *"Times-Dispatch* special correspondent."

It began, "This was comic opera day at the Federal Trade Commission's power trust investigation as two young men told how the International Paper and Power Co. had played Santa Claus for them in the realization of their dream to acquire a chain of Southern newspapers.

"The principal actors in this comedy were William Lavarre and Harold Hall, who told the story as witnesses under oath; Archibald R. Graustein, president of the International Paper and Power Co.; S.E. Thomason and John Stewart Bryan, two other newspaper publishers, who were also acting for the paper company in this play of cross currents."

Manly's story told of two young men with no capital but sure that "somewhere in big-hearted New York they would find somebody to buy newspapers for them." Manly referred to Hall, business manager of the New York Telegram and president of the Scripps-Howard Supply Co., as "a young man who wears horn-rimmed glasses and looks something like Harold Lloyd [an American movie actor]." Manly told how Lavarre had hunted diamonds in South America and Africa for four years after finishing Harvard, "returning to New York some three years ago to become a high pressure newspaper circulation builder."

Manly went on to recite how Lavarre and Hall, with financial aid from the paper company, began touring the South, looking for papers although they had "no options, no capital and no experience in operating Southern newspapers."

While Lavarre and Hall were prospecting in the South, Manly wrote, they found that Bryan and Thomason were also searching for papers and were being financed by the same paper company. "President Graustein's right hand apparently did not know what the left hand was doing," wrote Manly.

He concluded, "Now every newspaper man in Washington is wondering why he too did not believe in Santa Claus and get his help to buy a few newspapers in the North, East, South or West with a drawing account . . . and unlimited expenses."

Graustein had testified May 1 that he had not met any editors of the newspapers in which his company had invested and wanted in no way to influence their news and editorial policies.

Two weeks later, Thomason said he and Bryan had bought the Greensboro and Tampa papers before any transaction with International Paper and Power Co. but had obtained backing from the company for the purchase of the *Chicago Journal*. He conceded that it was "a stupid and foolish thing" not to make public earlier International Paper and Power's financial interest in the *Journal*, but he had told executives of competing Chicago newspapers, he said.

In any case, Thomason testified, International Paper and Power was "just like a bank and they have no more control over the newspaper and its securities than banks have over securities which they hold as collateral."

On May 15, Bryan filed notice in Richmond's Law and Equity Court that he was suing the owners of *The Times-Dispatch* and Manly for $500,000. But apparently he calmed down. On June 1, the suit was dismissed by direction of the plaintiff's attorney, court records show.

Bryan and Thomason had long been friends—even before the joint search for new newspapers. In a *News Leader* editorial on June 18, 1925, Bryan said that the consideration of Thomason as president of the University of Michigan was "one of the most encouraging and stimulating evidences of real wisdom and insight on the part of the American people." He didn't get the job.

When Thomason died in 1944, editorial tribute appeared in both Richmond papers. Bryan's editorial in *The Times-Dispatch* said Thomason "epitomized freedom of the press and freedom of opportunity in America." Without mentioning himself, Bryan noted the success of Thomason "and his partner" in acquiring papers in Tampa, Greensboro and Chicago.

In October of that year, Bryan died after a couple of years of failing health. *The News Leader* editorial page said, ". . . As he lies today in the library of Laburnum, under the picture of his father, there are no secrets to hide, no vices to ignore, no basic weakness of character to gloss over with a varnish of shining words. Those of us who were awed in his living presence can look at him in triumphant death and we need not apologize for anything he did, as for aught that he was. . . .

"During the 44 years of his direction of Richmond newspapers, with his father for eight years and on his own account for 36, he witnessed half a dozen wrecks on the treacherous shoals of journalism in our city, but he steered always a clean, progressive course."

Tennant Bryan was chosen by Richmond Newspapers' directors to succeed his father as president and publisher. But as a Page One *News Leader* story explained on November 6, he couldn't take over right away. The directors gave him a leave of absence, since he was on active duty with the Navy.

D. TENNANT BRYAN

Like his father and grandfather and like many other scions of distinguished Virginia families, D. Tennant Bryan attended the University of Virginia. Unlike his father and grandfather, he did not graduate. He didn't come close to graduating.

"After about three years and two summer schools, I had something like three credits and realized the university life was not to be," he said.[28]

Did he have a good time?

"Yes," he said. "I had a good time except explaining it to my dear father when I got home. That was not much fun. But anyway, he tried to be understanding, and it was hard for him because he had been a hell of a good student himself."[29]

He also had been rector of the university.

Tennant Bryan had wanted originally to be a surgeon like his uncle, Robert Coalter. But, said Bryan, "He told me my skin was too dry. Surgeons in those days didn't wear rubber gloves. He said I'd be washing my hands so often the skin would come off."[30]

Having failed to acquit himself as a student at Mr. Jefferson's university, Bryan returned to Richmond and joined *The News Leader* as a reporter in October 1928. "I became an honest-to-God reporter," he recalled 64 years later.[31] "I was sent to do all kinds of different things that I never knew had to be done, and I loved it." After a couple of years, he moved to the circulation department. Or, as he said, he was "put into circulation" by his father.

"I didn't have anywhere else to go," he said. "I'm not sure anyone else would have hired me." He saw himself as the prodigal son, who said, "Father, make me as one of thy hired servants."[32]

"I no longer wanted to be called 'thy son,'" he said. "So make me as one of thy hired servants."

The boss of that new young man in circulation was Lee Sullivan, who had been brought to *The News Leader* from the *Chicago Tribune,* where he was assistant circulation manager. Everything was fine between John Stewart Bryan, the publisher, and his circulation manager until 1932, when Publisher Bryan decided that there had to be a reduction in payroll.

"I didn't agree with him at the time," Tennant Bryan said, "but that didn't make any difference."[33] The publisher and his colleagues—with the exception of Sullivan—agreed on the course to follow. Sullivan, recalled Bryan, said, "he'd come for a certain price and that he would not work for less than that. That was $10,000 a year. I remember that very well indeed."

Thus did Tennant Bryan become circulation manager of *The News Leader.* According to Bryan, Sullivan told the publisher, "'We've got some real good people down here who have a lot more experience than Tennant has, but he won't steal nothing.' He wasn't so sure about all the others. So they gave me the job, and I didn't steal anything."

Bryan moved up to vice president, assistant treasurer and business manager of *The News Leader* in 1934. Two years later he added the title of general manager. He held those posts until he became a naval officer in World War II. His next step was the big one—to publisher. John Stewart Bryan died October 16, 1944, a week before his 73rd birthday. Tennant, still on active duty, was named to succeed him.

By that time, John Dana Wise, who had been publisher of *The Times-Dispatch,* was vice president and general manager of Richmond Newspapers Inc. Wise had engineered the repurchase by the Bryans of majority interest in *The Times-Dispatch* and the creation in 1940 of that new corporation.

Bryan said that Wise persuaded Colonel Samuel Slover, principal owner of *The Times-Dispatch,* and two members of the Lewis family in Norfolk that "there wasn't going to be room enough for two highly competitive newspapers in a town that was not growing very much at that time, and that was Richmond.

"And he was right. But both sides resisted hell out of it. We resisted; *The Times-Dispatch* ownership resisted it. We didn't want it. We wanted to be competitive."[34]

Wise was highly controversial at Richmond Newspapers Inc. and elsewhere. Virginius Dabney, editor of *The Times-Dispatch,* disliked him intensely. Bryan considered him a born newspaperman and admired him greatly.

Wise was a self-made man who had been a Navy boxing champion in World War I and who made a mark in the business end of newspapers in Columbia, South Carolina. By the time Bryan ended his Navy service, Wise was running the business end of Richmond Newspapers Inc.

Like Wise before him, Alan S. Donnahoe ran the day-to-day business operations of Richmond Newspapers Inc. During the 1971 strike by the printers, Bryan, his wife and his daughter Polly worked briefly in the composing room—in a way showing the flag for other members of the corporation.

Donnahoe spent little time in the composing room, but he called the shots in dealing with the union. As the largest stockholder, Bryan could implement any policy he chose. He was the boss, but he didn't exercise all of a boss' prerogatives. He let Donnahoe do that.

• • •

Both in the office and away from the office, Bryan's manners were as impeccable as his clothing. He seemed not to know how to be impolite. Even those who disagreed with him on many things described him as gracious.

Bryan knew that Jane Dunford, wife of *The Times-Dispatch* city editor, was fluent in several foreign languages, He once asked her to translate some remarks he had to make into French.

She did so and they looked over the result. ("I think his French is as good as mine," she said later.) Nevertheless, several days later, Bryan telephoned and, after Mrs. Dunford declined any payment for her work, inquired, "Do you enjoy spirits?"

"Why, yes," she said and listed bourbon when he asked what kind.

Two days later, Bryan—impeccably attired as always, this time wearing a houndstooth jacket, gray flannels and highly polished tassel loafers—left his Mercedes with motor running at the curb and rang the Dunfords' doorbell.

The spirits he brought were a fifth of 100-proof, 16-year-old, bottled-in-bond bourbon in a bottle numbered by the distiller and wrapped in mesh.

• • •

The news staffs on both papers always appreciated that Bryan, fiercely conservative politically, never interfered with how stories were played. He was almost apologetic about even calling the news rooms—with certain exceptions. Those were the deaths of socially prominent people, especially an elderly one whom he thought the editors (mostly not from the same social milieu or even from Virginia) might not recognize. Usually, the staff agreed even in private conversation that the old geezer probably was worth "a couple of grafs."

Once, Bryan called the author when he was *Times-Dispatch* city editor, to tell him of the death of a servant, "a footman," Bryan said, for some old-line Richmonder. Trying not to sound remotely insubordinate, Dunford wondered how many readers had ever heard of the servant. "Mr. Bryan," he said, "it's your newspaper, of course, and we can do an obit on anyone you say, but this sounds a little Uncle Tom-ish."

"No, no; it's not my newspaper. It's the readers' newspaper," he said. "And you just may be right. But I've promised [Mr. Whoever] that we'd do an obit. So, I think a couple of paragraphs would do just fine."

Two paragraphs ran, perhaps the last time that the death of a footman was chronicled in a Richmond newspaper.

• • •

On July 1, 1990, Bryan stepped down as chairman of Media General, the holding company that was the parent of the papers in Richmond, Tampa and Winston-Salem. He turned over the title to his son, Stewart, who already was president and chief executive officer of the corporation and publisher of *The Times-Dispatch* and *The News Leader.* In an interview with Gregory Gilligan of *The Times-Dispatch,* published July 1, the elder Bryan said, "I haven't had a very exciting career. I've just had a lackluster career. I wouldn't even call it a career.

"I've done nothing except follow, as accurately as I could, the pathway that was laid out for me. I haven't had an original thought in 83 years."

JOHN STEWART BRYAN III

The two-column headline—

Richmonder, 3 Others
Hurt Near Roanoke

in *The Times-Dispatch* of October 30, 1959, and the Associated Press story beneath it were similar to many that readers saw every day.

"Two Hollins College girls and their companions—one of them a Richmonder—were injured when their convertible careened off a curve on the Woodrum Airport road near Roanoke and overturned late Thursday night."

But the second paragraph hit home at Richmond Newspapers Inc. It identified the Richmonder, who had serious injuries, as "John Stewart Bryan III, 21, a University of Virginia student and son of D. Tennant Bryan, publisher of *The Richmond Times-Dispatch* and *The Richmond News Leader*."

The seven inches of type—more than was normally devoted to out-of-town accidents in which no one was killed—quoted police as saying Bryan was the driver of the car that went off the road and skidded along the shoulder for about 210 feet before overturning. Three of the four occupants including Bryan were pinned beneath the car. Workers on a city water truck helped to right the car so rescuers could get to the injured.

A telephone call to the state desk of *The Times-Dispatch* was the reason for the detailed account. Jack R. Hunter, who spent 41 years at the paper before retiring as state-city news editor, recalls answering the call from Tennant Bryan.

"He told me about an event at the airport in Roanoke," said Hunter, "and made clear that he wanted a report in the newspaper. It was a minor little event that we ordinarily would not have carried. It was a minor little event involving his son. And to this day, it stands out in my mind as one of the great evidences that I personally experienced [of] the integrity of the publisher and the integrity of the newspaper and the honesty of its product."[35]

The News Leader also carried a detailed story on the crash, and both papers carried other stories with every minor development. By the time the case was concluded in court—with Bryan pleading guilty to reckless driving, being fined $250, losing his license for six months and receiving a suspended 60-day jail sentence—each Richmond paper had carried five stories.

It wasn't the first time that Bryan's traffic problems had been exposed to the public. *The News Leader* reported June 10, 1958, that he had been fined $75 and lost his driving permit for 60 days after a conviction of reckless driving. He'd been charged with going more than 100 miles an hour through a state police radar checkpoint.

Did the papers overdo his trouble in 1959—with five stories apiece? Did he feel crucified? he was asked in an interview.

"I was always brought up to believe," he replied, "that if you did something wrong, it was going to be in the paper. If you did something right, it probably wouldn't be in the papers."

Bryan acknowledged that he was "pretty well banged up" by the accident and couldn't think well for a couple of weeks, but he never gave the coverage much thought. "It certainly never bothered me," he said.[36]

Bryan volunteered that he was charged with drunken driving in Tampa in 1971. He was driving Red Pittman's car. Pittman was general manager of the Tampa papers.

"We had had a session with Alan [Donnahoe, Media General executive] earlier in the day, and he told us neither one of us had any sense, so we decided to go out and drink whiskey."

The morning after he was picked up, Bryan told the managing editors of *The Tribune* and *The Times* what happened and said, "You all do what you think is right." They decided to see which paper's reporters picked up the item, but no one did until the case went to court several months later and the charge was uncontested.

For the record, Bryan said he felt the publisher's arrest on such a charge should be in the paper, in the Metro section, but not on Page One as Eugene Patterson, publisher of Tampa's competing *St. Petersburg Times,* decreed should be the case when he was charged with drunken driving. Front page play like that is "grandstanding," said Bryan.

Whether he was publisher in Tampa or publisher in Richmond, "the part of the newspaper that I love the most," said Bryan, "is the news side—much more than the editorial side, much more than the advertising and the circulation side, although I've worked in all of them and they're all fun."[37]

After graduation from the University of Virginia and service in the Marine Corps, Bryan went to law school as "a way to prolong not going to work," but was bored by the routine. He told Tennant Bryan, "I'd like to go to work in the newspaper business, but I don't want to work for you."[38]

His first newspaper job was at the *Burlington* (Vermont) *Free Press,* where he sold advertising for two and a half years. Then he was a reporter on the *Tampa Times,* for almost three years. He joined *The Times-Dispatch* in 1967 as a reporter. The idea was that he'd learn about the area from the news side, then switch to editorial and help Virginius Dabney.

But there were problems in Tampa and he went there as assistant to the president, Alan S. Donnahoe. Up the ladder he went as vice president, executive vice president and, in 1976, publisher.

On January 1, 1978, he took over as publisher in Richmond.

Although Donnahoe had been president of the subsidiary publishing the Tampa papers, his office remained in Richmond. When Stewart Bryan took over as publisher in 1978, he had to deal regularly with Media General's president and chief executive officer, Donnahoe.

"Alan was not an easy man to get along with," said Bryan. "He had his ideas and he really didn't want many ideas from other people."

Bryan said in 1992 that Donnahoe was "a very bright fellow, but in the last two years that I've had this job [chairman] what I've spent most of my time doing is selling eight or nine of the companies that he bought, or closing them down. So I don't think our relationship was the smoothest. I don't think Alan liked the idea of another Bryan coming along. I think he sort of had the idea that maybe Media General would become a true public company and might even be sold one day to a bigger company. And that idea just didn't appeal much to me."[39]

Among the companies sold off in recent years were Onduline, a roofing manufacturer (1986), Media General Broadcast Services (1988), the Pomona mill of Garden State Paper Co. (1989), Highlander Publications and Golden West Publishing, which together published 36 weekly community newspapers (1990), Cliggott Publishing, which turned out medical magazines (1991), Technical Information Distribution Service (1991) and a minority interest in a Mexican newsprint mill (1994).

In 1994, Media General also sold its interest in Garden State Newspapers Inc. and bought 40 percent of the common stock of Denver Newspapers Inc., publisher of the *Denver Post.*

SECTION B

• Origins

The Times.

DAILY DISPATCH.

RICHMOND, VA., SATURDAY MORNING, APRIL 1, 1865.

EXTRA THE NEWS LEADER

EXCLUSIVE ASSOCIATED PRESS REPORT.

RICHMOND, VA., FRIDAY, MAY 7, 1915.

LUSITANIA TORPEDOED AND SU

TRIO TO FRAME

BERLIN WARNS GER

The Times Dispatch

Hundreds of Bargains are offered daily by Richmond's leading merchants in the Ten-Dee Want Ad. columns.

Promptness in Result is an established characteristic of the Ten-Dee Want Ads. Use them and see.

WHOLE NUMBER 16,593.

RICHMOND, VA., FRIDAY, JULY 15, 1904.

PRICE TWO CENTS.

SUMMARY OF THE DAY'S NEWS

OOM PAUL DEAD AFTER LONG AND FULL CAREER

Boer Leaders Mourn Death of Kruger.

He Had Been Gradually Failing for Some Months.

BE BURIED IN TRANSVAAL

Remains Will be Taken to South African Land He Formerly Ruled.

YIN KOW IN HANDS OF JAPS

An Important Strategic Point Taken Yesterday

NO MORE LIGHT ON JAPANESE LOSS

Incoming Reports Both Confirm and Deny the Late Rumors.

KUROPATKIN SAID TO BE IN DESPERATE STRAITS

Must Face Big Army or Retire From Southern Manchuria. Heavy Fighting Reported From Several Points. The Advance on Ta Tche Kiao.

CORRUPTION IS CHARGED

Action of Republican Chairman Williams Severely Condemned by Several Members.

HIS REMOVAL IS ASKED

FIVE ARE DROWNED WHILE IN BATHING

FABLES AND POLITICS.

There was once a tailor who made imperial robes for a king. As he was sewing a large, but thoroughly gentle elephant pushed his trunk through the window just to see what the King's tailor was doing. "Look at your master, you frumpy old furnisher of campaign necessities," said the tailor, and without a moment's hesitation he stuck the elephant with a needle.

(To be Continued.)

Distressing Accident to Party at Edgewater.

THREE SISTERS ARE AMONG THE VICTIMS

A Mother and Little Child of Westmoreland County Complete the Number.

WENT BEYOND DEPTH; COULD NOT BE REACHED

Willing Hands Near by, But Could Not Get to Them in Time—Great Sorrow in Washington, Where Misses Kemon Lived.

THE BIG CHIEFS PUT HEADS TOGETHER

OUTBURST OF WILD FURY

Enraged Mob Makes Demonstration Against Men Taken From Norfolk.

SHOTS FIRED AT THE CAR

"All Is Harmony Now," Says McCarren, of New York.

JUDGE PARKER MAKES SPEECH

Responds to Rousing Ovation Given Him, But Does Not Touch Politics

PRESIDENT WILL HEAR THE MINERS

GRAFTS PIG SKIN ON LADY'S SHOULDER

THE DISPATCH

The origin of the present *Richmond Times-Dispatch* goes back to 1815, but it was not until 1850 that an ancestor bore the name Dispatch. It was *The Richmond Dispatch,* founded by James A. Cowardin and William H. Davis. They had tried unsuccessfully to breathe life into *The Times and Compiler,* which traced its ancestry to *The Richmond Compiler* in 1815.[40]

The *Compiler* failed about 1853; meanwhile, Cowardin, who had tried banking and brokerage, had joined with Davis to start the *Dispatch* in 1850. The paper was unaffiliated politically, although Cowardin was a Whig member of the House of Delegates from 1853 to 1855.[41]

Success came quickly to the *Dispatch,* situated at 3 Governor Street, north of 12th and Main Streets. By January 1852, the paper bragged in a notice to advertisers at the top of the editorial page, that *The Dispatch* had a circulation "three times as large as that of any other Daily paper in the city of Richmond" and therefore was "greatly superior" to any other as a medium of advertising. That may well have been true, but the honor of being the pre-eminent paper of the city at the time belonged to the *Richmond Examiner.*

The Dispatch increased from five to six columns in the first month of 1852, because of the amount of advertising, and apologized editorially for the move. "We much preferred the smaller size," said the paper, "but could no longer adhere to it in justice to the public nor to ourselves.

"We shall now have more room for our advertising customers and more for ourselves; but still, let us assure them, that our room is not so spacious as to allow any long stereotyped advertisements to render our columns hideous by their everlasting occupation of one locality. The advertising in *The Dispatch* must be brief, pithy, and often changed, to accommodate itself to our space, and this is the only kind of advertising that is worth a rush to the advertiser."

Advertising and news departments may have been separate in the middle of the 19th century, but the ads were not relegated to secondary display status and, indeed, often dominated front pages.

In issue No. 170 of its first year (May 13, 1851), *The Dispatch* devoted all of its first two columns to ads, featuring the Monongalia and Delaware lotteries and the coming Broad Rock Springs races. Column three was headed by an ad for Ayer's Cherry Pectoral, "for the cure of coughs, colds, hoarseness, bronchitis, whooping cough, croup, asthma and consumption." Only column four of the five-column paper was devoted exclusively to news, this day including "Further News by the Europa." There were items from Britain, Ireland, France, Portugal, and Austria, Prussia, Russia and Italy— "With regard to their governments, we have many rumors."

The inside pages of the four-page sheet had as much advertising as news, with the latter including a report on "The Accident at the Coal Pits— Eight persons (one white man and seven blacks), lost their lives by the explosion at the Chesterfield Clover (known as Cox's) Coal Pits on Friday night last between 12 and 1 o'clock."

One-column classified ads, some as brief as a half-inch, were spread over much of the front page in those days. On January 14,1852, for example, the briefest of ads announced: "FOR SALE—A good MILCH COW.—Apply to O.A. Strecker." Accompanying the text was a small line drawing of a cow.

The front page also gave prominence to legal notices of dissolution of a partnership and creation by the principals of new partnerships.

Another ad, typifying the period, read: "Servants for hire—I have the following servants for hire, viz: two boys from the country, about 14 years of age, suitable for a brick yard or tobacco factory; also two girls about the same age, accustomed to house work, also one woman with three children, and one old man suitable for gardening or light work.—James T. Sutton, Jr., Corner of Bank and 11th streets.

"N.B. Also for sale, about $2,000 worth of Virginia Central Railroad Bonds, paying 6 per cent interest semi-annually; due, 1860."

Editorially, the paper was fiercely conservative. An 1852 editorial, entitled "Slavery an Economic Necessity," said that free labor could not turn out consumer goods as well as slave labor. It called Abraham Lincoln "a vulgar tycoon" and said at his inauguration, "We will stand in a solid phalanx in defense of the independence and sovereignty and the sanctity of Southern soil."[42]

In 1859, John Hammersley bought a half-interest in *The Dispatch,* which two years earlier had prospered so much that it increased its page size

The Dispatch Building at the northwest corner of 12th and Main Streets was the home of the paper from 1868 to 1900.

again, this time from six to seven columns. Hammersley and Cowardin were joint publishers until May 5, 1862, when no name appeared in the masthead. Hammersley then ran the Union blockade in 1864 and brought back new presses from England. Before he left, he sold half of his interest to James W. Lewellen.[43] Presumably the blockade was run through Wilmington, North Carolina, the only Southern port open to the Confederacy in 1864.

That year the paper defended Jews against charges of speculating. It continued coverage of the war, calling Union soldiers "thieves and cut-throats."

But the end was near. *The Dispatch* was operating out of a building at the northeast corner of 13th and Main Streets. On Saturday, April 1, 1865, the *Dispatch* began its account of news from "the Richmond and Petersburg lines," like this:

"All continues, and seems likely to continue, quiet on the north side of the James river. The enemy are expanding their activity on our right.

"Immediately at Petersburg, in front of General Gordon's lines, there has been no stir since the *feu d' eufer* of Wednesday night. The performances of that night are quite sufficient to last a considerable length of time. The heroes of that dark and sulphurous, but bloodless, field can afford to rest on their laurels for the present. General Lee, in his official report of this affair, which was received late Thursday night, and published yesterday, says:

"'General Gordon reports that the enemy, at 11 o'clock P.M. yesterday, advanced against a part of his line, defended by Brigadier-General Lewis, but was repulsed.'

"We have quoted this dispatch to call attention to the fact that, whereas it says the enemy advanced at 11 o'clock Wednesday night, the cannonade, as every one in Petersburg and Richmond, who is not deaf, knows, began before 10 o'clock, and was at its fiercest before 11. The report to the contrary notwithstanding, we cannot help adhering to our opinion, expressed yesterday, that there was no attack at all. Of course we do not think our officers willfully misrepresented the case, but that, in the shadow of that darkest of nights, they were mistaken. We look with interest to the Yankee account of the affair, which we will receive to-morrow. We should not be surprised if they have a flaming account of a repulse of the rebels, with the usual 'horrible slaughter'."

When "to-morrow" came, President Jefferson Davis was called from Sunday worship at St. Paul's Episcopal Church—only a few blocks from the White House of the Confederacy—and told the Confederate government should leave Richmond. Despite the bravado of the *Dispatch,* defeat was imminent.

The April 1 issue of *The Dispatch* was its last for more than eight months. The paper already had cut back from seven to six columns and since March was publishing only half-sheets. Inflation had driven the cost of a single copy to 50 cents. In the great fire of April 2-3 that wiped out the business section of Richmond, *The Dispatch's* office also was destroyed.[44]

Lester J. Cappon's history of Virginia newspapers says, "When General Lee surrendered at Appomattox on April Ninth, the Virginia press had already reached its nadir, and during most of that month of 1865, journalism in the Old Dominion was virtually at a standstill."[45]

On December 9, 1865, *The Dispatch* "is this morning restored to life," it said, noting that it had "met a temporary suspension of its existence in the expiring flames of the recent Confederacy."

"It is again endowed with the Promethean fire, and speaks to its readers as though it had never lost its breath or its voice. Welcome it, 'dear reader,' with the same kind and genial sensibilities which warm its own heart, and let there be established once more between it and thee the same confidential and affectionate relations which formerly existed, and which blessed and rewarded all its toil, all its struggles, through the thorny and flinty way of journalism.

"These Southern States have passed through an ordeal of trial and suffering seldom the lot of a generation of people. They entered upon a struggle, in which they failed, and in which these trials and sufferings were incurred. Unlike most rebellions, as they are called, especially when they have failed, those who undertook it were not merely a set of malcontents, recklessly resisting the clearly-defined political organisms of the country; they were fortified by a sense of rights under the Constitution and a conscientious conviction of the justice of their position, which had at least the semblance of support in the debates of our ancestors, who framed the Constitution itself under which the Republic was formed. Those truly great men left the question of the relations between the States and the General Government an open one. There were strong parties in the very convention which framed the compact of union upon the questions at issue touching those relations. The very able and patriotic men who figured in that body, after much debate, gave the question the go-by; and while they failed to settle it themselves, they appointed no umpire to which it could be referred. They thus left us as a legacy a bitter and disastrous war—a war which was fought, and fought bravely, to its final conclusion. The South entered upon it with more unanimity and determination than has been known to characterize the resisting party in any civil war that we read of. It fought through it, under its sense of constitutional right, with a courage and constancy which has challenged the admiration of other nations. But the question thus submitted to the arbitrament of war, was decided against them, and they submitted, like brave men ever submit, to the fates, which all their fortitude and power cannot control. They were overwhelmed by superior numbers and resources, and succumbed after a resistance which vindicated the honesty and sincerity of their intentions. Their heroism has lately received a tribute that is alike honorable to the head and heart of the magnanimous commander-in-chief of the powerful armies they encountered in the field.. . . "

Continuing, the editorial assured its readers that the paper "sympathized with the Confederacy, did all it could to cheer the hearts of the people in the struggle, and continued with it, and, we may say, fell with it in the calamitous fire of the 3rd of April. Its voice was heard up to that hour. [The last *Dispatch* was that of April 1.] While the carrier conveyed its communications to the public in one part of the city, its types and presses were melting in the fires of another."

The editorial concluded, "That our own townsmen and the good people of Virginia—God bless and preserve her!— may pass through their trials successfully, and become, as they deserve to be, prosperous and happy, is the devout prayer of *The Dispatch.*"

The cost of a single paper was 2 cents, compared with 50 cents for the last edition during the war.

In 1866, Lester Cappon writes,[46] Richmond had seven daily papers, five of them "carrying prestige from ante bellum days"—*The Dispatch,* the *Enquirer,* the *Examiner,* the *Whig* and the *Sentinel.*

The postwar *Dispatch* was situated at 12th and Main Streets, later the site of the Parcel Post Building. It fought reconstruction and opposed the 1868 constitution, which enfranchised blacks and appeared to give them control of the state. After amendments that did not disenfranchise whites, *The Dispatch* approved the document.[47]

The paper's editorial stances on the role of blacks was ambivalent in the postwar years. Although it opposed the Ku Klux Klan, it accepted its advertising in 1868. (That, of course, could have been argued as openmindedness.) It supported the idea of Negroes on juries, in the legislature and at political conventions, but it stated, in opposing William Mahone's political moves, "No Negro is fit to make laws for white people."[48] Mahone was a former Confederate major-general who led a coalition of Republicans and unhappy Democrats and wanted to "readjust" the state's antebellum debt.

With the enactment of the 14th and 15th Amendments to the Constitution and the end of Reconstruction, "*The Dispatch* had played a constructive and highly important role in bringing about this happy result."[49]

James Cowardin died in 1882 and was succeeded by his son Charles. As the paper backed off its support of Negro rights, it said that Rep. John Mercer Langston was "still a Negro, with all of a Negro's conceit, pomposity, credulity and stupidity."

THE TIMES

Major Lewis Ginter, who had a finger in so many Richmond pies, stuck one in journalism by establishing *The Richmond Times,* whose first issue was October 22, 1886.

"We christen our penny paper," said the lead editorial on the first day, "with the most familiar name in journalism to indicate that its spirit shall be representative of the advanced ideas of the present day, and that we will furnish our readers with an unprejudiced report of the happenings of each day without serving any interest but that of truth.

"As an organ of the conservative elements of all classes, and with the purpose of promoting healthy public opinion, we need only the support of the community to achieve a success in which the people of Virginia will be benefitted as well as the sponsors of our enterprise."

Its front page, like that of other journals of the day, was a mixture of social notes, advertisements, wireless reports from home and abroad and short news stories. The first issue made much of a brief visit to Richmond by President Cleveland, and there was space also on the front page for news of the annual reunion of the Army of Northern Virginia and the naming of Ginter to the executive committee.

The competing *Whig* was complimentary, and the third issue of the *Times* quoted the *Whig* as calling the newcomer "a neatly printed little daily of twenty-four columns, and the initial number is exceptionally bright. Captain [Page] McCarty is a clear and forcible writer, and his name at its head will be of great advantage to the *Times* in winning its way to public favor."

Like many a newspaper today, *The Times* ran a "telegraphic summary" in column one of its Sunday paper of items found in more detail elsewhere in the publication. In its third day of publication, *The Times'* summary included these items, among others, arranged in no logical order:

"Thomas Patintini, worth $100,000, blew his brains out in Philadelphia.

The city room of the Richmond Times *in 1897. Identifiable staff members include (fourth from left, seated) John S. Irby, managing editor; (standing next to him) Tom Barclay, artist and cartoonist; (standing near telephone), Henry D. Perkins, later managing editor of* The Norfolk Ledger-Dispatch; *(seated, right), John D. Murrell, state editor.*

"Near Detroit, John Wicker accidentally shot and killed his mother-in-law.

"In Danville, Va., C.M. Holden shot and mortally wounded Gus Walker.

"Rev. Dr. Woodrow, the South Carolina evolutionist, refused to resign, as requested.

"Blaine is expected next week to make a speech in New York in favor of Roosevelt for Mayor.

"In the great game of base ball at New York yesterday, the Brooklyns whitewashed the New Yorks.

"A Japanese prince, a near relative of the Mikado, has arrived in San Francisco and is heading this way."

The Richmond Times *was housed in this structure on Bank Street.*

After about a year, Ginter "lost interest as well as money in the enterprise" and gave it to Joseph Bryan, who was his lawyer and was much younger than Ginter.[50]

"Of course," said Bryan's grandson, D. Tennant Bryan, "my grandfather didn't have any money. He had whatever he earned from his lawyer's fees. He didn't have anything else. His father had everything taken away by the end of the [Civil] war, and there'd never been any times to get anything back, to accumulate anything. But. . . he felt that by diligent operation of *The Times,* he could stop losses of it; and he did eventually. It took a little while."[51]

An early editor of *The Times* was William L. (Buck) Royall, who about 1896 is reported to have told his publisher: "I have, Mr. Bryan, as you know, educated myself in all the great classics of the Greek and Roman times. I have read widely in the works of the great French and English essayists. I have found exceeding pleasure in the poets from Homer to Tennyson. But the greatest pleasure in reading that I have yet found is to take to bed with a pint of good whisky and read my own editorials."[52]

THE LEADER

On June 2, 1888, J.F. Bradley and Ben P. Owen Jr. published the first copy of *The Leader,* which, as they proudly noted, was "the first daily paper here since the founding of the city." It cost 2 cents.

The city of which they spoke was Manchester, south of the James River and not then part of Richmond. Indeed, the owners of *The Leader* noted, "Manchester has, during most of its history, been content to depend on Richmond for its news, its journalistic enterprise having been only three or four in number."

The Leader noted its short-lived predecessors—including the *Courier,* the *Virginia Sun* and the *People's Friend*—then plunged into providing Manchester residents with news and advertisements in its four pages. Editorially, the paper showed restraint. "*The Leader* does not expect to do more than other papers," it said. "It will not vaunt itself as an independent newspaper. Such a thing is impracticable and unpopular with our people. It proposes to be just, candid, and fair in its dealings with questions of public importance—never arrogant, but ever ready to accord justice to merit, reserving the right to speak plainly and in unprejudiced terms of men and matters, all the while clinging to Democracy."

For two cents a copy, readers got a quaint mixture of ads, telegraphed news of the outside world and homespun accounts of items great and small. Messrs. Bradley and Owen apparently figured their readers' minds well, for with Issue No. 58 on August 9, the paper grew from five to six columns.

In column one on Page One of Volume 1, Number 1 was "CITY NEWS, Nicely and Quickly Gathered by Our Reporters." The most interesting item was headed "A Shriek in the Night."

It read: "Murder, murder, murder.

"These three words rang out sharply about 3 o'clock this morning, and aroused citizens in the neighborhood of the Hustings Courthouse.

"Policeman Smith was on duty at the station-house, and he went to see

The Richmond Leader *was housed in this building on Hull Street before Joseph Bryan bought the paper in 1896.*

the cause of the cry. Up and down the street he ran trying to find out what was the trouble. After a while he saw a boy, about fourteen years of age, run out of Ninth street towards Decatur.

"'Halt! Halt!' cried Policeman Smith but. . . the boy hastened on, until a pistol shot in the air frightened him so badly that he could not run.

"The boy turned out to be a grandson of John Evans, who lives on Decatur Street between Sixteenth and Seventeenth, and his absence from home was said to have been on account of some slight trouble between himself and some member of his family.

"There was no real murder, but the little fellow was killing time."

In 1896, *The Leader,* then controlled by Raleigh Green, was sold to Joseph Bryan, who changed the name to *The Evening Leader.* Thus, Bryan had a morning paper, *The Times,* and an afternoon paper.[53]

A policy statement in an editorial in the first issue on, November 30, said that the paper would cover the news of both Manchester and Richmond and would go beyond most afternoon journals by being "a complete newspaper."

"It will print the news and all the news that is fit to print [a steal from the *New York Times?*], and both sides of the news impartially," said the policy statement. "As for its editorial opinion, that shall always be honest in sentiment and parliamentary in expression. *The Leader* will always be a guest whom you will not be ashamed to entertain at your fireside."

The Evening Leader spruced up its appearance quite a bit, with larger headlines and line drawings on the front page. Its first issue of 1899, for example, had three stories, each of which merited a one-column headline with five smaller headlines.

OUR FLAG NOW

FLOATS IN CUBA

said the story in column one, which began, "HAVANA, January 2—The sovereignty of Cuba passed from Spain to the United States at noon to-day, when the Spanish evacuated Havana."

In the middle of the page at the top, a story out of Albany, New York, was handled by a less than accurate speller, who produced this headline:

GOV. ROOSEVELT

INAUGERATED

The determination of the editors to achieve symmetry in its seven-column format—even if redundancy were required—is evident.

Under the main headline on the Roosevelt story are these lesser heads:

The Inducting in Office

Accompanied With

Ceremony

TAKES THE OATH OF OFFICE

Grand Parade of Civic and

Military Bodies

TWO GOVERNORS MAKE SPEECHES

---

and

The Keynote of Roosevelt's Speech Was That the Homely Virtues of Common Sense, Honesty and Courage Were Needed to Govern

The other major story—in the right hand column and what would be considered the "lead" position today—is an extended account of President McKinley's first reception of the year at the White House. "A brilliant assemblage," said the headline writer.

Perhaps even the great unwashed among readers of *The Evening Leader,* now published in "Manchester and Richmond, Va.," were interested in New York society. Bryan's editors apparently thought so, for they placed two-column pictures of Mrs. Henry Sloane and Matthew Sterling Borden at the top of the page, neatly separating the stories on Cuba, Roosevelt and McKinley.

Of Mrs. Sloane, the paper said, "New York society is generally distressed over the news that the great society leader has separated from her husband, who is to sue, it is said, for a divorce. Mrs. Sloane has the distinction of being the best-dressed woman in New York society."

Of Borden, "It is an ill wind that blows no one any good, and though the pain and privations borne by the gallant boys of the Eighth New York Regiment have been too terrible to picture, Matthew Sterling Borden has profited by them. For it was the news of his services among the sick at Camp Thomas and his own subsequent illness that caused his father to be reconciled to him—the parent having been estranged by his son's marriage."

THE NEWS

Of the newspapers that were forerunners of the present *Richmond Times-Dispatch,* the shortest lived was the *Richmond News.* It was established in 1899 by Harvey L. Wilson.

Wilson's *News,* selling for a penny a copy, was anything but conservative in its Page One makeup. The largest headline of the April 2, 1900, issue, for instance, is reserved for a local accident.

Spread across three columns was the headline:

BURIED UNDER
A FALLING WALL

Through that and smaller headlines, readers learned

Mr. Henry A. Flege
Fatally Injured
While Walking
Along Franklin
Street To-Day

SAD ACCIDENT

Although Bricks
Which Covered
Him Were Re-
moved Quickly
He Soon Expires

The busy reader going through all of those headlines may have bypassed the story itself, which began, "This morning at about 11 o'clock Mr. Henry A. Flege, who is employed by the establishment of Armour & Co. as bookkeeper, was caught by a falling wall and crushed to death. The young man in company with two others was walking down Franklin street, where workmen were engaged in tearing down the old buildings near Union street, and when in front of the building formerly occupied by The Implement Company, a crash was heard and before Mr. Flege had time to escape the building debris caught him and carried him to the pavement."

Like the *Evening Leader* of the same time, the *News* had a symmetrical front page of seven columns with two two-column drawings breaking up the type. At the *News,* however, a picture concerning a Chinese play is sandwiched between the headline and the story concerning a lynching in Emporia, Virginia. Similarly, the headline and story about the Boer War are divided by a picture of "the proposed Nicaragua Canal."

The final edition of the *News* was on Saturday, January 24, 1903. It contained eight pages. Still, a minute book of the *News'* board of directors shows meetings continued through January 20, 1910, although by that time there was not even a quorum present.

The *News* was sold in 1900 to John L. Williams and consolidated January 26, 1903, with Joseph Bryan's *Evening Leader,* thus making *The News Leader.*

That same day, Bryan's *Times* and Williams' *Dispatch* were consolidated into *The Times-Dispatch,* owned by Bryan.

Those consolidations set the pattern for daily newspapers in Richmond for almost 90 years. They occurred at a small dinner where participants discussed fund-raising for a YMCA building. Two powerful men essentially carved up Richmond's newspaper readership because (1) they sat next to each other and (2) there were no stringent anti-monopoly laws.

At the dinner, said Bryan's grandson Tennant, "My grandfather and Mr. Williams just happened to be sitting beside each other." And their talk turned to business, specifically the newspaper business.

"They were both losing money at the time," said Tennant Bryan, "and there were four newspapers, whereas if there were only two, they'd probably stop the losses. At that point, they agreed to make four into two—*The News Leader* and *The Times-Dispatch.*"[54]

In 1909, Bryan bought *The News Leader* from Williams, and John Stewart Bryan succeeded his father as publisher of both papers, although both had separate staffs until mid-1992. The Bryan family sold *The Times-Dispatch* in 1914 and didn't repurchase it until 1940.

From 1914 until 1940, *The Times-Dispatch* was under the direction of two Hasbrooks and a Slover.

Colonel Charles E. Hasbrook, who became publisher in 1914, was a founder of the Associated Press and earlier had been publisher of the *Kansas City Times,* the New York *Commercial Advertiser,* the *Boston Traveler,* the *Denver Republican,* the *Minneapolis Times* and the *Binghamton Press.*

Two years after taking over *The Times-Dispatch,* Hasbrook brought in his son, Charles Phillips Hasbrook, as business manager. The younger Hasbrook's earlier newspaper experience had been with the *Brooklyn Eagle* and the *New York Globe.*

Six years after coming to Richmond, the senior Hasbrook died, and his son took over. For the next 14 years—until 1934—Charles P. Hasbrook was publisher.

Hasbrook's main accomplishment in Richmond outside journalism appears to have been guiding the Community Chest, as general chairman, to a successful campaign in 1930, the first year of the Depression.

Indeed, *The News Leader* said that Hasbrook had built "a most admirable organization and then infused into it a spirit that would not even admit defeat as a possibility."[55]

Samuel LeRoy Slover, another colonel (because of his appointment to Gov. Westmoreland Davis' staff), became publisher of *The Times-Dispatch* in 1934, a year after gaining control from the Hasbrook interests.

Slover and the Bryans were not enemies, and the colonel remained a director of Richmond Newspapers until poor health forced him off the board in 1957. That was 17 years after the Bryans regained control of *The Times-Dispatch* and Richmond Newspapers became the parent of *The News Leader* and *The Times-Dispatch.*

Upon Slover's death in 1959, Tennant Bryan said, "Virginia has lost the last of her elder statesmen of the press."

At that time, Slover was still chairman of the board of Norfolk-Portsmouth Newspapers Inc., which he had helped form in the early 1900s. It published the morning *Norfolk Virginian-Pilot* and the afternoon *Norfolk Ledger-Star,* the latter an amalgamation of the *Norfolk Ledger-Dispatch* and the *Portsmouth Star.* He also had published the *Newport News Times-Herald* and the *Petersburg Progress-Index.*

The Times-Dispatch editorial on Slover's death traced the merger of the Richmond papers in more detail than readers normally find in the papers involved.[56]

"Richmonders will be particularly interested," said the editorial, "in Colonel Slover's acquisition of control of *The Times-Dispatch* in 1933 from the Hasbrook interests. From that date until 1939 the competition between *The Times-Dispatch* and *The News Leader* was so severe as to attract national interest in newspaper circles. When in 1939 it became apparent to publishers of both papers that neither could win and both must lose, John Stewart Bryan and Colonel Slover undertook to merge the two newspapers into a single operation, thereby utilizing the equipment and talents of both constructively. After a year of negotiations the newspapers were merged in 1940, Colonel Slover yielding control of the corporation to Bryan interests."

THE OTHERS

No one knows how many papers, including crudely produced, here-today-gone-tomorrow sheets, have been printed in Richmond over the years, although Lester J. Cappon lists 199 in his *Virginia Newspapers, 1821-1935*. Seven were in one way or another predecessors of today's *Times-Dispatch.*

Among the others were at least five German language papers, another (Beau Monde) that chronicled society events; the *Republic*, which in 1865-66 supported Andrew Johnson's Reconstruction policy; *Justice,* the official organ in 1898 of the Socialist Labor Party of Virginia; and numerous publications of various Protestant religious denominations.

The pre-eminent Richmond paper of the 1850s was the aforementioned *Richmond Enquirer.* Thomas Ritchie at age 28 founded the *Enquirer* in 1804 and edited it for more than 40 years.

Ritchie was an ardent supporter of the Republican Party in a city that was predominantly Federalist or Whig. He supported Thomas Jefferson and his party (later the Democrats) and accepted a party subsidy. He openly aligned the paper with the party and did the state's public printing.

He assailed slavery (even after the Nat Turner slave rebellion), pushed for public education, advocated a better deal all around for women and supported both the union and states' rights.

Virginius Dabney says, "It is to be doubted if any Virginia editor since his time has been so potent in the nation's councils." Frank Luther Mott in his history of American journalism is quoted as saying, "The greatest paper of the Southern states in those years was Thomas Ritchie's *Richmond Enquirer.*"[57]

Ritchie's words may seem strong today, but they were tame, compared with those of some of his contemporaries. He felt strongly that Aaron Burr was guilty of treason, so he demanded the impeachment of the judge at Burr's trial—John Marshall. Ritchie said Marshall's dining with the accused man was "a reprehensible and willful prostration of his own dignity and a wanton insult to this country."

President Andrew Jackson called the *Enquirer* "infamous," and the *Richmond Whig* said Ritchie was "an impotent dotard and driveller." On the other hand, his reputation was such that President James K. Polk asked him in 1845 to become editor of the Republican-Democrats' paper, the *Washington Globe*. Ritchie had turned down the editorship a year earlier, but that time the offer didn't come from the president of the United States.

So, Ritchie accepted Polk's offer, changed the name of the *Globe* to the *Union* and turned over direction of the *Richmond Enquirer* to his sons, Thomas Jr. and William, but they couldn't match their father as editors.[58] Furthermore, Thomas Jr. killed his rival editor, John Hampden Pleasants of the *Whig*, in a duel the year after his father went to Washington.

In 1857, the editorship of the *Enquirer* passed to O. Jennings Wise, a former diplomat and son of Gov. Henry A. Wise. Jennings Wise not only edited the paper; he also engaged in duels—eight of them. He never hit anyone and once, when his near-sighted opponent missed with his own shot, Wise fired into the air and announced, "Sir, I present you to your wife and children."[59]

Later editors of the *Enquirer*, before it died in 1877, included an Irishman, John Mitchel, and James C. Southall, a brilliant student while at the University of Virginia and editor of the *Charlottesville Chronicle* before coming to Richmond.

Like Thomas Ritchie, John Hampden Pleasants became an editor early. In 1824, at age 27, he founded the *Richmond Whig*. Although he passionately attacked Ritchie in editorials, the two men agreed on better treatment of women, a need for public schools and opposition to slavery. Both also felt that if more Northerners came to Virginia, the state would benefit from people of diverse backgrounds.

Politics was something else. When Ritchie's candidate for president was defeated in 1824, Pleasants ran a long editorial that, tongue in cheek, was titled "Death of Thomas Ritchie." It said, "He was so good a Republican that he refused to express any opinion. . . before he had clearly discovered on which side of the question public opinion was. His own sentiments were cheerfully sacrificed to those of the majority."

But, being a Whig, Pleasants took a more conservative approach than the Democrat-Republicans on protective tariffs. The party, after all, contained more people from the upper classes than did its opposition.

After the Nat Turner rebellion, Pleasants went to the scene in Southampton County and reported first-hand. He told of the "atrocities that have been perpetrated by the insurgents: whole families, father, mother, daughters, sons, sucking babes, and school children butchered, thrown into heaps, and left to be devoured by hogs and dogs, or to putrefy on the spot."

Still, he also wrote of retribution against blacks. "We allude to the slaughter," he wrote, "of many blacks, without trial, and under circumstances of great barbarity. . . Another insurrection will be the signal for the extermination of the whole black population in that quarter of the state where it occurs."

The *Whig* opposed expelling free blacks to Africa but supported the use of federal funds to end slavery. When the Virginia General Assembly passed legislation in 1835-36 that made printing anti-slavery tracts a felony, the *Whig* declared the action was "far worse than lynching and lynch's law, and a reflection on the state that such deformed crudities are submitted in the shape of bills."

As argument over slavery increased, the *Whig* said that low-grade whites were "a far greater pest" than free blacks in the state.

What led to the Ritchie-Pleasants duel in 1846 was an assertion in the *Enquirer,* under the pseudonym "Macon," that Pleasants was going to start an abolitionist publication. Pleasants denied it; whereupon Thomas Ritchie, Jr., called him a coward. Pleasants felt he must challenge Ritchie to a duel, which suited Ritchie fine.

Each man appeared with several weapons, but only Ritchie took aim. Pleasants fired once in the air, but several of Ritchie's shots scored. Pleasants lived only two more days.

Oliver P. Baldwin, former editor of the *Richmond Republican,* briefly followed Pleasants at the *Whig* and gave way to Richard H. Toler, who was succeeded by Alexander Moseley. Other editors followed, but when Robert Ridgeway strongly opposed secession on the eve of the Civil War, Moseley returned as editor and remained in that capacity until the end of the war. The *Whig* was the only paper whose offices were not destroyed in the great fire of 1865, but the paper reappeared as a Union publication. In 1868, Moseley was back as editor.

In the late 1870s, the editorship of the *Whig* passed to William C. Elam, whose political soulmate was William Mahone, like Elam a former Confederate officer. Mahone was a power in state politics. He was so close to Elam that he moved his headquarters to the *Whig* offices.[60]

Elam wrote vitriolic editorials aimed at competing newspapers and supported virtually everything Mahone did—including readjusting the state debt incurred in antebellum days. Elam left the *Whig* in the mid-1880s to start a Republican paper in Harrisonburg. His *Whig* in Richmond closed in 1888.

John Moncure Daniel, who seemed to oppose everybody and everything, was another young crusader. He became editor of the *Richmond Examiner* at age 22 in 1847. Although it lasted only 20 years, the paper made its mark. Daniel was "the most brilliantly slashing writer of newspaper editorials in Virginia in the 19th century." His editorial style was "both eminently readable and notably more vituperative than that of any of his contemporaries."[61]

Daniel found few things to like. He condemned the "essential stupidity" of the cornerstone-laying of the equestrian statue of Washington at the Capitol. When other papers hailed the movement to Virginia of farmers from the North, Daniel labeled them "fragrant hordes of adventurers fresh from the . . . codfisheries of the Bay State."

He also opposed marriage, saying that "there are but two ways to manage a woman—to club her or to freeze her."

After a stint in the foreign service, where he managed to alienate officials of various countries, he returned to Richmond in 1861 as the Civil War was brewing. Initially, he opposed secession but labeled two Richmond delegates to a peace conference in Washington "consummate traitors." After the war began, Yankees were "thieves upon principle, assassins at heart."

The South's Civil War heroes didn't escape Daniel's villification. When Robert E. Lee succeeded Gen. Joseph E. Johnston after the Battle of Seven Pines, the *Examiner* said, "Evacuating Lee, who has never yet risked a single battle with the invader, is commanding general." During the bread riots in 1863, the *Examiner* alone defied President Jefferson Davis and reported the event in detail.

On March 30, 1865, as the end of the Confederacy neared, Daniel died at age 39. The issue of the *Examiner* that announced his death was its last.

Of all the daily newspapers that graced the Richmond scene, perhaps none was more outrageous than the *Virginian,* the brainchild of Methodist Bishop James Cannon, manipulator of politicians and crusader for prohibition of alcohol.

The *Virginian* lasted only 10 years and its circulation probably never topped 16,000. Yet, Cannon was a major figure on the political-social-religious front. He had a host of followers—mostly Methodist and Baptist true-believers—and a host of enemies, including Richmond's other dailies.[62]

In 1911, when Dr. R.E. Blackwell, president of Randolph-Macon College, a respected Methodist institution for men, asked the editor of *The Times-Dispatch,* Major J. Calvin Hemphill, to be the commencement speaker, Cannon thundered, "There would have been equal fitness in selecting the editor of the Wine and Spirit Gazette." That prompted such a response by dry alumni of the college that Hemphill never gave the address.[63]

The first copy of the *Virginian* appeared Jan. 28, 1910. It was to appear each afternoon but Sunday, and it claimed that it "begins with the largest bona-fide subscription list ever acquired in Virginia by a new paper."[64]

Hypocrisy never bothered Cannon. He damned gambling but dabbled in the worst kinds of stock dealings. His paper reported professional boxing in detail, although he condemned the pastime and a proposed state athletic commission to oversee boxing. "Let there be no backward step, no yielding to the clamor for brutal and debasing exhibitions to line the pockets of a coarse crew who wish to exploit the young, the foolish and the depraved," said the *Virginian*.[65]

Cannon had always opposed Sunday newspapers, but that didn't stop him from switching the *Virginian* to a seven-morning-a-week publication in 1911. He and another cleric who was a major stockholder said two weeks before Sunday publication began that they were severing "all official connection with the paper." The paper announced it would take care to exclude "such features as are calculated to do harm, rather than prove uplifting."[66]

It was explained in the *Methodist Advocate* that Cannon still opposed a Sunday paper, but other stockholders overruled him. Cannon would not accept one dollar in profit from the Sunday paper, he said.

At first, the paper was in quarters near Governor and Ross Streets—only a brief distance from the city's red light district, but the *Virginian* gained some respectability by moving uptown to 7th and Franklin Streets. Yet, its reputation among the city's newsmen didn't change. "The city room reeked with whiskey," said one reporter.[67]

Perhaps the *Virginian's* finest hour was in 1916, when the General Assembly—with Cannon on the floor of the Senate near the sponsor of the Mapp Bill—approved legislation restricting severely the sale of alcohol in the state. It limited each person to a monthly import from outside Virginia to a quart of whiskey or three gallons of beer or one gallon of wine.[68]

The front page of the *Virginian* rhapsodized, "To the chorus of church chimes ringing and of factory whistles screaming in loud accord, Virginia freed her domains from the shackles of the saloon with a mighty stroke last night. For the first time since her glorious history was opened to the world, the Mother of States looks across her fertile lands and through her prosperous cities today to see a landscape freed at last from the pestilence of rum."[69]

"The *Virginian* went downhill gradually," wrote Virginius Dabney, author of *The Dry Messiah*, a biography of Bishop Cannon. "At the outset, the local staff, when sober, was able to hold its own with any of its Richmond competitors. In fact, it scored some impressive scoops over the opposition." But on May 14, 1920, it announced it had sold its subscription list and good will to the *Evening Journal,* which the *Virginian* carefully pointed out, had new management that was a “supporter of prohibition and of righteousness.”[70]

THE LAST MERGER

Daily newspapers across America—especially afternoon papers—had been closing during the 1970s and 1980s, so it was no surprise that *The Times-Dispatch* and *The News Leader* were merging. The only surprise to many, particularly staff members, was the time: mid-1992.

Media General's afternoon papers in Tampa and Winston-Salem had closed. Closer to home, papers in Norfolk, Roanoke and Lynchburg had merged or become round-the-clock papers, changing the nameplate but employing only one news staff.

With the merger in Richmond, there were obviously too many reporters and editors for even the larger *Times-Dispatch* that was envisioned. Advertising, circulation and production departments had been merged since the formation of Richmond Newspapers Inc. more than a half-century earlier. The same photography department served both news staffs.

Some experienced people took advantage of sweetened early-retirement offers. Others had new titles—even without added responsibilities. Still others had bruised feelings. After all, there would be only one senior political reporter. So, for instance, the man with the most longevity, Tyler Whitley of *The News Leader,* got the nod over Jeff Schapiro of *The Times-Dispatch,* who, despite writing frequently about politics, began writing more frequently about state employees.

Claude Burrows, a 32-year *Times-Dispatch* veteran with a steady record of accuracy and fairness but little imagination, was shunted off to a Plus section, which dealt with suburban matters of less than cosmic significance. The same thing happened to Hugh Robertson, who had spent almost 35 years with *The News Leader.*

The new *Times-Dispatch* became one of the few dailies of its size with two editorial cartoonists—Gary Brookins of the old *Times-Dispatch* and Robert Gorrell of the old *News Leader*—and two outdoors writers, Henry Christner of *The News Leader* and Garvey Winegar of *The Times-Dispatch.*

Two people covered television—Katherine Phillips of *The News Leader* and Douglas Durden of *The Times-Dispatch*. Louis Mahoney of *The News Leader* remained food editor; her *Times-Dispatch* counterpart, Jann Malone, became a columnist.

The day the end of The News Leader *was announced, Sept. 4, 1991. Far left is Jerry Finch, managing editor of* The News Leader. *Others in foreground: Margaret Edds of* The Norfolk Virginian-Pilot, *Earle Dunford, the author and retired city editor of* The Times-Dispatch, *and Mark Johnson and Tom Silvestri of* The Times-Dispatch *news staff.*

Ross Mackenzie, the fire-breathing editor of *The News Leader,* became editor of the editorial pages, and Ed Grimsley, who had the same title on the old *Times-Dispatch,* became chairman of the editorial board on the expanded paper. It seemed that Mackenzie's style prevailed over the equally conservative but less scathing preachments of Grimsley.

Jerry Finch, of *The News Leader,* was in his 60s and was senior to Marvin Garrette, his *Times-Dispatch* counterpart as managing editor. Garrette was named managing editor of the new paper. Finch took on the job that many editors had pushed for—and wanted: ombudsman or readers' editor, the person who answers complaints (some of them in a column) about how the paper handled news.

Although Publisher Stewart Bryan and Executive Editor Alf Goodykoontz gave the impression that the merger had been decided on less than a year before the announcement in September 1991, the decision was reached in mid-1990 by a committee that Bryan had named to look at the future of the papers.[71]

Garrette learned in September 1990 that he had cancer, and by the end of the year he was assured that he would be managing editor of the new *Times-Dispatch.* Meanwhile, he was instructed to work up a table of organization for the expanded paper.

About that time, Bill Millsaps told Goodykoontz and Bryan that he'd had enough of sports and wanted to get into management. He found receptive ears. Goodykoontz had long been an admirer of Millsaps as a person and as a newspaperman. And in Bryan, Millsaps had a late-night drinking companion.

Late in 1990, after his annual review, Tom Howard, assistant managing editor of *The Times-Dispatch,* was told by Garrette and Goodykoontz that the merger was coming. It was to be announced at the end of the next year, they said, and Howard was to keep the information secret. Few people knew of it, they said.

One of those who did not know was Jerry Finch, who as managing editor of *The News Leader,* was one rung higher on the ladder than Howard. In March 1991, when they were guests of Charles McDowell at the Gridiron Club dinner in Washington, Finch's wife, Nancy, heard Bryan and an editor from Greensboro, North Carolina, talking. The Greensboro man asked, Mrs. Finch recalled, "When are you going to get rid of that afternoon paper?"[72]

Bryan replied, "We're not getting rid of it."

And Mrs. Finch chimed in, "You'd be making a horrible mistake."

Five months later, the Finches were walking along a beach in North Carolina and the talk turned to newspapers. When Nancy Finch repeated Bryan's remark in March, Jerry Finch said, "He lied."[73]

Bryan said he couldn't recall the conversation but added, "I certainly wasn't going to announce it to the outside world before I announced it to the staff."[74]

Garrette's illness worsened in March of 1991 and Howard was assigned the job of compiling a table of organization. About the same time, Howard says, Millsaps was told that he was the heir apparent to Garrette and—assuming he didn't stub his toe—the successor to Goodykoontz when the executive editor retired at the end of 1993.

Another person who wanted the job of managing editor on the new paper was Nelson Hyde, longtime assistant managing editor of *The News Leader.* But on his 60th birthday he was told by Goodykoontz he was too old. Hyde came to the merged paper as a deputy managing editor but left after seven months when the paper renewed its retirement offer, which had been offered veteran employees at the merger.

He said there was "an over-all difference between the papers." *The New Leader* had been like a family, Hyde said, whereas he found animosity between reporters and desks on *The Times-Dispatch.*

Furthermore, he found Louise Seals, the old *Times-Dispatch's* assistant managing editor, abrasive; and there was too much micro-management.[75]

The official announcement of the pending merger came September 4, 1991, in the second-floor conference room at Richmond Newspapers. Years earlier, the room had been the site of Media General's annual meetings, but none of those was as well-attended as the session that day. The crowd of 150 to 200 was made up not only of reporters and camera crews from the papers' competitors but also of staff members of *The Times-Dispatch* and *The News Leader,* who had learned the news hours earlier but wanted to get every crumb of information they could from Bryan and Goodykoontz.

Bryan said that "more than 18 months ago" senior management decided, as a new building in Hanover County was progressing, "Look, we're going to have a world-class production facility. We can produce a newspaper or newspapers or other products that will be at least as good from a printing quality standpoint as anything produced in the world today. What are the products that we should be turning out? From that beginning, we expanded our group. These gentlemen you see here were part of that original group. Expanded it up to about 10 of the senior managers of Richmond Newspapers, and the decision which was reached some six months ago was that we needed a single morning paper."

That would have been late February or early March, but Howard said he was told of the decision by the end of the preceding December.

Bryan told a questioner that no single event caused the merger. It was a combination, he said, of various things, including *The News Leader's* circulation going below 100,000 and low third-quarter earnings during a recession.

Bryan also said, "More and more people want one daily newspaper." Richmond, he said, would not do as Roanoke and Norfolk had done—combine staffs and produce afternoon and morning editions, whether with a combined nameplate or changed nameplates. "It's not the death of *The News Leader,*" Bryan asserted. "It's the rebirth of the best parts of *The News Leader* in a new product."

The publisher also said he regretted that choices available to people deciding how to spend their time in the 1990s included not only newspapers, radio, television and leisure activities like gardening but also the choice of "not knowing as much as they used to want to know."

One questioner noted that Burt Sugarman, the company's *"bête noire,"* had said Media General management didn't act quickly enough on developments, but was reactive. Sugarman had led an unsuccessful move in 1988 to take over Media General. Bryan, although alluding neither to Alan S. Donnahoe nor James Evans, former presidents of the parent firm, said, "I never thought of Burt Sugarman as a '*bête noire.*' . . . The management that he accused of being whatever he accused us of being is gone and has been replaced by new management." Bryan had introduced himself as "the publisher of *The Times-Dispatch, The News Leader* and chairman and president of Media General."

Media General had already killed off its afternoon papers in Tampa and Winston-Salem. Bryan noted that the *Tampa Times* circulation had dropped to 19,000 before it closed. "I think we learned that while it is very sad to close a newspaper at any time, that it is much more humane to take a newspaper when it is still strong and vital and really a product that is worthwhile reading. Take the best of it and incorporate it into a new one. And that's what we're doing in this case."

Among Media General's three afternoon papers, *The News Leader* was the strongest in comparison with its morning counterpart. That's one reason it outlasted its sister PMs in Tampa and Winston-Salem.

The News Leader's peak circulation was 127,500 in 1965, the same year *The Times-Dispatch* had reached a peak of 150,910. But *News Leader* circulation trended downward steadily from 1965 to about 97,000 the day of the announcement, whereas *The Times-Dispatch* daily circulation started rebounding in 1975 and had reached 144,000.

In Tampa, the best the afternoon *Times* could claim was 46,282 in 1962, far more than double its circulation when it folded. By comparison, the morning *Tribune* circulated 202,363 copies in March 1982.

In Winston-Salem, the afternoon *Sentinel* had a circulation of only 30,959 when it closed in March 1985—down from its peak of 47,845 in 1973. The morning *Journal* had a circulation of 75,638 when its companion paper ceased.[76]

Bryan predicted the new *Times-Dispatch* would have a daily circulation of 200,000 within a year of the merger. Actually, it settled at 215,000 within several months after a brief "artificial" spurt.[77]

At a *Times-Dispatch* staff meeting immediately after the press conference, Goodykoontz said the new paper would be "very heavy on local columns." It was. There was considerable grumbling about the decision by some editors and many readers. As promised, the new paper had a full-time travel writer, a full-time writer for women's sports, a full-time business columnist and a special, investigative team of two reporters. New bureaus were opened in Northern Virginia and Roanoke.

Bryan was committed, said Goodykoontz, "to having the best medium-sized paper in the country, and we think we can deliver that."

With the merger, Goodykoontz went on, the news staff would be trimmed to 232 from the existing total of about 280. Twenty or so were eligible for early retirement, so he figured 30 to 35 would be laid off—"and that will not be pleasant."

The total included reporters, editors, library and photography staffs and people in community news.

A PAPER CLOSES

Even though it was the traditional thin paper of a Saturday, when *The News Leader* shut down after 95 years on May 30, 1992, it went out in style.

The entire front page and editorial page and two adless inside pages were devoted exclusively to the paper's history. In addition, there was an 84-page special commemorative magazine with each copy.

The next morning, June 1, the enlarged *Times-Dispatch,* printed on what Publisher Bryan called "the largest and best available [presses] in the world today," trumpeted its new appearance and then spent considerable space the rest of the week chronicling its circulation foibles.

"What happened at *The Times-Dispatch* late Sunday night and early Monday morning was almost a newspaper meltdown," Gary Robertson wrote in the Tuesday paper. A day later, Ray McAllister noted in his column that newsroom wags had come up with a *Times-Dispatch* slogan, "*The Richmond Times-Dispatch:* A morning paper delivered in the afternoon."

On Sunday, June 7, Executive Editor Alf Goodykoontz acknowledged that late delivery brought "thousands of calls" to the circulation department, "but another 2,900-plus readers called our editors' hot line to let us know what they like and don't like about the new paper."

On that last day of *The News Leader,* the front-page stories appeared with a banner headline that read,

'Nevermore'

Managing Editor Jerry Finch wrote the lead story that chronicled the paper's history. Even the turn took up more than a third of a page. Reporter Randy Hallman told what features of the dying paper would appear in *The Times-Dispatch.* One thing that would remain was a reminder of what had ended. Under the name, *Richmond Times-Dispatch,* on the front would be a smaller

Last day of The News Leader. *In front (from left): Jim Caiella, photo editor; Mary Mitchell, artist; Dean Levi, retired reporter, and Jane Zemel, assistant city editor.*

Pressman C.C. (Puffa) Rice, a pressman for 40 years, notes the final day of The News Leader.

VIRGINIA'S NEWS LEADER

Steve Clark, reporter and columnist, captured the atmosphere at his paper's final day. He noted that Hew Stith, a copy editor, wore a tuxedo and Jane Zemel, an assistant city editor, had a T-shirt with the slogan "WE DID IT IN THE AFTERNOON AND DIED."

Publisher Stewart Bryan came by and gave staff members dispensation to break the no-smoking rule for a day. Bryan himself "join[ed] some of the troops by dragging on a Richmond-made Merit," wrote Mike Allen in the next morning's *Times-Dispatch.*

The commemorative magazine that was part of the final *News Leader* featured a four-page retrospective, in which Bill Lohmann traced the history of the paper. He pulled no punches and covered the paper's treatment of desegregation head on. He quoted Tennant Bryan, the former publisher, as saying, "There was a time when I would have said that I was very proud of our stand on Massive Resistance. But the older I get [he was then 85] and the more that fades into the background, the less proud I am of it because I should have realized at the time that there was just absolutely no way. . . states' rights could have prevailed in that case.

"I guess I should have realized it was unrealistic, but I didn't, and neither did Jack Kilpatrick."

The Times-Dispatch of Sunday, May 31, was as much about birth (the "new" *Times-Dispatch*) as about death (the former *News Leader*). There was a 12-page special section—almost promotional—that featured stories on the new presses at the new building in Hanover County. The Perspective section, which normally led with a political "think piece," featured a column by Publisher Bryan that began, "The death of a newspaper is a sad and melancholy event. . . " It ended, "We hope your new newspaper will serve you long and well. That is surely our intention."

The front page of the main section told how *News Leader* staff members went about their chores on their last day. The story was by Mike Allen, who was on hand when the first people at his rival paper came to the office at 4:10 a.m. McAllister did *The Times-Dispatch's* version of *The News Leader's* history, and columnist Charles McDowell came close to being sentimental as he recalled the years 1949-1952 when he, as a young *Times-Dispatch* reporter, shared a house called Twin Maples with Bob McNeil, Bill Deekens, Andy McCutcheon and Martin Millspaugh of *The News Leader.*

Monday, June 1, gave *Times-Dispatch* editors the chance to show off their new product. They did. As is frequently the case on Sunday, there was little spot news, so the banner headline

A new newspaper is born

didn't seem too out of place. Two-thirds of the front page were devoted to the new *Times-Dispatch.* Readers were given telephone numbers for calling in their opinions on design and news presentation or on circulation. Two inside pages told of further changes, including a detailed story by Beverly Orndorff, veteran science writer, on use of fiber-optic technology in producing the paper.

The editorial writers went into explanations of their presentation—including a column by *The Times-Dispatch's* Ed Grimsley and *The News Leader's* Ross Mackenzie. One of the three op-ed page columns was by Gov. L. Douglas Wilder.

The paper let Ray McAllister get away with laughing about having so many editors and about "Stewart, Goody and Saps," the names by which the publisher, the executive editor and the managing editor were called.

Steve Clark, *The News Leader* columnist who moved to *The Times-Dispatch,* got into the "let's-laugh-at-the-new-paper" game on June 2 by telling how his paper hadn't arrived by 9 a.m. when he left for the office the previous day. "By all accounts," he wrote, "Murphy's law had kicked in at the birth of the baby and made it a most difficult delivery."

The final bit of self-examination was Goodykoontz's column of Sunday, June 7—the one in which he acknowledged the circulation problems. Further on, he said the paper had not "gone soft and fluffy," but that there was a lack of "blockbuster news," for which the paper was grateful.

And, he added, the extensive coverage of the new *Times-Dispatch* did not mean columnists were told what to write.

"As a matter of fact," said Goodykoontz, "I think I am about two of 84 with Steve Clark and perhaps three for 60 with Ray McAllister on column ideas I have passed along over the years."

The "world-class production facility" that Stewart Bryan had talked about in September 1991 when announcing the forthcoming merger was, indeed, impressive. The new presses cost $49,916,000, and there were futuristic robots moving rolls of newsprint across vast floors.

Still, with the distance between newsroom and pressroom about 20 miles instead of three floors, some things worked differently. Pages were still made up in the composing room, but "faxing" one page to Hanover County took several minutes. Page proofs were available to the newsroom in advance of printing, but the big difference was in the time before the news staff could get papers in their hands.

In the old operation, a clerk wheeled a cart of papers, still damp with ink, into the newsroom within minutes after the press start—which for *The Times-Dispatch* was about 10:50 p.m. With the new *Times-Dispatch,* the press run was 10:30, but the professional messenger who brought perhaps 50 papers to the newsroom in the heart of the city didn't arrive until about 11 p.m.

A copy editor did go to the plant as early as 9 p.m. to oversee operations and could, but rarely did, make changes immediately after seeing a paper come off the press.

Still, said Joe Gatins, an assistant city editor, "It is a drawback" not to have the real paper in your hands as soon as it runs.

Trouble or not, *The Times-Dispatch* maintained deadlines later than many on the East Coast. The final, city edition, was scheduled to begin rolling at 1:45 a.m. And it could routinely be replated for major league baseball scores from the West Coast or for major, breaking stories.

About the time the final press run begins, the first of 50 to 70 newspaper carriers begin arriving at each of 13 distribution centers in Metropolitan Richmond. They are not "newspaper boys," as in the old days, but mainly adult contract carriers who use their own vehicles. The routes are too long and the papers too heavy for most juveniles to do the job.

For delivery outside Richmond, the circulation department uses its own drivers; then local carriers take over. There are about 1,000 carriers, two-thirds of them in the Richmond area. The circulation department hopes all papers are delivered by 6 a.m. It advises subscribers who haven't gotten their papers by 7 a.m. to telephone complaints.

Richmond Times-Dispatch

144,496

Virginia's State Newspaper

Man Walks on Moon

Astronauts Begin Exploration Early

Luna Lower, May Overfly Eagle Site

Today's Events On Apollo 11

People Around ... Feat, Rejoice

Wheeler Says Lull Is No Peace Signal

The Inside Story

The City

The State

Business

Richmond Times-Dispatch

129,262

The Weather

Saigon Surrenders Unconditionally After Last Americans Are Removed

Lay Down Arms, Defenders Told

Ford Urges U.S. To 'Close Ranks'

The American Way Lured Some Right to the Last

Cambodia 'Expels' Foreigners

The Inside Story

SCC Opposes Plan For Approving Ads

Saigon Officers, Families Flee in Fighters, Copters

The World

The Nation

The State

The City

SECTION C

- Page One Stories

THE TITANIC

In the spring of 1912, you could buy a copy of *The News Leader* for a penny. *The Times-Dispatch* cost 2 cents. If you wanted a half-pint of Silver Leaf whiskey, you paid 25 cents.

It was still the era of "tombstone heads," one-column headlines on each of several stories set side by side. For the next 80 years, each of Richmond's principal daily papers went its own way, although the owners were the same beginning in 1940.

The best way to trace the publications is to examine how they covered the major events of the day—in the news columns and on the editorial pages. That is what this section does.

For several days in early April 1912, *The Times-Dispatch* led the paper with obituaries of Dr. Richard A. Patterson, surgeon, Civil War physician and tobacconist; Maj. Gen. Frederick T. Grant, son of the former president and Civil War leader; and Clara Barton, founder of the Red Cross.

The News Leader devoted a three-column headline on its seven-column front page to the forthcoming trials of the Allen Gang, accused of killing five people in a courtroom in Hillsville in Southwest Virginia.

On Monday, April 15, *The News Leader* was onto one of the great stories of the age but—like countless other papers—wasn't sure of the enormity of the situation. A banner headline over the nameplate read:

Richmond Man Escapes from Sinking Titanic Steamer

There were two pictures, three columns wide, of the ship.

But the lead story, in the upper right corner of the page, dealt with the state's desire for a change of venue in the Allen Gang trials.

The Richmond man who escaped the *Titanic* was Robert Williams Daniel. In the "off-lead" position in the upper left corner of the page, was a wrapup of the *Titanic* story, including the barest mention of Daniel. The story began with an account of a "wireless message" from the *Titanic,* noting it had struck an iceberg and was "in a sinking condition."

An explanation of *The News Leader's* hesitancy to lead the paper with the story could be found in the fifth paragraph: "A reassuring feature was that the weather was calm and clear, and help only a few hours away."

Thus a secondary headline read:

PASSENGERS ALL SAVED;
STEAMER REPORTED AFLOAT

But on Tuesday, April 16, readers of *The Times-Dispatch* were confronted with a banner headline that proclaimed:

Titanic, Giant White Star Liner, Sinks After Collision
With Iceberg on Her Maiden Voyage, and 1,800 Lives
Are Reported Lost in World's Greatest Maritime Disaster

The front page also carried a five-column photograph of the ship and six other articles, many continued inside, about the sinking. There was nothing on the seven-column front page but news of the *Titanic*. The entire paper consisted of only 14 pages.

The News Leader that afternoon noted, also in banner headlines:

1,302 Are Drowned or Missing
in Titanic Disaster, Latest Report

The News Leader's front page did carry three items unconnected with the *Titanic,* but it also carried a list of known survivors, who had been put aboard the liner *Carpathia,* plus a short story that the Richmonder, Robert W. Daniel, was among them. On Page 2, the paper placed a picture of the eight tallest buildings in the world. In the middle, standing on its stern, was the 882-1/2-foot *Titanic,* taller by far than even the 750-foot new Woolworth Building.

The News Leader carried banner headlines on the *Titanic* for six consecutive days but found room on the front page for other items—among them the new officers of the Grand Council of Royal Arcanum, then meeting in Richmond.

From New York, where survivors were taken by the *Carpathia,* a "Special to *The News Leader*" quoted Daniel as saying he was "a fair amateur wireless operator and tried to relieve the tired operator of the *Carpathia* and to send a complete list of names of the survivors to the shore.

The Times Dispatch

WHOLE NUMBER 18,957. RICHMOND, VA., TUESDAY, APRIL 16, 1912. PRICE TWO CENTS

Titanic, Giant White Star Liner, Sinks After Collision With Iceberg on Her Maiden Voyage, and 1,800 Lives Are Reported Lost in World's Greatest Marine Disaster

WIRELESS CALLS SEND VESSELS RUSHING TO AID OF SEA COLOSSUS

Through the Night They Drive With Full Speed to Reach Titanic.

MEANTIME, WORLD WAITS IN AGONY OF SUSPENSE

OF ALL ON BOARD ONLY 675 KNOWN TO HAVE ESCAPED DEATH IN OCEAN

Those Rescued Mostly Women and Children, Who Were Taken Off in Boats.

BITS OF WRECKAGE ALL THAT IS LEFT OF GREAT VESSEL

THE TITANIC

COL. JOHN JACOB ASTOR IS AMONG DROWNED

HIS WIFE IS SAVED

FINANCIAL BLOW IS VERY SEVERE

CARRIED NOTABLE PASSENGER LIST

OFFICIALS CONCEDE GREAT LOSS OF LIFE

PEOPLE ON SHIPS GET FIRST NEWS

STILL HOPING FOR BEST

PREVIOUS BIG SEA DISASTERS

"... But the amateurs all along the coast kept butting in and we could not do a thing."

By that time, Daniel was identified as a former Richmonder who had become a Philadelphia banker.

Generations of journalists have been awed by the coverage given the disaster by *The New York Times*. Meyer Berger's history of that newspaper details how it went. The *Times'* managing editor, Carr Van Anda, read an Associated Press dispatch at 1:20 a.m. Monday, April 15, reporting the *Titanic* had hit an iceberg. Officials of the White Star line were no help, but they knew the ship was "unsinkable." Van Anda reasoned that the silence following the *Titanic's* SOS meant that it indeed was sinking.

The final edition of *The Times* of April 15, on the press at 3:30 a.m., scooped the world. It said in a three-column headline:

NEW LINER TITANIC HITS AN ICEBERG;
SINKING BY THE BOW, AT MIDNIGHT;
WOMEN PUT OFF IN LIFEBOATS;
LAST WIRELESS AT 12:27 A.M. BLURRED

In an archaic journalistic style of putting all attribution before the news, The Times said, "HALIFAX, N.S., April 14—A wireless dispatch received tonight by the Allan line officials here from Capt. Gambrell of the steamer *Virginian,* states that the White Star liner *Titanic* struck an iceberg off the Newfoundland Coast and flashed out wireless calls for immediate assistance."

Walls of newsrooms and libraries around the nation often display *The Times* front page that carried these banner lines:

TITANIC SINKS FOUR HOURS AFTER HITTING ICEBERG;
866 RESCUED BY CARPATHIA, PROBABLY 1,250 PERISH;
ISMAY SAFE, MRS. ASTOR MAYBE, NOTED NAMES MISSING

The Times devoted its entire first eight pages to the *Titanic,* but that was the issue of Tuesday, April 16, the same day that *The Times-Dispatch* and other morning papers across the world dug into the story.

The Times-Dispatch, a regional paper no match for *The New York Times* except in price (*The Times* was still 1 cent—half the price of *The Times-Dispatch.*), ran virtually everything its editors could pull from the Associated Press wire and elsewhere.

For the next five days, *The Times-Dispatch* had banner headlines on the front page about all ramifications of the disaster. From Wednesday through Saturday, readers could find nothing on Page One but news of the *Titanic,* and on each of those days there were four more pages inside the paper devoted to the *Titanic*—nothing else.

Page 6 of the Friday April 19 *Times-Dispatch,* for example, had a banner headline:

Rescued Tell of Gross Negligence in Providing Means for Life Saving

News editors at *The Times-Dispatch* approved headlines for April 20 that dripped with emotion. Across the top of Page One was this banner:

J. Bruce Ismay Tells in Whispers How He Escaped Death
By Leaving Sinking Titanic in Lifeboat With Women

One secondary head was:

DRAGGED FROM HIS
LIPS THAT VESSEL
WAS BEING SPEEDED

Another head:

QUIETLY MEN WAIT
FOR CERTAIN DEATH
AS SHIP GOES DOWN

Inside was the touching story of Mrs. Isidor Straus, under the headline:

Chooses Death With Husband Rather Than Life Without Him

Finally, on Sunday, April 21, *The Times-Dispatch* noted on its front that Progressives had were winning Nebraska presidential primaries. But the *Titanic* story was worth another two-line banner, plus parts of five inside pages.

CAVE-IN

The effects of television and, earlier, of radio can be appreciated by looking at the newspapers of 1925. The newspaper was still the medium for spot news, the place where most people got their first information.

Results of World Series games in 1925 were routinely the lead stories in *The Times-Dispatch.* Not coincidentally, the newspaper operated a "Playograph," by which passersby on Tenth Street could keep abreast of games—play by play.

On October 9, the paper accompanied its story on the Washington-Pittsburgh game with a Page One feature on the Playograph. Two days later, *The Times-Dispatch* still led with the game and added a note that the Playograph would be suspended on Sunday for the Sabbath and gleefully reported, still on Page One, "If the excitement was any higher at Griffith Stadium [in Washington] than in front of *The Times-Dispatch,* the ambulance men must have had a busy afternoon."

In 1925 a copy of *The Times-Dispatch* (46,000 circulation daily, 55,117 Sunday) was up a penny to three cents. There was an eight-page section on the State Fair that season and on Sundays, a picture-filled rotogravure section, also eight pages.

The big story that month was local—the kind that still grabs readers almost 70 years later. Workers were trapped in a cave-in.

A railroad tunnel, unused for 10 years and running about a mile from 18th Street to 31st Street, was being repaired. There were days and days of front-page coverage, but there was nothing to match *The Times-Dispatch's* front page of Saturday, October 3, with two large pictures and three stories. The headline, across the top, read:

TWO MEN KNOWN TO BE DEAD; TWO INJURED;
SEVERAL OTHERS MISSING AS TUNNEL CAVES IN

Both papers used outdoor scoreboards to keep Richmonders updated on the World Series. In 1929, The Times-Dispatch *"Playograph" at the paper's building on 10th Street showed the progress of a game between the Philadelphia Athletics and the Chicago Cubs.*

INSET: Series Jam - This crowd of Richmonders gathered on Fourth Street, between Franklin & Grace, to receive news of the 1926 World Series between the New York Yankees and the St. Louis Cardinals. The Series scoreboard, then being operated by The News Leader, *is at the upper left.*

The staff must have been operating under the tell-it-all-in-one-sentence formula. The lead read:

"Two men met death, two others were seriously if not fatally injured, several others were slightly injured, and a number of negro section workmen estimated at from ten to fifteen were trapped under a falling mass of earth, when the Chesapeake & Ohio Railway tunnel, unused for several years caved in near Nineteenth and Marshall Streets shortly after 3 o'clock yesterday afternoon."

There was a thump from above and bricks began raining down on the workmen, who hurried to escape the tunnel. Most did.

Almost a quarter-century after the event, a writer pieced together, "based on contemporary accounts," a detailed story on the event and how three members of the train crew escaped.[78] Conductor C.G. McFadden suffered a broken arm when it was caught in falling debris and pinned on a flatcar. Nevertheless, he crawled under other flatcars and at the end of the train was helped to safety by C.S. Kelso, a brakeman, who also was injured. Another brakeman, A.G. Adams, also crawled under flatcars to safety. Some of those trying to crawl free had to feel their way almost a mile along the darkened tunnel. The electric lights had been knocked out when the cave-in began.

Fireman Benjamin F. Mosby also escaped and was taken to Grace Hospital "in a *News Leader* reporter's taxicab," that paper reported. But Mosby was badly scalded and died shortly thereafter.

The engineer, Tom Mason, died at the controls. His body was recovered October 11 after nine days of drilling more than 40 feet down. But the bodies of two black workmen, identified only as R. Lewis and H. Smith, were never found. Along with the locomotive, they were left inside the tunnel, which was sealed.

Although the C&O said after calling the rolls that only two workmen were missing, some said there were 10 to 15 men still in the tunnel. No one knows for sure. If so, they are still there, entombed with the locomotive behind the closed-off entrance to the tunnel.

STOCK MARKET CRASH

The fall of 1929 found Richmond and its daily papers doing well. The new Hotel John Marshall on Fifth Street was completed, and *The News Leader* carried a special section on the event. Generally business was fine.

Circulation of *The News Leader* was 73,704, and a single copy cost 2 cents, a penny less than its morning competitor. *The Times-Dispatch's* circulation was 67,580 daily and 71,549 Sunday.

Despite scary headlines and front page reports of a wild stock market, editorial writers did more than keep a stiff upper lip. At times, they pooh-poohed whatever gloom others showed.

On October 24, *The Times-Dispatch's* front page gave a clue of things to come. Under a two-column head (Stock Market Is/Demoralized By/Unexpected Drop), the lead story said, "Wall Street was thrown into the nearest approximation of a stock market panic experienced in years during the last hour of trading on the New York Stock Exchange yesterday."

The Times-Dispatch also played prominently a Carnegie Foundation report condemning the "glorification" of college athletics and calling for an end to the policy of paying coaches.

On October 24, *The News Leader's* front-page proclaimed:

STOCK MARKET SELLING NEAR PANIC PROPORTIONS

Yet, its editorial page said, ". . . The worst may be over and support may develop today.. . . but with factories busy and the general demand heavy, there is little reason to anticipate a general smash-up in the market."

The Times-Dispatch of October 25 went to an unusual three-column head that said:

Stock Market In Panic
As Billions In Profits
Vanish; Banks Halt Drop

There were two stories on the front page about the market, one with the imaginative head:

Police Battle Surging Throngs
Without as Bears Rage Within

That day's *News Leader* led with the conviction of Albert Fall, former secretary of the interior, for accepting a bribe. Its front-page story on the market merited a one-column headline:

Buying Orders
Seem to Check
Slight Losses

The Times-Dispatch by October 26 was giving the story still a one-column head, with three "decks":

Stock Clouds
Swept Away
By Bank Pool

Powerful Support Is
Thrown Into Market
With Gains Following

Trading Is Orderly

Brokerage Houses With-
Stand Attack; Business
Conditions Declared Fair

The Times-Dispatch editorial page voiced concern about another matter that would come to a head 25 years later. Commenting on debate in City Council, Harry M. Smith Jr., a lawyer, had told local realtors, "Segregation of races by municipal law, in my judgment, is doomed to failure. I believe the law will be held unconstitutional."

Praising Smith, the paper said that "when Council was debating the hopeless attempt to interpose a legal barrier between White and Colored residential sections, the basic trouble is the city's failure to provide adequate living facilities for the colored people."

But the gyrations of the stock market wouldn't end. *The News Leader* noted on Page One of October 28:

Stocks Break
Again in New
Selling Wave

And the next day, a banner head:

PANICKY SELLING BRINGS NEW BREAK IN STOCKS

That wasn't enough to alarm the editorial page, which said, "Thus far most of the profits that have been wiped out in the decline of the stock market have been on paper." It concluded, "The present period of uncertainty is not apt to last very long."

Things were indeed looking better. *The Times-Dispatch* of October 30 carried three front-page stories, one of them local, under a four-column head:

Barriers Of Buying Orders Set
Up By Bankers To End Stock
Panic; City Leaders Confident

The News Leader proclaimed on Page One:

STOCKS RALLY AS STRONG AID APPEARS

The Times-Dispatch came back October 31 with only a one-column head on its lead story:

Bank Group's
Help Brings
Sharp Rally;
Stocks Climb

The Times-Dispatch editorial page that day sniffed at "the few manipulators who sold stock short in the recent debacle at Wall and Broad Streets."

The News Leader's front page of October 31 said:

STOCK PRICES RALLY IN SPECTACULAR FASHION

Editorially, *The Times-Dispatch* tried reassuring its readers. "During the past two or three years," it said on November 1, "Americans have plunged into an orgy of speculation. Scarcely a man with $100 to spare has refrained from trying his luck in the stock market. . . . The business of the country is fundamentally sound. America has reserves and economic power the like of which the world has never known. Abundant work will be found for those who have been shorn in the market."

For sports fans, that same paper carried an interview by Sports Editor Richard V. Carter (later state editor) with Ty Cobb, in which Cobb said he was uninterested in returning to baseball.

Whatever was happening with the stock market, politics never ended, and Virginia was choosing a new governor. Democrat John Garland Pollard, strongly backed by *The Times-Dispatch* and *The News Leader,* trounced Dr. William Moseley Brown, a former professor of psychology at Washington and Lee University, who was supported by Republicans and by Democrats opposed to Al Smith.

The Times-Dispatch felt so passionately about the gubernatorial race that it ran a Page One editorial October 26 in which it lambasted Dr. Brown for refusing to say how he voted on "the so-called short ballot amendments" to the State Constitution.

"The professor thereby established a precedent in American politics," said the editorial. "Not even in Alabama, where the preposterous Tom Heflin holds sway, nor in South Carolina, where Coley Blease holds office by virtue of the appalling number of illiterate mill hands and pardoned convicts, has any candidate for so high an office as Governor deliberately refused to tell how he voted on any matter of public interest."

The editorial concluded, "On this date. . . the low-water mark in Virginia politics was reached. If Virginians fail to rise up and rebuke this trifler, this irresponsible manikin, then the very worst that can happen to the Old Dominion will be none too bad for it."

On November 7, however, a day after it reported Pollard's win, *The Times-Dispatch* announced on Page One, under a one-column head: "An unexpected and somewhat mysterious break in stock prices, rivaling in extent any heretofore recorded but lacking much of the hysteria of recent reactions, threw Wall Street into turmoil again today, as it was struggling to get back on its feet after the wild sessions of the previous fortnight."

Three days' headlines from *The Times-Dispatch* tell the story:

November 8 **Market Rallies**
Spectacularly
After Decline

November 12 **Seventy Stocks**
Hit Low Levels
In Late Break

November 13 **Stocks Crash**
To New Low
Price Levels
For The Year

Things would not look good again for a long time.

MAYOR BRIGHT VS. THE PAPER

In the depths of the Depression and the heat of a presidential race, Mayor J. Fulmer Bright took on *The Times-Dispatch,* and the story ended up in the lead position October 1, 1932.

The paper editorially had called for lower real estate taxes, appointment of a city purchasing agent and reduced salaries for city employees. It also had been critical of Bright's administration.

Bright thereupon ordered an end to the city's advertising in the paper. Advertising, such as that from the departments of Public Works and Public Utilities, was customarily split between *The Times-Dispatch* and its competitor, *The News Leader.* It accounted for a minuscule part of *The Times-Dispatch's* ad revenue. But Bright was determined.

"There will be no more city advertising for *The Times-Dispatch,*" he said. "I have taken this business from your paper because of your editorial criticism. This is the only way I can strike back."

Later, he changed his stance and said: "I don't care how much you criticize my policies, but I object to the insinuation that there has been graft in the administration and to criticism of my personal motives and character."

He told the newspaper's advertising executives, with whom he'd met, "Go back to *The Times-Dispatch* and tell them to laugh that off."

The paper replied that His Honor was trying to suppress a free press.

Vincent Byers, editor of *The Times-Dispatch,* contended that there was no quarrel with the mayor as a person. Indeed, Byers told the Virginia Press Association convention January 13, in Roanoke, the paper considered the mayor "as a gentleman of charm and ability. It has sought in its editorial criticism to distinguish between Dr. Bright the individual, and Dr. Bright, the Mayor of the City of Richmond."

Byers recalled for his fellow newsmen that *The Times-Dispatch,* which had campaigned for a central purchasing agent as a means of saving money, found that Bright and his predecessor had ignored a City Council mandate to do just that.

Then, said Byers, reporters were barred from examining departmental books on purchasing. There was already what Byers called a silence strike in effect, meaning the mayor would discuss publicly no issues before the administration.

The situation was aggravated when *The Times-Dispatch* chided the mayor for his dealing with one Abe Tomkin, an activist who had been denied use of the City Auditorium for a mass meeting and had sought out the mayor at his office. The mayor had Tomkin arrested on a charge of vagrancy—which a court threw out.

The Times-Dispatch denounced the mayor's action and the later arrest of the secretary of the Richmond Unemployed Council, whom the mayor ordered thrown out of his office by the "seat of his pants."

Editorially, the paper urged the mayor to play down the "Red menace" and said the city was not "in the midst of a Russian revolution."

Cartoons lambasting Mayor Bright stirred him, as had earlier editorials that hit at him for saying morality was at stake because of billboards advertising a tobacco product, Bull Durham.

A six-paragraph story at the bottom of Page One in *The Times-Dispatch* of July 31 began:

"Richmond's innocence, a fragile flower but lately saved from the wicked comic magazines, yesterday again was snatched back from the primrose path to perdition by prompt action by Mayor Bright in having removed the Bull Durham sign 'Her Hero,' which depicts the futile amour of a cow gazing rapturously at bovine beauty on a billboard.

"The Mayor regarded the advertisement as 'suggestive and offensive' and when his views were known the tobacco company assured that the bull must go, he said.

"Local historians said last night the demise of 'Her Hero' was the greatest victory for civic virtue since the plastering of the show girls' legs on the theatrical posters thirty years ago by Mayor Carlton McCarthy. This was in the Lillian Russell era when legs were limbs, but not bad at that. . . "

On January 3, the mayor announced he was severing "diplomatic relations with the press" because of "endless editorials of criticism." That was followed several hours later by an edict from Police Chief R.B. Jordan that all news of police activity except what he chose to release would be withheld from the press.

The Times-Dispatch promptly filed suit on that action and won a verdict in Hustings Court on January 13, the same day that Vincent Byers was addressing the press association. Judge John L. Ingram said that Chief Jordan's order "was an abuse of power and unwarranted in law." All police records, except certain unfinished police business that may be withheld temporarily, are public records, said the judge. He cited "the constitutional rights of petitioners and the security and protection of the public and the arrested persons as well."

Byers concluded his talk to the editors: *"The Times-Dispatch* holds that a dangerous precedent would be established by permitting to escape without legal challenge the action of a City administration which permits its chief of police to retaliate for editorial criticism by withholding public documents.

"Public welfare demands that citizens be informed what is taking place in the City, what arrests its police department has made. This is not darkest Russia, where a man may be sent into exile with no one the wiser. This is Virginia.

"It is only to clear the abuses to which such a police order as that issued by Chief Jordan could be subjected. 'Reds,' whom Mayor Bright, and not the press, put on Page one, could be arrested by the score—if a score of 'rcds' could bc found in thc City of Richmond. A 'ccnsorship'—which is what Chief Jordan's order means—cannot and will not be tolerated in an American city of the Twentieth Century."

The competing *News Leader,* which had not sued the city, congratulated its rival in an editorial the day after Judge Ingram's ruling. It added:

"We have seen many mayors come and go in thirty years. There have been three chiefs of police in that time. We expect to be here, publishing the same newspaper, when there is a new mayor and a new chief of police. To make it quite sure that we shall not fail to accord the police all assistance, at all times, for the preservation of good order in Richmond, we are prepared to ignore the petulance and to forget the mistakes of officials."

TRI-STATE GANG

When editors and reporters show off their papers, they seldom choose Saturday editions. There's not enough room to tell the news because the big advertisers—especially in morning papers—hold off for the fat Sunday editions, and fewer ads mean fewer pages and the resultant smaller "news hole."

Even when there were many afternoon papers, there was a shortage not only of space but also of news. And many reporters had the day off.

But by Saturday, September 29, 1934, the five-day week was not the standard. Neither was *The Richmond News Leader* that day. It carried banner headlines that read:

LEGENZA AND MAIS SHOOT WAY OUT
OF CITY JAIL; WOUND 3; FLEE IN AUTO
U.S. Probe of Daring Escape Is Suggested

Beneath two more headlines, the lead story began: "Hours after they had ruthlessly shot down three men in a spectacular break from the Richmond city jail, Walter Legenza and Robert Mais, 'tri-state' gangsters condemned to death in the electric chair for murder, were still at large—in the biggest man hunt in the state's history."

By its final edition that afternoon, *The News Leader* had put together a newspaper of incredible detail. Virtually all of Page One and all of Page Five (which had only a quarter-page of ads) was devoted to the breakout.

The lead story, set two columns wide in bold type, was four columns long. There were five other stories, plus four pictures on the front and 14 (half of them head shots) on page five. The staff put out that mass of information about an event that had begun shortly after 10 a.m.

The other stories included interviews with witnesses and reports of a visit to the jail that day by Mais' mother and demands for an investigation of the breakout.

Robert Mais (left) and Walter Legenza, indicted for murder, walk handcuffed toward court hearing in 1934. They were Richmond's most celebrated criminals in a generation.

When the break occurred, Detective Sergeant O.D. Garton (who would become police chief years later) was in court seeking transfer of the prisoners from city jail. The director of public safety, Captain James R. Sheppard, Jr., had been urging a tighter guard over Mais and Legenza. The only person permitted to visit them was an elderly, white-haired woman, Elizabeth Mais of Philadelphia, mother of the defendant. She had taken the prisoners a can labeled "baked chicken," which investigators determined contained two pistols used in the breakout.

Among those shot in the escape was Patrolman W.A. Toots, who died several days later.

The escape came midway in an 11-month period that began with the murder of a Federal Reserve Bank truck driver and ended with the electrocution of Mais and Legenza. America was still in the Depression, and big-time gangsters were big-time news across the nation. Banner headlines became quite ordinary as Richmond papers reported the initial murder, the search for Mais and Legenza, their later murders and robberies, their capture and return to Richmond, their trial and execution.

The day-to-day accounts as execution day neared vied for readers' attention with reports of the trial of Bruno Richard Hauptmann for the kidnapping of the Lindbergh baby.

Richmond's involvement with Mais and Legenza and others in the "Tri-State Gang" began late on the night of March 8, 1934. E.M. Huband, the reserve bank employee, reached for the brake handle and stopped his truck near Broad Street Station when a large car appeared in front of him.

Legenza shot Huband and he and four other men hauled five mailbags from the truck, put them in their own car and drove to a back road. They unloaded the bags and found nothing of value—only canceled checks and letters. Abandoning the bags and their car, they jumped into a waiting truck filled with empty egg crates and headed north.

One witness said he heard a man say, "We got that fellow." and another say, as the mail bags were being taken from the truck, "We got enough; let's go."

George J. Seay, a Federal Reserve governor, announced that "a substantial reward" would be paid for return of the mail pouches and ridiculed the intelligence of the bandits. "If they had been as experienced and intelligent as we are led to suppose criminals are in these days," he said, "they would have known that nothing of value to third persons would have been sent either to the express office or to the mail trains unless guarded in more formidable manner."

In the months ahead, Mais and Legenza would be known as members of the Tri-State Gang, the Big George Phillips Gang, the Williams Gang or the Meadows Gang. *The News Leader* reported on June 4 that Mais, whom it identified as a member of the "notorious Meadows gang," and the man who was believed to have shot Huband, had been "probably mortally wounded" in Baltimore. In a gun battle with police there, Mais received six bullet wounds. Legenza gave up peaceably, and two other gang members were captured.

Of the myriad stories about Mais and Legenza in both Richmond papers, only a few carried bylines. One that did, by John Riis, son of Jacob Riis, the journalist/muckraker who gained renown by writing about New York's slums, appeared July 28 in *The News Leader.*

"The thin partition of an egg crate was all that stood between a Virginia state motor vehicle officer and instant death on the night of March 8, police here revealed today," said Riis.

Caught up in the drama, Riis continued, "Somewhere along the highways today this motor vehicle officer keeps his patrol, grumbling perhaps at the monotony of the blistering ribbon of concrete, at the dumbness of auto drivers and the public in general, and unaware that for the fraction of a second certain and horrible death stared him in the face."

Riis reconstructed the flight of the five men after the Huband murder in the truck filled with egg crates. Two men were on the front seat and three behind them and in front of the crates. A highway patrolman stopped the vehicle because of its speed.

The men in front said they were hurrying to market and the crates seemed harmless.

"Just to be sure, more from habit than anything else, the officer pushed one or two of the crates aside a bit," said Riis. "The two men on the front seat sat still. The finger of death hovered over the shoulder of the officer.

"Crouching in a nest between the egg crates sat three desperate men with machine guns on their laps, their trigger fingers twitching. Had the officer pushed his search among the crates just a little further, he would have fallen under a withering blast of gun fire!"

Brought back to Richmond after their capture in Baltimore, Mais and Legenza were convicted in late August of Huband's murder and sentenced to death. Mais' "lips curled in a bitter smile when he heard the pronouncement," *The News Leader* said. Mais contended he'd had no part in the killing; indeed, he said, he'd been watching a movie in Washington at the time. Both men contended in interviews with *The News Leader* that the convictions were a frameup. That paper also reported the not unusual rumor of intimidated jurors. They had been given a "threat note" during Mais' trial, the report went.

Following the jail break September 29, there were the standard false reports of sighting the escapees and the expected criticism by many newspapers in and out of state about inadequate security at the jail. Two days later Judge John L. Ingram, who had presided over the murder trials, disqualified himself in any grand jury investigation.

The News Leader bannered:

INGRAM ASKS PEERY TO NAME OTHER JUDGE TO SIT IN PROBE OF MAIS-LEGENZA JAIL BREAK

It was more than a week before the grand jury was named and almost a month before it reported, but there was no lack of news coverage of Mais and Legenza. *The News Leader* said that the commonwealth's attorney was investigating a report that Patrolman Toots, who then was still in a hospital, had been drunk on duty at the jail and with no bullets in his pistol when the escape occurred. The paper also said it had learned that "weapons which unarmed jail deputies might have used against the gangsters were within easy reach, but remained untouched when the two desperadoes blazed their way to freedom."

Adding drama to the event was the suicide October 14 of Richard C. Duke, a deputy city sergeant who had unlocked a jail door September 29 so Mais and Legenza could confer with their lawyer. Then they blasted their way out of jail.

The grand jury was composed 10 men whom *The News Leader* in a Page One story called "a representative group of Richmond business men whose ability and integrity assure a thorough and impartial investigation of all phases of the jailbreak."

Its report, which dominated three pages of *The News Leader,* indicted City Sergeant John G. Saunders for negligence and recommended dismissal of two deputies—Saunders' son, John H. Saunders, and T.F. O'Connor. It also reprimanded Judge Ingram for giving insufficient attention to security at the jail.

But Saunders was cleared by a jury in the Hustings Court of John Ingram, who continued to sit for years. The deputies kept their jobs.

After their escape and flight north, Mais and Legenza committed several other major crimes and had another shootout with police—this one in Philadelphia. Several of their accomplices were caught, but the men wanted in Richmond escaped again. It was costly; Legenza jumped 30 feet to a concrete street and broke a leg. Mais, according to Ben B. Dulaney's *News Leader* account of the criminals' violent behavior, "lugged his prostrate friend to an empty box car, threw him in and continued running. Two hours later, he returned in a stolen car, drove Legenza to New York and when the pain became unbearable, placed him in a hospital under the name of William Stewart."

Both men were arrested January 18, 1935—Mais in a Harlem flat after police had been alerted by a telephone call they intercepted in Philadelphia. Several days of questioning ensued, and the men were returned to Richmond January 22 in what officials had hoped would be early morning secrecy.

It was not to be.

"Other than the brass buttons of the railway men, there was not a uniform in sight,' reported *The News Leader.* "Local police, uninformed of the transfer, left the matter strictly in the hands of the men who moved the killers from New York."

Newsmen were among the "odd and silent gathering" of about 50 as the first section of the Havana Special rolled into Broad Street Station. "Few knew the time of the return," the paper said, "yet within the half hour before the arrival word spread quickly over the station and brought trainmen, Negro porters, cooks and other employes of stores across the street and a few persons who were waiting for other trains."

The gangsters were on the second section of the train, which arrived 15 minutes later, with shades drawn on the Pullman car. "Agents occasionally had to poke gun muzzles at the curious who ventured too close to the steps," added *The News Leader.*

The paper knew readers were almost panting for word on the killers, and it aimed to satisfy them.

"Nature today provided a fitting background for the next-to-last scene in the lives of the two gangsters who have caused Richmond police more trouble than any other criminals in the history of the state," said *The News Leader.* "At 6 A.M. Broad-Street Station stood deserted in a cold drizzle that hid the first hint of dawn. In the concourse were two local detectives who said they had not been notified of the projected return, but were just 'looking around.'

"Except for an empty stretcher and several overcoated individuals identified as government men from Washington, the platform was deserted when the first section of the Havana Special pulled in at 6:10. Trainmen said the gunmen and their retinue were on the second section.

"At 6:25 the other train slipped in. From the last two cars jumped men with automatic rifles and submachine guns. Others played searchlights on the dusky platform and searched beneath and between the cars. [A] cot was rolled up and Legenza, his thinning hair awry and his face a pallid mask, was lifted from the door. Both legs were wrapped in huge rolls of gauze and the left one, which is broken, stuck straight out. Tucked incongruously under a pink blanket, he was trundled quickly to the end of the platform.

"From the other end of the car, Mais, heavily shackled, was assisted to a wheelchair and rolled after his pal. In addition to his many chains, Mais was handcuffed to a government man who walked beside him as a shaking porter pushed the vehicle. The gangster seemed in a daze.

"All that was left of the debonair appearance which characterized him all through his trial here last summer was a pearl gray snap-brimmed hat. He wore an unpressed suit and a dirty shirt, open at the neck. Since the jailbreak Mais has dyed his hair and grown a small black moustache. He puffed a cigarette which the man with him removed occasionally from his mouth. The 29-year-old desperado was so heavily manacled that he could lift his hands to his face only with difficulty."

Escorted by four cars with agents, a makeshift ambulance had Mais and Legenza at the state prison 20 minutes after their arrival at Broad Street Station—a mere 50 yards from where they had gunned down Huband.

At the "pen," *The News Leader* said, "Frank X. Fay, undercover man of the department of justice who was instrumental in the captures, sat down with relief as the inner bars clanged behind his charges. With a 'tommy gun' across his knees he relaxed and talked—as much as a 'G' man ever talks.

"'Well, we got 'em here,' he said, and that was his only comment."

Four hours later, six carloads of Richmond police led the men to Hustings Court. *The News Leader* said Mais "was a sorry sight. With red eyes, scars on his neck and a three-day growth of beard," he faced Judge Ingram, who set a new execution date of February 2—11 days away.

Legenza, the paper said, "lay stolid and seemingly unhearing" as Judge Ingram set the same execution date for him. "It was the first time," said *The News Leader,* "that local officers had ever seen the man lose even a trace of the animal-like calm which characterized him during his trial confinement here."

Beneath a banner head,

MAIS AND LEGENZA SENTENCED TO DIE ON FEB. 2

The News Leader went all out with eight columns of pictures stretched across the top half of the paper and similar layout on Page 12, on which nothing but the crime story appeared.

With it all, no reporter or photographer rated a byline.

Accounts of activity at the penitentiary and how the convicts spent their last hours still were Page One news for *The News Leader* and *The Times-Dispatch.* On the day of the executions, February 2, *The Times-*

Dispatch's editorial cartoonist Fred Seibel showed the sun shining on "Gangdom" near a nearby "Underworld" hole. The caption: "The Groundhog Sees Its Shadow." The front page said Legenza was going to the chair with "cynical defiance," while Mais was repentant.

"No final words were addressed to guards who lifted him from his cot to a wheelchair," *The Times-Dispatch* said, adding that Legenza murmured, "Handle that leg easily, it's sore."

There were late "confessions," intended to divert suspicion of aiding their jail escape away from Mais' girlfriend, Marie McKeever, and direct it elsewhere. But the thrill was all gone; *The Times-Dispatch* reported 12,000 people viewed the bodies.

HOPEWELL BUS CRASH

Legend has it that Maurice Dean, *The Times-Dispatch's* earnest police reporter, was still in formal attire after a debutante party when he covered a highway crash that was labeled "probably the worst in Virginia's motor history."

"Thirteen persons, possibly more, were drowned Sunday morning about 8:58 o'clock when a Greyhound bus plunged through a drawbridge over the Appomattox River at Hopewell, the bridge having been opened to permit passage by a tug and a barge." So read the lead on an extra December 23, 1935. Text on the top half of the front page was set two columns wide.

The driver had been hurled through the windshield before the bus hit the water, and he died of shock and injuries a few minutes later. The bus sank in 30 feet of water.

By the final edition that Monday, *The Times-Dispatch* had a lead story and two sidebars, at least one of which had Dean's byline. The headline across the top of the page read:

14 Bodies Taken From River After Bus Plunges
Through Open Drawbridge Outside Hopewell

Dean's bylined story was virtually all quotes from the bridgekeeper, Lacy McNair, who said, in language suspiciously like that of most people in Dean's crime stories, "Those screams and cries of women as the bus hung on the edge of the bridge before its final plunge into the icy waters of the river—that was a half-minute I'll never forget."

The Times-Dispatch devoted all of Page Four to pictures and all of the next page to sidebars and more pictures. The accident occurred an hour after the bus had left Richmond and was caused by the brakes freezing as it moved at moderate speed toward the north end of the bridge, according to the state's Division of Motor Vehicles.

Emergency signals on the guard rail to the drawbridge were operating, the paper said. But, "It was then that witnesses were horrified to see the coach, apparently out of control, splinter the wooden panel which served as guard gate, and proceed to the brink of the open draw and plunge into the 30-foot channel."

THE SNOW OF 1940

The News Leader thought it wise to explain to its readers how handling news of World War II was difficult, so in a Page One "Our Report to You," on the first day of 1940, it did so.

"Not since 1918 have The *News Leader's* facilities and personnel had such a test," the paper said. "Never have dispatches required more careful handling and keen interpretation. Much of it we had to label: 'The British say. . . ' or 'The Germans say' as we matched wits with propaganda ministries. Still, we helped you find the truth in numerous obscure reports." And, the paper added, among its duties were "to cover Richmond like a roof."

The war in Europe was big news but not big enough to merit the lead story every day. On January 22, under a two-line banner head, *The News Leader* reported that an annexation court had awarded Richmond a segment of Henrico County containing 15,000 residents. Amazingly, the editorial page, which had supported annexation, carried a column-long editorial although the decision was announced that afternoon.

Both papers were carrying renowned national columnists. *The News Leader* had Drew Pearson and Robert Allen, Eleanor Roosevelt, Walter Lippmann and David Lawrence. *The Times-Dispatch* countered with Dorothy Thompson, Westbrook Pegler, Hugh Johnson, Walter Winchell and Ernest K. Lindley. It also was serializing Daphne du Maurier's *Rebecca.*

By the third week of January, Richmond had been suffering a severe cold spell. *The Times-Dispatch* said January 22 that some relief was expected—from the low of 7 the previous day to only 16 the following day. But by the afternoon of January 23, *The News Leader* warned, "A storm whipping in from the snow-covered far South tonight may bring Richmond it heaviest snowfall of the winter to date. The snow which started falling shortly after noon today is only a preliminary to what may be expected throughout the night, the Weather Bureau forecaster said."

The forecaster was right. Under a banner headline reading:

INCREASING COLD ADDS TO DIFFICULTY OF DIGGING CITY OUT OF 16-INCH SNOW

The News Leader reported, "Snowbound Richmond's third heaviest snowfall in its weather history is over. The task of digging from under 16 inches of snow will be made harder by increasingly cold temperatures, the Weather Bureau reported yesterday." The snow, which had begun at 12:20 p.m. the previous day, ended at 8:30 a.m.

Severe weather often brings out the best in a newspaper's local coverage. Virtually every staff member works on a weather story, several of which merit front-page play. Photographers have a field day, knowing their work will be displayed prominently. Sometimes a paper hams it up. Merritt S. Ruddock, a *News Leader* reporter, rode a mule to work from Bon Air, some 10 miles away, and was pictured on Page One.

Not every reporter could get to work. One who could was *The Times-Dispatch's* James Latimer, who walked to work from his apartment at 915 Park Avenue, less than a mile from the newspaper.

So, "I was the snow writer in the Great Blizzard of 1940," Latimer recalled.[79]

Latimer, who had written the annexation story for *The Times-Dispatch* two days earlier, had the lead again—this time on the storm—January 25. "The deepest snowfall since 1908 settled down over Richmond yesterday—a chilling blanket of white that held the city helpless and inert in the wake of Tuesday night's howling blizzard."

BUSINESS AND INDUSTRIAL LIFE OF RICHMOND HALTED; SCHOOLS CLOSED AS CITY BATTLES 16-INCH SNOWFALL

That was *The Times-Dispatch's* headline for Latimer's story, which spelled out gracefully and completely how severe the storm was. All highways but part of U.S. 1 were closed. There was minimal bus service in the city. Schools were closed. Most stores had closed but some would try to reopen that day. Twenty-nine trolleys were frozen on their rails. The 1908 storm to which Latimer referred had totaled 17.2 inches.

Dancers at Tantilla Gardens, a favorite night spot, were marooned overnight and didn't leave for home until noon the next day—some in evening clothes. At one intersection, five cars were abandoned, each pointed in a different direction. The bright spot was that trains were running.

True, the snow had stopped on the morning of the 24th, but the official temperature at the Chimborazo Park weather station was 2 above zero, while at Byrd Field it was 11 below—colder than Fairbanks, Alaska. Although county and private schools opened on Monday, January 29, the city schools remained closed until Wednesday—a total of four days' work missed. The superintendent, however, reminded everyone that schools had been closed 10 days in the great snowstorm of 1899. The total then was 16.3 inches.

As late as January 27, *The News Leader* editorially was urging Richmonders to restrict their use of automobiles because of ice and accumulated snow.

Although contemporary news accounts listed the snowfall as 16 inches, the Weather Service now counts the total for January 23-25 as 21.6 inches. That is because all data since 1930 have been corrected to account for conditions at Byrd Field, now weather station for the city. Total snowfall for all of January 1940 is listed at 28.5 inches.

There was other news in January 1940; a "society" wedding still counted for a lot in Richmond's papers. When Janet Keen Patton and Lawrence Lewis Jr. married, the wedding at St. Paul's Episcopal Church and the reception at the Commonwealth Club merited a six-column head and four pictures in *The Times-Dispatch.*

Also that month, *The Times-Dispatch,* which carried blistering editorials on big-time college athletics while Virginius Dabney was editor, let fly under a two-column headline, "Football—Wrecker of Honor Systems."

"Intercollegiate football in Virginia and throughout the nation," said *The Times-Dispatch,* "is a racket which is shot through with hypocrisy, deceit and deliberate misrepresentation." The tone of the editorial was similar to that 11 years earlier when the paper commended the Carnegie Foundation's criticism of big-time college football.

PEARL HARBOR

As the entry of the United States into World War II approached, even sports occasionally made the front page. On Sunday, November 21, 1941, *Times-Dispatch* editors thought the exploits of Bill Dudley in his final football game for the University of Virginia—a 28-7 win over North Carolina—merited a two-column headline and a picture on Page One.

Not everyone was sure that war was imminent for the United States. Syndicated columnists Drew Pearson and Robert Allen wrote in *The News Leader* on November 27, "After weeks of negotiation, actually beginning last May with the visit of Saburo Kurusu, Japan and the United States appear to be nearing an agreement in the Pacific."

There were five "provisional" points, said Pearson and Allen, which included Japan's withdrawal from most of Indochina and U.S. relaxation of its embargo on Japanese trade.

When Pearl Harbor was attacked on December 7, *The Times-Dispatch* published one of its rare extras, with a banner headline,

HONOLULU, MANILA BOMBED;
BATTLE NOW RAGING

The edition was put together so quickly that Fred Seibel's editorial cartoon showed a grinning Japanese on a pendulum labeled Far East Crisis swinging from "War Chatter" to "Peace Talk."

The regular edition (without the Seibel cartoon) had only one non-war story on the front page. It concerned John L. Lewis mineworkers' winning a union shop.

The headline for the war story had been changed to

JAPAN DECLARES WAR ON U.S.
AFTER RAIDING PACIFIC BASES

The News Leader's front page that day was all war news, except part of a news summary. The main headline:

WAR DECLARED ON JAPAN
BY SWIFT CONGRESS VOTE

Editorially, the paper sounded relieved. "If it had to come upon us, we could not have asked for conditions that gave us so just a case, so righteous a cause, at the bar of history and of conscience."

Richmond Times-Dispatch

91st Year — Richmond, Virginia, Monday, December 8, 1941

Weather, Forecast

On the Inside

JAPAN DECLARES WAR ON U. S. AFTER RAIDING PACIFIC BASES

British Are Attacked; Thailand Is Invaded; Naval Battle Raging

By The Associated Press

Japan assaulted every main United States and British possession in the central and western Pacific and invaded Thailand today in a hasty but evidently shrewdly planned prosecution of a war she began Sunday without warning.

Her formal declaration of war against both the United States and Britain came two hours and 55 minutes after Japanese planes spread death and terrific destruction in Honolulu and Pearl Harbor at 7:35 A. M., Hawaiian time (1:05 P. M., E. S. T.) Sunday.

The claimed successes for this first swoop included sinking of the United States battleship West Virginia and setting afire of the battleship Oklahoma.

From that moment, each tense tick of the clock brought new and flaming accounts of Japanese aggression in her secretly launched war of conquest or death for the Land of the Rising Sun.

The Record of Aggression

As compiled from official and unofficial accounts from all affected countries, the record ran like this:

Honolulu bombed a second time;

Lumber-laden United States Army transport torpedoed 1,300 miles west of San Francisco and another transport in distress;

Shanghai's international settlement seized, U. S. gunboat Wake captured there and British gunboat Peterel destroyed;

Capture of the U. S. Island of Wake;

Bombing of the U. S. Island of Guam;

Bombing of many points throughout the Philippine Islands;

Invasion of northern Malaya and bombing of Singapore;

Invasion of Thailand (Siam) and bombing of Bangkok.

Sea Battle in Progress

Declaration Expected Today

Hull Calls Japanese Liars

Berlin Comments Gleefully

Declaration By Britain Due Today

Parliament Is Called: Winant Sees Churchill

Note of Tragedy Comes With News

Tokio Declares War on U. S. And Britain

Togo Calls Envoys: Grew Is Handed Note

Continued on Page 2, Column 4

All Japanese Are Arrested In Norfolk as Precaution

Continued on Page 5, Column 2

Mr. Roosevelt To Address Joint Session

White House Meeting Hears of Pacific Loss

Lewis Wins Union Shop For Mines

Arbitration Board Vote Is 2-to-1

IT'S A LONG WAY TO . . . TOKIO—Three sailors from the Norfolk Naval Base, snatched off their week-end leave in Richmond to report at the base, wave good-bye from the bus window, above a significant inscription. Left to right, Blake Moe of New

WORLD WAR II

It wasn't as if *The Times-Dispatch* and *The News Leader* didn't cover World War II; they did. On many days, the majority of stories on the front pages were war stories, but they were all wire service stories—the Associated Press in *The News Leader* and the AP and United Press in *The Times-Dispatch*.

Although both papers had grown in size and prestige since World War I, when neither had overseas correspondents, they still were not large enough or wealthy enough to afford them. Both papers' staffs had been depleted by callups to the armed forces, and both had an increasingly large percentage of women reporters covering beats that had always been male domains.

The News Leader's Douglas Southall Freeman and *The Times-Dispatch's* Virginius Dabney, well-versed in foreign affairs, contemplated developments in the war in editorials that were long on reason and high on support of the Allied effort.

The Allied invasion of Western Europe began about 12:30 a.m. Eastern War Time, Tuesday, June 6, 1944. That gave *The Times-Dispatch* time in its Tuesday morning paper to set most of columns 7 and 8 on Page One two columns wide and in bold face type. There were six Associated Press stories, one from Washington, the others from London and Allied Force Headquarters.

The banner head read:

NORTHERN FRANCE INVADED

That afternoon's *News Leader* proclaimed:

ALLIES STORMING INLAND IN FRANCE
FROM BEACHHEADS QUICKLY GAINED

Seven AP stories from London or the new front in Europe made the front page.

By its final edition, *The News Leader* had completely remade its front page. The headline now said:

ALLIES SMASH ON IN FRANCE
REACH CAEN 9 MILES INLAND

One three-column picture showed an Army chaplain blessing troops headed to battle; another, reprinted in many history books, showed General Dwight D. Eisenhower, the supreme allied commander, meeting paratroopers before they dropped on France.

Catching up in all editions of Wednesday, June 7, *The Times-Dispatch* had a war-only front page. The lead story appeared under the headline,

ALLIES 13 MILES IN FRANCE

Tucked away in the lower right corner under a two-column head was a local story on reaction to the invasion.

It read, "'A day of solemn dedication' in military camps, classrooms, chapels and homes was observed throughout Richmond yesterday with little of the expected D-Day hysteria as banker, baker, soldier, sailor, wife and mother paused at least once in the day to celebrate the long-awaited event by attending church.

"There were no hilarious gatherings, but a rather quiet acceptance of the exciting news with silent prayers that the losses would not be too great."

The reporter was Lucille Wheeler, soon to be the bride of Corporal Chauncey Durden, sports editor of *The Times-Dispatch,* on indefinite loan to the U.S. Army. They married July 26 that year.

Editorially, *The News Leader* said, "This 6th day of June will be forever memorable in the history of Europe." It analyzed the sites of landings and worried that the public might be "swamped instead of served" by the outpouring of news. For its own part, said the paper, "*The News Leader* intends to condense as best it may the bulk of the report. We want to give the significant facts, but we do not wish to obscure by purposeless comment."

The Times-Dispatch of June 7 warned editorially of grave days ahead but said, "Like the hammer of Thor, the Allied Expeditionary Force struck the foam-flecked coast of France early yesterday, and the moment for which the civilized world had stood on tiptoe for months, had come. Mighty in its fire power and its armor, the great company of Anglo-American fighting men, perhaps a quarter of a million strong, made its way through the mine fields and tank traps, the artillery shells and the machine gun bullets, and established beachheads on the Norman shore."

EXTRA Richmond Times-Dispatch

Richmond 11, Virginia, Wednesday, August 15, 1945

Five Cents

JAPS QUIT

orean Port
f Seishin
aptured

Truman Declares
Two-Day Holiday

Darden Hails
Victory,
Asks Prayers

Fitting Tribute
To Fallen Urged

MacArthur Named
To Take Surrender
As Allied Leader

Offensive Operations Stopped;
Draft Inductions Ordered Cut

Enemy Flyers
Out in Force
Over Korea

Sixteen Japs Downed,
One Thunderbolt Lost

Americans, British Reveal Secrets of Radar;
Important Role in Peacetime Work Forecast

Nation Drops
All Controls
On Manpower

Petain's Fate
Lies in Hands
Of 24 Jurors

Truman Cuts
Draft Quota
To 50,000

hinese in South-Central Area Cut Off Escape
f Thousands of Japs in Tungan Attack

Premature Peace Celebrations
Break Out in Big Cities

The precise time of the invasion was obviously unknown to the Axis and to Allies. But Americans had been primed for it, as evidenced by *The News Leader* of June 6, the day of the invasion. Full-page advertisements from the two big department stores—Miller & Rhoads and Thalhimers—and lesser ads from Virginia Electric & Power Co. and Byram's restaurant, among others, all alluded to the invasion.

The News Leader ran a full page of pictures from its files of fighting men preparing for the invasion during maneuvers.

Both Richmond papers routinely carried stories throughout the war of local servicemen who had been killed or wounded or who had been decorated or gained major promotions. The News Leader went a step further.

Each Saturday, it carried a column, titled "Service Men's News," by Jack Kilpatrick, its star reporter and later its editorial page editor. Because of asthma, Kilpatrick had been classified 4F—unfit for military service. His column was a potpourri of local developments.

On September 18, 1943, he reported that "The Third War Loan campaign swung into full stride in Richmond this week, as thousands of persons dug deep to find cash for War Bonds and Stamps." In the same column he told of two men's convictions for buying liquor with someone else's ration book, of Virginia's production of 754,000,000 quarts of milk in 1942, "a tremendous lot of moo-juice," and of the election of "Mrs. M. Fontaine, popular English teacher," to sponsor the Thomas Jefferson High School Cadet Corps."

Kilpatrick's column ("Clip this out and mail it," readers were advised) continued throughout the war. Sometimes, even in days of a newsprint shortage, it was two columns long.

With World War II in full swing, the news staffs of both papers were depleted of males by call-ups to the armed forces. Recruiting experienced copy editors was a major headache. Increasingly, women were getting major reporting assignments, but there were few of them on the copy desks.

One recruit that *The Times-Dispatch* didn't have to worry about losing to Uncle Sam was Henry Bowles, who was all of about 5 feet tall and was called "The Midget" by everyone.

Bowles was a pretty fair headline-writer, but what distinguished him from everyone else on the staff was a routine he perfected for disposing of balled-up paper on the floor. Often, a harried copy editor would write out a headline, see it was too long and dispose of the paper on which he'd written by balling it up and aiming it at a trash basket. Often he missed.

Whereupon, Bowles would jump from his seat, walk to the paper and—maneuvering somewhat like a soccer player—work the paper ball between his heels. Then with grace, but considerable effort, he would jump and deposit the ball with his heels into a trash basket.

Many admired Bowles' expertise as a jumper; Richard V. Carter, the assistant city editor who sat a few feet from the copy desk, marveled at it.

One day in 1944, working on copy for the next edition, Bowles turned back a story to William G. Leverty, the news editor, who looked at it and snarled, "On *The Times-Dispatch,* we hyphenate 'co-operate.'"

One of the great news stories in Richmond newspaper history—the end of World War II.

Bowles replied, "There's no hyphen in 'cooperate'; only an idiot would hyphenate it."

Leverty, who brooked insubordination from no one, bellowed that if he wished to continue working for *The Times-Dispatch,* he'd hyphenate 'co-operate.' Bowles and his boss exchanged a few more words before Leverty announced, "You're fired" and chased him out of the newsroom.

It was Dick Carter's day off, and Leverty knew the firing would distress him. Somehow, he found a replacement.

When Carter returned to the office, Leverty told him, "Dick, I had to fire the midget." Carter was distraught. "But," said Leverty, "I've found a first-rate replacement."

Carter looked up, sighed and asked only one thing: "How high can he jump?"[80]

THE THALHIMER STORY

Although the war was over, the news of November 21, 1945 was anything but routine. Auto workers called a strike against General Motors, and George C. Marshall and Ernest J. King were being replaced by Dwight D. Eisenhower and Chester W. Nimitz as the top men in the Army and Navy.

Each story rated a banner headline in *The Times-Dispatch*. Yet, a story tucked under a two-column headline at the bottom of the front page cost the paper its managing editor and left a legacy of bitterness and gossip—much of it untrue.

The Associated Press story out of Cherry Point, North Carolina, ran only nine inches. It began: "Captain William B. Thalhimer, Jr., Marine Corps reserve officer from Richmond, Va., was found guilty by a general court-martial here yesterday of 'conduct to the prejudice of good order and discipline, culpable inefficiency and neglect of duty.'"

Only six of the nine inches of text ran on the front page. The decision to have a three-inch "turn" caused the trouble.

"Billy" Thalhimer was, in civilian life, a third-generation member of his family to be an officer of one of Richmond's major department stores, Thalhimer Bros. Inc. At Cherry Point, he had been in charge of several post exchanges. Among 24 charges against him were two that he switched goods between the store in Richmond and the Cherry Point post exchange branches.

Those were among 18 charges dropped at the outset of the trial. Four months later, Thalhimer was cleared of the final six charges and was restored to duty.

Still, after almost half a century, reports persist that Richmond Newspapers carried nothing on the trial or that the story was buried inside. Both are false.

The first story, seven inches of type under a one-column headline, ran November 9, 1945, on Page 7 of *The Times-Dispatch*. It said a court-martial was being convened to hear the charges. The story that caused the hullabaloo was the one 12 days later that started on Page One and continued.

One *Times-Dispatch* veteran who recalls the episode is Paul Saunier Jr., who returned to the paper after Navy service in World War II and was discharged in the fall of 1945, partly because of an injury. But while he was in the Navy, he heard about Thalhimer's troubles and alerted the newspaper when he returned. Ben Johnston, acting managing editor, thus asked the Navy for information when the outcome was determined.

Saunier recalls that the merchandise supposedly switched between Thalhimers and the post exchanges was stockings—cottons for nylon or rayon stockings.

When the court-martial result came in, said Saunier, there was considerable consternation among newspaper executives. Leon Dure was back as managing editor after three years in the Army Air Corps.

"The advertising manager, who was Dick Stevenson, had been under all sorts of pressure from the advertisers to either kill it or do something with it," said Saunier. "And what happened was that Dure held on very strongly and said, 'They can't pull their ads; there's no newsprint; they can't go anywhere else.'"

Saunier, recalling the incident, declined to identify D. Tennant Bryan, the publisher, or John Dana Wise, the general manager, by name or title. He called them "the top management guy" and "the second-ranking guy."[81] But everyone else familiar with the incident, including Bryan, identified them by name in interviews with the author.

Dure said, according to Saunier, "People will admire us for a long time if we run this and handle it big, and the top management guy said, 'Will the defense be on the front page?' or asked for it to be, and [Dure] said, 'Yes, it will.'"

Thus, said Saunier, a response was gotten from defense attorneys (one of whom, Lt. Cmdr. Alexander Parker, later became general counsel for Thalhimers). It was included in the story, all of which ran in the early edition on the front page.

Here recollections differ slightly. Saunier doesn't recall any picture. But he said that Wise called the newsroom and asked Dure where the story was played, to which Dure replied, "None of your damn business." It was a confrontation, says James Latimer, then and for years later *The Times-Dispatch's* top political writer, between two "very strong-willed, stubborn, opinionated men."[82]

Bryan saw the first edition with a front-page picture of Thalhimer and Parker at the Stork Club along with the story. Bryan thought the picture, a publicity shot sent to the paper from the club, was inappropriate and told Wise to get in touch with the news department.

Reflecting years later, Bryan said he wished he'd done nothing. "I asked Jack Wise to do it. I didn't do it myself; I was yellow." Bryan said Dure was "bitterly resentful and I don't blame him."[83]

Wise insisted on a two-column head on the front page and Dure wanted to keep the three-column head. Wise, as the boss, got his way. The two-column head was put on the story and the defense statement—which Bryan had been promised would be on Page One—ended up on the turn.

Saunier thinks Dure should have told Wise of his promise to Bryan that the response would be on Page One. "The point is that Dure was playing the game," said Saunier. "And the next day when I came in. . . 1 o'clock. . .there was a notice on the board saying that Mr. Dure has resigned as managing editor and Mr. Ben Johnston, who did so well standing in his absence in World War II, will now be the new managing editor."

Saunier is not alone in recalling that Dure resigned November 21, the day after the squabble with Wise. But *The Times-Dispatch's* two-paragraph story on Dure's replacement by Johnston came Dec. 6.

THE ASSAULT

A few American daily papers regularly print the names of rape victims. *The Times-Dispatch* does not and *The News Leader* did not.

But many readers thought *The Times-Dispatch* broke its own rule in the summer of 1946, when it explicitly identified a woman who was attacked by a man and then avoided naming her in every subsequent story—of which there were many. *The News Leader* never named her. In neither paper was the word "rape" used.

A socially prominent Vassar graduate and Junior League member, she was identified by name, age and address in the lead of an August 28 *Times-Dispatch* story, which said she "was badly beaten about the head with a piece of brick, stabbed twice in the neck and suffered other injuries about 8 o'clock last night when she was attacked in the rear of a house under construction at the intersection of Greenway Lane and Grove Avenue, in Westhampton."

It seems the woman had taken a streetcar to visit some friends in the West End, gone beyond the stop, gotten off and begun walking.

The story continued that "a Negro man ran from behind a house under construction and grabbed her from the rear, gagged her with a piece of cloth and dragged her to a point about 25 yards from Greenway Lane and a like distance from Grove Avenue.

"The Negro told [the woman], 'The only way I can get away with this is to kill you.'"

The story continued that he beat her and she became unconscious. She awakened two hours later, dragged herself to a brick wall and attracted the attention of a motorist. Her pocketbook and shoes were found at the point of attack and her knitting needles and a magazine were nearby. Police who responded called out bloodhounds.

Almost 50 years later, old newsmen recall pressure on the papers not to use her name, and the woman—now living out of state—says members of her family were friends of Publisher Tennant Bryan and Virginius Dabney, editor of The Times-Dispatch. Whether they were called, she is not sure.[84]

In any case, *The News Leader* of August 28 did not mention her name. Nor did *The Times-Dispatch* a day later, when it reported Mayor William Herbert had given $500 toward what he hoped would be a $1,000 city reward for information on the attacker. Governor William M. Tuck denounced the crime as "a most revolting one." Police said the woman had feigned death.

Late summer of 1946 was not a good time for black men to be walking around the West End of Richmond. Less than a mile from the point of attack was Westwood, a quiet, all-black section, where residents were queried at length by police.

The Hampton Gardens Citizens Association planned an "indignation meeting." Police Chief E.H. Organ said, "We have reason to believe the man we are after lives in the same section of town in which the attack occurred."

Police Captain O.D. Garton called the victim "remarkable" and said she reconstructed "the entire crime from beginning to end." The knife the attacker reportedly used was said to be "a small, rusty paring knife." The woman said the man was small and not very strong but stronger than she.

By the end of August, the local NAACP announced a $100 reward for the capture of the assailant. All police leaves were canceled. "More than 60 leads" were under way, the press reported.

There were no arrests, but rumors were rampant. The most repeated was that the entire story was a hoax and that the woman was protecting a former suitor who had beaten her. That report surfaced when, one day less than a month after the attack, a former Richmonder whom the woman had dated jumped to his death from the 76th floor of the Empire State Building.

One week later, the woman married a Baltimore man at St. James's Episcopal Church in Richmond. And six days after that, she went to Trenton, New Jersey, where she identified a Bahamian in a police lineup as her probable attacker, but, *The Times-Dispatch* reported, she wasn't positive.

Was her story made up?

In a telephone conversation, February 2, 1993, the woman said from her Delaware home that she was not raped, that her attacker was "absolutely a black man" and that she was "so badly hurt I hardly knew what happened" and she didn't think she'd live through the first night.

At the lineup in Trenton, she said, "My husband leaned over and said 'Is it the second [man] from the left?' and I said, 'Yes,'" But she could hardly talk afterward.

THE BEAUTY SHOP EXPLOSION

As night police reporter, Maurice Dean normally didn't report to work at *The Times-Dispatch* before 5:30 p.m. On July 29, 1947, his day began a good bit earlier—with a telephone from F.J. McDermott.

"Mac," The Times-Dispatch city editor, loved nothing more than City Hall politics except a good police story, and this was one of those. "Get out to the airport, Diz," growled McDermott, who always growled—a trait reporters traced to his Marine days in World War I. "Meet John Wood there; you're flying to Harrisonburg."

That, essentially, was the only direction McDermott gave Dean. He'd find out the rest from Wood, a Richmond Newspapers photographer and airplane pilot, who, like Dean, loved bourbon and good police stories.

At the airport, they took aboard a light plane a case of plasma. Wood informed Dean that there had been an explosion at a beauty parlor and several people were dead.

The next morning's paper looked like something from the war several years earlier. A banner headline read:

10 Women Killed, 19 Persons Injured Seriously
As Gas Blast Destroys Harrisonburg Beauty Shop

Dean's bylined story began: "HARRISONBURG, July 29—An explosion of block-busting force, believed to have been set off when a lighted match ignited gas in the basement under Pauline's Beauty Salon on South Main Street, today killed at least 10 women, seriously injured 19 other persons and inflicted lesser hurts on about 10 others."

Like most of Dean's stories, this was a rewrite. No one, including Dean, called him a writer. He was a reporter and he could gather facts in minutes that took others hours to obtain. His main story, from the front page through the continuation inside, ran more than two columns.

About two inches before the turn, a paragraph began: "The cause of Harrisonburg's greatest disaster, at first a mystery, was cleared up by bits of information pieced together from several sources tonight."

Then, "Fire Chief Louis Armentrout, who led the local volunteer fire department into action that quickly smothered small fires in the blast's aftermath, said that it apparently came from escaping gas in the building's basement.

"Coal trucks were unloading coal down a chute into the basement, the chief reported, and a workman below was working with a shovel at the bottom of the chute.

". . . Later it was determined that the workman in the basement was James Mullen. . . who was being treated at the hospital for serious injuries.

"Hospital attendants said Mullen told them, 'The last thing I remember was when I struck a match in the basement.'"

The operator of the coal company was quoted as saying just enough time lapsed between truck arrivals for Mullen to have lit and smoked a cigarette.

Newsroom legend has it that it was Dean who discovered the cause of the blast and traced it to Mullen. Dean is dead and so are many of his contemporaries. Others cannot confirm the report, but they say it sounds like Dean. He had a penchant for finding facts and letting principals in the story take credit for disclosing the information.

POLITICS, NATIONAL

Plenty of Virginia Democrats in 1928 didn't cotton to the idea of Al Smith as president of the United States, but to the editors of Richmond's dailies, voting for Herbert Hoover would be aberrant behavior.

For one thing, there was the anti-Catholic feeling, which each paper condemned pointedly and frequently. There also was the Klan. *The Times-Dispatch,* slashing at Robert H. Angell, the GOP state chairman, said editorially Nov. 3 that the Republican Party is "the Ku Klux Klan, anti-Catholic party in Virginia, if not in the United States."

The News Leader laid out its case November 1, "as a paper owned and managed by Protestants with no Catholic holding one dollar of its stock or exercising any measure of control over it whatsoever. *The News Leader* will not attempt again to warn Virginians of the baleful consequences that have followed religious proscription. *The News Leader* will content itself simply with reminding Richmond people of what happened 10 years ago at this very time."

Then it told how the city health director, a Baptist, in answer to a question from Bishop O'Connell about what help was most needed at a temporary hospital in the flu epidemic, replied that Negroes in the basement were "dying fast." Before 7 p.m. that day, said the paper's editorial, 12 Sisters of Mercy had arrived.

". . .In the name of all that is just," said the paper, *"the News Leader* must leave Richmond to decide what evidence she will take of what Catholics do—the evidence of anonymous slanders, with their babbling about illegitimacy and annulment of marriages, or the evidence of those 12 women defying the epidemic amid the darkness and the dying in that hospital basement."

The Times-Dispatch editorial page may have been carried away by its desire. On October 13, it declared that "Democratic leaders in Virginia, including Governor [Harry F.] Byrd, who is a most astute and discerning observer, are certain now that Smith will win the state by a comfortable margin." It noted that when Smith visited Richmond, "he was literally mobbed by hysterical men and women."

By 1928, responsible papers—including those in Richmond—were trying for total separation of news and editorial content. Yet *The Times-Dispatch* of October 24 was a Democratic chairman's dream. On Page One under a two-line banner proclaiming,

Glass Makes Attack on Hoover and Cannon;

Ridicules GOP Record; Challenges Wise

A non-bylined story read: "Herbert Hoover, Bishop James Cannon Jr., the 'Hooverites,' and the Republican party were given one of the most terrific verbal castigations ever administered to anyone in the United States last night by Sen. Carter Glass in an address of nearly two hours and a half duration before a widly cheering audience of approximately 5,000 persons which filled every seat in the Richmond City Auditorium and stood on the aisles and cheered."

Politics, of course, was not the only news that fall. An advance story in The Times-Dispatch of October 13 on a football game between John Marshall High School and St. Christopher's School merited a banner head in sports. On the entertainment page of *The News Leader* November 1, readers learned that Peaches Browning, "the most talked about girl in the whole wide world," was on stage at the National Theater "in person."

The lead story in *The News Leader* that day was of the Graf Zeppelin reaching Friedrichshafen in 71 hours and 12 minutes after leaving the United States for the first transatlantic commercial round trip by air.

But the paper's editorial page tried to put that in perspective after knocking "Mr. [Arthur] Brisbane's favorite prophecy of gigantic planes that will circle the globe in a day."

"Contrary to general belief," said *The News Leader,* "planes cannot be increased in speed and endurance in proportion to their increase in weight. At present, the maximum load of planes is 25 pounds per horsepower. . . . The navy speculates that a plane of 60,000 pounds would not be able to carry more than enough fuel to give it a cruising radius of 500 miles... . When man finds a way to break up the atom, world-girdling planes may come. Until then, cross-ocean flying in planes will be the feat of lucky aviators, not the routine of commerce."

But the election was *the* big running story and both papers were determined to tell their readers what was transpiring before the final voting tally.

The News Leader on election day invited people to the City Auditorium or to "News Leader Square" to "see the world's greatest searchlight flash the returns" or to hear NBC radio reports brought by *The News Leader*. *The Times-Dispatch* rented a plane that was to flash red, green and white lights in various combinations to show who was ahead in state and nation. The Times-Dispatch also flashed news bulletins on a screen at a Ford automobile agency near City Hall.

When it came to reporting results, *The News Leader*, an afternoon paper, was the winner. It put out a Tuesday night extra with the entire front page on the election and a three-column picture of Hoover.

HOOVER WINS COUNTRY
WHILE CARRYING CITY
OF RICHMOND AND VA

Under that headline ran the lead story: "Herbert Hoover is conceded by *The News Leader* to have carried the country, including the state of Virginia, in today's election."

The next morning's *Times-Dispatch* reported:

Hoover Wins in Landslide;
Carries Virginia by 20,000

The Republicans had carried all but one congressional district, plus Richmond and Henrico County. The off-lead story put it simply: "Virginia today is in the Republican column for the first time since Reconstruction Days."

By the next presidential election in 1932, the nation was in the depths of the Depression, and the editorial sentiments of the Richmond papers were never in doubt. It was the beginnning of a love affair with Franklin D. Roosevelt that continued through two campaigns. Both papers endorsed him all four times he ran, but for *The Times-Dispatch,* as Virginius Dabney acknowledged in an interview years later, the endorsement was a little more lukewarm in each of the last two campaigns.

On October 31, 1932, *The Times-Dispatch* said, "It must be admitted that the desire to oust Herbert Hoover from the White House is at least as strong as the wish to install Franklin D. Roosevelt." Another editorial blasted the *Los Angeles Times* for endorsing Hoover and trying to link Roosevelt with William Randolph Hearst.

A Fred Seibel cartoon on the Sunday before the election showed "Lord Hoover" handing up a sword to "General Roosevelt," who was on horseback. The caption: "What We Hope to See Tuesday." The accompanying editorial noted, "That great Christian statesman, Bishop [James} Cannon,

What We Hope to See Tuesday

has just told a waiting world that Mr. Hoover is the man who will get his support on Tuesday."

Virginius Dabney, rabidly anti-Cannon, couldn't have been happier with a choice of foes.

The day before the election, *The Times-Dispatch* rehashed Virginia's pro-Hoover vote four years earlier and stated: "That will not happen in 1932. Virginia is thoroughly repentant for her rash action."

The News Leader praised Sen. Glass for his blasts at Hoover, especially for saying Hoover had "converted the Treasury at Washington into a national pawnshop," in reference to Reconstruction Finance Corporation loans. "Senator Glass," said *The Leader,* "has put the final nail of conviction into the political coffin of Mr. Hoover and his party."

Again *The News Leader* put out an extra to annnounce the winner. Beside a five-column picture of Roosevelt was a mammoth three-column headline:

ROOSEVELT WINS ELECTION
BY TREMENDOUS MAJORITY

Page 2 was a picture page of Roosevelt shots, just as the page had been full of Hoover pictures four years earlier.

The Times-Dispatch's election head across eight columns:

Roosevelt Elected as Returns Swell Majority;
Landslide Sends Nine Va. Democrats to Capital;
Party's Control of House and Senate Is Assured

The presidential election wasn't the only event chewing up columns of Richmond papers in 1936. On October 24, scarcely a week before the election, *The News Leader* devoted most of a page to pictures of "society" babies, including one held by "the nanny of her mother." Four days later, an inquiring photographer had pictures and quotes from five people for a Page One feature on whether Britain's Edward should marry Wallis Warfield Simpson. On the more serious side, *The News Leader* commented editorially October 29 about the Spanish Civil War, "The war is Spanish, the horror is the world's, the disgrace is mankind's."

The Times-Dispatch now had Westbrook Pegler's column on the editorial page; four years earlier, his report of the Pittsburgh-Army football game was on the sports page. *The Times-Dispatch* also gave Page One treatment to an appearance before a labor group by the Rev. Ernest A. deBordenave, assistant of the then fashionable St. Paul's Episcopal Church. Mr. deBordenave said that "the whole process of the economic system is the process of the control of industry by a few. If it narrows down a little more, we would have absolute facism in this nation."

Editorialists of both papers, heartened by Roosevelt's actions of the previous four years, endorsed the Democratic ticket with gusto. *The Times-Dispatch* doubted the *Literary Digest* poll that had Alf Landon a winner and commented November 1, "So we look confidently for a decisive Roosevelt victory on Tuesday. And having strongly advocated his re-election throughout the campaign, we rejoice at the prospect."

The next day, a *News Leader* editorial said, "The average American, looking for a better day, is politically reasonable because he believes Mr. Roosevelt is determined that economic justice be done and that fair play prevails. Roosevelt, for his part, seeks to prevent revolution not by combating it, but by removing all justification for it."

On the morning after, *The Times-Dispatch* reported in an all-caps headline:

ROOSEVELT WINS IN LANDSLIDE

George Prince Arnold, getting a rare byline, reported, "Virginia's Democrats turned out in droves yesterday to give President Roosevelt the greatest majority the state has ever given any candidate for the presidency."

Editorially, *The Times-Dispatch* said, "If Governor Landon, with his fuzzy minded opportunism, had been elected to the presidency, the reactionary interests behind him would have been in the drivers' seat, the advances of the past four years would have been wiped out."

Without endorsing all Roosevelt had done, the paper said that "when the time comes for posterity to render its decision on his eight years in office, Franklin Delano Roosevelt will take his place among the great progressive leaders of America."

By campaign time in 1940, World War II was a year old. America was more than a year from entering it, but Selective Service was to call 4,874 Virginians by July 1.

What else was news? Edith Lindeman was informing *Times-Dispatch* readers that Shirley Temple, reigning child movie star, might earn $4,000 a week. Delmege Trimble, former news editor, was writing a column, "A Week Seen in Glimpses." On October 19, VMI's football team beat Virginia's, 7-0, and Washington and Lee edged Richmond, 3-0. Two local murders, including that of Patrolman J.A. Tibbs, merited a three-column, front-page headline in *The Times-Dispatch* of October 21.

Anti-third-term sentiment was building, as evidenced in a full-page advertisement in *The Times-Dispatch* of November 3 by "Democrats for Willkie." It was a harbinger of efforts, especially in the 1950s, by conservative Virginia Democrats to support Republican presidential candidates. Signers of the ad, who also supported Sen. Harry F. Byrd and Rep. David E. Satterfield, Jr., included Lawrence Lewis, a wealthy investor, and Thomas C. Boushall, president of the Morris Plan Bank of Virginia.

But the editorial course of the Richmond papers had been set. *The Times-Dispatch* said on October 23 that the South "will vote solidly for Roosevelt. He will deserve the vote, for he has done more for the region than any President since the War Between the States.

". . . Not himself a Southerner, Mr. Roosevelt may some day have it said of him by historians that he was the President who really introduced in the South a type of reconstruction which obliterated forever all the traces of a tragic era."

The News Leader, on the other hand, stressed foreign policy in its editorial the following day. It criticized the Republicans strongly and commended the Democrats. "In a period of immense difficulty, when totalitarians deliberately rejected all moral stands and employed every type of dishonorable deception," it said, "America has made few serious mistakes. Have we as a nation been brought close to war? We have. Has the fault been ours? It has not."

Democrats didn't escape *The News Leader's* editorial lash completely. On November 1, it hit the GOP for alleging that Rooselvelt was "dragging the country into war," but flailed the Democrats' vice presidential nominee, Henry A. Wallace, for "talking like a demagogue and a bungling demagogue at that" for saying Hitler favors a Republican victory.

On November 4, the eve of the election, *The Times-Dispatch* noted editorially that it "definitely prefers President Roosevelt to Mr. Willkie" but said America was "fortunate in having two reasonably qualified men to choose from in this critical hour." The editorialist couldn't resist a bit of borderline demagoguery of its own by saying Communist labor leaders like Harry Bridges of the longshoremen's union were leaning to Willkie.

In its own election eve editorial, *The News Leader* reminded its readers that defense was the major issue. "For the conduct of the national defense, at a time of extreme danger," it said, "procure the ablest, best qualified leeader—by voting tomorrow for Roosevelt."

The Page One banner headline in *The Times-Dispatch* of November 6 read:

ROOSEVELT WINS THIRD TERM

George Prince Arnold's off-lead story began: "Virginia's Democrats, unterrified over the third term tradition, gave President Roosevelt another sweeping victory yesterday and at the same time returned Sen. Byrd and the State's nine Democratic Congressmen to Washington."

The News Leader seven-column headline was:

WILLKIE CONGRATULATES ROOSEVELT ON SWEEPING VICTORY IN 39 STATES

By late fall of 1944, war news dominated everything. Allied forces were sweeping across Western Europe and the Pacific war was going well.

Occcasionally, something other than war and politics made it to the front page of *The Times-Dispatch.* An example was the concern of communicants of St. John's Episcopal Church, where Patrick Henry had made his "Give me liberty or give me death" speech. The rector proposed altering the narrow pews so as to permit kneeling, a proper Episcopal practice. But this was St. John's, and many members didn't like the idea—at all.

In the fall of 1944, James J. Kilpatrick was writing an outdoors column for *The News Leader's* sports page. But whatever either Richmond paper carried was influenced by wartime restrictions. *The News Leader* reported October 4 that, due to an "acute shortage of newsprint," it would no longer print the extras that it earlier had printed after World Series games. The edition of Friday, October 13, for instance, had only 28 pages.

One big story that didn't make *The Leader's* front page was the report that Miller & Rhoads proposed a 12-story building for its department store at 6th and Broad Streets following the war. It never happened, although the store—like its competitor, Thalhimers—did expand. After World War II, both stores opened suburban branches in Richmond and other cities. But, like many other retailers, both suffered downtown. Those stores closed and the suburban units closed or were sold to other chains.

In 1944, both papers supported Roosevelt for a fourth term but without great enthusiasm. *The News Leader,* on election eve November 6, praised Thomas Dewey, especially for his ideas on foreign policy. Yet, it said: ". . . American voters read the harangues of orators today and may listen excitedly to the radio tonight, but they have not forgotten 1932 or 1940. They will admit and deplore the mistakes of Mr. Roosevelt and they will shudder at the incomprehensible magnitude of the national debt. In the same hour, they will remember the rack from which they are hewn, and the 'hole in the pit' whence they have been digged."

The paper also recalled the "creeping paralysis of 12 years ago when Hoover sat helpless and hopeless in the White House. . . " and conditions in November 1940, when France was "prostrate and shackled," when "Russia was the ally, the arsenal and the granary of the Reich, Hitler's arrogant power was at its zenith."

Therefore, said *The News Leader,* "The contest today needs no description. It represents that labor and the resolution of millions of men. To no single individual goes even a tithe of the credit; but will anyone fail to place President Roosevelt among the half-dozen who have done more to raise the Allied cause from the depths of 1940 to the heights and hopes of 1944?"

The News Leader even had kind words for Harry Truman, the man whom it was to villify a few years later.

"The vice-presidential candidate," it said October 28, "is in actual fact, a man of character, earnest effort and singular devotion to ideals."

The Times-Dispatch on election eve noted that there had been four presidential elections in war years—1812, 1864, 1912 and 1944. "In the first three of these," it said, "the incumbents were chosen. Evidently, the people believed that it was 'best not to swap horses while crossing a river'."

The next morning's paper proclaimed in a banner headline:

ROOSEVELT IS RE-ELECTED

Editorially, the paper mused: *"The Times-Dispatch,* which supported him for a third term and also for a fourth term, did so because of the unprecedented issues which confronted the country in 1940, and again this year."

Further on, it tried to reassure conservative readers. ". . . As for those who permitted themselves to be frightened by the bugaboo of Communism, they should forget this synthetic issue. They should realized that Sidney Hillman and his Political Action Committee will not be the arbiter of our destinies during the next four years."

By campaign time of 1948, World War II was long ended and Harry Truman had been in the White House more than three years. Conservative Democrats in Virginia were most unhappy with the national political trend, and Republicans, greatly outnumbered in Virginia, still felt good about their chances in November as they assembled in Philadelphia in June.

On hand to report their deliberations was James Latimer. *The Times-Dispatch* had decided that after many years the time had come to have its own man there for the occasion. Latimer's first stories appeared on local section front Sunday, June 20. The lead read, "The vanguard of Virginia's delegation to the Republican National Convention hit Philadelphia today, ready to work for a State's rights approach to the civil rights platform plank and to urge greater GOP efforts in the South."

Another, quite short story on the same page said that the price of the Sunday *Times-Dispatch* would rise to 15 cents.

Virginians played no great role in the convention, but Latimer was there all week, scratching for whatever news there was. There wasn't much. His June 21 story on Page One said that no "smoke-filled rooms" were envisioned by Thomas Dewey, Robert A. Taft or Harold Stassen. Two days later, Latimer reported that Virginians met to poll themselves on how to vote on the first ballot, then changed their minds. It was scarcely attention-grabbing news.

Virginians assured Dewey, on the eve of his nomination, that he'd carry the state, since the Democrats back home had no one to vote for. As he swept the convention, Virginia gave him 10 votes; the other votes were Taft, 10, and Rep. Joe Martin of Massachusetts, 1.

Conservative Virginia Democrats were in a defiant mood as they arrived in Philadelphia in July for their convention. This time, *The News Leader* also had its man, Roy C. Flannagan, on hand. Latimer was back for *The Times-Dispatch*.

Flannagan reported first, on Saturday, July 10. "The triumphant Trumanites," he said, "were soothing the ruffled South today with vice-presidential talk and they mentioned among the Southern prospects, of course, Senator Harry F. Byrd of Virginia." The suggestion came from the old Chicago wheelhorse, Jake Arvey, an early anti-Truman man who'd changed his tune.

No one expected anything of the kind, since Byrd and Truman detested each other's policies. Early in the convention, Flannagan reported some Virginia sentiment for Ben Laney, a Dixiecrat favorite who was governor of Arkansas. Later, he said they were leaning to Alben Barkley of Kentucky.

Barkley did get the nomination for vice president, but Flannagan reported July 15, "The Virginia delegation to the Democratic National Convention moved homeward today, rebuffed on candidates and civil rights and uncertain of its future plans." The uncertainty would last a long time.

Latimer's first stories appeared Sunday, July 11, on the front page of the local section with the lead: "A demand that Virginia's anti-Truman delegation be required to take a pledge of loyalty to the national party before being allowed to take part in the Democratic National Convention arose today."

Martin A. Hutchinson, a leader of anti-Byrd Democrats in the Old Dominion, made the demand—one that Byrd followers would continue to fight in ensuing national conventions. Latimer reported the next day that Gov.William M. Tuck and Byrd "displayed an attitude of unconcerned silence" to Hutchinson's demand. The Old Guard had its way and the July 14 story by Latimer on Page One read, "Virginia's anti-Truman delegation today won the right to take part in the Democratic National Convention without being required to avow its loyalty to the convention or the national party."

They won that battle but lost the war. Virginia's 26 votes went to Richard Russell as Truman was renominated.

Editorially, Richmond's papers couldn't work up enthusiasm for any of the candidates. They were worried about a Fair Employment Practices Commission. *The Times-Dispatch* of November 1 said Dewey "is wrong if he thinks the Federal government can force the South, or any other part of the country, to adopt employment practices which are completely contrary to the customs of centuries. Yet there is reason to fear that he may follow that course."

Laughing Stock Of The Nation

On the same page, however, *The Times-Dispatch,* agreed with much of Felix Morley's column in the conservative magazine, *Human Events,* that blasted Truman and Dewey and praised Dixiecrat Strom Thurmond. Yet, said *The Times-Dispatch,* Thurmond "is also in the same political bed with an evil-smelling lot of Ku-Kluxers, Negro-haters and exploiters."

The News Leader of November 1 predicted a Republican victory, with 57 to 64 percent of the electoral vote. And if Truman is blaming defectors, said the paper, "Mr. Truman himself was more responsible for this division of Democrats than anyone else was. He guessed wrongly and he maneuvered badly. Tomorrow he pays the price. When he decided to cater to the Negro vote on the assumption that the South was his anyway, he made a gamble—and he lost."

Eating crow on the day after the election, *The News Leader* said, "Behind everything else, probably, was the continuing popularity of the New Deal political philosophy, even when its author and exemplar was dead.

". . . We thought Dewey had a walkaway—and we were as far in error as we well could be."

Richmond Times-Dispatch

Richmond 11, Virginia, Wednesday, November 3, 1948

Five Cents

Sharp Contests Mark Presidential Election Race; Early State Returns Give Truman Uncertain Lead

Mine Strike Fight Injures 22 in France

Pickets Attempt To Burn Police

Democrats Are in Front For Congress

Heavy Vote Cast By Virginians

Richmond Times-Dispatch

Dewey Takes Lead in Several Key, Big-Vote States; Victory For Truman in Virginia Is Indicated

Mine Strike

Democrats Are in Front

President Makes Fight In Big Cities

Richmond Times-Dispatch

7,000,000 Ballots Give Truman Popular Vote Lead; Straight Ticket Sweeps to Victory in Virginia

Mine Strike Fight Injures 22 in France

Pickets Attempt To Burn Police

Robertson Is Returned To Senate

Richmond Times-Dispatch

Uncertainty Marks Election With Half Votes In; Straight Ticket Sweeps to Victory in Virginia

Record Set By Voting In Richmond

Robertson Is Returned To Senate

GOP Overthrown In House Races, Democrats Claim

Neither Truman Nor Dewey Posts Decisive Margin for Presidency

The Times-Dispatch *for the day after the 1948 presidential election shows—through four editions—that the Truman-Dewey race was undetermined. The last edition shown here came off the press at 2:30 a.m.*

POLITICS, LOCAL

That 1948 election and its campaign skirmishing jarred what had been an amicable relationship between editorial writers for *The Times-Dispatch* and *The News Leader* and Sen. Harry Byrd. The papers had been unabashedly pro-Byrd—so much so that critics called them slavish followers of all Byrd organization policies.

But there were harsh words directed by the editorial writers at the organization in 1948.

Organization leaders in the General Assembly disliked President Truman, loathed Henry Wallace and hated everything associated with Joseph Stalin. Communists had staged a coup in Czechoslovakia, and there was a move in the legislature to outlaw the Communist party in Virginia.

Banner headlines in *The Times-Dispatch* on February 27 were:

Tuck Urges Truman, Wallace Elimination on Ballot;
Czech Reds Denounced by U.S., Britain, France

The lead on the Virginia story went: "A double-barrelled plan of legislative action by which Virginia could keep President Truman's name off its presidential ballot and also checkmate the Henry Wallace third party was urged upon the Virginia General Assembly yesterday by Governor Tuck.

"It was, in the Truman phase, a design whereby restive Democrats could 'hold their electoral votes in abeyance' to fight the Truman civil rights program and seek more influence within the party.

"And, where Mr. Wallace was concerned, it would allow no new political parties on the Virginia ballot this year."

Tuck's proposal, in a 17-minute appearance by the governor to a joint session of the legislature, was heard by the largest crowd at the General Assembly, *The Times-Dispatch* said, since Winston Churchill's appearance two years earlier.

Conservative editors were outraged. Douglas Freeman, in *The News Leader*, already was on a crusade against those in the House of Delegates who earlier in the session had voted themselves expense allowances of $300. Dr. Freeman said *The News Leader's* editorial page would run the name of each member who returned the money.

The same day that its front page announced Tuck's proposal, its editorial page called it an "attempt to solve the problem on an emotional rather than a rational basis.

". . .Banning people from the ballot because we don't like them is not the sort of thing the party of Thomas Jefferson ought to want on its record.

". . . But neither Virginians nor any other Southerners ought to be willing to abdicate their responsibilities as citizens by giving to a small group of politicians the right to decide after the November election for whom Virginia's electoral votes will be cast."

The News Leader on March 1 noted editorially that the governor made his proposal at 11:15 a.m. on March 26 and by noon the next day, "without any pretence of a public hearing, the bill, slightly amended, had been reported unanimously to the House of Delegates by the Committee on Privileges and Elections.

"That unanimous committee action, without 10 minutes' public hearing or any notice of an impending vote on the measure, gave you warning, we repeat, of the speed with which your liberties may be threatened. Virginians, shocked and startled, do not know what to expect next."

Letting the bill be returned to a committee, where it would sit until an outcry subsided, was not the way to act, said the editorialist.

"There is one answer only: DEFEAT THIS BILL NOW; defeat every other move to restrict the franchise; organize in every city and county in Virginia; protect your rights by re-electing vigilant Delegates and Senators; replace every compliant and incompetent legislator; start, pursue and complete a political revolution in Virginia. In no other way can you assure yourself a vote for the man you prefer for President, rather than for the man the State Democratic Committee, or the State Democratic Convention may name.

"Was ever such a proposal advanced to self-respecting, free-born Virginians as the one covered by the bill as originally drawn? You were bidden to sign a proxy, by which you were to permit the members of the State Democratic Committee to say, in effect, for whom you should vote! Had that bill passed, the wheels of the machine would have turned, after mysterious private meetings of a few powerful gentlemen, and you would have read, one day next Autumn, that you—a Virginian, inheritor of the Bill of Rights, were not to be allowed to vote for the nominee of the Democratic National Convention. You could vote for the man the Republican Convention named, but not for the Democrat. Under the terms of the bill as originally presented, Wallace might have been the favorite of 30,000 Virginians, but his name could not have been put on the ballot otherwise than as the Prohibitionist, Socialist or Socialist-Labor candidate. Those who wished to exercise their basic, constitutional right of a free franchise had to accept the label of one of those parties in order to have their ballot counted. As for you, a Democrat, you would have read the name of the man the State Democratic Committee had chosen, and you would have said to yourself, 'Oh, I'm for Mr. X for President, am I? It was nice of the committee to let me know'."

The Times-Dispatch kept it up, too. "Now," it said on March 2, "they [the politicians] are gathered in smoke-filled rooms trying to salvage something out of the wreckage. Further study of the measure convinces *The Times-Dispatch* that there is nothing in it worth salvaging. The last amendment that could be presented would be one amending the plan out of existence."

On March 4, *The News Leader* explained editorially how Virginia Democratic leaders, fearful of President Truman's civil rights plans, were trying to pressure the national party.

"The machine," said *The News Leader*, "believes in a 'white man's Democratic party' and it always has to take into account the sentiment of those Southside counties, commonly called 'the Black Belt' in which the Negroes are almost as numerous as the whites. The leaders of the machine decided that a filibuster in the Senate might not suffice to prevent the passage of the equal rights legislation. With passage probable, the men who frame party policy decided that the only way to reduce the chances of having the bills adopted at this session of Congress was to make it plain to the President that he would not have the support of the South in the National Convention and would not get the electoral vote of the Southern States even if elected.. . .

"This whole absurd scheme was not devised originally to take your freedom of choice from you but, as the gentlemen thought, to protect the 'white South' and defeat a man they consider a twentieth century carpet-bagger."

Even modification of the anti-Truman bill didn't satisfy *The News Leader*. A March 10 editorial envisioned a convening in August of the State Democratic Convention after Truman had been nominated. "Delegates will be told that the true prophet of Southern Democracy is Mr. X or Mr. Y, and that the electoral vote of Virginia will be cast for him. Four-fifths of the delegates obediently will shout 'Of course; he's the very man.'

"That afternoon, Mr. Voter, you will read for whom you will be voting when you go to the polls on the 2nd of November. You may or you may not be pleased; but if you do not want to vote for Prophet X or Apostle Y, the General Assembly will give you the special boon of scurrying around and of helping to get 1,000 names to a petition for someone else. You may draft it or sign a petition somebody else prepares or circulates. Others will be doing the same thing.

"By and by, election day will come. You will go to your precinct and get your ballot. If you can carry it to the booth without tangling your feet in it, you then will have your choice between a candidate named by the national parties and the machine-picked Special Vessel of Southern democracy."

The editorialist predicted erroneously (Truman carried Virginia) that with all the parties on the ballot, the president probably would be defeated. Virginia electors would vote for the machine candidate and come home.

"What, then, will the authors of the Tuck bill have done? They will have emphasized and perhaps aggravated the race issue; they will have contributed to the excessively dangerous, the potentially fatal split of American parties, with the resultant abandonment of the immense security of the two-party system; and, finally, these gentlemen will have preserved for themselves the label 'Democratic.' Wherefore we are led at last to the question. Is that label worth what the South will have to pay for it? We think not."

For good measure, *The News Leader* got in an editorial jab March 11 at Sen. Byrd. It noted that as soon as Gov. Tuck introduced his anti-Truman proposal, the senator, in Washington, endorsed it "without reservation." There are reports that the senator had not read the bill, said the editorial, but "we scarcely know whether it was worse to approve the bill when read or to endorse it unread."

As March wore on, *The News Leader*'s denunciation of the organization increased. "The notorious feature of the session," said *The News Leader* of March 13, "was the complete dominance of the Democratic State machine." A day earlier, it condemned what it saw as extravagances of the legislature. "With the State Democratic machine more completely and more arrogantly in control than ever it has been in Virginia history—

"With the interests of private business, of productive industry and of thrifty individuals completely disdained by the State Democratic machine in its surrender to office-holding pressure groups—

THE TIME FOR REVOLT HAS COME

"Virginians must bestir themselves, must organize, and must elect conservative, frugal men to the General Assembly. Unless this is done, and done at once, the plundering of taxpayers observed at this session of the General Assembly will be progressive."

On March 17, having again denounced Tuck & Co. for the anti-Truman legislation, *The News Leader* lamented the lack of a roll call on the $300-per-delegate expense package approved by the House. It said it would print a "roll of honor" of those who "sent back their checks and those who asked that their opposition to the resolution be made a matter of record."

By March 23, there were 37 names on *The News Leader*'s list. It said that pay increases delegates might vote for forthcoming sessions are one thing, but "Virginians were much more outraged by the manner in which the $300 was voted, in the middle of a term of office, than by the bill of $30,000 they had to meet to in this draft on the contingent fund of the House."

The blistering attack of *The News Leader* so unhinged the House of Delegates that its members approved a resolution demanding an investigation by the State Corporation Commission of Richmond Newspapers' monopoly in the news business here.

James Latimer, who covered the legislative session for *The Times-Dispatch*, recalled that John Dana Wise, vice president-general manager of Richmond Newspapers Inc., said, "I will take the front place at the door of the newspaper, and I'll have the honor of being the first man to throw the State Corporation Commission investigators out."[85]

Nothing came of the proposed investigation.

The Times-Dispatch, while not so moved over the $300 expense package, had little patience with a bill to outlaw the Communist Party in the state.

"Communism is an ideology rather than a political party," said an editorial on February 26, "and its defeat can most surely be achieved through the presentation of a saner program for the people than the Marxians can offer. Legislation which attempts to suppress ideology will get us nowhere."

MORE POLITICS, NATIONAL

By mid-1952, editorial writers at both *The Times-Dispatch* and *The News Leader* had had enough of Harry Truman. They supported his interventionist foreign policy, but they couldn't stomach his civil rights proposals and other domestic legislation—and certainly not what they saw as crookedness in many people in his administration.

In *The Times-Dispatch* newsroom, it was the first presidential election for Managing Editor John H. Colburn. When he found that both Dwight Eisenhower and Adlai Stevenson would speak in Richmond, he carefully "dummied" front pages for the papers that would report their appearances. It would be the same layout each day: two 6-column headlines of 72-point type, the lead story by James Latimer plus a four-column photograph of the assemblage and, in the lower right corner of the page, a two-column picture of the candidate speaking. Inside would be sidebars, more photos and the text of the candidate's remarks.

Colburn, the old Associated Press man, figured he could analyze as well as the next man, and on the Sunday preceding the election he wrote a Page One analysis of the election.

Although the editorialists endorsed the GOP ticket, they were undone by the news of a $16,000 fund set up by wealthy businessmen to offset the senatorial expenses of Richard M. Nixon, the Republican nominee for vice president. On September 20, less than two days after the first report of the fund, both Richmond papers urged Nixon to withdraw.

The Times-Dispatch said that the revelation could defeat Eisenhower "unless Nixon has the decency to resign at once as the vice presidential nominee." His explanation about "making ends meet" in that manner, instead of putting his wife on his payroll, "may be an explanation," said the paper. "It is not an excuse. Mr. Nixon is a lawyer. He cannot plead ignorance of the ethical code."

The News Leader's lead editorial September 20, was headed:

Senator Nixon Should Resign

It offered the advice "with [the] deepest sense of disappointment," saying, ". . .his acceptance of these postelection gifts cannot be explained away. It is utterly irrelevant that Sen. Sparkman's wife [John Sparkman, of Alabama, was Stevenson's running mate] is on the public payroll. It is beside the point that the story was broken by the left-wing *New York Post*. It is not demonstrable, as Sen. [Karl] Mundt loyally says, that this is merely one more attack on Sen. Nixon by the Communists who fear him. It makes no difference that the contributions apparently were gifts under tax law and not reportable as income.

"The acceptance of cash presents by a man already elected to the United States Senate stands admitted. It cannot be condoned, and if it can be explained, it cannot be excused."

Coverage of the candidates' appearances in Richmond went just as *The Times-Dispatch*'s Colburn had planned.

Stevenson was the speaker at the Mosque, a city-owned structure bought from the Shriners during the Depression. The hall became available when Democrats won a ruling from City Attorney J. Elliott Drinard that the gathering was "a Democratic Party meeting," rather than a public meeting; thus, state segregation laws didn't apply. Stevenson had said he would not speak to a segregated audience.

The Mosque, which seats about 5,000, was the site of performances by big bands, touring symphonies and traveling Broadway plays. In November alone, the Mills Brothers, Woody Herman, Dinah Washington and Sammy Kaye were to appear, as were George London, the opera star; plus Charles Boyer, Charles Laughton, Agnes Moorehead and Sir Cedric Harwicke in "Don Juan in Hell."

Colburn's design for identical layouts for the candidates' appearances in Richmond worked out precisely as he'd planned. The Nixon Fund became such a major story that it merited a two-column headline at the top of Page One in the same paper that reported the Democratic nominee's speech.

The six-column head read:

Stevenson Stands on Civil Rights Plank
In First Address to a Dixie Audience

James Latimer's lead read: "Governor Adlai E. Stevenson spurned 'beguiling serpent words' here last night and spoke up plainly in support of the Democratic platform's call for Federal legislation on civil rights.

"The Democratic nominee chose to meet the issue head-on in his first major campaign speech to a Southern audience."

To an unsegregated crowd of more than 5,000 people that overflowed the Mosque, he said, "In the field of minority rights, the Democratic party has stated its position in its platform—a position to which I adhere."

Latimer noted that Gov. John S. Battle, U.S. Sen. A. Willis Robertson and the acting state Democratic chairman, T. Nelson Parker, did not applaud.

Inside the paper were the text, a continuation of Latimer's story and a couple of other political pieces. The front page of the local section had a four-column picture, a two-column picture and a feature by Charles McDowell—all about the Democrats and their nominee.

The timing could not have been worse for *The News Leader*. Stevenson was to speak on a Saturday night, and the paper could give no report on the event until Monday afternoon. But its Saturday afternoon editions reported under a five-column, two-line head:

Adlai Comes to Richmond
For Major Speech Tonight

Along with that on Page One was a three-column photo of Stevenson at Quantico presenting a Marine commission to his son. Another major political story for Virginians was the death overnight of Lt. Gov. L. Preston Collins.

The Times-Dispatch paid tribute editorially to Stevenson, who, it said, "was his customarily eloquent self." The address was "eloquent and charming," but, it said, Eisenhower's views were more attuned to Virginia and the South."

Democrats could expect little more editorial praise from *The Times-Dispatch*. On November 2, two days before the election, it ran a two-column-long editorial that concluded: "It seems clear from the foregoing that, from many vital points of view, Dwight Eisenhower is the better qualified of the two candidates, for the presidency, and is entitled to win on Tuesday."

The Times-Dispatch saved its vituperation for Truman. The day before the election, it said, "Seldom, if ever, has a President of the United States stooped so low and has so deliberately distorted documentary evidence in an attempt to win votes for his party." It alluded to Truman's release of documents intended to show that Eisenhower was dovish on Korea.

Truman, said *The Times-Dispatch*, was "a shrewd and clever politician" who has "never hesitated to employ distortion as a weapon to kick his political enemies below the belt.... [He] has sunk to a level that will be remembered with humiliation as the low spot of the campaign of 1952."

Eisenhower spoke September 26 at the State Capitol.

The headline:

Eisenhower Calls for the Cancellation
Of Democratic 'Mortgage' on South

Latimer wrote: "Dwight David Eisenhower looked southward from Virginia's ancient State Capitol last night and called on Democrats and Republicans to join in canceling the Democrats' "heavy mortgage" on Southern votes.

"A crowd estimated at something between 10,000 and 20,000 roared its approval of the Republican presidential nominee's appeal to end corruption, to end waste and extravagance, to rescue our people from the squeeze of high prices and high taxes.

"They stood on the green slopes of Capitol Square and cheered happily as Eisenhower held up Sen. Byrd as a model of 'frugality and thrift'—a brief renewal of the more elaborate tribute he paid to the economy-minded Virginia senator in a whistle-stop speech at Petersburg earlier last night."

Latimer noted that Gov. John S. Battle, a Democrat, greeted the Republican nominee in Richmond.

The paper contained in addition to the large photograph and Latimer's story, three sidebars on Eisenhower (including one on the collapse of a ramp to the speakers' platform) and two Page-One stories on Stevenson's campaign. Inside were continuations and other political stories as well as the text.

An editorial on Sunday, September 28, ended: "It seems fair to say that the loud cheers for Eisenhower in Capitol Square on Friday night were given him, in part, at least, because his listeners were convinced that he meant what he said when he promised to clean up Washington, reduce waste, put a brake on centralization, and return to the principles enunciated by Thomas Jefferson.

"That, too, is our conviction."

The News Leader again was hampered in covering a night speech—this one on Friday. Saturday afternoon papers are traditionally thin. Guy Friddell, *The News Leader*'s political writer, filed an advance story Friday while he traveled north from Winston-Salem, North Carolina, with Eisenhower.

Friddell's Saturday story read: "Dwight D. Eisenhower's chief aides predict a Republican victory in November and say they sense an impending 'nation-wide landslide' for the GOP nominee for President.

"But—in the first reaction from local Stevenson supporters to General Eisenhower's speech here last night—John J. Wicker Jr. termed the general "nothing less than a political coward in being afraid to say one word about civil rights." Wicker was not a liberal integrationist.

Small paper or not, *The News Leader's* Saturday offering contained two sidebars on the event on Page One and a text and photos inside.

Editorially, *The News Leader* never backed off from supporting the GOP ticket. On Friday, the eve of Eisenhower's visit, it was tired of a variety of things, including "slick schemes and government by impulse," in 20 years of Democratic rule. It sensed a yearning for "government that is simply clean and decent and honest. That is our prayer for the general: That he can head up such a government. He speaks on historic ground tonight, and he holds in his grasp a chance to make great history."

A day later, *The News Leader* was unhappy. It said: "When General Eisenhower's speech on Capitol Hill last night is compared from a literary standpoint, with Adlai Stevenson's address in the Mosque a week ago, the general clearly comes off second best.

"Mr. Stevenson's talk was couched in faultless prose—parts of it could be scanned in perfect iambic pentameter. . . Bar none, Mr. Stevenson's address was the most polished political utterance heard in these parts in a couple of generations; the memory of man runneth not to the contrary."

The editorialist contrasted Stevenson with "an awkward, ungrammatical Eisenhower.

". . .At the end of every wild spree, the crushing hangover comes. We have a feeling that Ike will meet it with the cold shower treatment, harsh but effective, while Adlai tends toward just one more nip of the hair of the dog that bit us."

On election eve, *The News Leader* ran an 8-column headline over its editorial:

On the Issues, the Candidates, the Alternatives,

Dwight D. Eisenhower Remains Our Choice

It paid tribute to Stevenson's "remarkable appeal" but said, "we have watched him move progressively to the left.

"If we confessed pleasure at many aspects of Gov. Stevenson's campaign, we confess, as freely, a disappointment with General Eisenhower.

Yet, "We say, in sum, only that Eisenhower and his party seem to us far more likely than Stevenson and his party to set desirable forces in motion—to check alien influences, and to achieve a needed change in the Washington atmosphere."

Although James J. Kilpatrick was running the editorial page of *The News Leader*, his predecessor, Douglas S. Freeman, was still a major figure in Richmond. On September 16, a six-column ad for *LIFE* magazine featured a picture of Freeman, noted that his former paper was backing a Republican for the first time in 50 years and called attention to an article in *LIFE* by Freeman on why he supported Eisenhower.

The Times-Dispatch of Wednesday, November 5, gave the impact of the results in its front-page banner head:

Eisenhower Wins Landslide Victory for President,
Cracks Solid South, Sweeps Richmond and State

Inevitably, newspapers are accused of bias in their news columns by readers who are convinced there is collusion between editorial writers and reporters. Or the criticism may be that publishers, who can establish stances for editorial pages, tell news departments how to slant the news.

Both news and editorial departments vehemently deny such charges but often lack evidence to support those denials. In 1954, *The Times-Dispatch* found such evidence.

It printed on its October 17 editorial page, excerpts from a book, *One Party Press?*, by Nathan Blumberg, assistant professor of journalism at the University of Nebraska.

Blumberg had studied the coverage of the 1952 presidential election by 35 papers and found only six showing partiality in their news columns. *The Times-Dispatch* was not among them. In fact, said Blumberg, he found "no evidence of partiality in this generally excellent performance." He studied front pages of *The Times-Dispatch* from October 6 through November 4 and inside pages on three days in that period.

On the front pages, Democrats totaled 674 and 1/2 column inches to 504 for the Republicans; inside, the Democrats had a 224-221 edge. Republicans had 78 column inches of pictures to 60 for the Democrats on front pages, he found; however, in total column inches of news, the Democrats topped the GOP 734 and 1/2 to 580 on the front pages. Inside, the Republicans were ahead by 238 inches to 229 for the Democrats.

Blumberg's main criticism was that the paper "could have improved with more news space and less display emphasis to the Republicans."

"Despite its editorial support of Eisenhower," said Blumberg, "the *Richmond Times-Dispatch* devoted more news space on its front pages to the Democrats' cause than it did to the Republicans, largely because of extensive coverage devoted to [President] Truman."

Four years later, *The Times-Dispatch* still supported Eisenhower editorially, although K.V. Hoffman, one of its editorial writers, had become disaffected and let his sympathies show in his column written under the pseudonym of Ross Valentine. T. Coleman Andrews of Richmond, Eisenhower's former internal revenue commissioner who was running for president on the States Rights ticket, was Hoffman's man.

"He is running on a principle *you* believe in," said the column two days before the election.

The United States was caught up in two international crises—a Mideast war and the Soviet Union's tanks moving in Budapest—but the election obviously was the story on Wednesday, November 7. *The Times-Dispatch* head that day:

EISENHOWER WINS AGAIN

The paper had praised Eisenhower for keeping the United States out of the war and it had condemned the Soviets for threatening to intervene there. "All of us should be thankful that we have him to lead us at such a time," said the editorial the morning after the election.

Hoffman, however, after calling the Democrats and Republicans "as alike as two pcas in a pod," said "the States Rights' vote should be a small, bright candle of hope."

The Richmond dailies' editorial support of Eisenhower in 1952 and 1956 signaled their course in the years to come. Occasionally, they supported a Democrat in a local or statewide election (such as William B. Spong's futile bid for re-election to the U.S. Senate—supported by *The Times-Dispatch*—in 1972).

Neither paper identified itself as Republican, but each supported the Republican presidential candidate in every election beginning in 1952. That meant Richard M. Nixon three times, Barry Goldwater, Gerald Ford, Ronald Reagan twice and George Bush twice. After *The Times-Dispatch* and *The News Leader* merged in 1992, the editorial page of the new *Times-Dispatch* was a strong supporter of Republicans George Allen Jr. for governor and Oliver North for United States senator.

TORNADOES AND HAZEL

A weather story unique in Richmond history was reported in vast amounts of newsprint in 1951 but with little credit, by name, to any reporter or photographer.

The front page of *The Times-Dispatch* of June 14 told it:

Tornado Hits City; Scores Left Homeless

That was the banner headline, followed by:

Damage Estimated
From 2 to 4 Millions;
12 Persons Are Hurt

There were three Page-One stories, the main one leading with: "A tornado hit Richmond late yesterday afternoon and ripped out a million-dollar path of destruction.

"The big wind blew up suddenly from the west at about 4 P.M. Its twister cut a zigzag course over Byrd Park, swirled through the residential section to the east, crossed Monroe Park and finally spent its force across Broad Street in the area northwest of First Street."

The Times-Dispatch said the winds were "probably the strongest in the city's history," with gusts between 60 and 100 miles an hour.

As was the custom of the day, homeless whites were taken to the King Carter Hotel, blacks to Maggie Walker High School—a school for those of their race.

The most telling photograph was for some strange reason relegated to Page 6. Perhaps it was because the photographer was a free-lancer, William Edwin Booth. His picture, taken from the roof of Miller & Rhoads department store, showed the funnel. Also on the page was a first-person story by Louis Patterson, not a reporter but a Richmond Newspapers photographer.

Pages 7 and 8 were picture pages, with staff photographs credited to "Wood, Lynn, Patterson, O'Neil and Crawford." That meant John Wood, Carl Lynn, Louis Patterson and Richmond Crawford Jr. A Page One picture spread across five columns was taken by "Colognori"—Joseph Colognori, the chief photographer.

The News Leader, whose banner headline the next day read,

400 Buildings Damaged

was a bit more liberal than its competitor with bylines. John Wood, a photographer who also was a pilot, merited a credit, "Airviews by Wood," and Martin Millspaugh, a reporter, won a byline on his feature story.

Inside, the grand old man of *The News Leader*, R.B. Munford Jr., recalled in a first-person story the storm of 1896, when the steeple of Second Baptist Church fell and the city fathers forced the removal of spires from other historic churches, among them St. Paul's Episcopal, Broad Street Methodist and First Presbyterian.

Three years later, when furious weather again was the lead story, *The Times-Dispatch* was more generous with bylines. As was often the case, it called on James Latimer, Number 1 political writer, to do the big story. He wrote:

"Hurricane Hazel, riding northward on winds that blew in gusts up to 108 miles an hour, took a toll of at least seven lives and cut a broad swath of costly damage across Eastern Virginia yesterday."

Storm Batters State, Kills 7

read the banner headline and beneath it:

Thousands Are Homeless as Hazel

Rips Through 8 States, U.S. Capital

Even with staff members' stories and pictures of the storm dominating Page one and taking all of three inside pages, the most striking picture of all was by a free-lancer, Tommy Pollock, often snickered at by the newspapers' own photographers and editors.

Pollock came to the newspaper, developed his negatives and plopped on the city desk the pictures of the day. They showed the 226-foot steeple and spire of New Light Baptist Church, in several stages, falling from the force of the wind. The former Trinity Methodist Church, sold to blacks in 1945, had been a Richmond landmark for 88 years.

For some reason, the city edict of 1896 that forced several churches to remove their steeples didn't affect the old Trinity Methodist structure. Nevertheless, the city building commissioner had said a short time before the hurricane that the steeple should be repaired or demolished.

Pollock sold his photos to *The Times-Dispatch,* then took the negatives to both the Associated Press and United Press, which paid him more money than had *The Times-Dispatch.* He had the satisfaction of seeing clips of his shots from newspapers across the nation and abroad.

The mother of all tornadoes in *The Times-Dispatch* area occurred August 7, 1993.

Under a mammoth banner headline,

We just prayed

and a deck,

At least 3
people die
in twister

Mark Johnson's lead story began, "Swirling amid the relief of an overdue rainfall, a record-strength tornado killed at least three people in Colonial Heights—two in a Wal-Mart—and ravaged Petersburg's Old Towne yesterday on a 13-mile path of terror."

This was the new *Times-Dispatch,* combined with the old *News Leader* and redesigned. There were more pictures (all in color on section fronts), more space and bigger headlines. More than a quarter of the 16-page Saturday paper was devoted to the tornado—two stories and two pictures taking up two-thirds of the front page, plus four additional pages, without ads, inside.

Although there were only eight bylines and 10 stories, *Times-Dispatch* editors carefully toted up how many reporters were on tornado duty—22 plus a special correspondent—and duly noted for readers who they were. There were also a map, a chart and 16 photographs, including several from the air.

Sunday's follow-up disclosed, "Two tornadoes, not one as originally thought, spawned the violent winds. . . " Johnson's and Susan Winiecki's lead added that the death toll had grown to four. Furthermore, the 200-mile-an-hour winds caused at least $11 million in damage. The first and stronger tornado hit the Wal-Mart store, where three people were killed, and Old Towne. The second tornado, with winds up to 90 miles an hour, overturned trucks as it hit the Interstate 295 bridge over the James River.

As on the preceding day, *The Times-Dispatch* on Sunday allotted two-thirds of its front page and four inside pages to the tornado. This time, 17 reporters had bylines on 13 stories.

Colonial Heights is a mostly white city, cheek by jowl with predominantly black Petersburg—about 20 miles south of Richmond. This was an area with some of the harshest fighting in the final days of the Civil War. Preservationists had worked for years to resuscitate Old Towne, a favorite of tourists who come to look at battlefields. Established in the 17th century, the original Old Towne burned in 1815, but from the mid-1800s into the early 1900s the area thrived. Then its importance declined.

The Times-Dispatch gave heavy coverage to the effects of the tornado on Old Towne, but it devoted considerable space, too, to the effects on low-income residents, black and white. The front page of Sunday's paper carried a picture of Petersburg's black mayor, Rosalyn Dance, surveying damage with Virginia's two United States senators in shirtsleeves, John W. Warner and Charles S. Robb.

The National Weather Service determined that the first of two tornadoes, with winds up to 200 miles an hour, was an F4, making it probably the worst tornado to hit Virginia in recorded history. Earlier tornadoes rated no more than an F3.

As newspapers do, *The Times-Dispatch* dutifully noted on Saturday the "severe tornadoes" in the past in Virginia. Neither there nor anywhere else in the paper's grandiose coverage of the latest tornado was there any mention of the big blow in 1951, which then was *The Times-Dispatch*'s lead story.

PROBING THE POLICE

On January 22, 1960, agents of the Internal Revenue Service raided the office of Richmond Amusement Sales Co., which leased juke boxes, and the home of its president, Harry Donovan.

Because Donovan had been the reputed head of a "numbers" gambling ring for years, there was surprise among those in the know only that there had been a raid. Policemen as well as reporters knew Donovan's reputation.

The IRS promptly hit Donovan with a tax lien of $185,684.

Editorially, *The Times-Dispatch* answered its own uneasiness about warrants being issued from Alexandria, not Richmond, and about the absence of Richmond police by quoting IRS, which said nothing unusual was involved. "Jumping to conclusions is an unwise form of exercise," said an editorial January 27, "and shouldn't be resorted to in this case solely on the basis of the manner in which the federal men handled their job."

But *The News Leader* was more skeptical. Its lead editorial two days earlier said the "raid by Federal agents leaves an ominous and disturbing question in its wake: Where were the city police?"

Carl Shires, *The News Leader's* seasoned, talented police reporter, wrote on February 5, in a stilted fashion that was unlike him, "Richmond police division commanders are finding that many of their men visited a business office raided two weeks ago by federal investigators of alleged numbers writing."

So began the year's biggest local story, one on which Shires consistently scooped his opposition across the hall at *The Times-Dispatch*. One reason was that *The Times-Dispatch's* police reporter was not eager to alienate the police. He persuaded editors to assign the story to Ed Grimsley, who then covered City Hall, and Frank Walin, who covered federal courts. They didn't do badly, but Shires had contacts everywhere.

Much of his nine-year stint at *The News Leader* at that time had been spent on the police beat. A Phi Beta Kappa graduate of the University of

Richmond and of the Columbia University School of Journalism, Shires was charming but crude. He was unworried about offending anyone; he was faithful to his sources; he worked hard.

By mid-March, a federal grand jury had investigated all aspects of gambling in the city and had indicted Donovan on 11 counts of tax evasion and failing to buy a wagering stamp. Furthermore, it found an "appalling and flagrant disregard for law and order."

The grand jury had subpoenaed 105 policemen and, Shires reported, "it was believed that more than 60 refused to testify under terms of the Fifth Amendment."

How could Shires find out information about that most secret aspect of the American judicial system, the grand jury? He had a good source, whom he did not identify at the time: Joseph Bambacus.

Bambacus was the United States district attorney before the grand jury. The policemen hired one of the city's best criminal lawyers, Robert R. Merhige Jr., who later would become a U.S. District Court judge.

"Joe and I worked out a deal," Shires said.[86]

"The day they brought in all of the cops—I think I knew every cop on the force. . . and I sat in the hallway long before the grand jury. I'd write down their names on a yellow pad when they went in, and then I had a person [Bambacus] who escorted them in. If he came back out with his right hand in the pocket, they [the policman] took the Fifth and so I marked him down."

Thus, Shires could report in that afternoon's *News Leader* that "18 Richmond policemen pleaded the Fifth Amendment."

Richmond's director of public safety, William Groth, whose department oversaw police and fire bureaus, had been asking policemen questions on a form that the police dubbed the "Donovan royalty oath."

On March 18, Shires reported all 400 policemen were to be queried by Groth, who wanted to know "why there was such a tremendous splurge of Fifths." A *News Leader* editorial the same day, noting the existence of "an enormous numbers racket" and the fact that many police took the Fifth Amendment, said flatly, "Our police were blind, inefficient and stupid or some of our police were being paid off."

By early April, City Council was getting its own investigation under way. On March 27, a Police Bureau shakeup sent Chief O.D. Garton upstairs as an aide to Groth. Maj. John G. Hanna retired and Maj. John M. Wright became acting chief.

There was plenty of embarrassment to go around. T. Gray Haddon Jr., son of the long-time commonwealth's attorney, issued a six-paragraph statement complaining about a "whispering campaign" against his father but con-

Maurice Dean (left), former Times-Dispatch *police reporter and later a court clerk, chats in 1960 with Robert R. Merhige Jr., lawyer for many policemen during a City Council probe of the Police Bureau. Merhige later became a federal judge.*

ceding that the son had worked for Harry Donovan since October 1959 and had been installing vending machines.

The story was carried in *The News Leader*, although *The Times-Dispatch* had a chance to carry it first. Larry Weekley and the author, both of *The Times-Dispatch*, interviewed the younger Haddon at length at his home as he chain-smoked, perspired and explained his relationship to Donovan.

But Managing Editor John H. Colburn became quite cautious and sat on the story.

In testimony before a City Council committee, all but 10 of 389 members of the force appeared. Detective D.R. Duling—later to become the beloved, bearded "Sergeant Santa" at Christmas time—admitted borrowing $150 from Donovan but said he'd paid it back. Patrolman A.B.Cole III said Donovan had contributed to a fund set up by Cole's friends to defray hospital expenses after he'd had a heart attack.

The Times-Dispatch editorial page was pleased that only one policeman took the Fifth Amendment before the council committee but called for an independent investigation, since, after all, the federal grand jury had found "overwhelming evidence of appalling and flagrant disregard for law and order."

By late April, when City Council hired Robert Lumpkin, a lawyer and former FBI agent, to lead an investigation of police corruption, no one seemed satisfied with the situation. *The News Leader* editorial page was still perturbed that 62 policemen took the Fifth Amendment and wouldn't buy their explanations—which, *The News Leader* said, were that they acted on advice of counsel or their feet hurt or they were worried about personal questions.

Bambacus said reports of his asking "irrelevant questions" were a myth, and the recently retired Maj. Hanna accused three members of City Council of tormenting the Police Bureau.

Donovan's trial had been moved to Newport News, and on May 13, Shires reported that the defendant interrupted his trial to plead guilty to 11 counts. Shires also said that in a hall near the trial Garton, "who recently was kicked upstairs to the post of acting assistant to the safety director," was met by Donovan, who assured the former chief that there "had never been payoff money" for policemen.

Shires recalled in an interview that Donovan was angry over Shires' writing that, gambler or not, Donovan looked the part in a flamboyant array of "two-toned shoes, striped shirt, checked tie and sports coat and green trousers—or something."

The next day, Shires recalled, "He looked at me and said, 'You son of a bitch, do you like the way I'm dressed today?' He had on a sedate blue suit and a white shirt and a college tie."[87]

The News Leader editorial page didn't let up. Noting May 23 that Donovan had been sentenced to four years in prison, the paper quoted Bambacus' charge in court that "the entire vice squad of the City of Richmond Police Bureau was on Donovan's payroll."

It, therefore, asked, "Where were the Richmond cops all this time?

Why was Donovan able to operate unscathed? If out-of-town Treasury agents could gather evidence [in 72 hours] sufficient for conviction, what was wrong with the Richmond police? Were they deaf? Were they blind?

". . . The rumors that reached Mr. Bambacus on Main Street, loud and clear, never filtered through the walls of [the Police Bureau in] City Hall Annex on Broad Street.

"Incompetent? Or corrupt?"

The Times-Dispatch, although not so furious as *The News Leader*, said immediately after Donovan's plea, "What has been clearly demonstrated. . . is that a numbers operation of considerable size was carried on here, presumably for years, without any effective action being taken by city police to end it.

"Why?"

By May 25, *The Times-Dispatch* wanted to dispense with niceties in the Police Bureau, which it said should ask for explanations from those who invoked the Fifth Amendment before a legally constituted investigative body. If the answers were unsatisfactory, the cops should be fired for cause.

Through the summer conflicts continued. Safety Director Groth and District Attorney Bambacus feuded over co-operation or lack of same. Shires reported that at least 62 policemen who took the Fifth Amendment would be asked by Groth to take lie detector tests. Thirty policemen, including the top officers, were asked by Investigator Lumpkin to take such tests. All refused.

City Councilman J. Edward Lawler, a former FBI agent, wanted the investigation taken away from Lumpkin and turned back to the council and the commonwealth's attorney.

In mid-August, Lumpkin concluded in his 360-page, $45,000 report that "protection payments" to police were so routine as to be considered "fringe benefits." He said that Safety Director Groth and former Chief Garton must be held responsible for Donovan's multi-million-dollar operation, that the vice squad had a "bag man" and that there was a "pattern of corruption" involving "a large number" of policemen.

On September 1, Groth announced that Garton would retire at the end of the investigation. Bad health was given as the reason. By that time, *The News Leader* editorial page was in such a frenzy that it wondered why the city even needed a safety director. Norfolk, it noted, had abandoned the post 27 years ago. Richmond finally abolished the post in 1992.

On September 20, Groth opened his own investigation. Bambacus, invited to help out, said federal law prohibited his releasing his information. Finally, Groth disciplined four policemen and cleared the other 54 he was investigating. There was a lack of evidence of any multi-million-dollar gambling operation in Richmond, said Groth.

Meanwhile (on November 16), City Manager Horace Edwards said in a 781-page transcript of City Council's investigation that the alleged gambling could not have occurred without "police protection." But, it added, the Lumpkin report was "highly hyperbolic" in places.

By then all the juice had flowed out of the investigation. A Richmond Bar Association report on March 9, 1961 found no pattern of corruption then or in the past in the Police Bureau. Commonwealth's Attorney Haddon said there would be no call for a grand jury because "no good could be accomplished" and it would be a "waste of time and unnecessary expense."

Summing up, *The Times-Dispatch* said March 10, the bar association showed "no 'whitewash' of the charge of police corruption." Nevertheless, it said top police officers erred in not co-operating fully with Lumpkin, the bureau erred in not nabbing Donovan and Lumpkin erred in "making sweeping statements alleging corruption on the basis of unprovable assumptions."

THE KENNEDY ASSASSINATION

The assassination of John Kennedy, like the Japanese attack on Pearl Harbor, was one of those defining moments for all who lived through those days—newspaper people and ordinary citizens.

All knew what they were doing at the precise moment they learned of the president's death, but the news people also know exactly how their papers handled the event.

Staff members of *The News Leader* and *The Times-Dispatch* are virtually unanimous in saying both papers did a superb job. *The News Leader's* first (state) edition was complete when word came that the president had been shot; yet editors stretched deadlines and replated the front page several times so that virtually all its subscribers read about it. The paper, Virginia's largest afternoon daily, printed 152,000 copies, 20,000 more than usual.

The first replate carried eight inches on the shooting; a second, under a four-column, two-line head, reported the shooting of Kennedy and Governor John Connolly of Texas.

The late home, or next to last, edition carried a banner headline,

Kennedy Is Assassinated

plus a full column of text—all in bold face—from the Associated Press, despite the 2:37 p.m. time that two priests announced the president's death. The final, blue streak, edition had a complete Associated Press biography of Kennedy and a seven-column strip of pictures. Most of pages 1, 3 and 4 were devoted to the shooting.

The edition ran no more than five minutes late.

To Bob Hilldrup, perhaps *The News Leader's* most acerbic critic while a reporter and later, the handling of Kennedy's shooting was "probably one of the finest times" at the paper. That day, Hilldrup was covering the city desk between editions when a caller on the telephone asked, "What is this about the president being shot in Dallas?" When Hilldrup sounded unbelieving, the caller countered, "Why the hell don't you people turn on the television so you can find out what's going on?"[88]

Hilldrup rushed across the hall to the Associated Press bureau just as the first bulletin was moving. Larry Gould, *News Leader* city editor, recalled that "the main city edition," another name for the "late home edition," was on the press. "We just scrapped those newspapers in the hall," said Gould.[89]

At *The Times-Dispatch*, reporters and editors who weren't scheduled to be there until much later began arriving in the early afternoon. They had all afternoon and the early evening to prepare the Saturday paper, normally a thin one.

If the event was the biggest news story most reporters and editors had ever worked on, there was uneasiness because the number one man in the newsroom, John Leard, had been there only nine months. Furthermore, he'd been a *News Leader* man since before World War II. Only in February had he come to *The Times-Dispatch* as managing editor to succeed John Colburn, who had gone to Wichita as editor and publisher.

Leard acknowledged that "until then I was suspect, and I understood that and didn't expect anything else." He said people were co-operative, especially Bill Leverty, the news editor who had been passed over for the managing editor's job. "But then came the Kennedy thing, and I took charge, as I should have," said Leard, "and I think after we did a tremendous job on that, people just began to think, 'Well, maybe this guy knows something about newspapers.'"[90]

At the time, Omar Mardan, had his doubts. Mardan, who had been on *The Times-Dispatch* since his days at the University of Richmond in the 1940s, was perhaps the most admired man on the staff. His news judgment was good, everyone said. He had been a reporter, copy editor and sports staff member. He wrote headlines well and designed good-looking pages. He always worked nights and loved nothing better than to party all-night after work, then go and play golf before sleeping in the afternoon and coming back to work.

On November 22, 1963, his slumber was interrupted by a call from Harry Wyland, a copy editor, who told him of the shooting. "I came stumbling into work," said Mardan.[91]

What disturbed him, he said, was that Leard had assembled a mound of pictures from the photography department and told Al Wagner, an assistant city editor, to lay out a picture page. Mardan figured that was silly. "I thought somebody on the copy desk should handle everything, so it would not be any duplication of stuff. . . . This was a picture page; you wouldn't want a picture you'd also want for Page 2 or 3 or 4."

He and Leard exchanged some sharp words, although Leard was obviously in charge. The trouble, said Mardan, was "John Leard was an afternoon newspaper man, had been an afternoon newspaperman. His idea was to get it in the paper, and it didn't make any difference how you put it in the paper.

". . . His idea was to get something in the paper, whether it made sense or not."

Mardan's arguments with Leard were like those he had with the Circulation Department in bad weather. Circulation would argue for an early deadline. Mardan would reply with no attempt to hide the sarcasm, "Fine. Lock up *The News Leader* and put the T-D masthead on it and send it off. What difference does it make? If you are going to have a newspaper, you want some news in it. Well, you can't deliver them? . . . That is not my problem. My problem is to put the news in the paper."[92]

Mardan, even later as assistant managing editor, fought early deadlines. He, of course, compromised, but he reasoned that deadlines could be stretched in emergencies and that papers coming off the presses even a few minutes behind schedule and containing the latest news were a lot better than papers coming off early and omitting that news.

The Saturday morning *Times-Dispatch* the day after the shooting carried four front-page stories on the assassination, plus a reference to other stories inside, plus a brief item on the deaths in office of presidents elected every 20 years beginning in 1840. There were photographs of the president's car, of the swearing in of Lyndon Johnson with Jackie Kennedy at his side, of Lee Harvey Oswald and a black-bordered picture of John Kennedy.

The all-cap, banner headlines in the final edition read:

KENNEDY IS ASSASSINATED;

SUSPECT, 24, IS CHARGED

That bottom line was changed from

JOHNSON IS PRESIDENT

which any reasonably informed reader would realize was obvious.

Every story for the first eight pages was an assassination story. On Page 2, Charles McDowell told of Richmonders' reaction and noted how copies of Victor Lasky's rabidly anti-Kennedy book, *JFK, The Man and the Myth*, had been taken from the top of the book section at Miller & Rhoads department store and placed lower. James Latimer carried Virginia politicians' reminiscences of Kennedy. There were eight stories, along with a continuation, on Page 2. Related stories were in sports and business and as far back as Pages 20 and 21.

Miller & Rhoads and its competing department store, Thalhimers, carried full-page sympathy ads.

The News Leader of Saturday, November 23, carried eight Page One stories on the assassination, including an assessment of the late president, under the headline,

Kennedy

A Profile

In Courage

and a mood piece from Washington by Carl Shires. "A city sickened by sorrow got back its dead President last night," he wrote.

The banner headlines read:

Body of Slain President

Lies in Historic East Room

The slim paper devoted all of Pages 1 through 6 to the assassination, which also occupied part of two more pages and all of Page 11. The shooting also affected sports and society coverage.

The big *Times-Dispatch* for Sunday, November 24, had another two-line banner head,

Kennedy Will Lie in State at Capitol;

Johnson Will Proclaim Day of Mourning

plus eight stories on the front page. Except for Page 2, a full-page ad, there was only one non-assassination story in the first 12 pages. That concerned the report of a state sales tax study commission.

Monday's *Times-Dispatch*, of course, featured the fatal shooting of Oswald. Except for part of Page 2, there was nothing but assassination-related news in the first nine pages. *The News Leader* on Monday carried seven assassination stories on the front, including one by Shires in Washington. Virtually all of the first five pages were devoted to the shootings and related stories.

On Tuesday, *The Times-Dispatch* was unrelenting. Most of the first nine pages, including a front-page piece from Washington by McDowell, were Kennedy stories.

The editorial pages of both Richmond papers, which had opposed Kennedy's election, had kind words for him in death. *The Times-Dispatch* said "the people of the United States will stand together at the bier of the murdered President." More eloquently, *The News Leader* noted that it "fought him all the way." Yet, it added, "it is a measure of the character, the quality, and the charm of man himself, that Mr. Kennedy's stoutest political enemies were as shocked and saddened as his best political friends by yesterday's stunning events.

"The sense of keen regret in this editorial office most certainly was matched in other 'anti-Kennedy' quarters across this nation. Here was a man, God rest his soul, who fought fairly, not deviously; who kept a high heart and a lively sense of humor, who brought to his office a great warmth and vitality. You could not hate this man. You could disagree with him, fight his proposals, urge his defeat; you could fear the consequences of his ideas in areas of domestic government and foreign affairs. But the man himself had qualities that endeared."

Reflecting on *The News Leader's* coverage, Larry Gould found one "glitch." Shires' lead on the funeral was, "In splendid simplicity, they buried John F. Kennedy here yesterday."

Not long after Publisher Tennant Bryan read that, Gould said, Bryan called and said, "If that was a simple ceremony, I'd like to see something elaborate."[93]

Hilldrup, summing up, said of *The News Leader's* coverage, "There's not one-tenth of 1 percent of the people in the world who could do what we have just done, and there are damned few newspapermen who can do what we have just done. And I think that was the high point of any feel-good feeling at *The News Leader*."[94]

FLOODS

The Times-Dispatch of Wednesday, August 20, 1969, reported the victory of William C. Battle over Henry Howell for the Democratic nomination for governor of Virginia. Battle, who had been John F. Kennedy's ambassador to Australia, would lose the election in November to Linwood Holton, Virginia's first Republican governor in a century. Howell, from the liberal wing of the state Democratic party, would later become lieutenant governor—as an independent.

That afternoon's *News Leader* led with Carl Shires' election story, which said that Battle, "the finally-selected Democratic nominee for governor," was pledged the support "from both the Democratic establishment as personified by Gov. [Mills E.] Godwin [Jr.] and maverick Henry E. Howell Jr."

Tucked beneath the election wrapup was a story with no byline and the headline

Flooding Likely Here
As James Overflows

Normally, the Wednesday after an election is a day when a morning paper's reporters and editors who have worked overtime on Tuesday let up a bit. There was not a chance that August day. A banner headline in *The Times-Dispatch* of Thursday, August 21 read:

38 Dead, 32 Missing in State Floods;
Richmond Is Bracing for Record Crest

Larry Markley's lead story said, "At least 38 persons were reported dead, 32 others missing and scores homeless or without utility services last night as officials sought to cope with Virginia's worst flooding in years."

Richmonders were warned of the possibility of the capital city's worst flood in history. A Page 1 chart listed the record floods—the worst being a reading of 28.2 feet in 1870.

The News Leader of Aug. 21 topped its front page with an 8-column map of the James River. The headline,

Hundreds Flee Homes Here

As James Floodwaters Rise

was followed by the lead story of Dean Levi, the longtime "weatherman" of *The News Leader*. "Richmonders living near the swollen James River," he wrote, "were evacuating their dwellings today as the capital city prepared for the worst flooding in its history."

Flood stage at the city locks is 9 feet, and forecasters were looking for a depth of 34 to 36 feet. The river was rising a foot an hour.

Charles (Mike) Houston, senior reporter on *The News Leader* staff, toyed with a story on major flooding in 1936 and as far back as 1870. In that earlier flood, he said, a reporter in a boat was offered a drink by a man in a second-floor room on Main Street. "No, thank you," said the reporter. "I don't like so much water with so little whiskey."

The dire predictions for flooding in the city were correct. *The Times-Dispatch* of August 22 reported a reading of 30 feet at the city locks and the declaration by Governor Godwin of the state as a disaster area. What had hit the state was Hurricane Camille.

Ray Lovenbury, normally the night police reporter, was assigned by the city desk to be chief flood reporter. His lead read, "The James River, on its costliest and possibly its record rampage, built slowly to 30 feet at the city locks about 2 a.m. today."

As it normally did for weather disasters, *The Times-Dispatch* city and state editors assigned the bulk of their staffs to the flood. Lawrence Brown of the state desk staff told of the Virginia death toll reaching 46 and of 80 bridges having been washed out. Bill Millsaps of the sports department—later executive editor of the paper—wrote a sidebar on the flood of 1936.

Both papers had a difficult time pinning down the record flood. That Page 1 box in *The Times-Dispatch* on August 21 listed the 1870 reading of 28.2 feet. Lovenbury's story the next day that had the crest building to 30 feet said the river had passed "the flood record of 27.3 feet at the Richmond city locks set on Mar. 20, 1936." By Saturday, August 23, the paper reported that the river had begun ebbing from its crest of 28.6 feet. Mike Houston's August 21 feature in *The News Leader* had the record crest at 28.3 feet in 1936. He added that the crest then was the highest since 1870, but the record then was in dispute because of different methods of measurement.

The flood remained a front-page story for *The Times-Dispatch* seven straight days—through Tuesday, August 26, when Markley's story told of a death toll of 76, with 104 people missing. The final toll was set at 114. Overall damage in Virginia from Camille was $113 million, with 358 homes damaged.

For *The News Leader*, the flood was a Page One item through Friday, August 29. One of the most poignant stories was Bill Wasson's from Lovingston in Central Virginia on August 25. It told of the Davis Creek community, where 16 members of the Huffman family were missing, along with eight Perrys, five Martins and five Burnleys.

The 1969 flood was said by many to be a "once-in-a-century" flood. The century was severely condensed.

When the James River flooded, oil storage tanks in South Richmond were in the midst of the waters. This was in 1972.

Less than three years later, near the bottom of the front page of *The News Leader* on Wednesday, June 21, 1972, was a story by Jean Reed that began, "About 150 children and adults were evacuated from Camp Easter Seal in Craig County today as overflowing water from Craig Creek threatened the Barbour's Creek area. . . "

In *The Times-Dispatch* the next morning, Lawrence Brown wrote, "Six persons were known dead and there were unconfirmed reports of five other deaths last night as Tropical Storm Agnes intensified and dumped very heavy rains on already swollen Virginia rivers and streams and brought record flooding to some portions of the state."

That day's *News Leader* stripped two flood pictures across eight columns at the top of Page One. Hugh Robertson's lead story said, "Virginia's toll of death and destruction mounted today as Agnes fled northeastward." Bill Sauder's story on the same page said, "The advice to persons in Richmond's James River flood plain was 'head for high ground' today as the city braced for inundation. . . " A bulletin on Page One told of the closing of U.S. 1 and Interstate 95 because of flooding in Northern Virginia.

The papers had their own flood—of words. Brown's story in *The Times-Dispatch* of June 22 was one of four on Page One devoted to the disaster. All of Page 2 was a flood page. On Friday, June 23, the paper had an 8-column photograph of the flooded town of Scottsville, west of Richmond, and four Page One stories on the flood. In all, 10 reporters' bylines graced stories about the flood.

The News Leader of June 23 devoted its entire front page to the flood with the exceptions of a short on the Vietnam war and a story on President Nixon signing an education bill and condemning the busing of pupils for racial balance. Sauder and Steve Row combined on the lead story, which said, "A record-setting James River flood battered Richmond today, crippled its transportation and commerce and knocked its water treatment plant out of operation."

High-ranking city officials were at the plant, they wrote, when "waters engulfed its impoundment basins and swirled around its pumps at 9 a.m.

"They ordered all employees out and made a hasty exit."

The News Leader had two, no-ad pages inside devoted entirely to the flood.

On Saturday, June 24, Brown and Stephen Fleming wrote the state and local angles on the major stories in *The Times-Dispatch* about the flood, which at that point had caused $160 million in damage and 17 deaths. All of pages 6 and 7 and half of a women's news page were devoted to the flood. The number of reporters with bylines rose to 16.

In *The News Leader* of June 24, only a story about a bomb in a parked bus near Virginia Commonwealth University could crowd flood news off the front page. A brief story on the front told where Richmonders could get water from tank trucks. It also assured residents that water from all city springs was safe for drinking. In that thin Saturday paper, Page 12 was noth-

When the rains came, Tate Field—home of the professional Richmond Colts of the Class B Piedmont League—was flooded. This was in 1934.

ing but pictures and, in a rare departure from tradition, the entire editorial page was devoted to flood sketches by Jeff MacNelly, the Pulitzer Prize-holding cartoonist.

For nine consecutive days, the flood was Page One news in *The Times-Dispatch. The News Leader* also kept it outside nine days.

The flooding three years earlier was no longer a record. At the city locks, the crest was 36.51 feet, almost eight feet higher than in 1969. The city's reservoir went dry and stayed that way for more than four days, cutting off water for some 100,000 people. The National Guard patrolled downtown.

Three years earlier, Tropical Storm Camille had caused the destruction. This time it was Tropical Storm Agnes. Lawrence Brown wrote on Sunday, July 2, in one of many stories summing up the disaster, "Agnes, like her wicked sisters before her, was supposed to grow old and tired as she moved northward, but she was hellbent on writing new lessons for the experts to study."

For the record, Agnes was less severe than Camille only in the number of lives lost—22 vs. 114. But the total damage of about $330 million almost trebled that of Camille, and 6,000 homes were damaged, compared to 358 in Camille.

In about three more years, another flood came. But when the crest at city locks reached only 20.76 feet—or about 11 feet above flood stage, it seemed like a minor disruption.

THE I.T.U. STRIKE

Shortly after 7 o'clock March 31, 1971, just as *The Times-Dispatch* was nearing the first deadline for inside pages for the 72-page Thursday morning paper, a newsroom editor acknowledged a brief telephone call, turned in his chair and annnounced, "They just walked out."

The strike by 182 members of the printers' union was not unexpected. Ten days earlier Local 90 of the International Typographical Union had voted 149 to 8 to strikc Richmond Newspapers Inc. The old contract had expired September 30, and negotiations on a new one had been going on since August.

Still, the walkout was the first by any union against *The Times-Dispatch* and *The News Leader* in 75 years.

Exactly how long the strike lasted is difficult to say. A year after it began, printers were still picketing the newspaper building at 333 East Grace Street but it was obvious in less than a week who had won. Neither paper missed an edition and other unions who had signed contracts did not honor the picket line.

How did the papers do it, when typesetting machines were intricate devices that could not be mastered in a few short lessons? Even before the printers walked out and after some equipment was damaged, said Gerald W. Estes, vice president-general manager, people from advertising, circulation and news received "extensive training" on teletypesetting machines that used tape instead of the more involved manual keyboards that used hot metal.[95] Those people started work in the composing room as soon as the printers stopped.

Ironically, Media General, the parent corporation, had sent 15 employees each from papers in Richmond, Winston-Salem and Tampa to Oklahoma to learn how to run presses. It was wasted effort; members of the pressmen's union crossed the printers' picket line. Lee Painter, a union printer for 20 years before he walked out for good, said his colleagues had been assured that the pressmen's union would honor a picket line but learned later that the pressmen had specifically said they would not and that the ITU leaders "kept it to themselves."[96]

With more than the usual number of typographical errors, *The Times-Dispatch* of April 1 came off the presses three hours late. The lead story was the life sentence given Army Lieutenant William L. Calley Jr. for the murder of at least 22 Vietnamese civilians at My Lai. The off-lead was the strike. James Latimer, the senior reporter on the staff, had a byline under the two-column headline,

Printers Strike

Newspapers Here

There was a short "To Our Readers" notice from management, above Latimer's story and, beneath the story, a four-column photo by Carl Lynn of pickets outside the production building.

The night of the strike was a newspaper version of rich folks going slumming. Publisher D. Tennant Bryan, President Alan S. Donnahoe and Bryan's daugher Polly were in the composing room—working. (Donnahoe also went upstairs to write the lead editorial for the April 1 *Times-Dispatch*. It was duplicated in that afternoon's *News Leader*.) Bill Leverty, who had retired as *The Times-Dispatch*'s assistant managing editor, was back as a proof reader. Donnahoe's wife, Elsie, "was a pretty good typesetter," her husband said, "but. . . after she worked for about three weeks, I told Jerry Estes 'you have to get rid of my wife. I'm tired of her being down here.'"[97]

Many people—editors and reporters—finished their newsroom chores on the third floor, then went down one floor for a session in the composing room. Weeks later, they received extra pay for those chores. Some newsroom editors who also worked in the composing room may have been ordered to do so, but reporters—and any editors eligible to join their local union—were not compelled to be part-time printers.

Two days after the strike, the papers announced they were seeking permanent replacements for the strikers.

As is the case in most strikes, a key point of disagreement was wages. There was also contention on retroactive pay raises. A third issue—about which both sides felt passionately—involved the printers' right to continue reproducing or resetting type for advertisements that had been produced outside the shop.

The practice, known throughout the industry as "bogus," was labeled "make-work" and "featherbedding" by management. To the union, it was "a unique but necessary form of job insurance" that it said was worth $500,000 to its members in accumulated work.

Ed Bryant, a printer who joined Richmond Newspapers in 1947 and stayed on during the strike, said that the union's demand for reproduction was "unfair. . . unscrupulous." That was one reason that Bryant felt the union had "outlived its usefulness." Nevertheless, because he came from a union family and had "strike immunity" since he'd become assistant foreman, he kept paying ITU dues for two years in case the union ever came back.

Bryant also contended that some of the abrasiveness in negotiations could be traced to "tramp printers" on the negotiating committee. They came to town, showed their union cards, got jobs at the paper and moved on when the strike occurred, he said.[98]

Lee Painter remembers the strike somewhat differently. "Strong people who had been there for years" were pushing for the strike, he said. They figured they had built up retirement benefits and they had their union cards, enabling them to travel to other jobs. "The local was pushing more than the international" to walk out, said Painter. He said the international saw the coming technological advancements and "tried to reason with us not to go on strike."[99]

Far and away the major issue in negotiations was a process that was to put printers in the same league with blacksmiths and shove type-casting machines into newspaper museums. The century-old process by which newspapers had been produced was ending. The electronic age had arrived.

Donnahoe recalled in an interview that Media General had been experimenting with publishing a daily financial paper. "Word had leaked out," he said, "that we had this new process, which was indeed new and there was nothing like it before in the history of the world. And we could print this newspaper almost wholly by computer and do it with incredible speed."

The union's response, Donnahoe said, was concern over the procedure "and we would pretty soon be publishing newspapers and they would all be out of a job."

The union "demanded jurisdiction" over that paper, the *Financial Daily*, said Donnahoe, but management would never agree.[100] Estes said, "I told the international that if the strike happened, we'd publish without them and we'd hire replacements."

Skeptics are sure that management was determined to break the union. Yes, Estes said, it was true the company wanted to break the hold the union had on reproduction and the ITU's aim at jurisdiction on new equipment, "and they'd never come back." But he qualified his response by saying the company could have kept on dealing with the union on economic issues. Still, said Estes, "it would have taken years to get where we did" after the strike began.[101]

Bryant, the assistant foreman who remained with the papers until retiring in 1990, agreed that the union wanted not only reproduction rights but also control of all the new technological process. Bryant said he tried learning some of the new process and got in trouble with the ITU because he was doing it on his own time and not getting paid for it. "They were going to fine me rather heavily," he said.

Painter, who commuted to Washington where he worked mostly for the *Post* and some for the *Star* after the Richmond strike, said the ITU was "brainwashing" its members and that in the long run he thought the company was fairer than the union.

Each side tried convincing the public it was right. The union had its picket line and a request from the state AFL-CIO to its members that they cancel subscriptions to *The Times-Dispatch* and *The News Leader*, "two of the most anti-labor publications in the nation."

But management had the editorial pages of both papers and free advertising space. Donnahoe's editorial April 1, entitled "A Regrettable Strike," noted that the printers had a 37.5-hour work-week and that the company had offered a wage increase of $12 a week until September 30 and another $11 a week for the next year. That meant a 14 percent increase. Printers then were making $163.50 a week on the day shift and $170.50 on the night shift.

The union wanted an increase of $17.50 as of the previous October 1 and another $18 a year later.

The April 1 editorial said the company liked "harmonious relationships" with its employees. "We are, for example," wrote Donnahoe, "the only company in the newspaper industry with a long-term Thrift Plan that enables any employee to become a stockholder in the company, by matching his investment in the plan with a fifty percent contribution that vests gradually over a ten-year period."

The next day, another editorial paid tribute to those who helped the papers to continue printing, including "other union members who have honored their contracts." The editorial explained that many in the composing room were "not experts in typesetting, and we ask your tolerance, in this interim period, for typographical errors that may occur."

In an unmistakable warning to printers who remained on strike, the editorial added, "We shall hope to correct this situation as rapidly as we can, by the employment of replacements for composing room jobs."

President Tommy Thomasson of the printers' union local, in a letter to the editor of *The News Leader* on April 8, chided the writer of an editorial entitled "Heroic Publishing Effort" for saying "some machinery was in a disabled condition."

In reality, wrote Thomasson, "this is the most complicated and delicate machinery ever designed by man, with the possible exception of the Lunar Modules. If inexperienced people attempt to operate this machinery, chaos is the normal and to-be-expected result.

Veteran printers like these manned typesetting machines before strike in 1971.

"Whether any semblance of a miracle was present or not we don't know. But many people have called to say that children scratching on a mud fence could probably give the public more intelligent information."

On April 18, management staked out its position in a full-page ad. Three months later—on July 13—in another ad, it listed what it said were 66 instances of coercion of newspaper employees or damage to their property. And it offered $1,000 for information leading to the arrest and conviction of any perpetrator.

Donnahoe said that the striking printers "poured some Coca-Cola in some of the typesetting machines" as they left.[102] Ed Bryant said there was little of that and the damage was cleared up quickly. " I don't think there was much sabotage" in the composing room, he said, although a couple of windows at his home were broken and someone with bad aim tried to "paint-bomb" his house.[103]

THE WESTINGHOUSE CASE

Newspaper editors normally assign reporters for "gavel-to-gavel" coverage of court cases with high human drama—such as murder, rape, even custody fights or embezzlement. So when the first of 17 foreign and domestic utilities sued Westinghouse Corporation in 1975 over uranium shipments, it didn't appear that records would be set for column inches in *The Times-Dispatch.*

No one toted up column inches, but when the litigation ended six years later, scarcely a motion was argued that wasn't covered by Elliott Cooper, *The Times-Dispatch* business editor. In 1978 alone, Cooper had 49 stories on the Westinghouse case.

What caused the flap was Westinghouse's cancellation, in 1975, of uranium contracts with the utilities. Richmond-based Virginia Electric & Power Co., for instance, could—under its 1972 contract with Westinghouse—take varying amounts of uranium. The cost of uranium began to rise and Vepco began ordering larger amounts—more, in fact, that it needed for reactors at its nuclear power stations.

Westinghouse, operating under the doctrine of commercial impracticability, canceled its contracts. The utilities sued.

The News Leader gave sporadic coverage to the cases in stories by its business editor, Roger Kintzel; Kevin McCarthy, and Stewart Jones. But Cooper alone stayed with the case for *The Times-Dispatch.* There was grousing on the part of some *Times-Dispatch* editors and reporters that the case lacked "sex appeal" and wasn't worth daily stories that routinely ran a column or more.

Still, there was big money involved. In the case involving Kansas City Gas and Electric Co., for instance, the settlement involved between $47 million and $94 million, depending on which litigant's estimate one accepted. The lawyers involved in that case were two of Richmond's best known—

Lewis T. Booker and John S. Battle Jr.—from two of Richmond's biggest firms. Booker represented many of the utility plaintiffs.

U.S. District Court Judge Robert R. Merhige Jr. handled all of the cases. Although the Richmond papers' editorial pages lambasted him regularly for his liberalism, especially a busing plan to integrate the city's public schools, reporters loved him. He was a great believer in openness and the sanctity of the First Amendment. He was not likely to compel reporters to disclose anonymous sources. And he was quotable.

When Westinghouse and Kansas Gas agreed on an out-of-court settlement, Merhige commented, "To reach a settlement in this case without loss of life is monumental. I congratulate all of you." A Kansas Gas lawyer had joked earlier that in his part of the country, people were shot for breaking contracts.

At another point, Merhige, who had been urging litigants to settle their differences, told a lawyer that those who want 100 cents on the dollar for their contracts weren't going to get it. "They're just plain damn fools," he said. "No other way to say it."

Merhige made plain how he felt in October 1981 when he ruled that Westinghouse would not be excused from honoring its contracts with seven utilities. That left unsettled the matter of damages, but Merhige that day ruled in favor of the utilities on each point.

Two years later, in a story on how legal paperwork mounts, Shelley Rolfe wrote in *The Times-Dispatch* that the Westinghouse documents filled four storerooms near Merhige's court.

KEPONE

In the summer of 1975, Beverly Orndorff, *The Times-Dispatch*'s science writer, dropped by the office of Dr. Robert S. Jackson, the state epidemiologist, and asked that most-often-asked question from reporters: "What's going on?"

"They've sent a couple of samples from Hopewell down to CDC," said Jackson, "but the readings are so high that we don't know if they're accurate."

Jackson told Orndorff that some workers at a chemical plant at Hopewell, about 20 miles east of Richmond, had become ill. Blood samples had been taken and sent, not to the state as was usually done, but to the U.S. Centers for Disease Control in Atlanta.

"Keep me informed," said Orndorff, who was leaving immediately for vacation. Jackson said he would.

A few days later, Jackson was at a conference out of town and told the group roughly what he'd told Orndorff. A *New York Times* reporter at the conference filed a story of several paragraphs, which was buried in a Saturday morning edition. National Broadcasting Company personnel read *The Times* and queried Radio Station WRVA in Richmond, saying it needed something for a slow weekend.

WRVA "broke" the story locally, and Jackson telephoned Orndorff on Monday morning. Harold Waters, a summer intern, took the call. Luckily, Waters, who held a Ph.D. in immunology from UCLA, was the first recipient of a journalism grant from the American Association for the Advancement of Science. Until he came to *The Times-Dispatch* for the summer, he was doing cancer research in Pittsburgh.

When he got all the information that Jackson had, he called Orndorff—who was on vacation—and was advised to go with what he had.

By August, eight employees of the chemical plant, Life Science Products Co., Inc., had been hospitalized because of chemical poisoning, and 10 family members of employees had been found to have "significant" levels of Kepone, a pesticide, in their blood.

Within the next year, at least 26 *Times-Dispatch* reporters wrote stories on Kepone, and the paper carried more than 500 major stories on the poisoning. Because the plant was in Hopewell, State Editor Thomas W. Howard directed most of the coverage, although city-based reporters—especially Orndorff, the science writer—did significant work on the developing story[104]

There was enough action for everyone on the paper. The governor at that time, Mills E. Godwin Jr., closed the James River and its tributaries to fishing in December after the Environmental Protection Agency reported contamination of aquatic life. In May 1976, a federal grand jury indicted Allied Chemical Corp., Life Science and their officials, plus the city of Hopewell on 1,097 counts of violating anti-pollution laws. Allied Chemical had developed Kepone and first produced it. It later arranged with Life Science to produce the pesticide.

In August 1976, U.S. District Court Judge Robert R. Merhige Jr. fined Allied Chemical, which pleaded no contest to 940 criminal charges, $13.24 million. It was, at the time, the largest fine ever assessed for violating federal water pollution laws. Four months later, more than 50 people, including Life Science workers and their families, reached agreement with Allied in their suits alleging negligence. An Allied official said the total settlement of those suits was more than $3 million.

When Allied Chemical gave $8 million to establish the Virginia Environmental Endowment, Judge Merhige reduced the fine from $13.24 million to $5 million.

For its efforts, *The Times-Dispatch* received a National Headliners Club award in 1976. Did the paper overdo its coverage? After all, no one died from the effects of Kepone, and most of those poisoned went on to other jobs.

Perhaps the paper did overdo, said Howard, but certainly not for the first the first six or seven months. He lists two reasons: (1) "EPA saying it's a terrible thing and Allied not coming clean" and (2) "the ineptness of state agencies" that were responsible for overseeing environmental concerns.[105]

At first, said Howard, Allied Chemical stonewalled inquiring reporters. Then, he said, the company "began to court us." At one point, Allied offered to fly James Ezzell, *The Times-Dispatch's* man in nearby Petersburg, to its New Jersey headquarters. Howard turned that down flatly, saying the paper would pay its own way when obtaining news.

"It was a classic example of corporate PR," said Howard. "If Allied had 'fessed up, we'd not have had such a story."

Nicholas Brown, a quiet, unprepossessing assistant state editor, showed great interest in the story from the start and was named by Howard as "the clearing house" for Kepone. Wilford Kale, in Williamsburg, covered the Virginia Marine Resources Commission; Bev Orndorff in Richmond kept tab on the State Health Department and the medical community. At the papers' bureau in Washington, Merrill Brown (no kin to Nick) followed federal agencies that were investigating the poisoning. He followed them so closely, said Howard, that Alan S. Donnahoe, president of the papers' parent corporation and the man who had pushed for a reporter to check on regulatory agencies, complained that Brown was spending too much time on Kepone.

Brown's reply, said Howard, was that "this was the hot stuff."

What Howard described as the ineptness of state agencies was pointed out by Nick Brown on January 18, 1976, in the first of a series of stories on Kepone. "The state agency empowered to protect the health of private industry workers in Virginia," he began, "did not know of the existence of Life Science Products Co. . . . until May 29, about 14 months after the plant began producing the toxic chemical."

Furthermore, said Brown, "the State Department of Labor and Industry also was oblivious to Life Science until the story of the plant's closing was published by *The Times-Dispatch.* The federal Occupational Safety and Health Administration (OSHA) discovered Life Science on July 29 in a telephone call from [a State Health Department official's] office, five days after the plant was closed."

One of the few heroes of the entire Kepone episode was Jackson, Virginia's epidemiologist. When he heard from the federal Centers for Disease Control about the poisoning of a Life Science plant worker, Dale F. Gilbert, he went to the plant. Gilbert had complained of twitching eyes, weight loss, tremors and chest pains. After a company doctor asked if he were a heavy drinker, he went to a Taiwan-immigrant doctor in Hopewell. Dr. Yi-nan Chou sent Gilbert's blood sample to the CDC.

Jackson had never heard of Kepone, but when he received the CDC report, he went to the Life Science Products plant. It was July 23.

Nick Brown wrote, "Wearing rubber galoshes, he waded through puddles of Kepone-contaminated water in a makeshift factory filled with Kepone-caked machinery. He examined 10 employees. Seven of them, he said, were 'clearly affected' by the pesticide. 'The first one I saw was hospitalized shortly thereafter,' he recalled recently.

"The next day, July 24, 1975, the owners of the small firm agreed to close under the threat of being forced to do so by the health department.

During the time it operated for 16 months, 149 employees were exposed to Kepone. The company would not reopen."[106]

STERILIZATION

Newspapers don't—or shouldn't—try to portray history as spot news. Yet, changes in public attitudes over the years sometimes make newsworthy the retelling of what was routine decades earlier.

Such was the case in 1980, when *The Times-Dispatch* pounced on another newspaper's account of how the Commonwealth of Virginia involuntarily sterilized thousands of people from the 1920s through 1972.

Many of *The Times-Dispatch* stories were so detailed that the newspaper's library couldn't file them routinely in envelopes but had to place them in a large, manila folder.

Virginia's sterlization law was enacted in 1924 and upheld by an 8-1 decision of the U.S. Supreme Court in 1927. The opinion, written by Justice Oliver Wendell Holmes, said, "In order to protect us from being swamped by incompetents, it is better for all the world, if instead of waiting to execute degenerate offspring for crime or let them starve for their imbecility, society can prevent those who are manifestly unfit from continuing their kind. . . Three generations of imbeciles are enough."

In February 1980, George Stoddert reported in the *Winchester Star* that more than 4,000 men, women and children had been sterilized over a 50-year period at the Lynchburg Training School and Hospital. The new director of the facility, Dr. K. Ray Nelson, had been doing research on the program and made public his findings.

Stoddert knew he was onto a fascinating tale and tried to pursue it. But, Stoddert's editors didn't want to invest the money that would be required, said Thomas Howard, state editor of *The Times-Dispatch* in 1980.[107]

Gary Robertson, of the bureau in Harrisonburg, wrote the first *Times-Dispatch* story, giving full credit to Stoddert (who later became press secretary to Governor Charles S. Robb). Howard approached Managing Editor Alf Goodykoontz and Publisher Stewart Bryan about *The Times-Dispatch* going all out and sending reporters on follow-ups. They agreed, and "I had Betty [Booker] and [Bill] McKelway on planes that night," Howard said.

One thing that Howard and others recalled easily was that forced sterilization of the feeble-minded and other "socially undesirables" had been instituted early in Nazi Germany. Booker noted in a story February 24 that Harry H. Laughlin, father of the eugenics movement in the United States, had been given an honorary doctorate by the University of Heidelberg in 1936 for his research on race improvement.

Laughlin was not alone among Americans pushing for involuntary sterilization. Dr. J.H. Bell, superintendent of the State Colony for Epileptics and Feeble-Minded, urged in August 1933 that federal legislation be enacted to sterilize hereditarily defective people. In February 1944, in the middle of World War II, Dr. J. Shelton Horsley, a highly respected Richmond surgeon, wrote in the *Virginia Medical Monthly* that compulsory sterilization of morons or psychotic persons before marriage was advisable.

"It is more important by far," he wrote, "to have a competent psychiatrist pass upon the desirability of a marriage than to have a blood test of the applicants made for syphillis."

He said that "probably the most important single factor (in a satisfactory peace) is the kind of people who must implement these agreements." His article was titled "Breeding Better People for Peace: Human Nature Can Be Changed."

Five years later, Dr. Joseph Barrett, head of the State Department of Mental Hygiene and Hospitals, recommended sterilizing not only children with inherent mental defects but also those with accidental defects resulting from infection or injury.

The latter group, he told a child research clinic, might be able to reproduce normal children but they were "incapable of raising them normally."

That first *Times-Dispatch* story in 1980, in which Robertson was aided by Booker, whose beat included mental health, noted that forced sterilization occurred at Lynchburg four years before it was authorized by the General Assembly.

Dr. A.S. Priddy, superintendent at Lynchburg in the early 1920s, wrote the secretary of the state hospital board in 1924, "I have sterilized 80 for infection within the last seven years and at least 60 of them have gone out, earned their own living and some of them have married men of their own mental level and have proven good wives.

"And while some of them have indulged in immoral practices, no one has come within the strong arm of the law and had to be returned to the colony."

To legitimize his program, Dr. Priddy built a case to try to show that three generations of the Buck family were feeble-minded. First came Emma Buck, who had had one illegitimate child, was considered a loose woman and was committed to Lynchburg. Then, Mrs. Buck's daughters, Carrie and Doris, were committed. Carrie had also had an illegitimate child, who was examined at age 8 months by a Red Cross nurse and determined to be "slow."

Thus, Dr. Priddy had his three-generation, feeble-minded family. When Doris, at age 16, was taken to the operating room at Lynchburg, she was told she was going to undergo an appendectomy. Instead, he Fallopian tubes were tied.

Fifty-one years later, in the course of his research, Dr. Nelson met Doris Buck Faggins and told her what really had happened.

The day after his first story on the sterilization program appeared, Robertson was back with another Page One story—this one on Doris Faggins. He interviewed her as she sat with her husband of 39 years, a retired plumber.

"I'm not mad, just broken-hearted is all," she said. "I wanted babies bad. Me and him tried and tried to have 'em. I just don't know why they done it to me. I tried to live a good lifc."

Unlike her sister, Carrie Buck Detamore knew immediately after her own sterilization November 12, 1927, what had been done to her. "All they [the doctors] told me," Mrs. Detamore told Robertson 53 years later, "was that I had to go get an operation on me. I never knew what it was for. Later on, a couple of the other girls told me what it was. They said they had it done on them."

Mrs. Detamore said that at Lynchburg, "They were as good to us girls as they could be. But on this operation, they done me wrong. They done us all wrong."

A 48-year-old man whose parents couldn't care for him recalled for McKelway how he was sent at age 8 to Lynchburg although he, like many others there, was not retarded. He spent 10 years at Lynchburg, which he said was "a good place that was like home to me. They fed me three times a day, kept clothes on my back, and we got paid a dollar a month for the painting work we did and upkeep and things like taking care of the dairy."

But when he was 15 and learned the basics of sex, "The girls told on us." He wasn't surprised when his name was called at his dormitory, for all the boys knew they probably would be sterilized, he said. He didn't complain.

The superintendent said, "Buck, I'm going to have to tie your tubes and then maybe you'll be able to go home." The 15-year-old watched the entire operation. Sometimes, he said, there was almost an assembly line for sterilizations.

The Times-Dispatch editorial page, considered by many in the news department to be slow to react—especially on staff stories, wasted no time on sterilization. It found concern over the revelations "justified." The stories, said the editorial, "have made shockingly clear, the Virginia law was sometimes interpreted to permit the sterilization of criminals and the sexually depraved, though the public may not have been generally aware of the practice at the time. In some instances, it seems, even the *suspicion* that a person may have been degenerate or mentally defective was enough to justify sterilization of that individual, who might have been misled about the nature of the operation."

It was "highly gratifying," the editorial said, that the mental health board had ended the practice in 1972. Yet, in conclusion, the editorialist felt it would be wise to have on the books a "carefully drafted law, with ample safeguards, permitting courts to order sterilizations in extreme instances in which every medical indication is that reproduction would result in another generation of persons gravely defective mentally."

On March 2, 1980, Booker and McKelway dusted off the history of Virginia's sterilization program and interviewed a nurse who had been at Lynchburg 30 years and had helped in the operating room. Sterilization, said Celia Vandegrift, was "for the good of the patient" and "for the unborn child." She stressed that not all patients were sterilized. Many who were not went back to the community "because there was not a genetic component involved," she said. As for those who were sterilized but who wouldn't be deemed retarded by more recent standards, she said, "It makes me feel so bad that I was part of that, but we were following the correct procedures as they were given to us."

Booker and McKelway traced the movement for sterilization in Virginia back to 1908 and to Dr. Joseph S. DeJarnette, director of Western State Hospital. "We bow to the laws of heredity in breeding our cattle, our hogs, our dogs and even our garden seed," he said then, "but man is left to his own device." A year later he asked the state legislature to prevent the birth of "the weaklings and unfit by some legal process."

With approval of even the U.S. Supreme Court, Virginia was in the eugenics business. Dr. DeJarnette was dissatisfied with the pace in 1934, when 1,600 had been sterilized. "The Germans are beating us at our own game and are more progressive than we are," he said.

The man who blew the whistle in 1972 on forced sterilization was J. Emmett Blackwell, a relatively new member of the State Board of Mental Health and Mental Retardation. He was called to sit in on a hearing about whether to sterilize four teen-agers.

"I don't want anyone to think I was a crusader on a white horse," he said. "I don't think most members of the hospital board were aware that any sterilizations were going on. When I told them, they acted quickly.

"I just didn't think it was up to us to play God in people's lives. We did not have that right. I looked at it from the viewpoint of human rights."

The Times-Dispatch project reached beyond Virginia. On March 16, Shirley Elder in the Washington bureau of Media General, the paper's parent firm, laid out the history of sterilizations in the United States. The story covered a half-page.

Bob Poole of Media General went to Montgomery, Alabama, where he reported on two girls, one 12, one 14, who had been sterilized after their illiterate mother had drawn an X in a consent box.

By March 23, McKelway drew together figures for involuntary sterilization across the country.

"A nearly centurylong experiment that sought to cleanse society of virtually every form of human maladjustment," he wrote, "led to the involuntary sterilization of as many as 70,000 mental patients across the country.

"In reality, it amounted to little more than a withering assault on a nation's defenseless incompetents in the name of science."

He noted that "Virginia was a leading practitioner of eugenic sterilization in the country for a half-century and was aggressively pursuing the practice long after dozens of other states were forced to cease the operations because of court rulings or public outrage."

His travels took McKelway to Sonoma, California, where he reported that perhaps 5,000 people were sterilized, most of them before 1960. Of the 70,000 people sterilized involuntarily in the nation, McKelway said, more than 20,000 were in California.

Not content to limit coverage to the United States, Betty Booker reported March 30, 1980, that the United States had spent $1.3 billion in the previous eight years to promote voluntary sterilization throughout the Third World—and "there are questions over just how voluntary many of the U.S.-financed programs are."

ONE CASE WON

Newspapers contend that they report the news, not make it. Yet, on occasion, they do make it, as *The Times-Dispatch* and *The News Leader* did on July 2, 1980. As in so many cases when the newspapers themselves are the center of attention, it was a court case.

On that date, for the first time, the Supreme Court of the United States ruled that the press and the public are constitutionally entitled to attend criminal trials. The 7-1 ruling, with only Justice William H. Rehnquist dissenting, put the Richmond newspapers on the front pages of virtually every daily in the United States.[108]

The ruling was a victory not only for the papers and its reporters, Tim Wheeler of *The Times-Dispatch* and Kevin McCarthy of *The News Leader*, but also for journalists across the land. A year earlier, the court had ruled in *Gannett vs. DePasquale* that some pretrial hearings could be closed. In the Richmond newspapers' case, however, the court declined to reverse itself on pretrial closings, although it cited the Gannett case.

Chief Justice Warren Burger said that unless a judge articulated "an overriding interest," which Burger did not define, "the trial of a criminal case must be open to the public."

Burger added, "We hold that the right to attend criminal trials is implicit in the guarantees of the First Amendment; without the freedom to attend such trials, which people have exercised for centuries, important aspects of freedom of speech and of the press could be eviscerated."

Concurring, Justice John Paul Stevens said, "This is a watershed case." He went on: "Today. . . for the first time, the court unequivocally holds that any arbitrary interference with access to important information is an abridgment of the freedoms of speech and of the press protected by the First Amendment."

Although arguments before the Supreme Court involved some heavy hitters (Virginia Attorney J. Marshall Coleman for the state and Laurence H.

Tribe of the Harvard Law School for Richmond Newspapers Inc.), the trial that gave birth to the arguments did not. It grew out of the slaying four and a half years earlier of the manager of a motel on U.S. 1, about 15 miles north of Richmond in Hanover County.

John Paul Stevenson and his brother-in-law, Howard Franklin Bittorf, were charged with murdering Lillian Emma Keller. They had been living in a motel apartment next to Mrs. Keller's. Her naked body, with stab wounds in the neck and chest, had been found by her son.

The judge of Hanover Circuit Court was Richard H.C. Taylor, member of a distinguished family in the county and great-grandson of a Virginia Supreme Court justice. But he had been on the bench less than a year after a quarter-century of legal practice, most of it civil. The Stevenson case was only his second murder case.

Defending Stevenson was C. Willard Norwood, insignificant in the Richmond area's legal power structure. The prosecutor was Patrick R. Bynum Jr., the county's part-time commonwealth's attorney. The one notable aspect of the case was its setting: Hanover Circuit Court, where two centuries earlier a young firebrand named Patrick Henry practiced law.

By September 11, 1978, Norwood had become irritated with the pace of the proceedings. Already, there had been three mistrials. First, the Virginia Supreme Court overturned convictions of both Stevenson and Bittorf because of introduction as evidence of a bloody shirt that police had gotten from Stevenson's wife. Next, a juror became ill and a mistrial was called. Thirdly, even before a jury was chosen, several prospective jurors said they had read a newspaper story about Stevenson's earlier trials.

Meanwhile, Norwood had asked the judge to exclude everyone from the courtroom, complaining about a woman he couldn't identify who was sitting with Mrs. Keller's family. When the judge asked if he meant also to exclude the press, Norwood said yes. Judge Taylor acceded to the request and ordered press and public out of the courthouse.

That third time when he declared a mistrial, Judge Taylor ordered the lawyers not to explain why. But, as is usual, there was a leak; and the newspapers' lawyer, Alexander Wellford, was dispatched to Hanover to discuss with the judge the papers' concern about court closings. Wellford returned to Richmond, assured that Judge Taylor distinguished between closing the court for jury selection and closing it for trial.

On September 11, Norwood, emboldened by his success in having the court closed earlier, asked Judge Taylor in this fourth trial to close the court. He didn't want anyone telling prospective witnesses what was occurring, Norwood said.

Taylor again ordered the court closed.

When McCarthy, covering his new Hanover County beat for the first day, told *News Leader* editors in Richmond that the court was closed, they were incredulous. Editors called Wellford, who went back to Hanover and tried to convince Taylor that closing the court during trial was "a novel form of censorship" and flouted the First Amendment. The judge didn't buy that.

Reporters McCarthy and Wheeler couldn't attend that hearing, because the judge said he considered it part of the trial. What was said came out in transcripts. Midway through the second day of the trial, Norwood cited what he saw as shortcomings in the commonwealth's case and moved to strike the evidence.

Judge Taylor agreed, telling the prosecutor, "You've got too many holes in your case." Turning to the defendant, he said, "You're a free man, Mr. Stevenson."

Thus after four tries, the murder case was over, but the newspapers' case was not. They lost on their first appeal as the Virginia Supreme Court upheld Taylor. And in arguments before the U.S. Supreme Court, the papers were concerned when Justice Lewis F. Powell Jr., a friend of the former publisher, D. Tennant Bryan, took no part in the case. They had figured he would come down on the side of openness.

The concern was unmerited when the court announced its decision. On the same day, the court also upheld the constitutionality of federal public works programs that reserved 10 percent of money for minority contractors.

The banner headline on *The Times-Dispatch* of July 3, 1980 read:

High Court Affirms Right of Access to Trials,
Upholds Racial Quotas for Granting Aid

A three-column subhead read:

No 'Overriding Interest'
Found in Hanover County

ANOTHER CASE, LOST

Newspapers routinely are threatened with libel suits. Few of the threats are carried out, and by the time that those that come to trial reach the appellate court level, the majority are lost.

In the summer of 1982, *The Times-Dispatch* was hit by its biggest lawsuit, and when it got to the appellate level, tradition didn't hold. The paper paid.

Two years earlier, the author noticed a stream of people dropping by the desk of Charles Cox, the veteran education writer. Then Cox and his callers would repair to a conference room for perhaps an hour or so.

When asked what was going on, Cox said, "This is the story I've been waiting all my life to write." What was involved, he said, was a series of parents of exceptionally bright students who contended that one teacher was hopelessly incompetent and that their complaints to the principal and higher-ups in the Richmond public school system had gotten nowhere.

There were unusual aspects to the case. Richmond's school system at that time was 83.7 percent black.[109] The complaining parents were mostly professional people, all white, who had been determined to leave their children in public school, specifically Thomas Jefferson High School. The person who brought the situation to Cox's attention was Dr. I. David Goldman, a teacher and cancer specialist at the Medical College of Virginia.

The object of the parents' complaint was Vernell M. Lipscomb, who headed Thomas Jefferson's English Department. The parents contended that Ms. Lipscomb's being black had no bearing on their complaints.

Morgan J. Edwards III, the principal, said the complaints were "unworthy of dignifying by replying." The parents said Ms. Lipscomb was late to class, left class often, was unorganized and intimidated especially bright students. Soon after Edwards' comments, William H. Hefty, the school board's lawyer, confirmed that city employees had been instructed to say nothing about details of the case.

It was the type of story that stirs the investigative juices of most good reporters. With Cox, it was like tossing meat to a lion. In his late 50s, he had been covering education and some politics for *The Times-Dispatch* since 1969. His reporting often raised the hackles of people about whom he wrote. Two who lost their jobs after his stories appeared—the president of Longwood College and the chancellor of the state community college system—were especially bitter. Cox contended he wasn't after scalps but after stories, and some of them involved people in power who were after scalps.[110]

Cox was one of those reporters to whom certain people would mail envelopes, with no return addresses, that contained copies of private correspondence. A member of one governor's cabinet routinely stopped his car late in the afternoon at the newspaper office on Grace Street to give documents to Cox. Then he'd speed away.

Cox could be difficult to deal with. He argued not only with public officials but also with editors. He was a former State Department employee. Many of his newspaper colleagues were convinced he'd been in the Central Intelligence Agency, although Cox would never acknowledge it. He once told the city editor that he couldn't write a piece of appreciation after David K.E. Bruce, a distinguished diplomat with years in intelligence, died because, "I think I once signed some paper saying I wouldn't do that." Cox had a temper that was difficult to control; and when he became upset, his language was X-rated.

It was his temper that would cost Richmond Newspapers Inc. considerable money.

After Cox finished his story on Ms. Lipscomb and it had been edited and inspected by far more editors than usual, Stewart Bryan, the publisher, read it and called for a meeting with all the news people involved and with Alexander Wellford, the main lawyer for the papers.

Wellford said the story was fine, but "You're going to get sued." Bryan replied that no good newspaper made a name for itself by running away from a good, accurate story because it thought it might get sued.

He suggested pulling some paragraphs from the quite long story and making them a "sidebar." He also wanted photographs of the leading characters—Ms. Lipscomb, the complaining parents, the school principal, the school board chairman and the students.

He got what he asked. The story led the paper of Sunday, August 16, 1981, under a banner headline that read:

Questions About Teacher Hard to Pursue

The story ran down four inches across Page One and continued to Page 2, where it occupied three-fourths of the page. Comments from parents, students, teachers and school system officials were included. Much of what the officials said was in correspondence to Dr. Goldman.

The story led to several others in the next few days, and there was considerable comment in the community. But almost a year passed before there was another development. Then, in early August 1982, Ms. Lipscomb sued the paper, alleging libel and asking for $6 million. If she had waited two weeks, there would have been no case because the statute of limitations on libel is a year in Virginia.

After an informal hearing before the case came to trial, newspaper representatives were elated. Circuit Court Judge Willard I. Walker ruled that Ms. Lipscomb, as head of the English Department of a public high school, was a public official. That meant, in light of a U.S. Supreme Court ruling, that the plaintiff had to show malice.

Before the case came to trial, depositions were taken. The procedure involved lawyers for both sides asking questions and getting answers from principals in the case. A stenotypist recorded everything. Cox, Ms. Lipscomb, students and parents quoted in the story and the author were among those whose depositions were taken.

Ms. Lipscomb's attorney, John H. OBrion Jr., handled Cox skillfully. In a casual, friendly way, he would read a quote from the story and ask something like "Was that a first-hand or second-hand quote, Charles?"

Cox, infuriated that anyone would believe he'd use second-hand information in a direct quote, replied sarcastically, "Probably seventh-hand, John. You know reporters always try to get as far from the original source as possible."

Wellford, the newspaper's attorney, frowned, shook his head and kicked Cox under the table. At recess, he lectured Cox on abstaining from sarcasm.

If Reporter Cox, Publisher Bryan and Attorney Wellford were happy with Judge Walker's ruling on Ms. Lipscomb being a public official, they were appalled when they saw the list of potential jurors. The names, addresses and occupations indicated that the overwhelming majority of people were blacks with little higher education.

Wellford figured, correctly, that in peremptory challenges, his counterpart, OBrion, would strike the whites on the jury panel. Although after the verdict at least one black parent called Cox to say Ms. Lipscomb had treated her offspring shabbily, none of the complaining parents quoted in the story was black; and newspaper representatives feared an all-black jury passing verdict on a white reporter of the "establishment" paper that had criticized a black teacher.

Several years later, John Leard, executive editor when the story appeared, said he thought the story was good but he had recommended in the last meeting of editors that people "on the other side" be interviewed. Ms. Lipscomb had been promoted, Leard said, so "she couldn't have been all bad." He was concerned that the parents interviewed were those who came to Cox and "were sort of a closed group."[111]

The case lasted three days and jurors debated about three hours before deciding August 12, 1983, almost two years after the story appeared, to award Ms. Lipscomb $1 million in compensatory damages and $45,000 in punitive damages. Judge Walker earlier removed the newspaper corporation, but not Cox, as a defendant in possible punitive damages.

Three months later, Walker said the award was not realistic, and in May 1984, he reduced the award to $145,000 from the jury's $1,045,000. The corporation, not Cox, paid it all.

Much of what Judge Walker, now dead, thought about the case is in the record: his decision that Ms. Lipscomb was a public official, his ruling out the newspaper as a defendant for possible punitive damages and his reduction of the jury award.

But in his chambers during the trial, he chatted with Claude Burrows, a veteran *Times-Dispatch* reporter assigned to the case. If Cox hadn't been so harsh in his deposition, with remarks that indicated malice, he would have thrown out the entire case, Walker told Burrows[112].

Cox contends, "The story that got us sued was the best story I ever turned out," because of the checking and the trouble involved. He added that there was nothing factually wrong with the story.

Finally, he said, "I think to the everlasting credit of Stewart Bryan, he thought it was important enough for us to go ahead despite the risk [of a lawsuit]. . . he backed it."[113]

ESCAPE FROM DEATH ROW

The newsroom staff at *The Times-Dispatch* had dwindled considerably by 10:30 the night of May 31, 1984. The first edition was locked up, and Assistant City Editor Keith Pritchard was working on stories for the next editions.

Something from a police dispatcher made him halt.

Experienced city desk editors and police reporters are unfazed by the constant chatter on police scanners. But they stop work and turn up the volume when a dispatcher—perhaps without raising his voice—says something that translates into news.

Pritchard heard something that night that made him call the state police. He recalls, "When I called the dispatcher, I said, 'Did I hear something about the Brileys escaping?'

"He said, 'You sure did.'"[114]

Pritchard radioed to Eric Sundquist, night police reporter, to hurry back to the office. They were onto the biggest escape in history from any death row in the United States. James and Linwood Briley, who with a third brother were believed responsible for 11 murders, has escaped from Mecklenburg Correctional Center in Boydton, along with four other murderers.

It was only the third week at *The Times-Dispatch* for Sundquist, who had recently joined the paper from the *Daily Press* and the *Times-Herald* in Newport News. Pritchard, who had been with the *Rochester Democrat-Chronicle* when the Brileys were in the news, had learned of them only through conversation with Tom Morris, a *Times-Dispatch* reporter who left Rochester for Richmond before Pritchard did.

Sundquist can't recall details of what the state police said, but, "They were fairly explicit that it was a big deal."[115] By the final edition, Sundquist had talked also with police in North Carolina, where the escapees had abandoned their vehicle.

With the help of Pritchard and Bonnie Winston, a general assignment reporter, Sundquist had a 10-inch Page One story for Friday, June 1.

By the next day *The Times-Dispatch* had eight reporters working on the story—in Richmond, in Boydton and in North Carolina. By Monday, *The News Leader* had five.

Besides the Brileys, the escapees were Derick L. Peterson, Earl Clanton Jr., Lem D. Tuggle and Willie LeRoy Jones. Peterson and Clanton were captured as they ate cheese and drank beer at a grocery-laundromat near a police station in Warrenton, North Carolina. They had about 18 hours' freedom.

The breakout from what some had called an "escape-proof" prison occurred mainly because the staff didn't follow established procedures.

Twelve inmates housed in second floor of C pod in Building 1 at Mecklenburg had been outside for recreation. As the last of them returned about 8 p.m., Clanton jumped into an unlocked toilet used by guards. It was about six feet from the control room. The other 11 prisoners were locked in a day room, but no accurate count was taken.

About a half-hour later, the control room guard stepped out to give a prisoner a book through the day room gate and left the control room door open. Clanton bolted into the control room and pushed buttons opening gates to two rooms. Other inmates jumped the lone guard in the day room and a corporal who had been called about a "plumbing problem."

Within two more hours, 13 hostages had been taken. All were tied up and some were gagged. Using various ruses, the prisoners took even nurses as hostages. At knifepoint, a watch commander was forced to tell a guard to open first-floor gates to outdoors.

Against the rules, a guard opened a control door for someone she didn't recognize—who turned out to be a prisoner in a guard's uniform. By then, the six who were to escape were all in guards' uniforms, wearing riot helmets with visors. They also had taken the guards' wallets, identification cards and money and had incapacitated the guards with their own rope and handcuffs. They put a television set from the day room on a stretcher, covered it with a blanket, sprayed it with a fire extinguisher and carried the "bomb" on the stretcher to a van.

Again against the rules, inner and outer gates were opened at the same time, and guards—who normally check who's on a departing vehicle—were told to stand back because a dangerous bomb was being taken out.

Conditions at Mecklenburg were not the best for the staff. Guards speaking anonymously told Betty Booker and John Hoke of *The Times-Dispatch* that morale was low, the staff was overworked, there were complaints about discipline and restrictions on dangerous inmates had been loosened.

As early as June 2, Michael Hardy reported in a copyrighted story for *The Times-Dispatch* that prison officials had been warned of a planned escape and that the Brileys were the leaders. Furthermore, they said weapons were being hidden on death row, Hardy said.

What alarmed Virginians, especially Richmonders, was not only the escape of six murderers but also the fact that two of them were James and Linwood Briley, who were generally considered two of the vilest criminals in the city's history.

Among the 11 murders they and their brother Anthony (who was serving a life term) were believed to have committed were those of a couple (the woman was five months pregnant) and their 5-year-old son. James Briley drew two death sentences in that trial. He also raped the woman.

Linwood Briley, whose capital murder conviction came from his killing a popular disc jockey, had been convicted at age 16 of fatally shooting an elderly woman, who, he reportedly said, "would have died anyway."

During his trial, prosecutors described him as "incredibly vicious" and "incredibly, inhumanly mean."

Prosecutors said the Brileys kept a boa constrictor, a tarantula, piranhas and a pack of dogs at their house. They amused their girlfriends by feeding mice to the snake.

For Ed Kelleher, Andrew Petkofsky, Rex Springston and Bill Wasson of *The News Leader,* nothing in the entire episode was timed right. The breakout was at night and all the arrests were at night or in the afternoon. *The News Leader,* not for lack of ability or effort, was compelled to go with leads about where police were looking for the escapees—Richmond, Portsmouth, Lake Gaston, North Carolina, and even in Quebec. As in virtually all escapes, those who fled were "positively" spotted in places they never ventured.

Tuggle and Jones were arrested June 8 about 100 miles apart in New Hampshire. Tuggle was stopped at a roadblock in a rural area after the robbery of a gift shop operator. Jones, on the advice of his mother, turned himself in four hours later to a Vermont state trooper.

The big boys, the Briley brothers, were arrested about 10 p.m. June 19 in Philadelphia; and *The Times-Dispatch* story, bannered on Page One, was written by Eric Sundquist, who wrote the initial story on the breakout. Reporters Frank Douglas and Bill McKelway, who were dispatched immediately to Philadelphia, helped Sundquist.

The arrests, by about 20 FBI agents and Philadelphia police, came at a garage that their uncle had persuaded to let his nephews use. While someone barbecued chicken and neighbors made small talk, a white truck and several white cars passed by.

"I thought it was a funeral," one neighbor told Springston and Kelleher of *The News Leader.* "[The cars] were all brand new."

"Suddenly," said Springston and Kelleher, "men dressed in business suits and armed with shotguns poured out of the rear of the truck and from the cars."

It was all over.

Douglas and McKelway reported in *The Times-Dispatch* that a telephone call from the garage to New York was the major break in the case. Investigators had zeroed in on Philadelphia for almost a week.

THE DALKON SHIELD

The A.H. Robins Co. was an old-line Richmond pharmaceutical manufacturer with a reputation of extreme concern for the well-being of its employees and a record of steady financial growth.

In summer months beginning in 1973, employees were given Friday afternoons off. That was because President E. Claiborne Robins Sr. had been taking those afternoons off since a heart attack several years earlier. One Friday afternoon, he tried telephoning several executives and learned they were doing the same thing. He figured that if executives were doing that, perhaps lower level employees should do the same.[116]

In pre-Castro days the entire staff was given a company-paid visit to Cuba and other places. Under Robins, grandson of the founder, the company had grown enormously. Robins, a prominent Baptist layman, gave his alma mater, the University of Richmond, $50 million in 1969—then the record gift by any alumnus to a private college in the nation.

In short, Robins the individual and Robins the company enjoyed the best of reputations.

But in 1971, the company began marketing a new product, the Dalkon Shield, an intrauterine birth control device. And shortly thereafter, women began having trouble. There were therapeutic abortions, inflamed genital areas and illnesses.

Lawsuits were initiated.

In the summer of 1984, Elliott Cooper, the business editor of *The Times-Dispatch,* was on vacation, and Thomas R. Morris, another business writer on the paper, became interested in the story when a federal judge in Minneapolis publicly berated company officials.

Depositions were being taken in Richmond, and company officials figured it was wise to invite reporters to attend the hearings. It was a bad mistake, said Morris. Robins acknowledged that it had bought the Dalkon Shield "without ever testing it, without knowing what they had."[117]

Morris kept attending hearings and writing daily stories, then Sunday follow-up stories. He also reported, from the evidence, how much the company was paying lawyers in the many suits that had been filed.

As the suits piled up, newspapers across the country began reporting the story because women in their hometowns were suing. The company hired Griffin Bell, attorney general in the former Carter administration, as special counsel. At *The Times-Dispatch,* Morris found himself devoting virtually all his time to the Robins story week after week.

Morris was a meticulous reporter who probably had fewer inaccuracies to be cleared up with corrections than any other reporter on the paper. He was not known for his sense of humor but was extremely confident. All that did not endear him to officials at Robins, who found much of what he wrote unsettling.

Several of them came calling on *Times-Dispatch* editors. After their visit, Morris recalls, Executive Editor Alf Goodykoontz called Morris in to a meeting, explained the Robins officials' visit with him and Managing Editor Marvin Garrette and then asked Morris if his father had ever been fired by Robins.

Morris was aghast. If such had been the case, he said, he should have been fired for a conflict of interests. What Morris got from Goodykoontz was that Robins officials said "some of our employees are concerned that Morris is the son of a guy" that Robins had caused to be fired.[118]

The closest connection his father had, said Morris, was working as a self-employed accountant, one of whose clients was a drug store that bought products from Robins.

Robins executives wanted Morris off the story, and *Times-Dispatch* editors said flatly that he would remain on the story. When the company filed for protection under Chapter 11 of federal bankruptcy law, more trouble developed. Morris went to the record and found that company officials had said in court papers that their cash position was so bad that they might not be able to make their payroll if the judge turned down a company request for a line of credit.

Morris called Roscoe Puckett, Robins' public relations man and a former *Times-Dipatch* reporter, at home on a Saturday and said, "Let me be sure that I'm keeping this in the right context."

When Puckett said he could only "quote from the file," Morris saw the screw being turned. Robins executives then said Morris was acting like a financial analyst—which he denied—and that they would no longer talk to him. They would talk to other reporters. *Times-Dispatch* editors said Morris would stay on the story and they would talk to him or no one.

Pressure also was applied to the publisher. William Zimmer, president of Robins, was then the father-in-law of Stewart Bryan and told him several times "he thought Robins was being crucified." Bryan replied, "I don't think that's what's happening. I'm not setting out to do it. We're trying to cover it. Your people won't talk to us. They're making it very difficult for us to find out anything."

Bryan relayed Zimmer's comments to editors but not to Morris. Zimmer, Bryan recalled, "told me he thought we were being mean and vindictive and we didn't need the coverage in the depth and detail we were covering it."[119]

Morris thought the company's concern perhaps stemmed from the complaint of one of its executives who said he was being shunned at church because of *Times-Dispatch* stories. Morris stayed on the story, tapped his many sources and had more than a column of type written on a court-agreed settlement before it became public.

The Dalkon Shield was taken off the market by Robins in 1974, but it had been the company's undoing. It filed for bankruptcy in 1985 and eventually was sold to American Home Products Corp. As part of Robins' reorganization, the Dalkon Shield Claimants Trust had been established to compensate women harmed by the device. By late 1994, the trust had paid out $1.3 billion to 166,000 claimants and 7,000 cases remained.

The American Bar Association recognized Morris' work with an award in 1986. He left *The Times-Dispatch* in 1989 and joined the staff of the Dalkon Shield Claimants Trust briefly before settling down with an advertising agency.

THE ROBB STORY

On May 3, 1987, *The Times-Dispatch* jumped onto a political story about which it was roundly criticized—even by its own editorial page. Years later, the news staff was still chortling about having been vindicated.

The story, which ran scarcely a column including the turn, was played under a three-column head on the front page of a Sunday paper:

Robb denies being at parties
at which cocaine was used

Charles Robb had concluded four years as governor, was in private law practice and was considering a run for the United States Senate the next year. The story came as federal prosecutors continued investigating cocaine trafficking. They already had won convictions in cases involving a former Norfolk prosecutor, a restaurant operator in Virginia Beach, a former all-state rugby player and the son of a Norfolk judge.

The story affirmed only that while he was governor, Robb "attended parties in Virginia Beach at which the illegal drug was used." There was no evidence, the story said, that Robb used cocaine and there was no chance of any charges against Robb.

Nevertheless, sources were quoted as saying that Robb was seen "over the past five years and on numerous occasions" as being at beachfront parties where guests used cocaine.

The decision to go with the story was not hurried. It was gone over by the publisher and company lawyers in addition to the city editor, the managing editor and the executive editor. The writers were two experienced reporters, Michael Hardy and Jeff E. Schapiro. Hardy had spent years with the *Norfolk Virginian-Pilot* and had numerous sources among law enforcement officials in the Hampton Roads area. Schapiro earlier had been with United

Press International and *Virginia Business*, a magazine published by Media General, *The Times-Dispatch's* parent.

Before the story ran, the paper followed its standard procedure in such cases and sought out Robb for comment. He first tried convincing the paper that every other news outlet in Virginia had followed similar tips and concluded there was nothing to the reports.

Schapiro, however, told the former governor that *The Times-Dispatch* had its own sources and was going with the story no matter what Robb thought. What the paper wanted was his comment.

Finally, Robb said he had a statement. The first words he read to Schapiro were that he had been faithful to his wife. *The Times-Dispatch* had not even asked any questions about that, although it had heard rumors—which it couldn't prove and didn't pursue. Considerably more on that would come in months and years to follow.

About his having attended parties where others were using cocaine, Robb asserted, "I'll tell you in no uncertain terms; it ain't so."

Robb did tell Schapiro that during his term as governor he had been warned about the reputation of some of his Virginia Beach friends and for a while had kept a distance from some of them. Like his predecessors, Robb spent some time at Camp Pendleton, a National Guard base at Virginia Beach.

The day after *The Times-Dispatch* story ran, Robb told Tyler Whitley of *The News Leader* that he was disappointed *The Times-Dispatch* had run a story based on rumors that others had investigated and dropped. As for seeing or knowing anything about drugs, it was a big negative—"absolutely, categorically, no ifs, ands or buts."

Three days after Hardy's and Schapiro's story, *The Times-Dispatch* editorial page concluded that it looked "distinctively, we're glad to say, like a non-scandal."

The editorial grouped the Iran-Contra fracas, the supposed sexual exploits of Sen. Gary Hart and the tribulations of Jim Bakker, a television evangelist, into a condition of "Scandal Overload."

Then it looked into the Robb story and said, "Our reaction to this supposed scandalous revelation is a big yawn."

It was entirely possible, said the editorial, that Robb may have been at large parties where others used cocaine while he knew nothing about it. The only question is whether he knew it and condoned it.

"Knowing what we do about Chuck Robb—his devotion to family, his interest in health and fitness, his concern for projecting a proper image, his basically cautious nature—that scenario does not ring true," it concluded.

The Roanoke Times & World News tut-tutted *The Times-Dispatch* as did the *Norfolk Virginian-Pilot*. The *Washington Post* ombudsman chastised his paper for reporting what *The Times-Dispatch* had said instead of avoiding it or doing its own story.

Sixteen months later, the *Virginian-Pilot* came out with its own story, on which it had long been working, that ran more than a full page and included direct quotes much more damaging to Robb than anything in *The Times-Dispatch* story.

With the later allegations of Tai Collins, a former Miss Virginia who posed nude in Playboy magazine and "told all" about alleged sexual relations with Robb, then a U.S. senator, it was open season.

A NEWSPAPER CRIPPLED

If a saboteur plotted to dismantle a morning newspaper in a metropolitan area, he probably would decide that the appropriate time would be about 10 p.m. Normally, that's slightly less than an hour before the first edition; the third and final edition is scheduled to begin rolling about three hours after that.

There was no saboteur at Richmond Newspapers Inc. on Thursday, May 25, 1989, but a series of explosions about 10 o'clock that night sent reporters, editors and pressmen out of their work stations and threatened—for the first time since the Civil War—to cancel a morning paper, a Friday edition scheduled to run 68 pages.

A 13,200-volt transformer encased in a 6-foot concrete cube beneath the sidewalk adjacent to the building blew up. Other explosions followed, sending flames 30 feet in the air, blacking out the newspaper building and severely scorching the structure. It did not damage the presses or the composing room.

Virginia Churn, a reporter returning from an assignment in Powhatan County, said in a "color story" in the Friday morning paper, "People dashed around, calling 'Get out,' some running to the fire and some running away from it."

The explosions not only drove newspaper employees out of the building but also produced traffic jams and police barricades. Frustrated staff members couldn't get back into the building. Executives—news people and non-news people—decided at 1 a.m. that the paper would be published, but it would be a 16-page affair, printed by Beacon Press, a subsidiary of Media General, the parent of *The Times-Dispatch* and the afternoon *News Leader.*

Executive Editor Alf Goodykoontz returned from his home in the far West End and set up a temporary city desk at Jefferson National Bank at Second and Grace streets, two blocks west of the newspaper. Unable to return to their own desks, reporters began using portable equipment and computer terminals in other buildings—such as a circulation department office two blocks away in a converted gasoline station at Third and Main Streets or in the office of *Virginia Business,* another Media General subsidiary, across Franklin Street from the newspaper.

Other reporters put notes together as they sat on walls and sidewalks, bathed in the glare of light from television cameras. Some reporters were sent home to work on portable terminals. The state desk headquarters was shifted from Richmond to Petersburg, 20 miles away. For several hours, the city desk was operated out of the Henrico County bureau some seven miles away.

About 2 a.m., 10 minutes after the final edition normally was on the press, 14 of the 16 pages of Friday's abbreviated paper had arrived at Beacon Press. Then word came that the staff could get into the building that that housed the presses. Luckily, as Bob Knight, a systems editor, explained in a house organ, a quarter-million-dollar piece of equipment designed to keep voltage steady to the computers during a power failure performed beyond anyone's expectations. Even luckier, Mike Snead and Todd Moschler of the engineering department sneaked past a police line and into the building to oversee the "Uninterruptible Power Supply."

There would be a 68-page paper, but it didn't begin to roll until 4:46 a.m. Luck still was with the paper. All three presses ran simultaneously, the second starting at 4:47 a.m., the third at 4:48. In 90 minutes, 119,800 papers were printed.

Michael Paul Williams' story of the explosion led the paper. In addition to Churn's feature, there were two photographs of flame and smoke. One showed what was left of the 1985 Chevette on which Skip Wood, a sports reporter, had recently made his last payment. Wood returned from covering a baseball game and parked his car on Fourth Street, near the transformer that exploded.

"I was the only casualty, so to speak," said Wood.

SECTION D

• The News Staffs

A year before his death at age 71 in 1936, Harry Tucker winds up his newspaper career at The Times-Dispatch, *which he joined in 1920. He went to work for Joseph Bryan's* Richmond Times *in 1895, then worked on other papers in Richmond. In his last years, he wrote a column, "Main Street." Covering City Hall, he was alleged to have arranged City Council's docket so the juiciest items were discussed in time for his paper's editions.*

THE NEWS ROOMS

Over the past 50 years, *Times-Dispatch* and *News Leader* newsrooms had their share of characters and cognoscenti, of air heads and eggheads. With stories to write and edit, with deadlines approaching, there wasn't much time for horseplay.

But when the last page was diagrammed and the last edition had yet to come off the presses, there were high jinks unimagined by the publisher or ranking editors—especially in the early morning hours at *The Times-Dispatch.*

The newsroom there once echoed to .22-caliber pistols firing at targets or a starter's pistol firing in a sports department caper. The managing editor's office often was the site of a poker game; later there were bridge and dominoes at the copy desk. Some copy editors worked printed cross-word puzzles or created their own.

Maurice Dean, a police reporter whose spelling was atrocious, answered a telephone call from an editor pretending to give a whimsical obituary notice for Aloysius So-and-So. "How do you spell Aloysius?" asked Dean. "The usual way," was the response. After several exchanges, Aloysius came out the best way that Dean could deal with it—which was not correct. And the "obit" never ran. Dean was better at craps than at spelling. Once, out on his beat, he made 12 straight passes and won the grand total of less than $20.

An editor deathly afraid of rats would occasionally shake a pneumatic tube from the composing room and find, not galley proofs, but a rat.

Late at night, the "pie man" from a nearby bakery visited the newsroom and sold piping hot small pies—two for a quarter. Other visitors might include bootleggers summoned when copy editors ready to leave work but not quite ready to go home realized they were out of whiskey.

Young, unsophisticated reporters were routinely intimidated by their editors. When Larry Prentice came to *The Times-Dispatch* in 1962, fresh out of Richmond Professional Institute, he was confronted by Ed Swain, city editor and a World War II veteran of many Pacific campaigns.

The Times-Dispatch *newsroom about 1950. From left, Ben B. Johnston, managing editor; Chester G. McCalley, (standing blurred), copy editor; Dick Williamson, assistant city editor (seated, white shirt); Maurice Dean (in vest), police reporter; F.J. McDermott (standing), city editor; Omar Mardan, reporter; Gip Ludwig, copy editor, Clarke Bustard, copy editor.*

At retirement party in 1977 for Norman Rowe of Times-Dispatch, *Publisher D. Tennant Bryan engages in a bit of unusual horseplay by wearing a printer's cap. Between Rowe and Bryan is Marvin Garrette, assistant managing editor of* The Times-Dispatch.

News Leader *newsroom in 1956. John Leard, city editor, is in glass-enclosed room of managing editor. Outside are Katherine Lewis Warren, who covered medicine, and Joe Marsh, who covered Chesterfield County. Other reporters and copy editors are in center and to right.*

Part of The Times-Dispatch *news staff in late 1950s: Clockwise: Richard Wilson, reporter; F.J. McDermott, city editor; Al Wagner, reporter; Jack R. Hunter, assistant state editor; Ed Swain (standing), assistant city editor; Alf Goodykoontz, reporter; James Latimer (right rear), political reporter; Omar Mardan, assistant city editor; Earle Dunford, reporter.*

Times-Dispatch *newsroom in 1966. Omar Mardan (foreground), assistant managing editor. Others include Marion L. Fairey (standing, back to camera), makeup editor, and David Livingstone and H.B. Parrott, copy editors.*

"You've got one job to do," Swain told him, "and if you screw up once, you've had it. Every night, you reach into this bottom drawer and you'll find $4.10. Take it and bring me back a fifth of Old Crow. Put it in a white paper bag. I want to reach into that drawer and wrap my hand around the bottle. You mess up and you're through; got it?"[120]

"I said, 'Yes, sir; yes, sir,'" Prentice said. "I came to work at 5:30 and the ABC stores closed at 6. I rushed down to the store and the clerk asked what I wanted, and my mind went blank; I clutched. I rushed out and called on the radio. 'Car 32 to city desk. What was that order again?'"

"'Ancient Bird, economy size,' Swain answered. I completed my mission and never had any more trouble." said Prentice. "The night I left the paper, Swain took me down to the garage, opened a paper bag, took out the bourbon and we both had a drink."

Even at 2:30 in the morning, there were things to do. One night, the night city editor, Omar Mardan, and the author—then police reporter—joined a city magistrate to commandeer a boat and rescue a despondent man who had jumped into the James River from an overhead bridge. On less eventful nights, the late crew repaired to Grant's Drug Store, open all night, where they ate, played more dominoes and swapped stories with the likes of a private detective, a druggist, various gamblers and policemen—off duty and on duty.

The News Leader had less time for horseplay because its work day was more compressed. People there generally worked between 6:30 a.m. and 3:30 p.m.—nine hours. At *The Times-Dispatch*, the first people working on, say, a Thursday paper showed up at 10 a.m. Wednesday and the last stayed until 2:30 a.m. Thursday—16 and a half hours later.

The News Leader was not without its characters. One who startled newcomers especially was a grizzled state editor, Robert E. Dickson, who kept a whiskey bottle and a tumbler in his desk. Before noon, he would cast an eye on the managing editor's office, see that he was busy, and down a large shot of bourbon.[121]

Guy Friddell, a political writer-columnist—renowned as a deadline pusher, would walk to the composing room and finish his story there, long after his deadline had passed. Friddell was the butt of many pranks from his colleagues. A favorite was to hide his shoes, which he often took off. One snowy day, the reporter—minus shoes—made his way to the State Capitol in bedroom slippers.

Friddell accompanied President Eisenhower to Mount Sidney, Virginia, birthplace of the president's mother. When the president finished planting a pine seedling, Friddell promptly stepped back and onto the seedling. The incident made the wire services.

Not many people were fired at Richmond's newspapers, but *The News Leader* let go a young woman with many problems, including an addiction to alcohol. The night she was let go, she returned, put a mark on the managing editor's door and a hex on the entire paper.

John Leard, *The News Leader* city editor, was, as some of his devoted but snickering reporters said, obsessed with trivia. He wanted "snow brights," little human interest items, when Richmond was hit by snow.

Reporters realized they could invent "brights." They did so and flooded the city desk with supposedly amusing incidents. When one reporter found he had to write a "Groundhog Day" story, he went to the library, found the previous year's feature, copied it and saw his bit of plagiarism appear in print.[122]

Even with a compressed work day, there was time for lunch. One *News Leader* copy editor—the "slot man," who checked other people's headlines—managed to get married on his lunch break and return for later editions.[123]

It wasn't all cynicism or tricks at *The News Leader*. There was even time for kindness. The beloved Bill Christian, managing editor for years, would never ball out an erring reporter. He'd tear a story out of the paper, scrawl notes on it and talk to the reporter about getting things right the next time. "It made you feel that you weren't all that horrible," recalled Sylvia Costen, longtime women's editor.[124]

And when Bill Sauder, a much admired reporter, was in his last months with cancer at age 40, Managing Editor Jerry Finch named him political writer, a job he'd yearned for.

Occasionally, a reporter or copy editor on either paper would submit an offering to the editorial department, a practice outlawed now and generally frowned on in days past.

A *Times-Dispatch* copy editor, hoping to get $10 for an editorial, submitted one in which he endorsed what appeared to him as the reasonable demand of the United Auto Workers in their negotiations with the companies. He was called to the office of K.V. Hoffman, the most conservative of the paper's editorial writers, and lectured on market economics. The piece didn't run.

Undaunted, the copy editor made another stab—an editorial on an anniversary of some Civil War action by Mosby's Raiders, the unit to which Joseph Bryan had belonged. It ran.

The copy editor/editorial-writer, not long out of Washington and Lee University, left journalism for law school and later the ministry. He is Peter J. Lee, now bishop of the Episcopal Diocese of Virginia.[125]

MARK F. ETHRIDGE

One giant of journalism who made a relatively brief but impressive stay in Richmond was Mark F. Ethridge, who came in December 1934 as general manager of *The Times-Dispatch.* He was promoted to publisher five months later and moved in June 1937 to Louisville as general manager of the *Courier-Journal* and the *Times*.

Later, he became publisher in Louisville and, after retirement in 1963, he was editor of *Newsday* on Long Island.

When he left *The Times-Dispatch*, its directors said that under him the paper's "circulation has reached its highest mark and his efforts have contributed substantially toward increasing [the newspaper's] effectiveness as an instrument for public service to this city and to the State."

Unlike many publishers, including the Bryans, Ethridge was frequently in the newsroom. He had started out in newsrooms in Mississippi and Georgia, and he always felt at home in a newsroom. But as publisher in Richmond, he was a frequent speaker at civic events. Often a reporter would cover his addresses, and it seemed that often Ethridge felt he was misquoted in his own paper.

Norman Rowe, who spent more than 40 years on *The Times-Dispatch*, recalled being "chewed out" by Ethridge for misquoting him. He was in the publisher's office and the door was open as usual, Rowe said. Jud Evans, the political reporter, stuck his head in and asked, "What's going on, Mark?"

"Young Rowe here made a fool out of me," said Ethridge.

"What did you expect for $20 a week?" replied Evans.[126]

Ethridge, began his newspaper career as a reporter in Meridian, Mississippi, his hometown. There was a cascade of honors for him in his 84 years. In World War II he was Fair Employment Practices Commission (FEPC) chairman for President Roosevelt.

Ethridge may have been a Southern liberal, but he alienated blacks at the first FEPC hearings by saying those who argued for all or nothing were "playing into the hands of white demagogues." Further, he wrote that Negroes "must recognize that there is no power in the world—not even in all the mechanized armies of the earth, Allied and Axis—which could now force the Southern white people to the abandonment of the principle of social segregation."[127]

By 1965, Virginius Dabney argued in the *Virginia Quarterly Review*, Ethridge had become "one of the most militant advocates of full integration in the United States." It just goes to show, he said, that with time Southerners would move "steadily in the liberal direction."[128]

The National Association of Radio and Television Broadcasters chose Ethridge Man of the Year in 1956, and he was a Distinguished Journalist of Columbia University. Honorary degrees came from Tulane and Harvard.

JUD EVANS

The love-hate relationship between politicians and reporters was no better illustrated than on February 20, 1936, when the Virginia General Assembly passed a joint resolution in tribute to A. Judson Evans, and six legislators plus the lieutenant governor hailed him as a noble human being.

For much of his eight years at *The Times-Dispatch*, Evans poked fun at public figures, including politicians. Many thought him cynical, but they roared at his jokes whether in print or in speeches.

"Always a hater of pretense and sham," said a *Times-Dispatch* editorial, "he was an inveterate foe of stuffed shirts and posturing pretense."

At *The Times-Dispatch*, he covered virtually anything. James Latimer, who joined the paper several years after Evans' death, recalled Richard V. Carter, then weekend city editor, telling Latimer how Evans tried getting polysyllabic words past F.J. McDermott, the city editor. He succeeded once in a review of a vaudeville show by noting the "undulating umbilicus" of a belly-dancer.[129]

Ed Brill, who had joined the paper in 1926, recalled that admirers said Evans "could get more over the telephone than most people could get going out and worrying somebody."[130]

Evans was only 34 when he died of complications from influenza. But he had "probably the largest acquaintance among American newspapermen of any man in Virginia," said a *Times-Dispatch* obituary. He also had worked for the *Lynchburg News*, the *Baltimore Evening Sun*, the *New York Herald Tribune* and the Associated Press.

The legislature's resolution saluted Evans as "a most beloved character, able writer and friend to mankind." Lt. Gov. James H. Price said, "*The Times-Dispatch* has lost a great writer and the State of Virginia a splendid personality. He never betrayed a confidence."

A. Judson Evans, greatly respected political writer for The Times-Dispatch *in 1920s and 1930s, died young.*

One of Evans' attributes was his appearance. He was blond, stood 6 feet tall and weighed almost 275 pounds. One of his mythical characters was the Honorable Obediah P. Horsfall, a dirt farmer from Southwest Virginia who opined on members of the legislature when they gathered in Richmond.

Evans was in demand as a speaker. Once, he addressed a traffic conference for five minutes as "the last surviving pedestrian."

Reporters in the 1930s did not make handsome salaries, but Evans managed to hold memberships in three clubs including the Country Club of Virginia—the city's most exclusive country club. He was Southern vice president of the American Newspaper Guild, a factor that normally would not endear him to publishers. But, at his death, not only *The Times-Dispatch*, but also *The News Leader*, praised him in editorials.

"If Death is a gentleman," said *The News Leader*, "he exchanged a few words with Judson Evans and learned to respect Mr. Evans' wit.

". . . A man who never worried about the enemies he might make, he had more friends than enemies even among those with whom he contended."

BOB GOLDEN

Many newspapers are best known for their local columnists, who, in turn, are known for their fictional characters. At *The Times-Dispatch* in the 1930s the writer was Bob Golden, whose column reported the goings-on of McGonigle Egg, Warpath Riley, and Doc Step-and-a-Half Johnson—all in the Henrico Sit, Smoke and Argue Club.

Golden was a small-boned man, no more than 5 feet, 8 inches, according to James Latimer, much younger than Golden and, for many years later, the paper's chief political writer. Golden was slender, almost frail, Latimer recalled. When Golden died, Latimer said, he and Richard Carter, then assistant city editor, were pallbearers. Carter, a short man also, was relieved at the relatively light weight of the coffin. "Good old Bob Golden," said Carter," accommodating to the last."[131]

When Golden answered the telephone in the newsroom, Latimer said, it was, "'Hello, Bob Golden.' It sounded like the NBC chimes."

Sixteen years after his death in 1941, Golden was properly memorialized by Charles McDowell, whose own list of characters included Aunt Gertrude, Reliable Source and the Candid Congressman—but not this time. The occasion of McDowell's column on Golden was the receipt at *The Times-Dispatch* of Golden's annual membership card in the National Headliners' Club, whose award he had won in 1940 for his column, "Oldest Man About Town."

McDowell traced Golden's career through the Jamestown Exposition of 1907, where he was a promoter, and more than 10 newspapers, six of them in Richmond. He came back to *The Times-Dispatch* in 1932 at age 60. One highlight of Golden's career, as reported by McDowell, was offering a safe scalping by Chief Red Cloud at a Wild West show at the exposition, which was suffering financially.

"I guaranteed," said Golden, "that his scalp would be immediately replaced and that the double operation under an anesthetic would be painless." When press services sent the story to newspapers throughout the United States, Golden got a call from Col. Joe Miller, who ran the Wild West show, and figured he was due for a raise. Instead, he was fired. Sensitive ladies' clubs had complained.

"You idiot," said the colonel, "If I ever see you on my show lot again, I'll cut off both your ears."

Back at *The Times-Dispatch*, Golden wrote on every conceivable topic. He also reviewed vaudeville shows. After seeing one that featured a Spanish lion-tamer with a chair, a whip and a pistol, McDowell said, "Mr. Golden wrote that the lions were old, tired and harmless and the whole thing was a fraud.

"The Spaniard stormed into the office the next day in high temper. He insisted that his lions were the most dangerous of man-eaters. Mr. Golden listened patiently for a while and then took the Spaniard in tow and walked to the theater. The dapper old man opened the door of the man-eaters' cage, strode in and kicked a lion full on the chin. Turning his back on the lions, Mr.Golden bowed slightly to the Spaniard and walked out of the theater with great dignity."

McDowell included in that column a verse by Golden that appealed to any reporter who considered his prose as deathless:

"Gadzooks! As I hammer the keyboard,
My gaze wanders over the room.
To that tragi-burlesque called the Rewrite Desk
Where the best stories go to their doom."

CHARLES McDOWELL

Charles McDowell is to writing what Joe DiMaggio and Willie Mays were to baseball. Each makes the difficult seem easy.

Until he gave up chain-smoking in the early 1990s, McDowell normally started a column, or even an election night story, by lighting a cigarette, typing a sentence or two, studying what he'd written, discarding it (ripping the paper from the typewriter in the old days, wiping words from the screen later), lighting another cigarette and repeating the routine three or four times before the first paragraph proved adequate.

McDowell's homespun humor might persuade some of his readers—and countless television viewers across the country—that he is a rural Southerner who somehow got into newspapering. One recalls the Watergate hearings where the late Sen. Sam Ervin, who had a law degree from Harvard, insisted he was "just a country boy from rural North Carolina."

McDowell is the son of a law professor at Washington and Lee University, where he spent most of his youth and from which he graduated. He has a master's degree in journalism from Columbia University. For 45 years or so, he has impressed politicians, academics, fellow journalists and assorted groups to whom he speaks as an astute observer of the American scene and a writer with few peers. He is seen frequently on the Public Broadcasting System program, "Washington Week in Review."

From the day he joined *The Times-Dispatch* in 1949, McDowell was given considerable freedom in his writing.

"From the first day I covered a spot news story," he said, "I was writing more than the tradition of the paper or journalism— about the funny asides in the legislature or the governor. I stopped the maturation of a major story on the General Assembly about the third paragraph. I might be into some witticism that was exchanged or how some guy looked. And I usually tried to describe people, rather than taking them for granted. I was a sidebar feature writer or whatever you call them no matter what I did."[132]

Shortly before finishing a year at Columbia, McDowell came to Richmond, interviewed with Ben Johnston, managing editor, and was told, "You get out in June, and we'll have a job for you."

When McDowell got out in June and came to Richmond, Johnston had been demoted to Sunday editor. His successor was a former Associated Press executive, John H. Colburn. McDowell recalls Colburn as "a strange man by Virginia tradition. He was much too brisk and sort of heartless and self-important and all kinds of things we didn't know. Turned out to be a pretty good guy in some ways."

Colburn dispatched McDowell to work under Johnston, which McDowell recalls as "like working with a great writing coach. He was just gentle and nice. His immediate assistant was Parke Rouse, [a] marvelous sort of encourager of a young writer."

As McDowell recalls, virtually everyone from Publisher Tennant Bryan down through the other reporters valued good writing, except General Manager John Dana Wise. "I never heard him show any interest in writing," says McDowell.

He was struck by "the terribly impressive Virginius Dabney," whose early editorials urging desegregation of public carriers impressed him as a youngster; of Chauncey Durden, the sports editor "with a real sort of literary feel," and across the hall at *The News Leader*, Jack Kilpatrick, "one of the best newspaper writers of my time."

Like many other newspapermen, McDowell was "profoundly influenced by New Yorker writers like E.B. White." He was looking for a style that incorporated "the tradition of reporting two days out of three, that wouldn't be an opinion column specifically but would be a kind of point-of-view column that would really concentrate on being kind of well done."

McDowell spent about a year working on the Sunday section, but Managing Editor Colburn was constantly insisting, "We've got to make [news stories] more readable," which meant that McDowell, a specialist in "color" stories, would go to cityside. For a while, he took over the police beat from Maurice Dean, one of the all-time *Times-Dispatch* greats on that assignment. Dean, McDowell recalls, "turned out to be hopeless at everything else." McDowell was a general assignment reporter again, and Dean was, happily, back on night police.

McDowell was still toying with his own style. Dick Williamson, the senior assistant city editor, would tell him, "Well, try it your way. Yeah, you don't have to put the lead on top, I don't guess. Try it." State Editor Dick Carter, says McDowell, "just suffused the paper with story-telling and gentle respect for the language."

For McDowell, as for other reporters, City Editor F.J. McDermott could be a problem. McDermott had been a marine in World War I and let no one forget it. "The great marine, tough, had to act tough," says McDowell, "and constantly was intimidating me about, 'Well, if you can't do it, I'll send a copy boy' and all that stuff. [But he] really let me get away with nearly everything."

McDermott, the hard-nosed hard news man, wasn't much for columns. When McDowell wanted one, "McDermott said it was much too early to waste a good guy on some damned fool column. And that was his attitude throughout: Why would you want to take a reasonably good reporter and make him a damned fool columnist?"

McDowell had a penchant for developing the off-beat story. Once, when business and industry were humming but various state operations were closed because it was Jefferson Davis' birthday, McDowell stopped 27 people on the street and asked who Davis was. Only eight knew.

Among those he asked were three well-dressed men who tried unsuccessfully to enter a state liquor store. McDowell wrote a front page feature on how ignorant residents of the capital of the old Confederacy were about its president. Among those who flunked McDowell's quiz was a man at the liquor store who said, "I don't know who he was, but whoever he was, he certainly messed up a party at my house tonight."

In the summer of 1952, John Colburn decided that *The Times-Dispatch* would send not one reporter, but two, to cover the national political conventions. "Lat [James Latimer] wrote this beautiful, regional kind of coverage of the convention," says McDowell, "and I was free to poke and fool and angle around."

McDowell's idea of color stories at conventions is not one of "the pregame songs and the pageantry and the demonstrations in the hall" unless they're keyed to the news. "A real sidebar," he figures, "reflects, enlarges, deepens real news."

Latimer, his guru, felt the same way. Without really instructing the young reporter, he let McDowell know, "without telling me directly, 'Be sure it reflects something important and isn't just about the head of the band or something. We don't want to hear a whole lot about the movie star that came to be in the gala. Let it reflect what's happening."

The big fight at the Republican convention in Chicago was in the credentials committee, where the forces of Sen. Robert A. Taft and of Gen. Dwight D. Eisenhower clashed over delegates from several states.

McDowell tried to cover the hearing but was barred. He wandered down a hall, found a guard who was a college student and began talking about being kept out of a meeting at his first convention.

The guard said, "You just go on and slip in this back door, and you can go in there and hang out in this huge hotel kitchen."[133]

McDowell struck gold. "This kitchen with huge sinks and huge signs above the sinks that said 'Keep It Clean' was where the members of the Credentials Committee would come off the floor, get a drink of water, stand and talk a minute, smoke cigarettes, make phone calls. I stayed in that kitchen three days. I went home and slept at night and wrote a piece and returned to the kitchen."

McDowell's story for the July 10 *Times-Dispatch* began, "The most important and dramatic 'smoke-filled room' at the Republican National Convention today was a smoke-filled kitchen on the second floor of the Congress Hotel.

'. . . The kitchen was a caucus room, a retreat from the floodlights where political strategists could talk and negotiate. Press, radio and television were largely ignorant of the kitchen's existence and of what was going on among stacks of banquet plates, glasses and silver."

McDowell wrote about the face-to-face conversations or telephone calls of Warren Burger of Minnesota, a Stassen supporter, who supported the Eisenhower position on contested delegates, and of Rep. Clarence Brown of Ohio, a leading Taft backer.

". . . [T]he competing political factions did not indulge in 'cynical deals' or any particularly sinister maneuvers," McDowell wrote. "They used the kitchen as a place to talk—a place where the day's most important negotiations took place more or less privately. As for the cooks, they appeared to keep the potatoes clean and to ignore the cigar-puffing politicians completely."[134]

McDowell was enjoying the whole episode tremendously. "I can remember Herb Brownell [later Eisenhower's attorney general] and Everett Dirksen [Illinois senator] and all kind of people," McDowell recalled. "By the second day they were speaking to me and saying, 'Good morning, son.' I'd say, 'How are you, Senator? Good morning, Governor.'"[135]

McDowell also was witnessing an epoch-making event: the power of television on the political scene. "I'm listening to the members of the Credentials Committee talking to their staffs over at the hotel and in Washington and turning to one another and saying, 'We sure are getting a lot of calls saying that it's a dirty trick to keep this Eisenhower from winning.'

". . . That had never happened in American politics, where what happened was seen by people at home and fed back into the process. They picked up the phone and called their senator and said, 'I'm for Eisenhower.' Y'all are doing me out of it.'"

Charles McDowell had few peers as a writer. He also achieved fame as a regular on Public Television's Washington Week in Review.

Television was kind to McDowell, too. Some 20 years after that convention, McDowell became a regular on "Washington Week in Review" on public broadcasting. The host of the show was Paul Duke, who had worked for the Richmond bureau of the Associated Press in the building of Richmond Newspapers Inc.

Appearances on that program produced invitations to speak to groups across the country, many of which pay handsome fees for celebrity speakers. McDowell also has done other public television work, including a major speaking role in Ken Burns' series on the Civil War.

JAMES LATIMER

At newspaper parties, even late at night after drinks had been flowing for hours, it was still impossible to find out what James Latimer, the dean of Virginia's political writers, really thought about any politician. Lat had no bad guys and good guys. He treated them honorably and expected to be treated the same way.

He was never accused of breaking a confidence or taking sides. Conservatives and liberals, Democrats and Republicans, blacks and whites, all trusted Latimer.

Latimer came to *The Times-Dispatch* in 1937, a time when Managing Editor Leon Dure decided he'd had enough of reporters who came in from the North, stayed a while and left. He'd hire some Southern reporters. Latimer had a friend on *The Times-Dispatch* copy desk, and soon Dure offered Latimer a job at $40 a week, which was better than he was doing at the *Chattanooga News*, where he'd been three years.[136]

Latimer found Dure to be "a very strong character in that he was very opinionated. . . nevertheless, very tolerant of everything." For the paper, he was interested in words, in writing and in makeup—not in slant or political ideology.

Ben Johnston, who had a falling out with his superiors at the *Macon* (Georgia) *Telegraph*, where he had been managing editor, was brought to Richmond by Dure and was a strong influence on Latimer.

"He taught me, for instance," said Latimer, "that one politician with one voice cannot buy a salvo, and that a replica is an exact copy of the original and that it is made by the maker of the original. You cannot have miniature replicas or anything like that. And he suggested that you be careful when you used phrases like 'since Reconstruction,' because it means different things to different people."

A year after arriving, Latimer was covering the Virginia General Assembly with George Prince Arnold, a former William & Mary quarterback

James Latimer spent 44 years with The Times-Dispatch *and was dean of state's political writers.*

who lived at the Commonwealth Club, and Virgil Carrington (Pat) Jones, later a historian and aide to Rep. William M. Tuck.

Covering the General Assembly has always been considered a plum for *Times-Dispatch* reporters, but Latimer was pulled off the 1940 session because he'd been assigned the court case in which Richmond was attempting to annex part of Henrico County. He was off state politics briefly, but the annexation case led him to friendship with "a very nice, young lawyer" named Lewis F. Powell Jr.

In his 44 years with *The Times-Dispatch*, Latimer was the reporter editors called in for truly big stories. One of those times was in 1971, when President Nixon nominated Powell to the U.S. Supreme Court.

In the early 1950s, Latimer was detached from his regular duties to report on a proposal for a downtown expressway, which involved demolishing All Saints Episcopal Church. The proposal was fought heatedly and successfully by a group headed by a former mayor, Dr. J. Fulmer Bright. A decade later, an expressway was built through the central city. It came nowhere near All Saints, which had already moved to the western suburbs.

James Latimer (center), interviewed former Govs. Colgate W. Darden Jr. (left) and William M. Tuck in 1975 for a series that appeared on public television.

About that time, Publisher Tennant Bryan had offered his ancestral home, Laburnum, as the site for a new hospital. There was federal money available through the new Hill-Burton Act for hospitals, but it soon developed that Richmond was far down the priority list.

The Times-Dispatch editorial page was strongly in favor of funds for the new Richmond Memorial Hospital, and Dr. Harry Warthen, a local physician, dug up statistics to show Richmond wasn't being treated fairly. He fed the figures to the paper. John Dana Wise wrote blistering editorials, alleging prejudice against the new hospital by key people at the Medical College of Virginia Hospital in Richmond and the University of Virginia Hospital in Charlottesville.

Latimer wrote news stories, pointing to Dr. Warthen's figures and noting "very casually" that the governor, then John S. Battle, was from Charlottesville.

The money came through for Richmond Memorial Hospital.

Latimer's biggest scoop was national, and it came on the political beat. In 1952, members of Virginia's delegation to the Democratic National Convention were almost thrown out because of the refusal to sign a "loyalty oath" to support party nominees. The man who prevented their ouster was Battle.

In the Democrats' convention four years later, the civil rights plank in the platform was the major issue. What the wording would be was of paramount importance to delegates and to reporters. But the leaders at the convention were not giving out details on the compromise that had been hammered out.

Luckily for Latimer, Battle was on the platform committee. The two men got together and the reluctant Battle gave the report to Latimer "on condition that I would not use it until the city edition of *The Times-Dispatch*."

It was about midnight, approaching the deadline for the final edition. Latimer read the report, called his office in Richmond and dictated the details of the civil rights plank—something no other reporter had found out.

The copyrighted story, of course, led the paper. Under a five-column head,

Rights Plank Compromise

Is Reached by Drafting Body

and Latimer's byline, it began: "CHICAGO, Aug. 15 (Wednesday)—A civil rights plank that mentions but does not affirm anti-segregation 'decisions' of the United States Supreme Court will be recommended to the Democratic National Convention's Platform Committee Wednesday.

"This formula, which is expected to be approved by a committee majority, was worked out by the 16-member subcommittee. It seeks to settle the main civil rights issue that threatens to split the Democratic party wide open. The issue is: Whether the party should endorse and pledge enforcement of the Supreme Court's school desegregation decision."

Managing Editor John Colburn arranged for copies of the city edition to be sent by air, where delegates read *The Times-Dispatch* by 8 or 9 a.m.

In his last years at *The Times-Dispatch*, Latimer became increasingly irritable with editors who wanted to trim his prose. Usually, the editors gave in to a much greater extent than with other reporters. An example was Latimer's obituary on Colgate W. Darden Jr., former governor and former president of the University of Virginia. *The Times-Dispatch* then was an eight-column paper and Latimer's obit on Darden ran about six columns. Latimer felt, correctly, that Darden was perhaps the outstanding Virginian of our time.

RICHARD V. CARTER

Alumni of Virginia Military Institute are known for their loyalty that sometimes borders on obsession. None was more loyal, more enthusiastic than Richard V. Carter, who never even finished.

Dick Carter was enthralled with VMI and any of its activities. When the trip wasn't too far, he'd go to the Keydets' football games, usually supplied with at least a pint of bourbon. He had a hollowed out radio in which he kept his bottle.

At one game, a spectator on the row behind Carter at Lexington tapped him on the shoulder and asked, "How's Virginia doing?"

"This radio doesn't carry the Virginia game," Carter replied.

Carter worked two years for the Associated Press and joined *The Times-Dispatch* two years later at age 22. He became sports editor, assistant city editor and state editor. Legend has it that he went away on vacation as city editor and returned to find that F.J. McDermott had been named city editor and Carter state editor.

As state editor, Carter turned on the teletype printer and greeted correspondents at various bureaus each morning. Then it was scanning papers, chatting with McDermott, whose desk abutted Carter's, and talking with state desk staff members about what was doing. By mid-afternoon, he had probably finished his first pack of cigarettes of the day.

Copy editing was done cursorily. The guys on the copy desk who write headlines could do the fine tuning.

When Carter left early each evening, the routine rarely varied: Out to the soft drink machine into which he pumped the necessary coins for one can, then to the back steps where he opened the pint of bourbon in the pocket of his jacket, took a large tug from the bottle followed by a gulp from the soft drink, replaced the bottle in his jacket, set the almost full soft drink can on a ledge and proceeded downstairs.

Occasionally, he would drop in at Chiocca's, a restaurant half a block away, and down one or two glasses of wine. Then to home.

Carter retired in 1972 at age 66, and the boisterous retirement party was perhaps one of the most liquid in recent *Times-Dispatch* history. Bill McKelway, a lanky Washington & Lee graduate who was one of Carter's favorites among state desk workers, drove his boss to the party in a rented limousine.

One year and one heart attack later, Carter was dead.

Away from the state desk of The Times-Dispatch, Richard V. Carter was likely to be found at something involving Virginia Military Institute.

MARION L. FAIREY

If Hollywood picked out a grizzled newspaperman, who drank on the job, chain-smoked, told outlandish stories that no one could believe and tried to intimidate printers for the sake of editors and editors for the sake of printers, the critics wouldn't buy it.

But the critics didn't know Marion L. Fairey. He was all of those things. He was tall and thin and his face looked as if it had deep creases sewn in. His neck was long and scrawny, and some said he looked like a pelican before his goiter was removed.

He came to work at 6 p.m. and left about 2:30 a.m. In between, he was the liaison man between the newsroom and the composing room. He shouted from the composing room to editors that they had better get that last bit of copy downstairs or there'd be a hole with "Compliments of a friend" where a story should be. He bellowed from a phone in the third floor newsroom to printers a floor below that they'd crossed their hands and they'd better look at Page B-3 and see what an abortion it was.

Fairey, known as "Doc," usually killed a pint of bourbon on the job each night. He hid it in the trash basket in the office of an editorial writer who'd gone home hours before. After each edition, Doc would slip into the office and take a couple of slugs. Sometimes after an edition, he would take the bottle downstairs, hide it and go back to it when he felt the urge.

Occasionally, Doc would be weaving in the news room between the "one star" (penultimate) edition and the city edition. Somehow, he'd negotiate the stairs to the composing room, deal with the printers and make it back upstairs. The final edition looked fine.

One night, John E. Leard, the managing editor, decided to check up on Fairey, whose reputed drinking habits worried him. Leard slipped into the composing room, followed Fairey each step he made and found nothing improper. Somehow, Fairey had learned the boss was on the way before he ever got to the composing room.

Monday was routinely one of Fairey's days off, and he usually went—often with a couple of printers—to racetracks in Maryland. He took with him money that reporters had given him to bet on this horse or that. No one ever complained that Fairey had pocketed the money because all winning bets were paid off the day Doc returned to work. Still, his fellow employees were never convinced that Fairey himself really won as often or as much as he claimed.

Gambling was as natural to Fairey as was eating or drinking. Printers and others who worked late often played poker after the last edition was done. Legend has it that one night Fairey, out of cash, endorsed the stub of his paycheck, bet it and ended up a winner.

Fairey equaled Baron Munchausen as a teller of tall tales. Late one night after a long session at the Press Club, the author and his wife were on their way home and he told her that Doc embroidered his stories considerably.

"Oh, I didn't really believe them," she said, "but he does such a beautiful job that I loved every story."

WILLIAM G. LEVERTY

Bill Leverty had a reputation of eating copy boys alive and spitting enough of them back so they could do the newsroom chores. Like many an apparent tyrant, Leverty was charming away from the office and, on occasion, pleasant while at work.

His workweek began Sunday afternoon; he would have just returned from relaxation at his cottage off the Rappahannock River. He would walk to his seat on the copy desk, deposit two packs of cigarettes thereon and drop his ample frame into a chair.

His extended arm would sweep everything—old wire copy, notes, whatever—from his desk area, and he would bellow, "Copy." The nearest copy boy (there were no copy girls in William G. Leverty's day) would quickly but quietly come to Leverty's chair and wait for orders for anything from a cup of coffee to a copy of that day's *New York Times*.

Not only copy boys but also copy editors and reporters lived in fear of Leverty. Usually they got over it in a year or so. Some graduates of Washington and Lee University, where he taught a class on Friday (one of his days off), would come to work at *The Times-Dispatch* and be dismayed that the charming instructor in class was a raging terror in the newsroom.

L.M. Wright Jr. was one of many reporters who came to the paper in the 1950s and spent a few weeks on the copy desk to learn *Times-Dispatch* style before joining the reportorial staff. After Wright had spent several days on the job, Leverty asked, "How do you like working on the copy desk?"

Being addressed by Leverty after days of non-talk, Wright brightened and said, "Fine, Mr. Leverty. . . " He wanted to go on, but Leverty's attention then was elsewhere.

A week or so ensued before Leverty broke the silence between them again. "So you like the copy desk, do you?"

No one in the newsroom ever questioned Leverty's news judgment. He always seemed to cynical reporters and editors to have almost perfect judgment in assessing a story—especially one that was bound to develop into something major.

So it was a disappointment—at times, almost a distress—to hear Leverty late at night calling Managing Editor John Colburn at home to get approval for changing the front page as news developed.

Party time at The Times-Dispatch *in the 1960s. Seated: Edith Lindeman, movie reviewer; William G. Leverty, assistant managing editor; standing: Helen McCarthy, secretary for news and editorial departments; Richard V. Carter, state editor; Joseph Colognori, chief photographer; Norman Rowe, amusements writer.*

GUY FRIDDELL

Guy Friddell followed Nikita Khrushchev across the United States, covered national political conventions, scooped *The Times-Dispatch* on major news stories and was the appointed interviewer of visiting intellectuals.

But he is best remembered by his contemporaries as the reporter who trampled on a tree that President Eisenhower had planted at his mother's birthplace.

In October 1960, late in his second term, Eisenhower planted a pine seedling at Mount Sidney, Va. "As the crowd surged forward," the Associated Press reported, Friddell, "unaware of frenzied cries of 'watch that tree, watch that tree,' stepped on it and undid most of the President's handiwork."

That act was so Friddellian. It was like his forgetting appointments, or wearing mismatched socks or wearing slippers to the Governor's Mansion because reporters had hidden his shoes.

Friddell can write seriously and playfully. His columns for *The News Leader* and the *Norfolk Virginian-Pilot* are mostly in the latter category. So are many of his eight books. But, as his former managing editor at *The News Leader*, Jerald Finch, said, Friddell "did the most beautiful interviews you've ever seen."[137]

Indeed, once, when one of the world's foremost authorities on Voltaire visited the University of Richmond, Friddell was the sole interviewer from the press. *The Times-Dispatch* had no reporter who knew what questions to ask about one of the greatest of Frenchmen.

When John Leard was asked to name some truly outstanding reporters whom he had overseen as *News Leader* city editor, Friddell's was the first name mentioned. He was "a good reporter and a good writer," said Leard, knowing that the combination is rare.[138]

On the other hand, said Leard, Friddell was "kind of footloose. We had to get a commitment out of him to turn in his column on Friday for

Monday, and usually about a quarter of 8 on Monday, I'd go over and look at his page and he had nothing but three rows of X's because he'd X through what he'd written already.

"He had also some slight memory failings because he concentrated on the things that were important. He could remember a significant quote for a political story from five years ago, but he couldn't remember, as he did one day, where he'd left his car. He invited three of us to ride home. . . and we started walking down 4th Street, and he'd say, 'Gosh, I didn't bring my car today.'"[139]

Friddell, the absent-minded reporter, cared little about his appearance or that of his car. Finch recalled the day that his fellow car-poolers decided something had to be done about the disreputable-looking car that Friddell drove. Finch thinks it eventually was given to the State Fair for a car-bashing contest.

But on that particular morning, the car stopped to pick up Carl Shires. "Carl came running out with a pail and a hose," said Finch. "Everybody jumped out of the car. Somebody took Friddell's keys out of the ignition, and we started washing and cleaning the car—in about three or four minutes.

"Everybody just jumped in. Friddell never moved. He sat . . . with his hands on the wheel and never acknowledged anything was going on. Anyway, we cleaned the car. Shires took the hose back, the pail back; we all got in the car. Somebody gave the keys back. We sat back. Friddell started the car, and we drove to work and not a thing was ever said."[140]

Friddell could play the game, too. Once, when the car-poolers became weary of listening to City Editor Larry Gould regale them for three days about the great biography of John F. Kennedy that he was reading, Friddell asked to see the book. Gould, who was driving, handed it to Friddell, who tucked it away and opened an old textbook about the same size.

"I opened it and said, 'Oh, that's crap,' tore the page out, ruffled it a bit and "Listen to this. What possesses the man?'" Friddell continued tearing out pages and throwing them out the window. Gould screamed, "Friddell, you fool." And Friddell finally tossed the entire book out the window. Gould stopped the car, picked up the mutilated book and realized what had gone on.

"He never resorted to physical violence," said Friddell.[141]

Having graduated from the University of Richmond in his hometown and having received a master's degree from the Columbia University School of Journalism, Friddell nevertheless went into public relations for a year at the Virginia Museum of Fine Arts.

He was offered a job by John Colburn, managing editor of *The Times-*

Guy Friddell, a versatile News Leader *reporter, later editorial writer and columnist.*

Dispatch, but Leslie Cheek, Jr., director of the Virginia Museum of Fine Arts interviewed Friddell in New York.

"I didn't know anything about art," said Friddell, "but I was kind of intrigued with him—so creative." So Friddell went to the museum. One of his jobs was taking news releases to *The News Leader* and *The Times-Dispatch*. "The attraction was just too much. One day I just stayed there. I asked John Leard [city editor of *The Leader*] if he had an opening, and he did."

Friddell's way of informing his wife, Virginia, of his job shift was to walk into the hospital where she was resting with their firstborn, Rusty, and say, "Well, Gin, I left my job today." He explained later that he had another, and she took it well, he said.[142]

Shortly thereafter, he was assigned Capitol Square, the governor's office and assorted state agencies. "And, boy, it was fun," he recalled 40 years later. City Editor Leard always impressed Friddell. "He was the sun of that universe, the newsroom," said Friddell. "Everything reflected John and he reflected us. He was tremendous, just the ideal center for a newspaper."

Friddell loved politics. Scarcely a year after joining *The News Leader* he was in Chicago, covering the Democratic National Convention. Liberals wanted delegates to swear a "loyalty oath" to support the convention's nominees. Many Southern conservatives wanted to walk out of the convention. But Gov. John S. Battle, head of the Virginia delegation, wanted neither a walkout nor a loyalty oath.

Battle spoke three times to the convention, and Friddell, although in the midst of the Virginia delegation, thought he was in heaven.

"So, Battle got up and made these three wonderful appearances, and I sat by him the entire night. I stood by him, and there was this vast plain of faces. We all stood, and up in the middle, it looked like skyscrapers on a distant plain with the Virginia delegation just standing there all night.

"I stood there and took notes all night. Finished about 1. I just wrote until I gave it to Western Union at 6 in the morning. But I enjoyed it thoroughly, and Battle, when he got up to the forum, his face was just like a fist. I mean to tell you he was eloquent. I had a lovely time. That was my first convention, and it meant so much to me that it was almost like a baptism."

When the move to expel Virginia and several other states began, Friddell said, Battle spoke about "the sunlight striking the dome of Monticello" and "I hold this seat that Thomas Jefferson. . ."

"My God, they went wild," said Friddell.[143]

When he was the chief political writer for *The News Leader*, Guy Friddell scooped his friend and rival, James Latimer of *The Times-Dispatch*, on two of the biggest news stories of 1958—Sen. Harry F. Byrd's decision not to run for re-election and his change of heart 13 days later.

Friddell's lead story in *The News Leader* of February 12 began, "Sen. Harry Flood Byrd, Virginia's United States senator for 25 years, said today he would not seek re-election in the July 15 Democratic primary."

After a quote from Byrd's formal statement, Friddell wrote, "The senator bears his 71 years lightly, his cheeks rosy as one of his Winesap apples, his blue eyes clear as a baby's. In the recent race for Governor, the senator waged for the Democratic ticket one of his fiery, pepper-pot campaigns."

The announcement caused great consternation in the Byrd machine, or organization. Which of two former governors would succeed him—William M. Tuck or John S. Battle?

Reporters thought Friddell had one of the scoops of the decade and wondered how he had outdone Latimer, dean of Virginia's political writers. Friddell won't say, other than to note that *The News Leader*, as an afternoon paper, had early deadlines and, "So, I just hounded him to death."

Byrd's announcement set off not only speculation on his successor but also pleas for him to reconsider. So, on February 25, again in *The News Leader* ahead of *The Times-Dispatch*, Byrd's announcement of his change of mind appeared in an un-bylined story. The senator said he was responding to public and private appeals and had the consent of his wife to run again.

When Nikita Khrushchev arrived in the United States, Friddell covered the event for *The News Leader* and Charles McDowell was *The Times-Dispatch*'s reporter. The appearance of Khrushchev with a head that "looked like the moon" and wearing a beige suit that "jumped around like a tag team was inside it," told Friddell that lots of good copy was bound to come from every appearance the Soviet leader made across the country. He telephoned Leard that first day and asked to stay on the story. After calls between *News Leader* and *Times-Dispatch* editors, the return message to Friddell was "both of you are going the rest of the way."[144]

Good reporters find ways to beat the system, and Friddell showed during the Khrushchev visit that he was nothing if not enterprising. Under the system devised for the press, there would be a four-man pool that supposedly would accompany Khrushchev everywhere and give the horde of reporters details of events that all couldn't attend.

But Khrushchev and company moved so rapidly that often there was no time for a briefing before the press had to board buses. At an IBM plant, Friddell figured out—correctly—which of several buildings Khrushchev might visit and immediately went there himself.

He found a mimeograph machine, threw his coat over a chair and grabbed a piece of paper and walked into the rear of the office that Khrushchev was to visit. When he and other dignitaries arrived, Friddell—holding his sheet of paper—drifted up and listened to Khrushchev pepper an employee with questions about his salary, his automobile, his home payments and so on.

"I don't know why people didn't just throw me out," he said. "I guess it's because I've always looked just sort of vacuous and vapid and harmless, like someone who ought to be working at a place like that."

Khrushchev impressed Friddell as a reformer, a forerunner to Gorbachev. "My God, the man was determined to learn about us," said

Friddell. "And that was what I learned about him. That was why I had so much hope."[145]

Friddell's sharp, detailed coverage of Khrushchev was consistently lively as was that of McDowell for *Times-Dispatch* readers. In New York, McDowell reported on the reactions of residents there, including a Bronx dentist who said he thought Khrushchev had "a class three malocclusion."

"That refers," said the dentist, "to the relationship of the mandible and the maxilla, the lower and upper jaw bones. Khrushchev's lower jaw thrusts forward. The protruding lower lip is the tipoff."[146]

What other newspaper's readers got a dental report on the Soviet premier?

At *The News Leader*, Managing Editor Charles H. Hamilton wanted a local story leading the paper as often as possible. In the late 1950s, Arnold Toynbee was a visiting lecturer at Washington and Lee University, and Friddell was dispatched to Lexington to interview him. Friddell found him delightful and willing to expound on everything from segregation to space exploration.

As for the latter, Toynbee said, "Well, it's something to do on the risk, on the edge, on the margin. But much better to be spent at home." Friddell found that Toynbee was accessible at virtually any time for comment on virtually anything. City Editor Leard would ask Friddell to phone Toynbee for comment on, say, an African rebellion.

"I'd call him and I'd get him. I'd get him in the morning, I'd get him in the makeover [second edition]. Sometimes, if it was a developing story, I'd call him three times a day. . . . Hamilton was joyous because we were localizing everything on the globe."

About six years later, the great Englishman was back in Virginia, this time in Williamsburg. Friddell found where he was staying and was there when Toynbee and his wife arrived. Mrs. Toynbee gave a glance toward Friddell, turned to her husband, and said, "Dear, here's the young man who called us at breakfast, lunch and tea."[147]

CHARLES W. (MIKE) HOUSTON

One of the few complaints that his colleagues on *The News Leader* had about Charles W. (Mike) Houston was that they couldn't walk the half-mile or so with him from the City Hall-State Capitol area back to the newspaper in a reasonable time.

It seemed that every block along the way someone would greet Mike and start a conversation. Someone might be almost anyone, for Houston wrote for *The News Leader* for 40 years.

From the time he joined the *Alexandria Gazette* in 1921, until he died immediately after writing a column for *The News Leader*, he'd spent 54 years as a newspaperman. After only 17 years in the business, he had had such a varied career that his city editor compelled him to write a first-person story about it. Houston noted then that he had "seventeen years of thrills (and drudgery) on seven newspapers in six cities—Alexandria, Baltimore, Pittsburgh, Norfolk, New York and Richmond."[148]

His last managing editor, Jerald Finch, said that Houston used to joke that "he started out as managing editor and he's been going uphill ever since."[149]

He was managing editor of the Alexandria paper before becoming a reporter for the *Baltimore American*, a deskman for the *Pittsburgh Gazette-Times*, a reporter for the *Norfolk Virginian-Pilot*, a sports writer for the *New York Evening Post*, sports editor of *The Times-Dispatch* and, finally, a reporter for *The News Leader*.

His one claim to national fame came in 1933 when he, alone among "baseball experts," correctly predicted that the New York Giants and the Washington Senators would win pennants.

In his 1938 reflections for *The News Leader*, he recalled "traipsing out to sea 200 miles to meet Lindbergh on his triumphant, but modest, return from Paris aboard the U.S.S. Memphis, and to help take his first colonel's uniform to him."

A large chunk of The News Leader *news staff gathers around Douglas Southall Freeman (in suit), presumably at his retirement in 1949. At Freeman's left is Charles H. Hamilton, managing editor. To Hamilton's left with woman's arms around his waist is Charles (Mike) Houston, city hall reporter.*

Houston had been trapped in a burning skyscraper in Pittsburgh and "[had been] too dumb to be scared stiff during the Los Angeles earthquake in 1933." Later, he wrote, "My greatest thrill was that earthquake—11 seconds of terror."[150]

In his 1938 reflections, Houston told of the time he had written of a suicide-murder that involved an illicit love affair. "I wrote the story, and the boy's family, for some reason, objected. . . They sent me out to straighten up matters. .. The body was in the living room, and in the dining room, where we sat to talk, there was a bottle of Scotch. . . We might not have been absolutely respectful of the dead, but when I left we were the best of friends. . . and they'd agreed my story was correct. . .

"It's a good thing a reporter can't remember too much. He'd go nuts. I've had to break the news of sudden death too often, and that's the most unpleasant job any reporter ever has to do."

Houston said he'd known the baseball greats—Babe Ruth, Tony Lazzeri, Herb Pennock, Joe McCarthy, Bill Terry. "I knew them all, and a lot more, and I miss 'em in a way, too, but there is nothing in baseball to be sad over."

As a reporter at *The News Leader*, Houston covered the General Assembly for years and later was the City Hall reporter. Competing against *The Times-Dispatch*, which routinely had first crack at spot news coverage—for most City Council meetings were at night—Houston often outsmarted new reporters for *The Times-Dispatch*. The morning paper sent two reporters to the council's meetings, so that one could file a story while the other kept tab on other goings-on.

When the senior *Times-Dispatch* reporter went out to file a story, the green, number two man covered the council. Often he'd keep an eye on Houston when some arcane issue arose. If Houston was whittling with his pocketknife on a pencil, the *Times-Dispatch* man was relieved.

He shouldn't have been. For the noon edition of *The News Leader* the next day often splashed a front-page story on that arcane item, which Houston understood but the morning paper's man didn't.

Houston began writing his "Sidelights" column for *The News Leader* in 1960 and did three a week until his death in 1975. The only two he missed were in 1973 when his son, a vice president of Mary Washington College, died unexpectedly of heat stroke after cutting his grass.

Houston had a home on Church Hill in Richmond and a retreat at Barboursville in Orange County. More and more in his later years, the column was datelined there. In his final column, he complained of not having felt well over Labor Day weekend. "It is always my luck," he wrote, "that when I get sick, it is on my own time. It was nothing really, I suppose, and by Monday morning I was ready to get back in harness again."[151]

Several paragraphs later, he said, "This is sort of like beginning a new year when no resolutions are expected or made. It is the beginning of the end of the year when winter will come to be wished away in favor of spring."

Managing Editor Finch recalled that Houston wrote the column and "fell backwards—massive heart attack—and died."[152] He was dead by the time he got to the Medical College of Virginia Hospital. For Finch, it was the second time he had to tell Houston's wife, Louise, about a Houston death.

The first time was at a dinner party at the Finches' home, when another *News Leader* editor, Dick Payne, called and told Finch of the death of Houston's son, Michael. Louise Houston "went absolutely to pieces," said Finch, but her husband "was just like a rock."

After the father died, *The News Leader* carried a column with Louise's byline that thanked all the people who had helped her "through the ordeal."

Actually, Finch wrote the column, "but I tried to write in the style Mike would have written," he said.

ROY C. FLANNAGAN

One of the best reporters on either Richmond paper, it was universally agreed, was Roy C. Flannagan, who worked for *The News Leader* from 1923 until his death at age 54 in 1952.

A World War I fighter pilot, Flannagan joined *The News Leader* in 1923 and covered labor, City Hall, mental health and politics at all levels. In World War II, he was back in the Army in the Mediterranean, European and Pacific theaters.

With the cessation of hostilities, he was a newspaperman again, as well as a novelist. His books included *The Forest Cavalier, The Whipping, Amber Satyr* and *County Court*. At his death, a *News Leader* editorial called Flannagan "one of the ablest newspaper reporters and most competent novelists in the South."

Jack Kilpatrick, who came to *The News Leader* as a reporter and became editor, said Flannagan was "first rate, absolutely first rate" as a reporter. "And a wonderful human being."[153]

James Latimer, who covered the Richmond-Henrico annexation trial in 1939-40, marveled at the way Flannagan, his competitor, covered the event for *The News Leader*. "He had this legal pad," said Latimer, "and he would take little notes over here and he would be writing a running story right then, while they were talking."[154]

Flannagan wrote clearly in longhand, said Latimer, and as the deadline approached for the afternoon paper, Flannagan would write a lead on his running story and hand it to a messenger, who would head back to *The News Leader*.

ROBERT B. MUNFORD, JR.

Every newspaper needs its institutional memory in the form of someone who can tell the young reporters and editors that the person whose death is shrugged off today was truly newsworthy a couple of decades ago.

For almost a quarter of a century at *The News Leader* that person was Robert Beverley Munford, Jr. His main task was to write obituaries, and for years after his death old Richmonders would complain that "no one writes obituaries any more like Mr. Munford." Indeed, no one did.

Mr. Munford, as everyone knew him, was, as Jack Kilpatrick wrote in a long, touching editorial obit, "never, in truth, much of a reporter as the term ordinarily is employed." But, said Kilpatrick in that editorial upon Mr. Munford's death at age 73, "He was the best-loved man in the city room, and perhaps the most indispensable editor on the staff. He was the city desk's link with the past—with Old Richmond—and he had in his head, or in his meticulous files of clippings, an encyclopedic knowledge of old families, old buildings, old customs."

He spent the last 24 years of his life at *The News Leader*. Thus, he was considerably older than most of the reporters, whom he loved to take on walks through the city, pointing out to them what used to be here and who used to live there.

The reporters responded with respect but also with tricks. Andy McCutcheon, who called him "the most unforgettable character at *The News Leader* I ever met," said that Mr. Munford on occasion would fall asleep at his desk. Whereupon, some youngster would apply part of the contents of a paste pot from the copy desk to the earpiece of Mr. Munford's telephone and then ring the extension of the sleeping obit writer. Other times, McCutcheon said, reporters on out-of-town assignments would send him dirty postcards.[155]

Robert B. Munford Jr. came from an old Virginia family and had encyclopedic knowledge of other old families.

If he was upset, he restrained himself. However, he could not restrain himself when one's manners were bad. Mr. Munford, like any proper Richmonder, had been brought up knowing manners were important.

Kilpatrick recalled in that editorial obituary that someone once complained in a telephone call that a lodge notice he'd sent the paper had not appeared. Mr. Munford said he hadn't seen it.

Then he said, his voice rising, "I see on my desk an envelope from your order addressed to a Mr. Montford. I have not opened that envelope. My name is Robert Beverley Munford, Jr., and I have been here for 125 years and everyone ought to know it by now."

The favorite story at *The News Leader* about Mr. Munford, and one included in Kilpatrick's editorial, concerned the time Mr. Munford listened to a bishop condemn prohibition laws during a Lenten service at St. Paul's Episcopal Church. Mr. Munford routinely was assigned to the five-times-a-week services.

He wrote no story on the sermon and was asked after the next day's *Times-Dispatch* carried an account why he hadn't reported the bishop's remarks. Mr. Munford said the bishop had no business saying what he did, that it was in bad taste, and, therefore, he wasn't going to dignify the remarks in print.

"Much of Old Richmond has gone, and now Mr. Munford has gone, too," Kilpatrick wrote. "With his portly figure (he used to insist, pointing to his waistline, that the Lord must have intended him to be a bishop), his courtly demeanor, his old-fashioned courtesy and wit, he often seemed lost in a civilization bereft of civility."

BEVERLY ORNDORFF

One of the stars of *The Times-Dispatch* for almost four decades wrote about the stars—and about anything else scientific or medical.

Beverly Orndorff, who began his *Times-Dispatch* career chasing fire engines, covering courts and writing about local politics in the Charlottesville bureau in 1957, spent the bulk of that career in Richmond. He was one of the few reporters who could almost set his own agenda.

He also won a lifetime honorary membership in the Virginia Academy of Science—something no one else has ever received. He wrote a science column for years, and, early in 1993, after the merger with *The News Leader*, the paper began a science page once a week with Orndorff as the main contributor.

He had a degree in physics from the University of Virginia but no graduate degrees. Yet, doctors and scientists in Virginia and elsewhere had no compunction about talking to Orndorff about the most complicated procedures.

He covered some dozen space shots, including Mercury, Gemini, Apollo and Challenger programs, over more than a quarter-century. He explained heart transplants, weather phenomena and mathematics theories so the layman could understand them.

One project that stymied him was a series on cigarettes and health. Alan S. Donnahoe, president of Media General and a chain-smoker, had long doubted the surgeon general's report on the dangers of smoking. About 1971, he suggested re-interviewing one scientist on the surgeon general's panel. As Orndorff recalls, he thought the idea of re-interviewing all the panel members was good, especially since the end of radio and TV advertising of cigarettes had just begun.[156]

He wrote a series and waited. Executive Editor John Leard called him one day and had extensive notes from Donnahoe, Orndorff said. Donnahoe was "very, very critical" of the Orndorff's series, even objecting to calling the Tobacco Institute "a lobby," Orndorff said.

Orndorff concluded his series with up-to-date comments from all the panel members but the one Donnahoe had suggested. He could not be reached. And the series went to Managing Editor Alf Goodykoontz, who, Orndorff recalled, told Leard to deal with him, not with reporters, when he had concerns about stories.

In any case, the series never ran. Orndorff said Goodykoontz kept saying, "It's on my desk," and that he would get to it. Then a printers' strike occurred, and attention was devoted elsewhere.

Orndorff never was sure why the series didn't run. But the author, who was city editor at the time, recalls that Goodykoontz objected to Donnahoe's fly-specking and decided to kill the project rather than knuckle under to Donnahoe. Goodykoontz can't recall the details.[157]

Donnahoe, a two-to-three-pack-a-day smoker for years, routinely scoffed at smoking links to cancer and other ailments. In 1964 and 1965, he testified before congressional committees on the subject. In his earlier appearance, he said that statistics in a U.S. Public Health Service report "can only be described as haphazard and unscientific." The link between smoking and cancer, he said, "is not so much scientific method as it is scientific guesswork."

In March 1965, two months after the surgeon-general's report on smoking and health, Donnahoe, a statistician, said that the report contained "many frailties and inconsistencies in the underlying statistical data."

But more than 20 years later, Donnahoe changed not only his mind but also his habits. "I had a little heart attack in 1988," he said. His cardiologist told him, "You don't give up smoking, you'll be back here in 12 months."

The chain-smoker became a non-smoker.

He still hadn't changed his mind by 1990 about the statistics—"they were weird then, and they're weird now."

But, he went on, "Since that time, they've come up with a lot of biological proof, which is quite different from [the statistics]. . . And I figure it would be kind of hard to maintain that cigarettes are not injurious today."[158]

FRANK J. McDERMOTT

When F.J. McDermott, the feisty city editor of *The Times-Dispatch*, died, the paper was scooped, editorially, by its sister publication across the hall.

On March 30, 1966, Jack Kilpatrick, editor of *The News Leader*, wrote, "Frank J. McDermott, who died last night, was a city editor in that great—and vanished—tradition. . .

"Mr. Mac was built close to the ground like a good bulldog, and he even looked a little like a bulldog. His cigar was his billyclub, baton and barometer. In the T-D city room, he was The Boss and a succession of managing editors and reporters never forgot it. He was the mother bear to the cubs and holy terror to press agents. For these latter, he reserved an eye as cold as a hard-boiled egg. Yet under the layers of lava was a great kindness and gentleness that became more evident toward the end of his life."

Two days later *The Times-Dispatch* noted editorially that a retirement party for McDermott was carried off only after the honoree was lured under pretext to a restaurant.

Times-Dispatch reporters loved to tell of McDermott's sending them off on stories without the slightest indication of what might be involved. A police reporter would be dispatched to a fire; before he arrived, the city editor would be on the car telephone demanding to know how bad it looked.

Cub reporters were terrified of McDermott. If they didn't understand an assignment bellowed to them in the newsroom, they would quietly seek out a veteran reporter for a little more information before departing.

McDermott was without a college education but not without knowledge of proper English. Ed Brill, who joined the paper as a 19-year-old in 1926, recalled how proud he was of a murder story he'd covered as a young police reporter. One Morris Rohn had been found dead in his home, and Brill had worked on the story until 2 a.m. or later. As he came to the office about 12 hours later, he was congratulated by the head of the refer-

F.J. McDermott, the cigar-chomping, longtime city editor of The Times-Dispatch, *who was really softer than the image he tried to convey.*

ence department. When McDermott called for him to come over to his desk, the $15-a-week Brill thought it was for more congratulations.

"Did you write that story about Rohn that I read in the paper?" asked the city editor. "Yes, I did," replied Brill. "I was police reporter last night."

"Well, you know you called him a prominent leather dealer," said the city editor. "If the man was prominent, you didn't have to say so; and if he's not prominent, you're a liar if you say so. Never use that word—as long as you work with me—again."[159]

Although it is recorded nowhere that McDermott ever used a camera, he and the photographers were soulmates. That meant they could trick him whenever they liked. They knew he was a weather buff, so one day the poured soap flakes from their office, one level above his, and telephoned him about covering the unexpected snow. When they learned he was fascinated about reports of flying saucers, they rained down pie plates and called him again.

McDermott was so attuned to fires that tbe photographers gave him a fire helmet, which he kept in the city desk. The helmet had "St. Luke's Hospital" marked on it, and each time the fire box near the hospital sounded—usually a false alarm—the photographers added a star to Mr. Mac's helmet.

City Hall politics and police beat stories were Mr. Mac's favorites. It took a mighty good story to make him miss his homeward-bound 8 p.m. bus. One time that occurred was during a series of fires that police believed an arsonist had set.

When the author was police reporter, he was eating dinner at home three blocks from the paper one night when McDermott phoned and told him to leave immediately for a fire at an apartment house. A second alarm had yet to be turned in, but McDermott was insistent on the reporter's departure right away.

When he arrived in no more than 10 minutes, it was evident a major fire was under way. Occupants were evacuated, a gas line exploded—raining bricks down on the aging fire chief, John Finnegan—and multiple alarms were sounded. Luckily, the reporter had parked the *Times-Dispatch* police car near the scene and could race back to it and dictate updated stories for later editions.

When he returned to the office after midnight to top the story for the final edition, there was McDermott still at the city desk—having written a new lead attributing the blaze to an arsonist.

Happily, a telephone call to fire headquarters elicited for the first time the cause of the fire as arson. McDermott was almost in heaven.

CHARLES H. HAMILTON

On January 21, 1960, *The News Leader* editorial page carried a 30-inch report of how its news department handled a major story several days earlier. The dramatic account, in which one telephone "crackled" and another "shrilled insistently," was by Charles Henry Hamilton, a staff member for 43 years and at that time the managing editor.

The incident about which he wrote was the crash near Richmond's main airport of a Capital Air Lines plane, killing 50 people. *The News Leader's* performance was indeed impressive—16 stories and 16 pictures together accounting for 21 columns. The staff of *The Times-Dispatch* thought it had done a pretty good job itself, since the crash occurred at 10:30 p.m. and the next morning's paper had six columns about the crash—a main story of about two columns, two brief sidebars, head shots of the crew and a six-column photograph of the wrecked plane.

But Hamilton's account in *The News Leader* went into great detail about telephone calls between reporters and editors and co-operation all around.

"And the editions rolled," he wrote. "On their toes, as they seem to be in every big emergency, every mechanical department turned in a bang-up job. Engravers, stereotypers, compositors, pressmen, circulation personnel—all ahead of the clock, all ahead of the job. The presses rolled 16 minutes early for the first edition.

". . . At the end, the managing editor got out a memo to all concerned. It said, 'Thanks to all for a magnificent job of teamwork. Our coverage ranks with the great jobs of the past' [which he recounted] . . .

"And that is all the staff wanted to know."

One reporter singled out in Hamilton's account, and amused with the credit he was given, was George Gill, who said in an interview that he was "half in the bag" late that night when he heard of the crash. Gill was at a farewell party. He was leaving *The News Leader* for a copy desk job at the *Louisville Courier-Journal*, where years later he became publisher.[160]

Wise guys in both Richmond newsrooms took delight in some of Hamilton's dramatic prose, but what produced howls of laughter was the start of one paragraph: "When the sun took a toe-hold in Tuesday's sky. . . "

Reporters were so impressed that at a Newspaper Guild party soon thereafter they devoted an entire skit to "He's got a toe-hold in the sky" to the tune of the gospel song, "He's Got the Whole World in His Hands."

Hamilton took pride in his writing and indeed did sell articles to *The Saturday Evening Post* and *Reader's Digest*. He was chairman of the writing committee of the Associated Press Managing Editors Association (APME). In one of his APME accounts, he told how instead of simply saying "it rained," it was more descriptive to write, "rain dimpled the dust."

From the founding of *The News Leader* in 1903 with the merger of The News and The Leader to its end in 1992 in the merger with *The Times-Dispatch*, *The News Leader* had a life of 89 years. Hamilton's 43-year stint meant he was there for almost half of the paper's life—or, if his five additional years as assistant to the president of Media General are counted, more than half its life. He was reporter, sports editor, city editor, managing editor.

His former colleagues' assessments of his performance in the last two posts vary widely. Some recalled him as pompous and removed from the individual reporters. Other said he was a fine editor and a diligent worker. Not surprisingly, the assessments often seem based on how enjoyable one's experience at the paper was.

Robert Hilldrup is one of the embittered former reporters. "I enjoyed being a newspaperman," he said, "but you couldn't be a newspaperman at *The News Leader*."[161]

Why?

"I think Charlie Hamilton as much as anything else."

Hilldrup said his lack of respect for Hamilton was universal among reporters, although he admits, "It's not that Charlie wasn't smart; it wasn't that Charlie didn't write some good stuff." Rather, said Hilldrup, it was his behavior in such instances as insisting the paper carry a long, "embarrassingly bad" account of "one of those boondoggle trips" to a Latin American nation.

Hilldrup, regarded as a chronic complainer by many of his former colleagues, said he should have known he was in the wrong place when, two months after he joined the paper in March 1960, he received a note from John E. Leard, city editor. It said, "C.H.H. has been bothered by stomach cramps for about 10 days. They're general but painful. A neighbor complained of the same thing starting the same day. . . . CHH wonders if by any chance chemicals put in the city water would get concentrated at all while spreading generally through the water supply. . . . Please check. . . Keep me posted."

Hilldrup, per instruction, got in touch with the city's director of public utilities, who, astounded by the question, told Hilldrup, "You go tell Charlie Hamilton the reason he's got stomach cramps is he's as full of shit as he's always been."

Several former *News Leader* staff members said Hamilton resisted digging into possible racial prejudice in the area. John M. Lee, the former business editor who became an assistant managing editor of the *New York Times*, said Hamiliton "wasn't interested in accelerating integration in public life in Virginia." He had a hangup, said Lee, on the term "freedom riders," preferring, "so-called freedom riders."[162]

Hilldrup wanted to check into "block-busting" in neighborhoods that

Charles Henry Hamilton spent 44 years with Richmond newspapers, most of them with The News Leader, *where he was sports editor, city editor and managing editor.*

were turning from white to black. Real estate records were public, and Hilldrup asked Hamilton about pursuing the story, he said, only to be told, "We don't report this thing. You're making the news."

Hilldrup approached Robert J. Grey, head of the Urban League in Richmond, about the situation. He said he and Grey agreed that neither would want to live in a certain poor neighborhood.

Grey's comment, as Hilldrup recalled, was, "If the only place I can find decent housing, if I have to live next to a white person to find it, I'll just have to put up with it."

Hamilton killed the story, said Hilldrup, as he did proposed stories on grocery chains that reportedly had different prices in white and black neighborhoods and on whether some automobile inspection stations were cheating motorists.[163]

The Hamilton response invariably, according to Hilldrup, was that *The News Leader* was to report news, not make it.

Unlike Hilldrup, Guy Friddell found *The News Leader* "a great place to work. All those people. It was like coming to a picnic every morning. Hang up your coat and meet your deadline. Everybody hollering and laughing. The place, from the first time you got [there], was all action. Seven thirty was already close to 10:20," the first copy deadline.[164]

Friddell found Hamilton "sort of magisterial. I don't mean that he wasn't a good managing editor. . . . He wasn't hands-on, but he was aware of what was going on. He was quick to make a correction. He would do it in a half-sarcastic, half-humorous way that made you remember."

Hamilton wanted a "bright," a light piece of several paragraphs, on the front page every day. Friddell satisfied him once by writing of "a passerby" who emptied a water pistol in the face of a "freckled-face kid" on a bus who had a water pistol himself and challenged a man on the sidewalk to "stick 'em up, Mister." Passerby Friddell responded with a weapon he'd bought for his son.

Larry Gould, who succeeded Hamilton as managing editor and worked under him in lesser positions, said Hamilton "tended to be grumpy from time to time. He was very stern. He didn't take any foolishness or anything like that."[165]

Gene Miller, who wrote mostly features or real estate stories for *The News Leader* in his three years on the staff, recalled Hamilton as "a horse's ass," who once trimmed to "a few grafs" a story about a Boulevard Bridge guard firing at a car whose occupant failed to pay his toll. Miller and another reporter, John Connors, had written a colorful story, but, said Miller, Hamilton "questioned our news judgment" and whacked the story down. The bridge was owned by the Bryan family, one of whose members was the publisher of *The News Leader*.[166]

Jack Kilpatrick, whom Hamilton classified as the best reporter he ever had, was full of praise for Hamilton in an interview. "It was Ham," said Kilpatrick, "who corrected me or made suggestions to me when I was writing these long, long sentences." Hamilton referred the young reporter to periods.

"They're down there at the bottom of your typewriter," said Hamilton, then city editor. "Join right on in. There's a key that I have a feeling you can make good use of any time."

Continuing, Kilpatrick said, "I never found him difficult to work with at all. Well, except when he would come over with a little clipping of some kind in his hand that he thought might spark a light story, and he'd put his hand on my shoulder as I'm hunched over the typewriter and say, 'Here, be funny, Kilpatrick.' The worst instruction I ever received.

"Oh, no. I dearly loved Ham. He was a great teacher. I don't know how he ranks up there in the annals as a managing editor, but I expect pretty good in terms of meeting his budget and keeping costs controlled. Like other great teachers, though, he himself was not a particularly gifted writer."[167]

The methods Hamilton employed to meet the newsroom budget were one thing that irked Carl Shires, a veteran police reporter and later political reporter. Once, said Shires, when he had been without lunch on a cold winter day, he paid a boy 50 cents to fetch something for him while he was reporting on a car with three occupants that had gone through an open drawbridge.

"Charlie Hamilton called me in," said Shires, "and gave me a reaming because I had put 50 cents on the expense account." The same thing occurred, he said, when after working overtime on a story, he went "to what was considered the best restaurant in Baltimore with a couple of other reporters and put down dinner: $8. He gave me hell."[168]

Both Richmond dailies had automobiles equipped with police radios and telephones for use by their police reporters. But Shires contended that *The News Leader's* police reporter was lucky to get it one day a week, since even the women's news reporters seemed to have higher priority.

After covering an explosion on one particularly hot day and walking back to the newspaper, Shires said he went straight to the fourth floor and into the office of Alan S. Donnahoe, executive vice president. "Do you realize that the police reporter on this paper doesn't have a vehicle?" he asked Donnahoe. "I'm supposed to go to every crime, every accident, every fire and I have to call a cab or bum a ride with a cop or a fireman. I said, 'Do you realize that?' He said, 'That will be corrected in less than a week. The police reporter on *The News Leader* will have a car.' And the next afternoon, Charlie

Hamilton called a staff meeting. And he said, 'I have been arguing with the fourth floor for months that we needed another vehicle, and I want you to know that they finally acceded to my demands and there will be a vehicle. It's on order for the police reporter."

When Donnahoe a short time later asked Shires about the car, Shires recounted the word at the staff meeting. "He said, 'That Charlie Hamilton's something, isn't he?' That's all was said."

Hamilton, like John Colburn, his counterpart on *The Times-Dispatch* in the 1950s, made a major production of presenting the Christmas bonus checks—usually about a week's salary—to staff members.

Once during that period, Shires recalled, *The News Leader* had been waiting a long time for a new reporter. The paper was understaffed, but Hamilton assured everyone that things would improve when one Scott Waffle arrived. Waffle, however, was seriously injured in an automobile accident and his arrival was delayed. Finally, he joined the staff, but "became disenchanted" and left after a few months.

When Christmas bonus time arrived, Shires said, Hamilton assembled the staff, handed out envelopes and came to one with Waffle's name on it. He said, "This guy didn't have the courtesy to come by my office" before leaving. So Hamilton tore up the check.

"I stewed about it a long time and went into Hamilton's office and told him he was a cheap son of a bitch," said Shires, wondering why Hamilton didn't fire him.

"And I sent Waffle a check myself."[169]

Sylvia Costen, longtime women's news editor, thought that Hamilton cared much more about sports than about her department. And, she said, "He was a very economical person; he didn't like to spend money." She said Hamilton gave a talk to the Associated Press managing editors entitled "Women Are Just No Damn Good." She was convinced he was "totally serious."[170]

On the other hand, she never forgot his standing by her on a story that she chose to run over his objection. It concerned a man who became so distraught when the grocery chain for which he worked began pre-packaging meat that he went to a psychiatrist. Costen questioned the reporter and the psychiatrist. Still a bit concerned, she showed the story to Hamilton, then city editor. He said, "I wouldn't touch it with a 10-foot pole," she recalled. Yet, she thought, "What the heck. He's just a city editor. He's not my boss. I don't work for him."

She ran the story. Lawyers for the chain threatened a suit. Then Bill Christian, the managing editor, died of a heart attack. The lawyers came to the office to see Hamilton, who succeeded Christian. And the man who had spurned the story stood by Costen, defending the story in its entirety. There was no lawsuit.

Conventional wisdom about what journalists should and should not do changes over the years. In an interview, Hamilton spelled out his ideas, some of which differed from convention and some of which changed over the decades.[171]

One that didn't change was what makes a good reporter, who "may not be the noblest work of God, but he is certainly one of the rarest." Hamilton singled out Jack Kilpatrick, Roy Flannagan and Bill Foster.

To the good reporter, said Hamilton, you "explain the story that you want; here are the things that you want to cover. And then you can just forget it because it's going to be covered; everything will be complete; there'd be no unanswered questions in the story."

Hamilton, or *The News Leader* under Hamilton, permitted certain practices that other papers, including *The Times-Dispatch* would not. When the first regional shopping center in the area opened, Bill Bien, *The News Leader's* business editor (a reporter not admired by his compatriots) wrote not only news stories about the development but also—with his bylines and picture—an advertising flyer put out by the shopping center.

Some papers are picky about what editorials, if any, reporters can write. Many reporters cringe at the thought of expressing opinions, even anonymously in editorials, on controversial matters they cover.

Hamilton saw no problem with a reporter doing straight news stories and editorials on the same subject. "I don't see why not," he said. "He's got more intimate knowledge of it than anybody else. The question is the content. If he's out there to try to get somebody, I don't think that would be approved, but if he has knowledge nobody else has got, I don't see why not use it."

Yet, Hamilton felt so passionately about separation of news and editorial operations that for years when he was city editor he did not vote.

Many editors shy away from holding office in any organization that might make news. But Hamilton was proud of the eight years he spent—some of the time as chairman—on the Federal Home Loan Bank Board based in Greensboro, North Carolina. He said the board made little news, but he was worried that someone might bring up the fact that Donnahoe—"Brother Donnahoe," Hamilton called him in an interview—was on the board of Security Federal Savings and Loan Association and of the predecessor of Crestar Bank.

"I was scared to death. . . that was going to come up," said Hamilton, pointing to a regulation prohibiting membership on boards of an S&L and a competing commercial bank.

Had the matter come up, he said, "as chairman of the board, I guess I would have had to act on it, which would have been bad, but he would have acted on me right after that." (Donnahoe said there was no problem because he was "grandfathered" in both spots when the legislation was approved.)[172]

Hamilton did end up in the news—and on Page One—in 1959 when he, the bureau chief of the Associated Press and an ad department executive were charged with illegally baiting ducks. Some old staff members said Hamilton was happy when the city manager and others had been charged in a similar, earlier incident. They were gleeful when the same thing happened to Hamilton, and the arrest was the subject of another skit at the 1960 Newspaper Guild party. Opinions differ on how Hamilton felt the story should be played, but he takes credit for its being on the front.

"I was directing it," he said. "I was the managing editor."

Early in his *News Leader* career, Hamilton also did radio work. He was at a track meet as a sports writer in 1927, when a radio man heard his voice, liked it and suggested he become an announcer. Hamilton said he handled football play-by-play, the local opera and even the first airplane carrying mail to Richmond.

From 1927 to 1934, he worked for Station WRVA. "It suddenly dawned on me that I was working both sides of the street," he said. Given his choice, he opted for newspapering.

Like most editors and reporters, Hamilton thought his paper was superior to its competitor. "We never had much use for each other, and you know *The Times-Dispatch* thought *The News Leader* was stodgy and not alert and a lot of stuff like that," he said. "But we thought that they sat on their butts and that we printed 90 percent of the fresh news that there was to be gotten, and we just relished the idea of even competing against them."

Hamilton gloried in the days before the merger of the two papers in 1940. Counting replates, Hamilton said the Leader had 11 editions. It had a football extra Saturday nights. With the move of *The Times-Dispatch* to *The News Leader* building at Fourth and Grace streets, he said, Publisher John Stewart Bryan told the *News Leader* staff, "If there's any question as to who gets first choice on anything, give it to your guest. I want you to try and make them feel at home because it's not going to be easy in any way that you look at it."

Editor Douglas Southall Freeman said, Hamilton recalled, "The day of *The News Leader* is over."

The day of neither paper was over, and the news staffs fought as if they were in different buildings with different owners. Hamilton's impressions of how *Times-Dispatch* and *News Leader* personnel felt about each other is epitomized in his own assessment of John Colburn, *The Times-Dispatch's* determined managing editor.

"Oh, I liked him," said Hamilton. "And we went on trips together to the APME and did that kind of stuff. He was the driver. I never thought he was much of a newspaperman, if you want to know the truth of it."[173]

JOHN H. COLBURN

In May 1949, Ben B. Johnston, the easy-going, beloved managing editor of *The Times-Dispatch*, who had taken over after Leon Dure's leaving, went around the newsroom with a younger man, whom he introduced to reporters as "my replacement."

The younger man was John H. Colburn, 37, a veteran of the Associated Press—first as reporter, later as foreign correspondent, then as an AP executive. In that last post, he had visited Richmond's daily newspapers.

Colburn was a native of Columbus, Ohio, and had studied at Ohio State University there. He knew little about Virginia, but Paul Saunier, a former *Times-Dispatch* reporter and inveterate student of newspapers, thinks Colburn did know that lots of fine race horses were raised in Virginia.[174]

That, in any case, is how Saunier figures Colburn decided on the front page of May 8, 1949, when he had been at *The Times-Dispatch* scarcely a week.

Ponder, Paying $34, Wins 75th Kentucky Derby;

Capot Is Second, Palestinian Third Before 90,000

That headline, stretching across eight columns, was what confronted Sunday readers of *The Times-Dispatch*, which in a most un-Virginian departure from tradition, led with the Derby.

Saunier recalls Chester G. McCalley, a veteran of the copy desk, saying, "People been calling in saying, 'I didn't get my paper; I only got my sports section.'"

Colburn, who stayed 14 years before becoming editor and publisher of the *Wichita* (Kansas) *Eagle & Beacon*, was a workhorse. He often put in 12 hours a day, ordering stories, diagramming the front page, going home for dinner and returning to edit galley proofs and, sometimes, remaking the front page.

John H. Colburn, managing editor of The Times-Dispatch *for 14 years.*

He delegated little authority to his subordinate editors, some of whom felt they couldn't assign long-range stories without Colburn's OK. He was curt and often abrasive. But he was fair, complimenting a reporter today whom he had unmercifully criticized yesterday.

B. Drummond Ayres Jr., who stayed at *The Times-Dispatch* from 1959 through 1962 before departing for Columbia University's Graduate School of Journalism, recalls Colburn with awe. "He's dead and gone, God bless his soul, and I'm still scared of him," said Ayres 30 years after he left the paper.[175]

Ayres moved to the *Washington Post* and then to *The New York Times*, where he has been a reporter more than a quarter-century. "One thing you were always aware of on *The Times-Dispatch*," said Ayres, "was that it was an upholder of journalism standards." The paper, Ayres continued, "was very, very strong on fairness, accuracy and professional ability. Colburn insisted on constantly trying to get the writing. . . stronger on the paper. And you came out of here very, very well grounded."

William G. Leverty, who as news editor and later assistant managing editor was the No. 2 man in the newsroom, sneered at Colburn behind his back and called him "Blue Eyes." So did others. Many thought Leverty was intimidated by Colburn. He'd been around a lot longer than Colburn and had a great sense of what was news. Yet, if a late-evening development necessitated a change in Page One, Leverty routinely telephoned Colburn at home.

Newspaper reporters, no less than other people, second-guess their bosses away from the office. Nothing could have been further from the office than the annual party put on by the Newspaper Guild, the reporters' union, the winter of 1960.

There was the inevitable parody of the newsroom. Ed Grimsley, then City Hall reporter and later editorial page editor, portrayed Colburn. A team of *Times-Dispatch* reporters, with Charles McDowell in the lead, worked up a version of the song "Blue Skies," which became "Blue Eyes," a natural for spearing Colburn.

One line went, "Missed the Nixon story, flubbed the Suez, played the Russian Sputnik under his fez."

That was intended to show that Colburn's news judgment was severely flawed in handling the Nixon "slush fund" of the 1952 presidential campaign, the Israeli advance against Egypt in 1956 and the Soviets' launching of the first unmanned satellite in 1957.

How bad was his judgment?

The first Nixon fund story in *The Times-Dispatch*, Friday, September 19, was under a one-column head on Page 18. But by the next day, there were two stories about the fund on the front page. By comparison, *The New York Times* saw it as a better story that Friday, but still relegated it to a two-column headline on the front. (*The New York Post* had broken the story.) By Saturday, *The Times* also gave the story bigger play—three stories on the front page.

As for the Suez story, *The New York Times* devoted it more space, but *The Times-Dispatch* gave it major attention, too. That occurred, moreover, at the same time as the Soviet Union said it would remove troops from Budapest and as the U.S. presidential race neared its end.

On October 29, *The Times-Dispatch* said under five-column heads:

Russians to Leave Budapest;
Israel Mobilizes Its Reserves

The Times' front page used a three-column banner headline on the Hungarian situation. It used only a two-column head on the Mideast:

Israel Mobilizes Reserves;
Gets Eisenhower Warning

The next day, Israel's advance into Egypt merited banner headlines in both papers, and for days the situation was the most important story in Richmond as well as New York.

About the same time, *The Times-Dispatch* did give major play (more than perhaps any other paper) to a political story with local flavor. T. Coleman Andrews, a Richmonder who had been Eisenhower's first commissioner of internal revenue but who had become disenchanted with the Republicans, sought the presidency himself on the States' Rights ticket.

Thus, *The Times-Dispatch* of October 16, proclaimed in a four-column, front-page headline:

Andrews Accepts Draft,
Notes Socialistic Trend

There was more merit in the criticism of Colburn for his play of the Sputnik. After several calls at home from the copy desk, Colburn still wanted to lead the paper with a story from Frank van der Linden, a part-time Washington correspondent with deep conservative instincts. So, under a three-column headline:

Byrd Criticizes
Army Secrecy
On Riot Order

the Sputnik was relegated to a two-column, "off-lead" position and a secondary feature on its passing over the United States.

The New York Times, by contrast, went all out. Its banner headline:

SOVIET FIRES EARTH SATELLITE INTO SPACE;
IT IS CIRCLING THE GLOBE AT 18,000 M.P.H.;
SPHERE TRACKED IN 4 CROSSINGS OVER U.S.

"Shorty" Powers, the public information officer at Langley Air Force Base, where the astronauts were stationed, was asked for his reaction. "I don't know," he said. "We're all asleep here."

By the next day, Sunday, *The Times-Dispatch* was devoting the top half of its front page to the satellite. Newsroom cynics said Colburn spent the next several months trying to atone for his poor judgment on Sputnik. It seemed that every mention of satellites merited the front page.

Perhaps the performers at the Guild party ran out of verses, but there was no mention of another questionable call by Colburn. The paper of Sunday, June 25, 1950, had a front-page story on the biggest international development of the day. The headline said:

South Korea

Is Invaded

From North

and the story went on, "The North Korean Communist regime declared war early today on the American-sponsored Republic of South Korea."

But that headline covered only one column and the story ran less than a column long.

By Monday, there were banner headlines and lots of copy. The editorial page commented, "It remains to see what the next stop will be. The dangers in the situation are obvious, but they need not lead to another World War. We must keep our heads." Two days later the editorial page endorsed President Truman's ordering ships and planes into action.

ALF GOODYKOONTZ

At the end of 1993, the second executive editor in Richmond Newspapers' history—Alf Goodykoontz—retired, closing a career of more than 41 years with the papers.

Although he had put on weight and his hair had turned gray, he looked a bit like that raw-boned 23-year-old from Radford in Southwest Virginia who came to the paper in late 1952. The reason was his crew cut. Several weeks earlier, as more than 200 looked on, Goody was roasted at a dinner at the Commonwealth Club. During the ceremony that featured six speakers, he sat on stage while a barber trimmed his hair to the way it looked in 1952.

From his high school days, Charles Alfred Goodykoontz had wanted to be a newspaperman. He had gone to Emory and Henry College, a small, Methodist institution, for two years and had dropped out to work full time on the Radford paper. There he met Ed Swain, who by 1952 had joined *The Times-Dispatch* and had gotten the paper and Goodykoontz together. Swain later was the paper's city editor.

In the next 41 years, Goodykoontz climbed the summit, not only locally but also nationally. He was active in Sigma Delta Chi, the honorary organization that changed its name to Society of Professional Journalists. He became its president in 1977.

At *The Times-Dispatch*, he was reporter, assistant state editor, state-city news editor, women's news editor, special projects editor and, in 1969, managing editor. He held that post more than 12 years before going upstairs as executive editor.

Goodykoontz was not without reportorial experience, but he made his mark as an editor. He worked hard and long, and he was good at management. He was determined to keep anything approaching opinion out of the news columns, and he put great emphasis on newsroom ethics.

Goodykoontz was a John Leard protege, although Leard came from "across the hall" at *The News Leader* in 1963 to become the *Times-Dispatch* managing editor.

Goodykoontz recalled that "I went in to see John one day to complain about something, and he said, 'Goody, quit your griping; I've got some news for you. I'm moving upstairs, and you're becoming managing editor on January 1.'"[176]

Thanks to Leard, Goodykoontz rose on the ladder at Richmond Newspapers—despite leaving *The Times-Dispatch* (for all of three weeks) in 1963 and despite an explosive temper.

His brief departure was to Rock Hill, South Carolina. "I had in the back of my mind that what I really wanted to do was to run a small-town newspaper," he said. "I'd grown up in a small town and thought that was where I really wanted to spend my life and career. But it turned out that wasn't so." Goodykoontz won't go into detail, but apparently he and the publisher disagreed on who was to decide what was news.

So, Goody called home. His wife, Jean, got in touch with Leard, who said, "Come on back. We'll find a spot for him," Goodykoontz recalled.[177]

The temper was something else. Staff members knew that when Goodykoontz' lips drew together in a straight line and the back of his neck began to redden, the air might be shattered by a voice bellowing outrage, likely peppered with profanity.

The outburst might occur at a meeting of editors or at the edge of the copy desk. Once, Leard, Goodykoontz and the state and city editors of *The Times-Dispatch* met in Goodykoontz's office to discuss pictures taken by a Richmond Newspapers photographer of the Chesapeake Bay Bridge, which had been struck by a ship.

The long-standing rules were that on a spot news story, the next paper to publish got first crack at pictures, unless one paper had made a specific assignment. Goodykoontz knew that *The Times-Dispatch* had assigned a photographer to the accident before *The News Leader* and, therefore, should get all of the shots from that photographer.

But Leard decided the pictures should go to *The News Leader*, since it was the next paper to publish.

Goodykoontz was so angry that he was quivering. The facial expressions common in such instances appeared. He stood up, screamed at Leard, ordered him to perform an anatomically impossible act and stalked out of the office, telling State Editor Tom Howard and the author, then city editor, to follow him. They did not.

Goodykoontz was asked in an interview years later about his "legendary" temper.[178]

Alf Goodykoontz started with The Times-Dispatch *in 1952 and retired as executive editor of both papers in 1993.*

John E. Leard joined The News Leader *in 1938 and became its city editor before going "across the hall" as* The Times-Dispatch *managing editor. He retired as executive editor of both papers.*

"It may be legendary," he said, laughing. "I think it's been vastly overstated. I guess I maybe lost it two or three times in the past 10 years, but when I came to the fourth floor, Stewart Bryan said 'You can't afford to lose your temper up here.'. . . I've done pretty well. But my good friend Bill Millsaps told me one time, 'Don't lose all your red neck.' When those veins in the neck start popping out, he said people know to pay attention. I promise you: it was never done for effect."

Goodykoontz doesn't talk a lot about it, but he probably had more than anyone else to do with tightening *Times-Dispatch* policy on ethics. Traditionally, standards were high on fairness in presenting the news, honesty with sources and accuracy in expense accounts. But for many years, there were free tickets to ball games, circuses and concerts. Goodykoontz ended that.

Someone reviewing a concert or covering a basketball tournament still got a press pass, but the days of "freebies" being passed around the office ended. "I think a lot of that coincided with my involvement with the Society of Professional Journalists," Goodykoontz said.[179]

When a movie theater operator objected to a review and noted that the reviewer had a free ticket, Goodykoontz said that the reviewer from then on would pay her own way. The days of reporters who covered professional baseball getting extra pay from the league for being official scorers also ended. Christmas presents from sources were discouraged, although small presents were not outlawed.

Unlike many papers, *The Times-Dispatch* forbade its reporters to take free trips and write travel stories. Expenses involved in covering political campaigns were paid by the paper. (News department employees made no secret of their disapproval of editorial writers taking expense-paid trips to Taiwan, Israel and elsewhere.)

Goodykoontz and Leard, his predecessor as *Times-Dispatch* managing editor and as executive editor of both Richmond dailies, say that tightening standards of conduct was an evolving process, not an edict decreed overnight. Leard thinks that studies by the Associated Press Managing Editors had something to do with it.

In any case, by 1972, when Leard was on the fourth floor and Goodykoontz was managing editor of *The Times-Dispatch*, news department policies of all Media General papers—those in Richmond plus the two in Tampa and the one in Winston-Salem—were laid out in a thick notebook.

There was no intent to impose Tampa's policies on Richmond or Richmond's on Winston-Salem—only to let everyone see what the other guy was doing. In general, the policies of both papers would have to be considered strict, although *The Times-Dispatch* was in some cases even stricter than *The News Leader*.

The Times-Dispatch accepted free tickets for press coverage only, whereas *The News Leader* accepted "a small number of complimentary tickets. . . to some events, like football games, primarily so the man covering can take his family with him."

There was divergence also on how to cover industrial development. *The Times-Dispatch* said, "On major new plants, we try to publish ahead of formal announcement if we are sure of our facts. Industrial development people claim premature publication hurts industry, but we know of no instances in which publication of a story has adversely affected industry's location in the state."

The News Leader said sometimes rumors were so prominent that secrecy is "obviously voided." But, generally, it said, "We try not to make premature plant announcements if they might queer the deal."

Those were the days of "women's pages," and Richmond's dailies had at least one small difference in coverage. *The News Leader* said, "Brand names are not used; store names are not used, [but] store names are used when it is important to the story."

On the other hand, *The Times-Dispatch* reported, "Brand names are used on a limited basis; we generally use store names rather than saying a downtown department store."

There was no problem there 20 years later, for there was no such thing as "a downtown department store."

Goodykoontz took pride in improving sections on both papers, such as the tabloid business section on *The News Leader* that was carried over to the new *Times-Dispatch* and expanded sections on food and entertainment. He was deeply involved in improving consumer reporting and in expanding television logs.

He insisted on digging on major stories such as the Kepone pesticide in the James River, but "I don't think I've ever told anyone how to cover a story."[180]

The further away a newspaperman gets from covering a beat, the more removed he is from the news operation. "I think that even when I was managing editor," he said, "I had become more of an administrator than an editor, and it's certainly true now [as executive editor]."

Did he miss being in close touch with breaking news?

"I think the biggest satisfaction in our business," he said, "is the good story. There is no excitement like working on a major weather story, or hurricane, or snow storm or something that gets all the juices flowing and everybody involved in the operation. Election night's the same way."[181]

After 41 years with *The Times-Dispatch*, Goodykoontz wrote a farewell column several days before his retirement that contained large amounts of standard corporate confidence: "the new information highway," "outstanding leadership," "more female and African-American staffers mov[ing] into roles of ever-increasing importance."[182]

But the column also laid out where he thought *The Times-Dispatch's* emphasis should be. "The daily newspaper, in our community and throughout the nation, remains the dominant LOCAL news and advertising medium despite all the broadsides hurled against it over the years.

"Our franchise is LOCAL NEWS, and if we pay close attention to it, we're going to have a long and productive future."

THE COLOR BARRIER

In October 1969, fresh out of North Carolina A&T College and with no newspaper background, Al Johnson was hired as a general assignment reporter by *The News Leader.*

Other blacks' bylines had graced the pages of *The News Leader* and *The Times-Dispatch* over the years, but Johnson was the first African-American to become a full-fledged reporter on either paper—with all the rights, privileges and hangups pertaining thereto.

Johnson stayed eight years before moving to the *Charlotte Observer*, where he became assistant to the editor; then to Gary, Indiana, and the *Columbus* (Georgia) *Ledger-Inquirer*, at both of which places he became executive editor.

If he had any troubles breaking the color barrier at *The News Leader*, he doesn't recall them. "Maybe it's good I was so young," he said. He started out, as do most green reporters, on general assignment, then went to "that old urban affairs thing [a newspaper term for black affairs]" and later to state government and city hall.

How was his reception? Twenty-five years later, he can say, "It was pretty warm. I did not feel uncomfortable. I did not feel my life was more uncomfortable [than white colleagues] as a reporter. I was supported and nurtured."[183]

At *The Times-Dispatch*, Managing Editor Alf Goodykoontz told the author one morning in 1971, "You've got a new reporter. Mr. Bryan hired him."

"Mr. Bryan" was D. Tennant Bryan, the publisher, who was not in the habit of hiring reporters or even junior editors. The "new reporter" was Sid Cassese, a tall, smiling, black man with an Afro hairdo, prominent teeth and a ready smile, who was serving time for armed robbery.

Cassese was on work release and had heard that Bryan was the sponsor of a prison play. The computer printout training program in which Cassese was enrolled ended when the firm moved to Chicago; so, at the suggestion of a man who had helped produce the prison play, Cassese asked Bryan for a job.[184]

They talked and Cassese took a 50-word spelling test at *The News Leader*. "But they already had a black reporter, so I came to the T-D," he said.[185]

Cassese had a nose for news and a good vocabulary, although it was loaded with sociological jargon. He, too, started on general assignment. He covered some "social services" stories, other stories at City Hall, features and, "if it was black, I covered it." But that wasn't necessarily bad, he said later.

After a couple of years, he told the author, "I don't want to be your BLACK reporter." Meanwhile, he made sure he met the governor. That wasn't difficult, for the paper was happy for Cassese to accompany any reporter on a beat.

Each day after pursuing whatever story he was on, Cassese was driven back to the lockup by a reporter (generally Larry Hilliard). Suddenly, that ended. Linwood Holton, the governor whom Cassese had been careful to meet, responded to pleas from *Times-Dispatch* editors and others and pardoned Cassese.

As for *The Times-Dispatch* years, they were "a great learning experience," said Cassese. "I got lots of support. And, of course, some people [unnamed] never spoke to me the whole time I was there. But if it hadn't been for the newspaper people, I'd never have gotten my pardon."[186]

Cassese was the subject of a *Time* magazine article when he was still on work release. After the pardon, he left Richmond for a reporting job on *Newsday* on Long Island and a stint as a Nieman Fellow at Harvard.

For several years later, his was still a familiar face in the newsroom in Richmond as he stopped off as a special correspondent to review the Hampton Jazz Festival.

Some of those earlier blacks who earned bylines in *The Times-Dispatch* wrote for a "colored" section that appeared weekly in the 1930s. Much of the work was done by Roscoe C. Mitchell, whose son, Thomas, was later a special *Times-Dispatch* correspondent for athletic events involving black schools and colleges.

That early section was often referred to as the "Jackson Ward Edition," because a heavy concentration of blacks in the city lived in Jackson Ward. It was the subject of considerable comment from blacks and whites. One Theodore W. Jones, in a letter to the editor January 29, 1935, said, "[T]he new page for colored people edited by colored people receiving compensation for their services, will more than double or treble the circulation of the paper among colored readers."

He added, "Ten years ago *The Times-Dispatch's* new deal for the Negro would have astounded the country." Jones was sure that from the new section, "you will learn that weak as the Negro race is, weakest of the five races of mankind save one, yet it has many elements of strength, and that it has contributed a part in the making of American history."

Decades after the section ended, both local dailies still segregated classified advertising death notices by race and declined to run black women's engagement and wedding pictures although they ran those of virtually all white women in their circulation area. Those practices didn't end until the 1965.

Bonnie Winston, who joined *The Times-Dispatch* in 1979, is convinced she became the first full-time black on the paper, since Cassese was classified an intern. In any case, she was an immediate hit.

Winston was from an old Richmond family, the daughter of a physician who had died early. While she was a student at Northwestern University, she had been a summer intern. Her hiring came not long after graduation.

During her seven years as a reporter, she became the first woman to work the 5:30 p.m.-2:30 a.m. night police beat two days a week. She also did outstanding stories on migrant workers and a combination of stories on how one family lived in a public housing project.

For that assignment, she recalled several years later almost in embarrassment, she searched the department stores successfully for pajamas with feet in them because she didn't want to walk on what she was sure were roach-infested floors.

"I don't remember seeing any roaches while I was there," she said, "but I remember being awakened one night by gunshot and that really frightened me."[187]

On the police beat, Winston brought out an element that, until then, was too seldom reported: the way of life of poor, decent people in crime-infested neighborhoods. On a hot, summer night in a black neighborhood where a resident had been gunned down, Winston faced a situation that had confronted police reporters over the years: a street crowded with people, none of whom knew anything about the shooting.

After all the adults walked away from this young woman with a notebook and a walkie-talkie, a girl about 6 said of the shooting, "I heard it." The privileged college graduate couldn't believe that someone that young could identify gunfire. "I can't readily identify if something I've heard is a gun or a car backfiring," she said.

"And I remember thinking, 'My God, children are growing up like this. Is this really what people want their children exposed to?' I don't know. It was just very, very sad."

Meanwhile, back in the newsroom, it was Winston's idea to present a "gorilla-gram" to Publisher Tennant Bryan on his 75th birthday. Senior editors did not think that was the urbane Mr. Bryan's cup of tea, but Winston would not be dissuaded. When someone dressed like a gorilla showed up with a birthday message that Monday morning, she and Ed Briggs, the religion writer, accompanied him to Bryan's fourth-floor office.

Executive Editor John Leard was on hand with a camera; by contrast, Managing Editor Alf Goodykoontz was so outraged by the idea that he had told subordinates to talk Winston out of the idea. After the event, Bryan wrote a note thanking the participants in the presentation. "I remember thinking 'Goody is so stuffy,'" Winston said.

Winston left *The Times-Dispatch* early in 1986 for the *Boston Globe*, switched to the *Norfolk Virginian-Pilot* after several years and rejoined *The Times-Dispatch* in 1994 as an assistant city editor.

From the start, Winston had no trouble fitting in at *The Times-Dispatch*, but she couldn't understand remarks from women in the Lifestyles department who would say something like "Oh, you're so bright," as if she weren't supposed to be. Then there was the remark at a staff meeting that more coverage of the black community was needed. It was phrased this way: "We need to cover the prisons and [public housing] projects more."

To a cityside colleague who seriously worried that Winston might "feel funny" coming to work each day and seeing "all these white faces all the time," Winston replied disarmingly, "Well, I think of all of you as my friends."

For newspaper executives who complain about the dearth of qualified black reporters, Winston cautions not to concentrate on visits to majority-black campuses where there is insufficient training in journalism. Instead, she said, go to conferences where there already are practicing black journalists—"and aim for them."

In early 1995, there were 17 blacks among the 199 editors and reporters at *The Times-Dispatch*, according to Michael Paul Williams, a black columnist.[188]

SECTION E

• Sports / Entertainment / Photo

Sportswriters were often at City Stadium for football, track, auto racing and, here, the Police Boxing Show.

SPORTS

The sports department of a metropolitan newspaper is often derided by those in other divisions of the news operation as "the toy department." All they write about, say those on the national or metro staffs, are "men in short pants" or "people chasing a little ball."

Yet, outside of Walter Lippmann, what pundit of the middle or late 20th century was held in higher esteem than the *New York Times'* James Reston, who started out as a sports writer? When the old *New York Herald Tribune* wanted a colorful report from the National Democratic Convention in 1956, whom did it send but Red Smith, its renowned sports columnist.

On January 1, 1994, the man who moved to the executive editorship of *The Richmond Times-Dispatch* was its managing editor, Bill Millsaps, most of whose career had been in sports writing.

One of Millsaps' predecessors was Jimmy Jones, whose employment as sports editor in 1935 was deemed so important that the publisher, Mark Ethridge, wrote the by-lined story. Jones was hired from the *Atlanta Constitution.* Earlier, as sports editor of the *Macon Telegraph* he wrote a popular column. "His mail," wrote Ethridge, "was even heavier than the lovelorn columnist, indicating either that Jimmy had transcended in interest the boundaries usually prescribed for sports editors, or that the readers of the paper had no tangled love troubles."

At *The Times-Dispatch,* Jones was renowned for his writing ability and his forgetfulness. Max Ailor, who worked under him, recalled Chauncey Durden's telling him that Jones frequently forgot that he'd written his column. "He might have three columns over in the composing room at one time, and they'd have to call back, wanting to know which one he wanted to run."[189]

Durden, who became sports editor when Jones left in 1939 for the *Louisville Courier-Journal*—where by that time Ethridge had gone—told anecdotes about his predecessor when Jones died in 1977. By that time, Durden was sports editor emeritus of *The Times-Dispatch.*

Jones once left his press card in Richmond when he'd gone to New York to cover one of Mike Jacobs' boxing cards with three or four "championship" bouts. At one Army-Navy football game, when the weather in Philadelphia was zero and the press box was open to the weather, Jones stayed on manfully and filed his story even though he'd left his overcoat in Richmond.

Jones was a deadline-pusher, Durden recalled, and often would deliver his column by hand to Al Petzold, a printer. One night, with cigar clenched in his teeth, he headed for the composing room, reading his column as he went. To get there, he had to go through the Associated Press office, where months earlier a door had been shut off as the AP bureau was undergoing renovation.

He plunged into the wall, knocking his glasses askew and smashing his cigar. As fellow reporters roared, Jones returned quietly to his desk, saying only, "I would have sworn there was a door there."

Another time, Durden accompanied Jones to dinner at Pete Arrighi's restaurant, a favorite newspaper hangout. Jones ordered oyster stew and immediately became absorbed in a magazine he'd picked off a rack. Arrighi served the oyster stew, which Jones polished off without taking his eyes off the magazine.

When he finished the article, he asked, "What about my oyster stew, Pete?"

"But, Jimmy, you ate the oyster stew," said Arrighi.

"How could I," replied Jones, unconvinced. "I was reading."

Like other papers, *The Times-Dispatch* has a sports staff and a share of the "news hole" that, arguably, are out of proportion to the importance of sports to other events of the day. But the sports section is the one to which a sizable percentage of readers turns first.

One of the sins of many sports journalists has been "boosterism," the unapologetic promotion of hometown teams. Some aspects of boosterism include playing down or omitting unfavorable news of the home team and collaboration with sports promoters on plans for new arenas, stadiums or teams.

There have been many improvements in the last couple of decades in the behavior of sports journalists. No longer in Richmond and many other cities do reporters covering the professional baseball team also serve as official scorers and get extra pay. The longtime practice of teams' "papering the office" with "freebies" seems to have ended. The only people who routinely get free tickets are those writers reporting on the games.

Reflections of two former sports staff members for Richmond's dailies show how, almost 40 years after the Richmond's entry into the Inter-

Laurence Leonard (top) of The News Leader *and Chauncey Durden of* The Times-Dispatch *head off to another sports event.*

national League, they differ on the wisdom of their own participation in the episode.

Shelley Rolfe spent more than 20 years in the sports department of *The Times-Dispatch* as reporter and columnist before being wooed to the city staff in 1969. He retired in 1987. Laurence Leonard spent a year on *The Times-Dispatch* before going in the service in World War II and was sports editor of *The News Leader* from 1947 to 1968.

Richmond had been a member of the Class B Piedmont League in professional baseball for decades. But as the major leagues shifted franchises to different cities—such as the St. Louis Browns to Baltimore, where the team became the Orioles—openings appeared.

Richmond began agitating for a spot in the AAA International League, and as Leonard said, "Chauncey and I were in on it from the start." Chauncey Durden was then the sports editor of *The Times-Dispatch*.[190]

"Oh, we sat on a powder keg," said Leonard, "because Eddie Mooers [owner of the existing Class B Richmond Colts], once said to me, 'Hell, are you still sports editor? I thought you were real estate editor, trying to develop that franchise.' I mean he took it hard."

Principals included Harry Seibold, who had owned the Richmond Rebels professional football team; City Registrar Vernon Davis, Dr. Edward E. Haddock, who was Richmond's mayor, and others. The sports editors were cheerleaders, too. Leonard exaggerates when he says that sports writers, city editors and managing editors and others in the news business all played a part in getting the franchise.

Nevertheless, he says, "I think the corporation deserves a lot of credit for it."

Did he sit on stories he wished he could get in print?

"Sure, because we needed to get public support behind it."

Shelley Rolfe, who says he was "the secret link for bringing Triple A baseball here," looks at the situation differently. Before joining *The Times-Dispatch*, Rolfe had worked for the *Columbus* (Georgia) *Enquirer* and had known Bing Devine, then with the St. Louis Cardinal farm team there. Devine and Rolfe were at a minor league meeting in Baltimore, Rolfe recalls, where Frank Shaughnessy, president of the International League, said, "I've got to have Richmond and Norfolk in my league."[191]

Rolfe became an intermediary in various meetings, only one of which he reported on in *The Times-Dispatch*. In any case, says Rolfe, he is "ashamed now" of whatever role he played.

Leonard and Durden also covered what was probably the biggest athletic scandal in Virginia's history, and both of them, according to Leonard, sat on that story. At the College of William and Mary, the nation's second oldest institution of higher learning—where Leonard earlier had been sports information director for a year—it developed in 1951 that academic transcripts of various football and basketball players had been altered.

Rube McCray, the football coach, and Barney Wilson, the basketball coach, were immediately fired. There were reverberations across the state, demands for an end to athletic scholarships and the forced resignation of Dr. John Pomfret, president of the college. He left to head the Huntington Library in California.

Leonard broke the story on a Saturday afternoon and is still sorry he did. "I knew about this. Chauncey knew about it. We were sitting on it because it had been arranged that they [McCray and Wilson] were going to be let go at the end of the year. The integrity of the college would be maintained and the only reason we had to go with it. . . is because of some eager young reporter trying to prove himself at Newport News.

". . . I heard that was going on, so I went into Bill Christian [*News Leader* managing editor] and said, 'We're going to run this.' We did on the front page. It's a shame it worked out that way. It was all blown out of all proportion."

Leonard maintains that "some members of the board of trustees" and President Pomfret knew about the scandal but wanted to keep it under wraps until the end of the year.

"We were trying to save embarrassing a lot of good people down there," says Leonard, "maintain the good name of the college."[192]

Did Durden also know about the story and sit on it? "I would deny that," said Shelley Rolfe. "Chauncey had lots of faults as an administrator. He might hold a story for a day or so, but he wouldn't sit on something like that. . . . Chauncey was honest, and he made sure everyone in his department was."[193]

No contemporaneous sports editors could have been more dissimilar than Leonard and Durden.

Durden, was a graduate of the University of the South, where he majored in Latin. He was a voracious reader and an immaculate dresser. Leonard said, "I don't think there's been a better writer, from the standpoint of English grammar, anywhere, than Chauncey Durden—now and forever."

However fine a writer Durden was, he was no manager. Rolfe says that he was "terribly unorganized" and that the sports department schedule would be posted "by midnight Saturday for the following week."[194]

Max Ailor, who joined *The Times-Dispatch* in 1946 and covered everything from high school sports to wrestling to professional football and hunting and fishing, said Durden was "just lazy." As the youngest man in the department for a while, Ailor said he made up weekly schedules and helped answer Durden's mail. "He never answered letters," said Ailor.[195]

Ailor liked Durden and said he was "straight as could be." Ailor recalled a promoter who came to the sports department and turned in a program for a coming event. "Chauncey opened it up and there's $50 in there," said Ailor. "Chauncey grabbed the guy and threw him out before he could turn around."

Still, said Ailor, Durden let the sports department accept hams, turkeys and other food at Christmas from Bill Lewis, the wrestling promoter. The paper carried little about the results of wrestling matches, but it carried advance stories on them.

Ailor complained about the lack of serious coverage of the Rebels football team and won his point, but he said he almost lost his job. He also complained about the sports department covering professional wrestling. It ought to be in entertainment, said Ailor.

But, Durden replied, Ailor said, "Bill Lewis is a friend of this department and me. When I first came here, I couldn't find a place to live, and he let me move in with him. And as long as Bill Lewis is promoting wrestling, he'll find a place on the sports page."

Leonard turned out news stories and columns rapidly. Some of his columns, however, were little more than collections of names of people to whom he sent greetings. Leonard was ruddy, slightly overweight and not always careful in his choice of friends. When the University of Richmond played its home basketball games at the Richmond Arena, Leonard often sat not with other newsmen but with a small group of gamblers.

He also had a reputation as a skirt-chaser, which he disavows. "I could say I was a Lochinvar, but I never was," said Leonard. "I always admired the girls and women, and I liked to compliment those that I thought were attractive, but I never made myself a masher."[196]

That's not the way some others recall Leonard's activities. Ailor said that Charles Hamilton, Leonard's superior at *The News Leader*, was dispatched once to Lexington to check up on Leonard's behavior. Jennings Culley, Leonard's successor as sports editor, says the incident occurred before he joined the paper, but he'd always heard it involved Leonard's slapping a waitress.[197]

Hamilton returned and gave Leonard a clean bill of health.
Leonard's memory of the event was sketchy and he said the report was "probably exaggerated. . . . Hamilton may have come up to check up on me on some report that I was drunk, but I wasn't drunk."

Did he have any trouble with a waitress?

"Well, I don't know," he said, "but it wasn't anything major at all."[198]

Leonard has nothing but praise for the sports staff under him at *The News Leader*. "I've always been proud of the loyalty and effort of each of those individuals," he says. "There was no bickering, no jealousy, to my knowledge. We did work under duress sometimes, and maybe I was sort of tough. I didn't intend to be, but we had to save money."

Culley says, "His managerial style was one of intimidation." Yet, at the annual Christmas party, he says, Leonard was so kind to the reporters' wives that they couldn't understand their husbands' complaints.[199]

Andy McCutcheon was a *News Leader* sports reporter under Leonard from 1949 until he left in 1960 to work for Rep. J. Vaughan Gary. "Nobody could be nicer to me and my family—particularly since I left," said McCutcheon.

But, he added, "He was in lots of ways very difficult to work with, and I better leave it at that."[200]

McCutcheon and *The Times-Dispatch's* Shelley Rolfe both covered International League baseball when Havana had a franchise. Every time he went to Havana, Rolfe said, he had to bring back a six-pack of rum for Bill Leverty, the assistant managing editor, and others in the news room. When the availability of good, cheap rum became known, he said, he had so many orders that he persuaded baseball players to pack some in their bags for him to bring back.

Although Richmond Newspapers paid for the travel of its baseball writers, Rolfe recalls once when the league flew some reporters from Miami to Havana, where they stayed at the Cuba Libra Hotel. There were lots of East Europeans there, too. The aim of the trip was to assure North Americans that all was well for baseball in Castro's Cuba.

Havana did stay in the league for a part of the 1960 season, but then the franchise was moved. And that provided McCutcheon with what he still thinks may have been his best story. It was a column telling the feelings of a young Cuban baseball player who had to move his home to Jersey City because of international politics.

McCutcheon spent only 11 years with *The News Leader*, but he says he constantly tells young people that "the most gratifying job I ever had was in the newspapers. Because you come in every day and you write something, and you pick it up and look at it, and it may be good and it may be bad. But it's there, and you see it. And the next day you do it again."

Did he ever regret going into newspapering?

"Never," he said. "And I still believe it's the most satisfying work."[201]

THIS IS ENTERTAINMENT

Long before the "new" *Times-Dispatch* assembled a Flair section staff of about 35 and long before the "old" *Times-Dispatch* and *The News Leader* had sizable staffs of people who wrote about entertainment, Edith Lindeman and Alton Williams were writing about plays and films.

Williams, a professor of drama at the University of Richmond for 39 years, wrote for *The News Leader* from 1942 to 1974. For much of that time, he chose to write under the pseudonym of Will Whiteside—to distinguish himself from "Prof." Williams—although all of Richmond knew who Whiteside (his middle name) was.

Edith Lindeman Calisch wrote under her maiden name from 1933 to 1964. Like Williams, she covered both movies and plays. She also was a song-writer and collaborated with Carl Stutz of Richmond in composing "Little Things Mean a Lot," the top popular song of 1954.

There was nothing mean about either reviewer in person or in print. Unlike many of today's critics, Mrs. Calisch was harsher on foreign films than domestic fare. "There's an audience for every movie," she said. "I've tried to approach each movie with a fresh and open mind, looking for something that will appeal to someone. I think I always find it."[202]

The News Leader obituary on Williams on February 14, 1981, several days after his 77th birthday, said he was noted for his Christmas Day open houses at which "his signature drink" was a Tom and Jerry, "a steaming concoction of milk, water and bourbon."

Williams routinely wrote his reviews of plays immediately after the production. Anyone who ventured into *The News Leader* newsroom at that late hour could find Williams by the odor of bourbon or the heavy layer of cigarette smoke.

Mrs. Calisch and Williams made frequent trips to Hollywood in the old days when studios paid their way and later when the newspapers decided in the mid-1960s that wasn't proper and the papers paid for the trips.

Williams' wife, Mildred, was food editor of *The News Leader* from 1946 to 1976.

After Mrs. Calisch and Williams retired, reviewing often went to people with other assignments. Jon Longaker, art critic for *The Times-Dispatch*, also reviewed theater; but that became a problem at the Barksdale Theater, where his wife was involved with sets. Roy Proctor reviewed both films and plays for *The News Leader* until Daniel Neman took over films. At the new *Times-Dispatch*, Neman does films and Proctor does theater.

Carole Kass spent 28 years with *The Times-Dispatch*—starting as a general assignment reporter who, although quite green, filled in for specialists when they were on vacation. Later, she found her niche reviewing plays and finally—doing what she loved most—reviewing movies and interviewing actors.

Robert Merritt, a refugee from *The Times-Dispatch* sports department, where he covered stock-car racing, moved into amusements, where he wrote an art column, reviewed plays and became book columnist.

Society, with a capital S, figured prominently in Richmond's dailies for decades. The prominence, critics said, was far out of proportion to the number of readers involved or even interested. Each paper had a writer who chronicled the comings and goings of Richmond's—and to some extent, Virginia's—upper crust. On *The News Leader* over the years were Adelaide Rawles Goolsby, Maria Sheerin (wife of an Episcopal clergyman), Eleanor Knox and Charlotte Massie. On *The Times-Dispatch* there were Corbin Old, Bernard Nash, Frances Claiborne Guy and Louise Ellyson.

Each was appropriately connected socially and each worked out of her home and usually took her copy to the newsroom.

On *The Times-Dispatch*, Dorothy Robertson probably drew more letters than any other member of the women's news department, but not because of her column on food. For 25 years, ending in 1963, Mrs. Robertson wrote advice to the lovelorn under the pseudonym of Betty Bly.

A highlight of her career came in 1941 when several University of Richmond students formed a Society for the Prevention of Betty Bly and picketed the newspaper building because of her advice on good-night kisses. A questioner had asked, "How many dates should a boy and girl have before they kiss?" Betty Bly didn't give a specific number but warned against letting kisses become so routine that they are "no more fun."

Continuing to provide her anonymity, a two-column long story at her retirement did not identify her.

In the 1920s, '30s and '40s multi-column photographs of socially prominent people at parties were spread across pages. Debutante parties were covered extensively, as were vacations (always after the people had returned home, so as not to alert burglars) and the return home from college of various young ladies.

Mention would be made that the Misses A, B and C were home from Sweet Briar or Hollins. The Misses Y and Z might also be home from the same colleges, but if they were not in the social spotlight, there visits would be unreported.

Both Richmond dailies, like most other American newspapers, devoted considerable space to engagements and weddings. For many years after the papers merged in 1940, a paper would not carry both engagement and wedding pictures of the same woman. Thus, it was likely that a woman's engagement might be in *The News Leader*, and her wedding photo would be in *The Times-Dispatch*. Although both papers carried wedding and engagement pictures more than one day a week, it was *de rigeur* to have one picture in the Saturday *News Leader*.

Traditionally, some weddings merited more space than others, on the same rationale that some people's obituaries are longer than others'. In the mid-1970s, however, Alf Goodykoontz, managing editor of *The Times-Dispatch*, decreed that all pictures would be the same size—slightly less than a column wide. *The News Leader* continued its old policy. By that time the number of black women's pictures had grown considerably from the mere handful in the early 1970s.

It took two and a half years after the 1992 merger for the new *Times-Dispatch* to change its policy radically on weddings and engagements. At the start of 1995, some of the news columns in *The Times-Dispatch* were for sale. You could have a free wedding or engagement announcement if the total, including the photo, was no more than 15 column lines. Anything more cost—from $60 to $395.

Arguments for the change included (1) other papers—including the *Washington Post*—had charged for such announcements for years and (2) weddings and engagements were eating up too much valuable news space. Opponents of change argued that (1) other papers announced that all, not just some, announcements were advertisements and therefore paid for and (2) selling ANY news space is unethical.

Those paying for the announcements have considerable leeway. Many pictures now have bride and groom. And the wording of the announcements varies considerably. There is still much of the traditional.

But a mid-1995 wedding account included the names of the flower girl and "the bubble girl." It ended, "The sun shone brightly and a light breeze moved gently through the dogwood trees and azaleas which were in full bloom. The ceremony was brief, but beautiful. The reception was also held in the garden where guests dined from an elegant lunch buffet. There was much dancing and merriment had by all. As the bride and groom left the premises, the guests blew a shower of bubbles into their path. The party continued at another location.

"If the groom passes through immigration, the couple will enjoy a honeymoon in Belize and return to Richmond where they will live happily ever after."

PHOTO

Decades before the merger of *The Times-Dispatch* and *The News Leader* in 1992, one photography department had served both papers. The setup, in place ever since the Bryans reacquired *The Times-Dispatch* and created Richmond Newspapers Inc. in 1940, no doubt made sense economically and pleased management. But news staffs on both papers despised it.

The photographers, in general, tried to play by the rules. In a spot news situation, the next paper to publish got the choice of pictures. But if one paper made a specific assignment in connection with a story, especially not a spot news story, it had first crack at the pictures.

Some photographers acknowledged that they preferred their pictures go to *The News Leader* because it displayed them bigger and better than *The Times-Dispatch.*

The man who as chief photographer for 33 years tried to please two sets of reporters and editors was Joseph Colognori, who had joined *The Times-Dispatch* in 1926 and retired at the end of 1973. Colognori not only presided over a photography staff that invariably included some heavy-drinking, sexually aggressive men, but also took pictures himself.

Before the staff's steady growth, Colognori spent as much time taking pictures as did his underlings. In 1958, when shooting at the Oyster Bowl football game in Norfolk that featured the University of Virginia and Virginia Military Institute, Colognori ventured too close to the action and was run down by Virginia's Sonny Randle who had just caught a pass. The head injuries that sent him to a hospital were not serious.

The most newspaper attention Colognori ever received was early in his career when he accompanied Ed Brill, *Times-Dispatch* police reporter, to Fredericksburg for the trial of a Sunday school superintendent, who had a girlfriend and a wife. The man was accused of poisoning and trying to murder the latter.

Papers from as far away as Philadelphia were covering the case, and the judge ordered no one to enter or leave the courtroom during recesses. At one recess—a lunch break—Colognori entered the room and took a picture of people eating their lunches. Unfortunately, the judge entered the court about the same time and ordered Colognori locked up for more than two hours.[203]

Photographers from Washington papers gleefully shot pictures of Colognori behind bars and one picture ended up on a front page.

A bigger "character" than Colognori was Harvey Worthington South, who spent 54 years as a photographer, 28 of them with Richmond newspapers before retiring at age 74, less than a year before his death.

South was known by the great and not so great in Richmond—a fact more understandable when the number of news photographers was negligible. Once, South missed a picture because he was greeted, "Hello, Harvey," by a friend in a parade that he was covering. He turned, dropped his camera and responded, "Hello, Jim," to the Hon. James H. Price, governor of Virginia, who was riding in the back of the open, lead car.[204]

In the fall of 1936, South accompanied Jimmy Jones, sports editor of *The Times-Dispatch,* to Williamsburg for pictures of football players at the College of William and Mary. Jones' successor as sports editor, Chauncey Durden, recalled how South talked at length to Jones, as they rode to Williamsburg, on preparation.[205]

"In my business," said South, "you have to have good equipment to get good pictures. I would not dare go on an assignment without proper equipment."

After they arrived at Williamsburg and talked with athletic department officials, Jones became concerned at the time South was taking to retrieve his equipment from his car. Jones found Smith, with a wild look in his eye and a brick in his hand.

"Don't hit me, Harvey; don't hit me," implored Jones.

"Hit you!" South replied. "I'm going to beat my brains out. I came off and forgot my camera."

South was known widely by horse and dog people not only because of his pictures of the animals but also because of his knowledge. He also was known in his later years for hitting the bottle heavily—even when on duty. During the 1930s, South had been convicted of drunken driving, and he had to call on someone else to drive when he went on an assignment.[206]

Another story, related by sports fans, was that South stationed himself at the goalposts during football games so he could support himself while taking pictures.

Photographic staff in 1970 included (left to right), Dave Harvey, P.A. Gormus, Bob Jones, Bob Brown and Bill Lane.

SECTION F

• Editorial

Overton Jones (left), Virginius Dabney were backbone of Times Dispatch *editorial staff in 1960s.*

VIRGINIUS DABNEY

In 1922, Richard Heath Dabney, a faculty member at the University of Virginia, asked his son Virginius, "Did you ever think of going into journalism?"[207]

The younger Dabney, 21, was teaching at Episcopal High School, from which he had graduated in 1917 before entering the university. By the time the father suggested journalism, the son had earned a master's degree. But he had never had formal classroom education before going to EHS, since his father tutored him at home.

He took his father up on the suggestion about journalism and visited John Stewart Bryan, publisher of *The Richmond News Leader*. On July 1, he began work at the paper for $20 a week ($5 more than reporters generally were being offered). *The News Leader* was in "a somewhat ramshackle structure on the east side of Eighth Street just north of Main Street."[208]

"From that time on," he wrote, "I knew that I wanted to be a newspaperman."[209]

He remained one for 53 years. During those years—47 of which were spent with *The Times-Dispatch*, mostly writing editorials—he championed labor unions, increased rights for blacks and early U.S. preparedness in World War II. *The Times-Dispatch* supported Franklin D. Roosevelt for president four times. It generally endorsed the conservative Democratic political organization headed by U.S. Sen. Harry F. Byrd—although not always.

"Byrd was very hostile to almost the whole New Deal, so we criticized him considerably at that time," said Dabney. "Nevertheless, he sent me a bushel of apples every Christmas."[210]

The high point of Dabney's journalistic career, he said, was in 1948, when he was awarded the Pulitzer Prize, but he can't understand the award and said he submitted no editorials for consideration. The award was presented for "a body of work."[211]

Dabney said one book reported that Frank Kent of the *Baltimore Sun*, a Pulitzer Committee member, opposed an award for Dabney because Kent thought Dabney opposed Harry Byrd. By 1948, that opposition had virtually disappeared.

As the years passed, Dabney and *The Times-Dispatch* became increasingly conservative. The darkest period for Dabney was the paper's support—over his objection—of Massive Resistance to racially integrated schools.

Was it fair to say, he was asked, if the one-time liberal had become a conservative editor?

"I think I was certainly more liberal in the early days," he said, "and I think that later on I believed in more or less the same things that I believed in the 30s, but they were not liberal any more."[212]

Two issues about which he said he felt strongly were labor unions and race relations. "I was in favor of labor unions and in favor of better facilities and more fair treatment for the blacks," he said. "I believed in those then—which was regarded as a parlor pink [sort of thing]. . . and I still do. Of course, I don't think that everything is being done in either case as to my liking.

"The labor unions have gone too far, and I think they have done a lot for us newspapermen; they certainly got those low wages up. And the race issue, I think now they [blacks] want the moon practically, and I just don't favor that either." Those were the sentiments of Dabney at age 88.[213]

As a young *News Leader* reporter, he did what most young reporters do—a little bit of everything, much of it boring. Yet, "I learned more about the world around me in my first six months at *The News Leader* than I did at any similar period in my life," he said.[214]

"I was totally green and didn't know beans about reporting," he said. "They were silly enough to put me on a complicated bank failure case when I had been there three weeks."[215]

The Mechanics Savings Bank, a black institution headed by John Mitchell Jr., publisher of the *Richmond Planet*, had closed; Dabney was sent to the State Corporation Commission to follow up on the failure. He encountered Chairman Berkeley D. Adams, who explained that valuable securities had been replaced by worthless ones, adding, "I wouldn't use this if I were you."

The cub reporter took no notes. When he returned to the newsroom, City Editor William J. Robertson asked, "Where's that bank story?"

Dabney replied, "Well, Mr. Adams said he didn't think it would be a good idea to publish it."

Robertson obviously had different ideas. "He did? Well, can you write it?" he asked.

Virginius Dabney won a Pulitzer Prize for his Times-Dispatch *editorials.*

Dabney replied that of course he could. "So I proceeded to get it wrong in the worst possible way. I quoted Mr. Adams as saying, 'John Mitchell took valuable securities out of the bank's portfolio and put worthless securities in.' That came out on the front page of *The News Leader*, and all hell broke loose."

Adams, quite unhappy, said correctly that he had been misquoted. Robertson, Managing Editor Robert M. Lynn and Publisher Bryan were also unhappy. Dabney figured he'd be fired, but two things worked to his advantage. The one-year statute of limitations for a libel suit passed with no suit filed, and what Dabney wrote turned out to be true, although Adams had been misquoted.

A formal state report found "an unsound credit and investment policy, mismanagement, falsification of records and dishonesty."

The great lesson to the young reporter: Take notes.[216]

In 1928, Dabney shifted to *The Times-Dispatch*, where he found "more money and more stimulating work."[217] The paper was "in a barn-like structure on Seventh Street south of Main." Dabney became chief political writer and had a signed piece on the editorial page each Sunday. And he was an enthusiastic supporter of Al Smith for president.

He also was one of the earnest Southern liberals who argued vehemently against the Twelve Southerners or the Agrarians—John Crowe Ransome, Allen Tate and Donald Davidson, who gathered nine soul mates and published *I'll Take My Stand: The South and the Agrarian Tradition* in 1930. Their opposition to further industrialization in the South was countered by the liberals.

The Times-Dispatch sponsored a meeting that filled all 3,500 seats at the City Auditorium that year and brought Ransome face to face with Stringfellow Barr, assistant editor of the *Virginia Quarterly Review*. Dabney couldn't attend, but the audience included H.L. Mencken, Virginia's governor and Sherwood Anderson, the novelist, who was moderator.[218]

In his first six years in journalism, Dabney railed at the injustices of society.[219] He campaigned in print against anti-union tactics of various companies, for a better deal for blacks in voting and for the black Scottsboro defendants who were dragged from a freight train in 1931 in Alabama and accused of raping two white women who worked at a textile mill.

"Despite my previous indifference to the plight of the Negro, I became his advocate," he said.[220]

That was the antithesis of his father's position. During a state constitutional convention in 1901-02, Richard Heath Dabney wrote to the Richmond Times that only hatred and conflict could result from black-white competition and, thus, education for Negroes should end and they should be disenfranchised.[221]

Virginius Dabney began work in 1929 on a biography of Methodist Bishop James Cannon but couldn't get it published, he said, because of publishers' fear of libel. Twenty years later, *Dry Messiah* was published by Knopf.

Dabney was becoming bored with reporting at *The Times-Dispatch*.[222] He wrote occasional editorials and sought the job as editor, but "each time, management got somebody from New York who knew little or nothing about

Virginia." He sounded out Arthur Krock of *The New York Times*, because Dabney had doing articles for *The Times* since 1929. No dice.

In 1934, Dabney won a grant from the Oberlander Trust of the Carl Schurz Memorial Foundation and went to Austria and Germany. The foundation's aim was to promote German-American relations, and Dabney was not to get involved in Nazi propaganda one way or the other.

"They wanted to announce," he said "that I was going over there to study periodical literature, which was the last thing I was interested in. I went to the library once and asked for a copy of *Harper's* and the *Nation*, but they didn't let me have either of them because they had anti-Nazi articles. . . That's why I wanted to see it. I went to the library once; that was my six months' study of periodical literature."[223]

While abroad, he wrote once a week for *The Times-Dispatch* editorial page. "But I did not discuss the Nazi movement," he said. "I did not want to get the foundation in trouble, because they'd know I wasn't studying periodical literature. So as soon as I got back here, I let out all my pent-up feelings on the Nazis."[224] In 1933, Dabney had cautioned skepticism about reports of Nazi atrocities, recalling overblown accounts of German atrocities in World War I.[225]

Dabney talked to lots of Germans, some of whom thought Hitler "was not going to start anything." But Dabney was there when the Nazis "murdered all those people. . .and also when [Chancellor Engelbert] Dollfus was murdered by Nazis in Vienna." Those murdered June 30, 1934 were leaders of the Brown Shirts or storm troopers.

By that time, "I was violently anti-Nazi and predicted Hitler was going to start a war. Some people thought I was wrong—I usually am—but I wasn't that time."

While he was in Berchtesgarten, Dabney was offered a job as chief editorial writer on *The Times-Dispatch* by Charles P. Hasbrook, the publisher. If his work was satisfactory, he would get the title of editor.[226] He accepted and succeeded Vincent G. Byers on October 1, 1934. Several days earlier, he read that Hasbrook had resigned, but the job offer held. Mark Ethridge succeeded Hasbrook, and he and Dabney worked well together. They teamed up in clashing with Harry Byrd for his attacks on Franklin Roosevelt.

In 1936, Ethridge left for the *Louisville Courier-Journal* and was succeeded by a South Carolinian, John Dana Wise. A handsome, craggy-faced man with a white mane, Wise had strong opinions, and he and Dabney would have unpleasant confrontations as the years passed. But he quickly named Dabney editor.

One of Dabney's assets from Day One was Helen McCarthy, who already was on the secretarial staff. When he came back to the paper in 1934, he asked her to be his secretary. She accepted and held that position in addition to being secretary to the managing editor for many years until her retirement in 1971.

"He was a gentleman always, a very understanding person," said Mrs. McCarthy. "We worked together. I never worked for him. We were friends; we were associates. We honored each other's integrity, and he left a great deal to me to do things. And I would confer with him, and if it wasn't OK, then we would work it out."[227]

She always knew where he was (and called him at lunch at the Commonwealth Club the day of President Kennedy's assassination). She typed not only his correspondence but also all of his books. And she was godmother to his oldest daughter.

Dabney was really moving. He was tall, trim, soft-spoken, aristocratic, confident. He replaced his one assistant, William B. Southall, whom he called "notoriously lazy," and hired William Shands Meacham as his replacement. Southall became a reporter—the concern of the news department.[228] Meacham would later become editorial page editor of the *Norfolk Virginian-Pilot.*

Dabney's editorial series on the appeasement of Germany "brought what was the largest reader response ever evoked by any series of mine," he said.[229] One editorial on September 30, 1938, was entitled "The Sellout to Hitler" and "may have been the best editorial I ever wrote."

One prophetic paragraph read: "The year 1938 will mark the beginning of the end of the British Empire, the decline of France as a world power and the rise of a German empire far mightier than that of Charlemagne."

Still, Dabney opposed U.S. intervention in Europe's war as late as December 1939, three months after Germany had invaded Poland. "The way to destroy American democracy is for this country to be dragged into another World War," *The Times-Dispatch* said. A year later, Dabney changed his mind and supported aid to England at any cost.[230]

On the domestic front, Dabney was in his liberal phase. *The Times-Dispatch* campaigned for a 9-hour day, 48-hour work week for women instead of a 10-hour day and 60-hour week. The legislature obliged.[231]

By 1942, Dabney had his second book, *Below the Potomac*. Ten years earlier he had written *Liberalism in the South*. In each he espoused his fervent liberalism. One of his heroes in the earlier book was his former boss at *The News Leader*, Douglas Southall Freeman, whom he described as "another inveterate foe of meddlesome clerics and demagogic pseudo-statesmen." Freeman had blasted the Methodist clergy in Richmond for demanding the re-election of a certain judge.

"Few editors in the South are so consistent in their championship of the Negro or belabor the patrioteers and the industrial Bourbons with greater regularity," Dabney wrote. "*The News Leader's* prestige is further augmented by virtue of the fact that its publisher is John Stewart Bryan, one of Virginia's foremost citizens." [232]

Dabney concluded his book, "The South may well rejoice that the social attitudes of its leaders and its people are coming to be more and more shot through with liberalism. In that fact lies the South's hope of future greatness."[233]

In *Below the Potomac*, Dabney's idealism seemed to conflict with reality when he discussed race and education together. "The possible admittance of Negroes to the white universities is the most controversial and challenging of all the interracial questions now pressing for a solution," he wrote.[234]

But he envisioned the "persecution of Negroes on a wide scale" in a state if courts ordered a university to admit one or two blacks. Hundreds or thousands might suffer, he reasoned, because one or two might exercise "their undoubted legal right to the same graduate and professional training as that provided for whites."

Still, he said, ". . . the democratic ideal is at war with the thesis that American citizens can be placed in separate pigeonholes and given varying educational and social advantages, depending on the color of their skins. Any discrimination among citizens of this country for reasons of race or religion is undemocratic." Truly, he said, the South "inherited a problem of tremendous complexity and difficulty at the close of the Civil War."[235]

Morton Sosna's *In Search of the Silent South: Southern Liberals and the Race Issue* includes a chapter titled "Virginius Dabney, Publicist for a Liberal South." Sosna says Dabney envisioned a Silent South made up of "the spiritual descendants of Thomas Jefferson—an elite of educated humanists who exercised a liberalizing influence far out of proportion to their numbers."[236]

Sosna notes that Dabney's call for a federal anti-lynching law caused Walter White of the NAACP to label it "one of the most significant positions taken by an American newspaper since the Civil War." In 1943, when *The Times-Dispatch* editorialized for an end to Virginia's law compelling racial segregation on street cars and other common carriers, Dabney drew praise from Roy Wilkins of the NAACP, from the *Pittsburgh Courier*, a black newspaper that Dabney frequently criticized as "sensation-mongering," and from Oswald Garrison Villard of the *Progressive*, who said Dabney had taken "a statesmanlike and far-seeing stand."

But an article in *The Atlantic Monthly* in January 1943 cost Dabney the lasting respect of many liberals. It was the middle of World War II, and many blacks were agitating for an end to all segregation. A march on Washington was proposed. Dabney's article, "Nearer and Nearer the Precipice," said, "A small group of Negro agitators and another small group of white rabble-rousers are pushing this country closer and closer to an interracial explosion which may make the race riots of the First World War and its aftermath seem mild by comparison."

Sosna concludes, "Despite his brief campaign against segregated public transportation, Dabney's wartime stand against black militancy tarnished his reputation as a liberal. In continuing to insist that separate could be made equal, he would not win it back."

When Dabney retired from *The Times-Dispatch* in 1969, *The New York Times* noted that he concluded his editorship "with little notice or lament from the South's progressives and liberals, among whom the editor was once a hero."[237]

Dabney was one of the founders of the interracial Southern Regional Council, but his influence was minimal. He argued in vain in December 1944, before the council was a year old, that it should back segregation. When the council condemned segregation in 1947, Dabney resigned.[238]

In 1940, with the merger of *The Times-Dispatch* and *The News Leader* into a single corporation with separate papers, John Stewart Bryan became publisher of both. But, said Dabney,[239] Bryan "agreed that he would hold to a minimum his participation in the formulation of *Times-Dispatch* editorial policy and such formulation was left almost entirely to me. . . . I cannot recall that he took issue with any of my editorial pronouncements."

The paper endorsed Roosevelt four times, "with diminishing enthusiasm each time," he said. Dabney argued strongly against Roosevelt's scheme to pack the U.S. Supreme Court in 1937,[240] but he said, in reply to a letter-writer the next year, the paper was not turning to the right. "Since we are still in favor of what we understand to be the Administration's objectives," he wrote, "we do not consider that we have turned either to the Right or to the Left."[241]

John Dana Wise, then vice president-general manager of Richmond Newspapers, was becoming a bigger headache for Dabney. They fought over Westbrook Pegler's column, "which the paper carried and which I detested,"

John Dana Wise. A self-made man, whom some—like Publisher D. Tennant Bryan and Editor James J. Kilpatrick—admired greatly, and others—like Editor Virginius Dabney—disliked intensely.

said Dabney.[242] The paper dropped the column, but Bryan brought it back after reader complaints.

Wise accused Dabney of "notorious intolerance" and "puritanical intolerance" and said Dabney was "dragging *The Times-Dispatch* down to oblivion." Dabney replied: "I confess myself baffled when a person who has been cynical, bitter and super-critical of practically everything that has happened in Washington over a period of years begins lauding the virtues of 'tolerance.' When, in recent years, did you exhibit that characteristic in your comments on public affairs?"[243]

In the late 1940s and early '50s, Dabney said, Wise "took a terrific dislike to me and everything I did was wrong. . . I think he was the most unpopular man in Richmond. He was critical of everybody. He knew everything.

". . . Everybody else was stupid and he was brilliant, and he just antagonized all the leaders in the community." Wise, however, held several important positions in Richmond affairs, including the top post in the Community Chest at one point in World War II.[244]

Dabney was so antagonized that he went to Philadelphia to talk about a job on the *Saturday Evening Post*, but there was no offer.[245] At *Reader's Digest*, DeWitt Wallace said, "[He] didn't think I'd be satisfied if I got on there, that I wouldn't write but about once a month and he doubted if I wanted it. He didn't offer me anything, either."

During their confrontational period, Dabney said, he won three national awards. "Jack Wise made some sneering remark about it, and Tennant sent me a bunch of flowers."[246]

When the University of Virginia announced it was planning a graduate school of business, Dabney recalls, Wise said, "That's the most idiotic idea I've heard of—imagine having a graduate school of business in Charlottesville. Of course, it's absolutely absurd."

Dabney disagreed. "I went ahead and wrote an editorial backing it up, and it turned out to be a very good school of business—one of the best in the county."[247]

In 1989, Dabney had mixed emotions about the nation's press. As for his 47 years at *The Times-Dispatch*, "I'd describe them as very exciting and rewarding, except for those interludes that I mentioned. I'm not very enthusiastic about the way the press is behaving today."

He felt that "investigative reporting" went much too far in probing into private lives, yet comparing today's papers with those of 20, 30 or 40 years ago, "I think they do a better job. They overdo it but they certainly present more news and a broader picture of what's going on in this country and abroad."[248]

OVERTON JONES AND ED GRIMSLEY

When Dabney left *The Times-Dispatch* after 47 years, he was succeeded as editor by his longtime associate, Overton Jones, whose appointment as "chief editorial writer" was announced January 6, 1969.

One year and two weeks later, Jones' name went off the masthead. Less than three months after that, April 15, 1970, Ed Grimsley, who had been writing editorials for a year but who earlier had received plaudits from his newsroom colleagues for outstanding coverage of City Hall, was named "editor of the editorial page."

What happened to Jones, who had joined the paper in 1937, become an editorial writer in 1949 and associate editor in 1957?

Essentially, it boiled down to how conservative the editorial page would be.

"Because of V Dabney's prestige in the community and in American journalism," Jones wrote the author in an undated letter, "there was a limit to the influence that could be brought to bear on the *Times-Dispatch* editorial page from outside the department. When Dabney retired, the opportunity arose to make the *Times-Dispatch* editorial page a twin of the ultra-conservative *News Leader* editorial page. I had hoped to avoid this happening."

Personalities were involved also. Jones said that he considered Publisher Bryan "just the finest gentleman anywhere around."[249] And Jones continued to work on Grimsley's editorial page until he retired in 1982. He remained as a part-timer handling letters to the editor until *The Times-Dispatch* and *The News Leader* merged 10 years later.

Yet, Jones was anything but a fire-eater as an editorial writer. Reporters snickered that the only thing for which he crusaded was highway safety, a bit like motherhood, flag and apple pie. Like Grimsley, he had been City Hall reporter early in his *Times-Dispatch* career, but when he succeeded Dabney, he had been writing editorials 20 years.

Grimsley, however, had a reputation as a digger. Covering City Hall, he had a way of getting "in with the outs." No closed door meeting prevented his finding out what City Council members were up to. Early in his reportorial career on *The Times-Dispatch*, he disclosed that "a whole nest of city and state employees" had gotten paid leaves of absence and then gone to work for the General Assembly, thus drawing two paychecks for the same period. Eventually, they were required to reimburse one public treasury.[250]

Another time, Grimsley found that Richmond's city assessor, J. Edward Rountrey, had been paid both by the city and by a professional association for a speech he made in New Orleans. Grimsley confronted him with a photostatic copy of the city check and confirmation from the professional group that he had been paid there. Rountrey said it was all inadvertent but he was forced out of his city job. He set up a highly successful professional assessment firm.

What could have been one of Grimsley's best stories—an exclusive with perhaps national or international repercussions—he passed up. As city hall reporter, he was assigned to the annual meeting of the Virginia Municipal League. One of the speakers that year was Sen. John F. Kennedy of Massachusetts. After the senator's address, Grimsley followed the accepted routine of a reporter who had taken notes and asked Kennedy for a copy of his speech. Kennedy said he had none, that he had spoken from notes.

He added, said Grimsley, "Here's my briefcase. My notes are here. You can borrow them for a few minutes." Grimsley accepted the offer and, "Lo and behold, there in his briefcase was a transcript" of the minutes of a Senate committee private meeting with Nikita Khrushchev.

"So what did I do? I ignored it because he had given me his briefcase to look at those notes. He obviously had not remembered about this [transcript]."[251]

On the *Times-Dispatch* editorial front, Grimsley said he had "absolutely nothing to do with what was going to happen with Overton."[252] Not from the fourth floor and not from Jones, Grimsley said he had the impression that Jones was not going to be named editorial page editor. He understood, said Grimsley, that some executives "who were responsible for establishing the editorial policy of the newspaper felt that Overton might not be as conservative on many issues as they would like."

Jones was "very supportive and very helpful," Grimsley said, when he moved from the newsroom to the editorial department. "I could go to him sometimes when I was doing something very impetuously, and I benefitted quite a bit from having Overton's sage advice."

Grimsley also found that he, Bryan and Alan Donnahoe "were in agreement on major issues."

That's where Grimsley and Jones differed—at least in degree. Jones realized that when he was put in charge of editorials, it was on a trial basis.[253] He was not invited to join the Forum Club, as editorial page editors normally were. "I was determined," he said, "to make it a moderately conservative paper, if I could, "and I didn't want the job under any other conditions."

His troubles with the fourth floor came early. In April 1969, Bryan asked Jones to reprint a *Chicago Tribune* editorial on anti-ballistic missiles (ABM's). Jones sent Bryan a memorandum saying he'd like not to reprint it for one reason: the final sentence in the *Tribune's* editorial said senators opposing the ABM were taking their cues from the Russians.

"This is the kind of extremism I would like to see us avoid," Jones wrote.

"Well, you could imagine his shock," said Jones. "And it was probably the first time in the history of Richmond Newspapers that an editor had not quickly acceded to his request to do something."[254]

Jones would agree to carrying the editorial with a disclaimer as to the last part. Bryan disagreed and sent the editorial to *The News Leader*, which carried it in its entirety.[255]

There was a problem, too, in the 1969 Democratic gubernatorial primary. William Battle, son of a former governor; State Sen. Henry Howell, a liberal; and Lt. Gov. Fred Pollard were the candidates. *The Times-Dispatch* supported Pollard, a Richmonder, but he lost. In the runoff, Jones had no trouble backing the more conservative Battle "to save us from a fate worse than death in the election of Henry Howell."

Battle won and faced Republican Linwood Holton in the general election. Management wanted to support Holton, said Jones, who reasoned that the paper had supported two Democrats and, now, surely should not support the Republican. Bryan was "very disappointed that I took that position," said Jones. But Jones had his way, and *The Times-Dispatch* supported neither man, although *The News Leader* vigorously backed Holton, who won and became Virginia's first Republican governor since Reconstruction.

On a Saturday early in January 1970, Jones was in the office and went upstairs to see Bryan on some minor matter. When that was done, said Jones, "he said he wanted to try Ed Grimsley in charge of the editorials. Of course, Ed was working with me at that time. [Bryan] said, 'You can be in charge of the rest of the page.' He said, 'We won't make any announcement; nobody will know it. Your name will stay up there, and we will just try it this way.'"

Jones needed no more than the weekend to consider his position. Bryan was not in his office, so Jones sent a message to Donnahoe. It read: "At Mr. Bryan's direction, I have relinquished control over the editorial columns, effective with tomorrow morning's issue of the paper.

"I respectfully request that during this and any other period when I am not in charge of the editorial columns that my name not appear on the masthead as chief editorial writer. In Mr. Bryan's absence today, I will greatly appreciate it if you will authorize the deletion of my name."

That was January 19, the last day Jones' name was in the masthead.

It was too much for Mrs. McCarthy, the longtime secretary to Dabney and other editorial writers. "Ovie," she wrote in a memo on copy paper, "I am simply stunned over what you have told me. I can't imagine anything like it. You've worked so hard and at such a disadvantage. I just hope and hope that they change their minds. What am I to tell people when they notice your name is missing from the masthead? That is unbelievable.

"I don't know whether I can take a new boss or not.

"May admiration [Apparently she was upset enough to make a rare typing error.] for you through the years is great, as you know and I have always loved you.—Helen"

DOUGLAS S. FREEMAN

Douglas Southall Freeman wasn't cut out to be a newspaperman. He was too orderly.

Every minute of his day was organized. He allotted two minutes and 40 seconds for cooking breakfast and 17 minutes for driving to *The News Leader*. Fifteen minutes were devoted to reading the morning *Times-Dispatch* and two and one-half hours for writing two columns of editorials.[256]

In writing his four-volume biography of Robert E. Lee, he set aside at least 14 hours a week.[257]

He stopped smoking because he figured the time spent on all the doings for cigarettes amounted to 8 and one-half hours a week.[258]

A sign over his office clock read, "Time alone is irreplacable; waste it not." Office wags said inserting the missing "e" would have consumed too much time.[259]

In his editorial tribute June 15, 1953, two days after Freeman's death, Virginius Dabney, wrote in *The Times-Dispatch*, "Dr. Freeman was so many-sided, his capacity for work was so prodigious, and his ability to parcel out his time on a precise schedule for 24 hours of each day so amazing, that he accomplished more in one lifetime than three men could normally do."

A regular day for Dr. Freeman (he was "Dr. Freeman" to most people; *News Leader* staff members referred to him behind his back as "the Doc") began at 2:30 a.m. That's when he arose. He cooked breakfast, ate it, drove to his office and was at his desk at 3:15.[260]

By 6 a.m., he had completed two columns of editorials, which he revised for 40 minutes. About 15 more minutes went into note-taking for a radio broadcast, then an hour for writing by hand on his biography of George Washington.

At 8 a.m. he was on the air for his daily newscast—"without sign of a manuscript and usually without notes," according to Dabney. He strode into the studio just as the announcer was saying, "And now, Dr. Freeman." [time]

ABOVE: *Dr. Douglas Southall Freeman (far right) called members of the news staff at* The News Leader *his eyes and ears. From left: R.L.C. Barret, Robert E. Dickson, John Riis, Charles H. Hamilton, William T. Christian, Roy Flannagan and Charles W. Houston in 1939.*

Douglas Southall Freeman, scholar, historian, biographer and News Leader *editor.*

That was accomplished by knowing precisely how many minutes were necessary to gather whatever notes he needed and to traverse a catwalk from the newsroom to the WRNL studio.

After the broadcast came the daily session with key members of *The News Leader* staff—the city editor, the managing editor and four or five key reporters.[261] Each was supposed to have a "tidbit" to pass on to Dr. Freeman.

One day when he was city editor, Charles Henry Hamilton reported a bit of news from Main Street and was brought up short by a dozing reporter, who blurted out, "Hey, you stole my tidbit." James J. Kilpatrick, Dr. Freeman's successor, recalled those meetings in *The News Leader's* editorial obituary. "The powwows were known irreverently downstairs as carrying wampum

In 1936, Virginia newspaper editors honored the rangy John Stewart Bryan (center), publisher of The News Leader, *at a dinner given by Douglas Southall Freeman (left), editor of the paper. Others, from left, J. St. George Bryan of* The News Leader, *Louis J. Jaffe of the* Norfolk Virginian-Pilot, *Douglas Gordon of the* Norfolk Ledger-Dispatch, *Virginius Dabney of* The Richmond Times-Dispatch, *William B. Smith of the* Roanoke World-News *and Robert Glass of the* Lynchburg News.

to the great white father," he said, "but the fact is that more often than not they were fun."[262]

By 9:45 a.m. Dr. Freeman was in the composing room to check on the editorial page layout. Then it was back to writing on Washington. At 11, he took a 15-minute nap, then saw visitors for 40 minutes. Then it was off to WRNL for a noon broadcast.[263]

Dabney said that Dr. Freeman had half of Richmond's radio audience at a given time. His speaking voice was soft and to some it was sugary or even oleaginous, but people listened.

He went home for lunch with his wife each day. Then it was a brief nap and back to work on Washington for two and a half hours.[264] His daughter, Mary Tyler Cheek, recalled, "He never set an alarm for himself and would wake up in exactly a quarter of an hour. He said one needed only to lose consciousness to refresh the brain.

". . . Dinner was at six o'clock, and Father would go to bed at eight-thirty. He got up at three-thirty and in later years at two-thirty. . ."[265]

From 1934 to 1941, he taught at the Columbia University Graduate School of Journalism, and he had an intricate schedule worked out for that. "[H]e would write his editorials," said Mrs. Cheek, "get on the night sleeper, get off at Pennsylvania Station in the morning at six o'clock, go to the Hotel Pennsylvania, have a shower and eat his breakfast, take the subway up to Columbia, teach all day, then get on the eight-thirty southbound train, get off at three-thirty in Richmond and go right to the office."[266] His other teaching included 17 years at the Army War College.

Dr. Freeman didn't plan to enter journalism. He finished Richmond College in three years, picked up a Ph.D. in history from Johns Hopkins University and returned to Richmond. He taught a bit at a Miss Jennie Ellet's School (forerunner of St. Catherine's School) and went to work for the State Department of Taxation.

While there, he was recommended by the chief librarian to *The Times-Dispatch*, which wanted someone to write editorials on taxation. He joined the paper for $7 a week and later became its chief editorial writer.[267] When John Stewart Bryan sold his interest in *The Times-Dispatch* in 1914, Dr. Freeman followed him to *The News Leader*.

He became its editor in 1915 and held the post until his retirement in 1949. Kilpatrick figured that Dr. Freeman wrote nearly 600,000 words a year. He had "Twenty Rules for Good Writing," which *The News Leader* reprinted on occasion. The first three were (1) "Above all, be clear," (2) "Therefore, use simple English" and (3) "To that end, write short sentences." He may have been inspired to list those rules, in the 1920s, by an experience he had as a graduate student.[268]

Mrs. Cheek said in reflections on her father's life that after turning in a paper at Johns Hopkins, he was upbraided by Dr. James Curtis Ballagh of the history department, who said, "Freeman, the research on this paper is excellent, indeed most exceptional. But you will never make a writer. Your purple prose is execrable."[269]

Among staff members at *The News Leader*, Dr. Freeman was held in awe. The combination of erudition, orderliness, writing ability and the magnitude of output was overwhelming. He was a stickler for accuracy. Charles Henry Hamilton recalled his earliest days on the *Leader*. He had been assigned a story on Poe House, the oldest home in Richmond. (It was named for Edgar Allan Poe, although he never lived there.)

Soon after the story appeared, Dr. Freeman was in the newsroom and called to the city editor, "Sowers, who wrote this story?" Earl Sowers, whom Hamilton described as "just a dynamo, a bundle of nerves," jumped up and replied, "Why, sir, we have a new man here, Hamilton, who wrote it."

Freeman's reply: "Hum. Tell him the next time to find out how to spell the name of what he's writing about." Like many another young reporter in the decades following, Hamilton had written Edgar Allen Poe.[270]

John Leard's early days on *The News Leader* (he later was its city editor) involved working up a news digest of the week that appeared Saturdays. Then unmarried and able to set his own hours for the research, Leard often arrived at the office at 5 a.m. on Fridays so as to have the summary ready for Dr. Freeman at 1 p.m.

Dr. Freeman would tell Henrietta Crump, his secretary, to "go get John" whenever he had a question. "I'd stand in front of him and he would say, 'John, is this what you really meant to say?'" Another day he asked Leard, "Can you justify using the Russian invasion of Finland as your lead item for this week?"

Leard liked the challenge. "I justified it; no problems on it."

Dr. Freeman's relations with the news staff were unusual then and would be almost unheard of today with the separation—and sometimes antagonism—of news and editorial staffs. But *The News Leader's* reporters were Dr. Freeman's eyes and ears locally. His morning sessions for "tidbits" also included a critique of the previous day's paper and often of that morning's rival *Times-Dispatch*. His summaries were typed, single-spaced.[271]

"He would go through the paper and read every story and then criticize it and what was left out of the damn thing and what was missing and any mistakes or anything else," said Hamilton.

". . . He also criticized *The Times-Dispatch*, which he didn't do as thoroughly but just pointed out that they had missed this story or how did they get that? Or why didn't you get it?"

The News Leader was so concerned that a major story not appear first in the fat *Times-Dispatch* on Sunday that it required its reporters to check every news source Friday afternoon. Then, if a major story appeared Sunday, the source would be confronted on why he held out when asked by *The News Leader* reporter Friday.

"We really had a go-round if we missed a big story," said Hamilton.

Dr. Freeman's courtliness included quiet behavior and usually patience, but, said Hamilton, "He had a very quick temper which he kept under control pretty darn well; he was too darned smart not to." Yet, Hamilton said, "He did not have good telephone manners. . . He was kind of gruff."

One day during a conference in his office, he answered the phone with an abrupt "hello." Dr. Freeman began getting tense. The caller identified himself as "Mr." and called Dr. Freeman by only his surname. "Look a here," he said. "I am Dr. Freeman to you and if you want to talk to me, you'll hang up and call me and address me properly."

"Then", said Hamilton, "in just a flash, he recovered and then he apologized and said, 'I'm sorry I lost my temper. I shouldn't have done that.'"

Dabney recalled an instance when he was a young reporter for *The News Leader* when Dr. Freeman "should have given me hell because of one thing I did, but he talked to me very politely about it."[272]

Dabney was covering the governor's office and also writing occasional pieces for the *Baltimore Evening Sun*. When Gov. E. Lee Trinkle nominated Sen. Carter Glass for president, Dabney correctly quoted Trinkle as saying, "Nobody will point the finger of scorn at Carter Glass except with pride."

The governor, said Dabney, was "sore as the devil," and Dr. Freeman "just politely admonished me that if I was assigned to that office, I ought not to be taking out after the governor."

When each was a nationally renowned editor, Dabney said, "We were very friendly. He was extremely nice to me."

Yet, "he was very much older than his years. He just seemed like 70 years old when he was 35. It really was ridiculous.. . . When I was 40 years old, I walked into his office one day, and he said, 'How are you, my sweet boy?'"

Dr. Freeman's stature as the ranking Civil War historian of his day, or certainly the ranking historian of the Confederate side, was unchallenged. But his knowledge was accompanied by a passion. His tipping his hat to the Monument Avenue statue of Lee each morning as Dr. Freeman drove to work was only one manifestation of his passion.

J. Bryan III, a cousin of the publisher and a young editorial writer for *The News Leader* in the 1930s, described that passion. "I was our third-stringer, and if there had been four of us, I'd have been fourth string," he wrote.[273]

One day at the editorial conference, R.L.C. Barret, the number two man, asked Dr. Freeman if he hadn't forgotten an anniversary. That produced a listing of events over the centuries that had occurred on the specific day, but Dr. Freeman thought none deserved "engraving on our editorial tablets."

Sen. Barret (he was a former member of the Mississippi State Senate) said, "But surely we're going to have our regular editorial about the little Chandler girl? It's her birthday today."

"The Doc leaped from his chair and pumped the Senator's arm, crying, 'My children will arise and call thee blessed! O my learned colleague, if I had forgotten that girl today, the pallet of my conscience would have been stuffed with peachpits for all eternity!' (I'm not making this up.)

"He flung himself on his typewriter, and the Senator and I retired to ours. I could hardly wait for the noon edition. When it finally came up, I didn't even glance at the headlines. I turned straight to page eight, the editorial page. There it was, leading the column: *A Little Maid of Old Virginia*. It appeared that when Stonewall Jackson was accidentally shot by his own troops at Chancellorsville, he was carried to the Chandler farm, where little Lucy Chandler, twelve years old, took his dying head in her lap and wept, 'Would God that it had been me!'"

At his retirement from *The News Leader*, Dr. Freeman was still teaching an evening current events class, which had begun 34 years earlier and still had some of its original members—all invited. He continued his 8 a.m. daily news broadcast and a Sunday morning "Lessons in Living" broadcast, which was 20 years old. But he reserved most of his time for more volumes in his life of Washington.

In 1953, campaigning in Richmond for the presidency, Gen. Dwight D. Eisenhower said that it was Dr. Freeman who first gave him the idea of a political career.

And it was Douglas Southall Freeman, who, nine years earlier, had suggested to Franklin Delano Roosevelt that "liberation of Europe" sounded better than "invasion of Europe." The president agreed.

His publisher, D. Tennant Bryan, summed up Dr. Freeman: "I never knew anyone like him—even close. He seemed to me to be encyclopedic in his knowledge. He knew something about everything and a hell of a lot about most things."[274]

JAMES J. KILPATRICK

In March 1941, an eager, green Oklahoman who had recently graduated from the University of Missouri School of Journalism joined *The Richmond News Leader* as a reporter. Before he left 25 years later, he'd made a lasting impact on the city, the state and the South.

It could be argued that James Jackson Kilpatrick had more influence than even his predecessor as editor of *The News Leader*, Douglas Southall Freeman, or Virginius Dabney, editor of *The Times-Dispatch*. They made their marks as editorial writers, although Dabney had briefly been a reporter.

Kilpatrick, on the other hand, was an outstanding reporter before he began writing editorials. Charles Henry Hamilton, who as city editor and managing editor supervised Kilpatrick, said he was one of just a handful of "the good reporters I encountered or worked with." He was probably the only reporter Hamilton ever had "who asked permission to come in on his day off and go around another beat with another reporter" so he could learn what was going on.[275]

He became editor at age 28 and achieved influence and fame—some would say, notoriety—by his determined fight against racial integration and his fight for "interposition," whereby the threatened Southern states would interpose their sovereignty against the federal government.

In an article that was part of a *Times-Dispatch* series in late 1988 and early 1989 on bygone days in the city, "Kilpo" recalled how his application for a job was answered by Hamilton's telegram: "Are you interested in job possibly only for year at thirty-five per week? If interested, when could you report?"

The reply: "Will report Monday. Kilpatrick."

When the United States entered World War II less than nine months later, Kilpatrick tried enlisting in the Army Air Corps and was turned down because of bronchial asthma—the reason for his discharge the preceding summer from ROTC.

James J. Kilpatrick, as editor of The News Leader, *led fight against racial integration and later moved to the center.*

Thus he was classified 4F and spent the war as a *News Leader* reporter. City Editor Hamilton kept saying, "Every man a tiger." There weren't many women on city staffs then.

"I got shifted around from one beat to another because it was pretty tough in those wartime days to cover the whole city," said Kilpatrick in an interview. "I covered City Hall, I covered police. On anybody's day off, I would go in and cover police and fire, or I would cover City Council." For a while during the war, he wrote a weekly summary of Richmond happenings, which readers were encouraged to clip out and mail to servicemen in their families.[276]

He was a stickler for detail. Traipsing through the Hotel Jefferson the morning of March 11, 1944, after a fire had killed six people, including the widow of Governor James H. Price, Kilpatrick took copious notes.

He wrote, "On the sixth floor, in Room 615, a friendly poker game was in progress. The sixth floor is made up principally of suites, and Room 615 contained two single beds, a large round table, a refrigerator, a dresser and a desk. Around the table were Senator Aubrey G. Weaver of Front Royal, and a number of fellow legislators. It was 11:47 p.m.

"A glance around the room before daylight this morning told a tragic story. Senator Weaver's familiar gray hat, crumpled but superb, lay in lonesome dignity on one bed near his gray tweed overcoat. The Senator's bamboo cane, which had thumped through the corridors of the Capitol since 1912, rested on the other bed. On one wall was a framed photograph of members of the Senate at this session; and a row of ties hung cheerfully over the dresser mirror.

"The table was cluttered with cards and poker chips. Apparently, the game broke up just after the fourth card had been dealt in a hand of stud poker. Half a dozen bottles of milk stood about the table, and the refrigerator contained a bowl of eggs, some mustard and some more milk. Scattered among the chips were memoranda relating to the budget bill and a statement of Commonwealth finances."

In his later years, Kilpatrick would become one of the nation's foremost writers on writing—in columns and books. Even as a youngster, he knew the right words to capture the mood of an event. Hamilton recalls a murder case, to which another reporter, Roy Flannagan, was assigned.

Hamilton recalled a 12-year-old uneducated mountain boy who owned nothing and who "always yearned for a bicycle so he could get around the mountains, so he murdered the storekeeper and stole all the money that the guy had [at] some little mountain store, and he went somewhere and bought a bicycle and he was riding around the mountains when they caught him. It made quite a story."

Kilpo went along, with no assignment, but came back with a "perfectly beautiful story" about "a mystical little boy on his bicycle in the mountain roads." That, too, appeared in *The News Leader*.

The versatile Kilpatrick was assigned once to review a vaudeville show. Recalling some horses he'd seen at Fort Riley, Kansas, he wrote, "For a moment last night at the National Theater, we thought Astor Girl and Hannah had slipped the corral. Then the lights came up and it turned out to be a couple of girls in the stage show. There's not one good-looking girl in the outfit, and we'll draw a curtain of mercy down on their collective figures."

When the girls, in scanty costume, descended on *The News Leader* the next day, Hamilton ordered Kilpatrick to do another piece. Dutifully, Kilpatrick wrote, "The girls looked a lot better in the *News Leader's* city room than they did on the National's stage."[277]

When Kilpatrick was covering the Virginia Supreme Court, he thought he found something fishy in the trial record of Silas Rogers, who had been convicted of murder.

"The more I looked into that case, the more convinced I became that this kid had been railroaded by the Petersburg police," Kilpatrick recalled. "He'd killed a police officer, and you know what that is. . . . For an itinerant black hobo who was kind of an odd-looking duck anyhow, for him to be charged with killing a police officer in Petersburg was just right straight to the chair. Verdict first and evidence afterwards."[278]

A witness in the case swore he'd been in a first-floor hospital bed and had seen Rogers running down a path from the hospital.

"Well, I went to the hospital," said Kilpatrick, "and I went to the first-floor room and I got down on the bed. And it was way up. The first floor must have been 10 or 15 feet up off the ground, and the walk was right close by the building. There was no way on God's green earth that he could have seen someone running down that walk."

Kilpatrick kept after the case, writing editorials and "nagging" Gov. John S. Battle, whose office he was covering at the same time. Battle relented and pardoned Rogers.

Charles McDowell wrote in *The Times-Dispatch,* "Silas Rogers, his gold tooth gleaming like a Christmas light, walked to freedom in a new blue suit yesterday after two years in 'death row' and seven more as a lifetermer in the Virginia State Penitentiary."[279]

It was a big story not only locally but also nationally. Kilpatrick was pictured shaking hands with Rogers, who was then off to New Jersey, where he was lionized and interviewed on television and radio. Then, less than three years later, he was convicted of rape in Newark.

But, Kilpatrick will tell skeptics, "He was not guilty of the Petersburg murder."

Kilpatrick had attracted the attention of Freeman, who, in January 1949, "press-ganged me, or asked me or whatever, would I like to consider writing editorials for him. And I said, of course, I would. . . You know, at that time we all revered the old gentleman. So I said I would give it a try."

Freeman was impressed. Six months later, he went to the publisher and announced his retirement. "And that was it," said Kilpatrick. "Then the

Doc spoke to me. I was pretty stunned and flabbergasted because the Doc told Tennant he wanted me to succeed him."

However, there was at least one person with whom the publisher discussed the position. That was Harry Ashmore. Ashmore had been named editor of the *Charlotte News* by Thomas L. Robinson, who bought the *News* in 1947.

As Ashmore told it, the meeting went this way:

"Before the change in management at the *News*, I had been asked by Virginius Dabney to come to Richmond to discuss the opening on *The News Leader* left by the retirement of Douglas Southall Freeman. I was flattered, but convinced in advance that this would turn out to be a clear case of incompatibility. My instinct was confirmed in the course of a pleasant luncheon with D. Tennant Bryan, publisher of the Richmond newspapers, and his general manager, John Dana Wise. After an exchange of views on the issues of the day had established a yawning void, Wise, a native South Carolinian, shook his head and said, 'I thought so—we've never had any luck with these Tarheels.'

"I headed back to Charlotte reminded of the old saw that characterized North Carolina as a vale of humility between two mountains of arrogance. *The News Leader's* editorial pulpit went to James Jackson Kilpatrick, who in the years to come would employ it to urge defiance of the United States Supreme Court in his anointed role as the father of interposition. In his autobiography, *Across the Years*, Dabney told of a bitterly personal running campaign waged by Wise to force his resignation. Bryan refused to go along, and tolerated the divergent editorial views of his morning and afternoon newspapers until the Supreme Court's school desegregation ruling forced a showdown on the racial issue. At that point, the publisher exercised his prerogative as the final authority on policy."[280]

". . . At the tender age of 28," Kilpatrick recalled in his syndicated column nearly 40 years later, "I became the fire-eating editor of *The News Leader*. There wasn't a topic under moon or sun on which I could not deliver a definitive opinion. I laid upon my enemies with shillelagh, tire iron and bung starter. Those were glorious times—10,000 words of copy a week, half a million words a year. Ah, the stuff I turned out in the old days."[281]

When Freeman retired, Kilpatrick recalled, he reminded his successor of his unlisted telephone number but promised never to set foot in the building at 4th and Grace streets except for quarterly meetings of the corporate board. "And he put on that old felt hat and picked up his lunch pail and off he went, and he lived right up to it," said his successor.[282]

On occasion, Kilpatrick needed that unlisted number, especially if some prominent Richmonder died who merited an editorial obituary. He would call Dr. Freeman, who would say, "'Well, I think you might want to say something along this line.' And then he would dictate to me. I would take this down just as fast as I could, and have to say, 'What was that again, Dr. Freeman?' I never called him Doc. 'What was that again, Dr. Freeman?'

"'Well, my boy. . . ' I'd thank him politely, and then all I had to do was type it up, send it to be set. Tennant Bryan would say, 'That sounds just like Dr. Freeman would write it.' And I'd say, 'Yes, sir.'"

Settled into the editorship, Kilpatrick began an annual summary of how he'd done—or how the year had been and how *The News Leader* editorial page had behaved.

On January 1, 1953, for instance, he said, "We wrote too much and too warmly about Georgia's senator Dick Russell as a presidential hopeful. And we wrote too much, and too critically, about General Pick of the Army Engineers and Major-General Robert W. Grow of Moscow Diary fame. Since we teed off on those gentlemen, evidence has come to light that the Moroccan air bases are not as faulty as Senate investigators had feared, and there is some reason to believe that General Grow was the victim of forgery."

A year later, he conceded, "We were too critical of the efforts to develop educational TV; the longer we think about this move, the more it seems to us that the effort merits encouragement instead of cold water."

On the other hand, "We were too enthusiastic about some things. Looking back to last January, we doubt that President Eisenhower's inaugural address will rank 'among the top state papers of this generation.' We were too enthusiastic about Mr. Eisenhower as a whole; his administration still seems to us as improvement, but his leadership has been far from inspiring."

On the first day of 1955, Kilpatrick noted the "changing concept of the nature of government. . . not only in Congress but in the Supreme Court also." This was early in Kilpatrick's feud with federal authorities on any level about racial segregation.

Continuing on January 1, 1955, he wrote, "For most of us in the South, the year will be remembered longest as the year of the decision in May on school segregation. Yet another opinion of the court in its November pronouncement on urban development was almost as significant. And it is profoundly sobering to note that both opinions were unanimous opinions. Not a single member of the court voted to uphold concepts of State's rights and property rights that once were a vital part of the American tradition.

"We acknowledge this trend not in pessimism, but in honesty. This is the way things are going. . . . "

The way things had been going domestically wasn't appealing to *The*

News Leader's editorial page. An editorial referred to a new book on the late Sen. Joseph McCarthy, the Wisconsin Republican who seemed to find Communists everywhere.

"Gradually, ever so slowly," said the editorial, "the McCarthy years are coming into perspective so that rational men may distinguish who was persecuting whom. The evidence is mounting that a courageous American was driven to an early grave as a sacrifice to 'liberal' self-esteem; that a myth was made by the small-souled men who could not accept even the possibility that they may be wrong."[283]

Kilpatrick the conservative was also Kilpatrick the conservationist. Federal slum clearance programs upset him; so did slum housing. By attacking the latter, he incurred the wrath of some of the Establishment.

"One of the leading slumlords in the city was a fellow who was in the right clubs and socially very prominent," said Kilpatrick in an interview. "He had a beautiful house. . .

"John Pearsall. . . was not at all pleased. Hell, I'd been in these lousy, miserable houses and smelled them, and tried to keep from falling through the rotting floorboards. These houses he was renting out were disgraceful. I did a pretty hard-hitting editorial series."

That series, Kilpatrick recalled, resulted in "a little eyebrow-raising from the fourth floor." He thinks it was from John Dana Wise, the general manager.

It also was Wise who introduced Kilpatrick to Edmund Burke's *The Reflections on the Revolution in France*. "I was thunderstruck," said Kilpatrick. "All of a sudden I began to get some intellectual grounding, my conservative instincts."

It was Wise who, early in Kilpatrick's editorship, began leaning on him for *The News Leader's* carrying Walter Lippmann, whom Kilpatrick called "the most prestigious columnist in the entire country." Wise asked Kilpatrick, in what the editor called a Socratic dialogue, about the function of an editorial page. "Was it not," he recalled Wise as saying, "to lead our readers in the directions that we believed to be politically, economically and philosophically sound?"

"Yes, Mr. Wise."

"Now, Mr. Lippmann. Mr. Walter Lippmann. The famous Mr. Walter Lippmann. You've been carrying his column regularly, and I gather from what you've told me about your own political philosophy that you must be in regular disagreement with Mr. Lippmann."

Kilpatrick said that was the case sometimes.

"But you believe that your own views reflect those of the management of Richmond Newspapers, and that these are sound views?"

"Oh, yes, Mr. Wise."

"And yet you are publishing Mr. Lippmann, whose views you find are unsound."

"Yes, Mr. Wise; sometimes that's true."

"Well, let's go back to the function of the editorial page. It is to lead our readers in directions that we conceive to be sound, and yet when you publish Mr. Lippmann on your editorial page, you are leading them in the other direction. Is that not so?"

"I said, 'Yes, Mr. Wise.' Well, I could take a hint as well as the next man, and that was the end of Walter Lippmann. We dumped him. I mean we dumped him. We were the only paper that would ever cancel Walter Lippmann."[284]

Not quite. *The Times-Dispatch*, which picked up Lippmann in the '50s, canceled his column in the late '60s. The column was in varying lengths and often arrived late. Yet, by then Lippmann was a leading opponent of continuing American participation in the Vietnam War, which editorialists on both papers supported.

John Dana Wise was a power at Richmond Newspapers for a quarter-century. He came in 1936 as publisher of *The Times-Dispatch*, effected the merger of *The Times-Dispatch* and *The News Leader*, then rose to business manager, vice president and, in 1942, to general manager.

"Jack Wise brought us together," said Tennant Bryan in an interview. "He was a great man in my book."[285]

"He [Wise] was an absolute capitalist," said Kilpatrick. "He hated the labor unions. He thought that the papers ought to turn a 25 percent profit. If they weren't turning a 25 percent profit on an investment a year, something was wrong, and he was the one who was going to set it right. He was a patrician looking fellow. He had a very limited education in public schools. He had his nose broken in a fight once in the Navy, so he had one of those noses that you see in the old Renaissance portraits of Italian masters. Handsome guy.

". . . He couldn't stand the unions, and so they deserved each other in a way. He believed passionately in the free enterprise system, capitalism—the least democracy, the better. He felt that Harry Truman was leading the country right down the road to socialism and ruin. So he took a shotgun and stopped the world and got off."[286]

That was in 1963, 10 years after Truman's presidency. Wise had retired and was ill. He committed suicide near Callao on the Northern Neck of Virginia.

Although Wise was a favorite of Bryan and Kilpatrick, Virginius Dabney, *The Times-Dispatch's* editor, disliked him intensely. *The Times-Dis-*

patch editorial obituary said that Wise was "a dynamic man, mentally and temperamentally, a perfectionist of unshakable convictions, which he expressed forcefully and with articulate clarity."

Those were the words not of Dabney, but of K.V. Hoffman, an editorial writer with the same rock-ribbed conservative convictions as Wise.

On *The News Leader*, Kilpatrick had a succession of associates on the editorial page who went on to establish names for themselves elsewhere—generally in writing.

Richard Whalen wrote for *Fortune* magazine and is the author of *The Founding Father*, a biography of Joseph Kennedy, and *Catch the Falling Flag*, a story of his disillusionment with the White House staff of Richard Nixon.

Guy Friddell became editorial page editor of the *Norfolk Virginian-Pilot* and wrote several books on Virginia.

Louis Rubin Jr. taught English at Hollins College and the University of North Carolina, founded Algonquin Books in Chapel Hill, North Carolina and is recognized as one of the nation's foremost authorities on Southern literature.

James Lucier worked for Sen. Jesse Helms, (R-N.C.) and was minority staff leader of the Senate Foreign Relations Committee. He occasionally writes special articles for *The Times-Dispatch.*

Garry Wills is the author of *Nixon Agonistes* and other books and teaches at Northwestern University.

Friddell spent only about a year on *The News Leader's* editorial staff. He left before a possible disagreement with Kilpatrick over desegregation. "I never had a conflict with Jack," Friddell said. "He was a splendid person to work for, and we continued to go to national conventions together just for fun."[287]

Kilpatrick recalls Friddell as "a fabulous character" but unable to be mean to anyone and, thus, not suited for editorial writing. "The guy had no instincts for the jugular," he said.

Wills, a onetime conservative, did a 180-degree turn at the Democratic National Convention in 1968 in Chicago, Kilpatrick recalled.

"He got so repelled by the sight of the cops hitting some of these flower children that almost overnight it was like Saul on the road to Damascus. . . . I trembled. Next thing I knew, Garry was dragging me off to some left-wing meeting there in Chicago, and he went completely over to the other side at the time."

Still, said Kilpatrick, Wills is "a brilliant scholar." He was a "very fast writer," who would turn out "solid editorials and then he'd go home." He and his wife worked together on other articles, and Kilpatrick recalls Wills "treated his work as an editorial writer for me as a part-time affair."

Rubin had done book reviews for *The News Leader* for years before he began writing editorials in late 1955. With Kilpatrick and Publisher

Bryan absorbed in domestic affairs, Rubin wrote about foreign affairs. "I got us involved in all sorts of things and spent the next few years backing off," he said.[288]

He wrote one editorial on the Suez Crisis in 1956 supporting President Eisenhower's position and thus opposing Britain, France and Israel. One editorial was headlined "Britannia Waives the Rules."

He was ready as a young man to do all the editorials in the fall of 1955 when Kilpatrick planned a vacation, Rubin said. But Kilpatrick had already done all the editorials on the Gray Commission plan for desegregation.

When he moved back to Richmond in early 1956, Rubin said, Kilpatrick had repudiated his earlier position and begun to endorse Massive Resistance. Rubin wrote one editorial endorsing that position, but it didn't run. "In two weeks," he said, "I was ashamed of it."

Rubin liked Kilpatrick, ate lunch with him and went to ballgames with him. But, he said, "Working with him was different. It was a one-man show. He was hard to work for."

Writing pseudonymously was not for Rubin. Once, he said, he did an editorial on Shakespeare, which Kilpatrick wanted to change. "My God," said Rubin, "do we have a policy on Shakespeare?"

Kilpatrick enjoyed his 25 years at *The News Leader*, but some things didn't work out as he'd hoped. He figures he was ostracized by Old Richmond by not being invited to join the Commonwealth Club, which is THE club for men in the city. Kilpatrick figured he was "blackballed" by Louis Ballou, president of the club and the architect for a new City Hall, whose appearance *The News Leader* had denounced.

"The editor of the paper ought to be a member of the club in Richmond," said Kilpatrick. "And not being admitted to that was a little sting. There was a little hurt there. And by the same token, Marie [his wife] should have been invited to become a member of the Woman's Club, and she wasn't. Marie was getting progressively unhappy. She thought she was getting snubbed.

". . . Richmond had been very good to me on the whole, but socially I was never there. I was still the Oklahoma boy."

His departure from *The News Leader* followed a disagreement with Alan Donnahoe, president of the corporation. Something Kilpatrick had written upset Donnahoe, who called Kilpatrick to his office and, as Kilpatrick recalled, "closed the door and for about five minutes he read me the riot act on who was in charge of Richmond Newspapers Inc.[289]

"And it was in a tone that was absolutely just like taking a thrashing.

If he'd used a cane and beat me, it would have been the same kind of thing. And I walked out of there, and I had little tears in my eyes, and I said, 'This is it. I've had it.'"

Luckily, his column—first with *Newsday* and by then with the *Washington Star*—was catching on. So he quit.

Kilpatrick still rages at mention of Donnahoe, who, he says, "was a pluperfect son of a bitch. An absolute bastard. And that asshole gave me more trouble than anybody. He was so arrogant and domineering, so absolutely God-damned certain of the rectitude of his positions, and I finally got to the point that I couldn't take any more of Alan Donnahoe."

In a subsequent interview, Donnahoe could recall nothing like the contretemps with Kilpatrick and said they generally got along well. Besides, said Donnahoe, "He didn't work for me; he worked for the publisher. Why get so upset with me? I don't understand it, frankly."[290]

But Donnahoe wrote some editorials and prides himself on once winning a Virginia Press Association award.

"He couldn't write his way out of a paper bag," said Kilpatrick. "He was not a good writer. He had no felicitous touch at all. I think his economic thinking is probably very good, but as a writer he was nothing, and as top boss, he had none of Jack Wise's courtliness or gentility. . . . You could live with Jack Wise in a way, even though he was pretty rough. Donnahoe was just crude in all kinds of ways."[291]

Three days after the second interview with the author, Donnahoe expanded, in a memo, on his relationship with Kilpatrick.

For two or three months after his joining Richmond Newspapers [as director of research in 1950], Donnahoe said, he shared an office with Kilpatrick while his own was being remodeled. "I wrote about as many editorials as did Kilpatrick," said Donnahoe. "In all of this, of course, he approved, and seemed to be very happy about this arrangement."

Even though he moved to his own office, Donnahoe said, Kilpatrick for several years "would plead with me to take over the editorial page for a week or two, so he could get a vacation." It was during one of those periods, Donnahoe said, that he received a first place award from the Virginia Press Association for editorial writing." The VPA later changed its rules so only full-time editorial writers could win that award.

Elaborating in his memo on his inability to recall any reason for Kilpatrick's "deep malice, over a long period of time," Donnahoe wondered if perhaps it was caused by Kilpatrick's longtime association with only one company—whereas other people move around.

"So," said Donnahoe, "his experiences there were his sole criteria to make his comparisons thereafter. And, of course, he also had little knowledge of the non-editorial operations of a newspaper, which made it difficult foar him to see the whole picture.

"Beyond the Publisher himself, one wonders if Kilpatrick ever had any understanding or real friendships for anyone in *The News Leader*. This may or may not be so, but perhaps it is the reason for his bitterness and malice for so many years."

GROVER HALL, JR.

To succeed Kilpatrick, corporate executives thought they had just the man in Grover Hall, Jr., son of a Pulitzer Prize-winner, a staunch conservative and, until shortly before his appointment in Richmond, the editor of the *Montgomery Advertiser*.

Hall had quit the *Advertiser* in late 1966 after its new owner endorsed a liberal U.S. senator, John J. Sparkman, whom Hall had opposed.

Writing in *The Times-Dispatch*, Virginius Dabney welcomed Hall as "an eminent exemplar of the editorial writing profession" and a man "who is steeped in the Southern tradition."

Dabney noted that Hall was "a personable bachelor who wears $150 suits [and] is a real addition to the community."

"The editorial styles of Messrs. Hall and Kilpatrick are similar," continued Dabney. "Each writes vividly and incisively, with a slashing belligerence, and each is knowledgeable on public affairs, and takes a distinctively conservative stance."

It sounded like a perfect fit, but Hall remained only a year. On January 6, 1968, *The News Leader* announced his resignation, saying Hall would announce his plans after a Florida holiday. Tennant Bryan said in an interview that Hall left "very largely on his own motion" and was not fired. His health already was bad, Bryan said.[292]

Some in Richmond said Hall had an aversion to hard work. Others said he drank too much. In any case, he became a columnist based in Washington and had agreed to work for George Wallace, when he was hospitalized after being arrested on a charge of drunken driving.

Tests showed that he did not have a high level of alcohol in his system, and he was hospitalized. That was when a brain tumor was found. He died a year later, in September 1971.

Another version of Hall's departure comes from a former high-ranking *News Leader* editor who said Bryan was averse to firing anyone but indeed did fire Hall because of Hall's lack of interest in a local story.

In that version, Hall parked his car one morning near the newspaper office on the way to work and fell in step with an advertising department employee. The ad man asked Hall what he thought about a local election the next day. Hall replied, "I don't give a shit." The ad man was so appalled at that idea from the editor of the afternoon paper that he told Bryan precisely what Hall had said and Bryan fired Hall.

After Hall's departure, Ross Mackenzie and Ann Lloyd Merriman were put in charge of *The News Leader's* editorial page. He was put in charge in August 1969. On the new *Times-Dispatch,* Mackenzie runs the editorial page and Merriman runs the book page and edits the Commentary section in the Sunday paper.

CARTOONISTS

Two members of the staffs of Richmond's newspapers with the widest appeal were neither reporters nor editors, but editorial cartoonists—Fred O. Seibel, who spent 42 years with *The Times-Dispatch*, and Jeff MacNelly, who won two Pulitzer Prizes with *The News Leader* before he was 31.

From 1926 until 1968, when illness forced his departure, Seibel drew 14,866 cartoons for *The Times-Dispatach*. MacNelly joined *The News Leader* as a 23-year-old in 1971 and left 11 years later to devote more time to his comic strip, "Shoe," but his syndicated editorial cartoons still appear in the new *Times-Dispatch.*

Modesty was a trait of both men, and neither was inclined to eviscerate the object of the day's cartoon, but there the similarities stop. Seibel stood barely over 5 feet and both his nose and his glasses seemed overly large. He wore suspenders. Whenever he padded around the newspaper building to look over out-of-town papers, he rarely struck up a conversation.

MacNelly is 6 feet, 4 inches tall and weighs about 220 pounds. He has an unruly shock of hair, seems totally at home in a pickup truck and, as his former editor at *The News Leader*, Ross Mackenzie wrote July 1, 1981, "[A]round the office and over Heaven-knows-how-many beers, he has been a stand-up comic."

Seibel came to *The Times-Dispatch* after 10 years with the *Albany Knickerbocker-Press.* As a youngster, he witnessed President McKinley's assassination in 1901. He claimed to have been a boilermaker's helper, apprentice machinist, photographer, clerk in a law office, laborer in an arms plant, bookkeeper, shoe salesman and commercial artist. While he held that last job with the *Utica Herald-Dispatch*, he submitted some cartoons. Some were published. That was no doubt a boost to his ego, for he had attended the Art Students League in New York before holding all those other jobs.

After Utica came Albany and Richmond. Upon Seibel's retirement in 1968, Editor Dabney of *The Times-Dispatch*, wrote about "the dizzy speed with which this up-state New Yorker was transformed into a Confederate. He hadn't been in Richmond a week before he sounded like an unreconstructed rebel after Appomattox. Before anybody could as much as say 'Damyankee,' Seibel had learned how to draw the old Virginia colonel with his goatee, to wave the Confederate flag in his cartoons on appropriate occasions, and to throw in a Virginia 'you-all' when the situation warranted."

On May 22, 1927, Seibel's cartoon in *The Times-Dispatch* celebrated Lindbergh's arrival in Paris and showed an eagle circling the Eiffel Tower. It was entitled "A Great Eagle With Great Wings Came," and Seibel thinks that was the one that drew wide attention to his work.

Early in his career, a little bird began appearing in each cartoon. As a youngster in upstate New York, Seibel had had a pet crow, and, as the years passed, "The Crow" appeared in his cartoons. Later it was named Moses Crow. Whenever a cartoon without Moses Crow appeared, readers became concerned.

"What in the world happened to Mr. Crow in Fred O. Seibel's daily cartoon of July 5?" wrote a reader in 1951. "Did he get clobbered on the Fourth by the wreck in the cartoon?"

An editor's note explained that the Crow was always the last thing Seibel drew in his cartoon. Sometimes he couldn't find an appropriate spot for the bird and sometimes—such as cartoons on the deaths of famous people—an appearance seemed out of place.

Seibel, who described himself as "a restless migratory bird," once wrote out for readers this explanation of Moses Crow. "The little bird that appears in my cartoons is a caricature of a crow. This is my trade mark. Outside of that it does not represent anything and has no significance.

"For the sake of variety, I change the attitude and expression of the crow from day to day in order to make it fit the idea of each cartoon, which makes him appear like a sort of interested spectator or innocent bystander who 'watches the passing show from day to day but doesn't quite know what it is all about.'"[293]

When Seibel had just finished 30 years at the paper, Charles McDowell wrote a long "personality profile" of the cartoonist.[294]

McDowell noted how people with virtually no interest in politics loved Seibel's cartoons. "His bewildered elephant and silly donkey, his stuffy little congressman in chin whiskers, and his wistful 'We the People' in sideburns and a high collar are symbols that everyone understands."

McDowell pried out of the cartoonist this idea of his work: "I think every cartoon should do at least one of three things. It should make the reader

"A Great Eagle With Great Wings Came"

laugh or cry or think. I usually try to make him laugh a little whether I can make him think or not."

Like *The News Leader's* editor, Dr. Freeman, Seibel followed a spartan regimen, although he did not, like Freeman, arise at 3:15 a.m. McDowell chronicled a typical Seibel day. Arise at 7 a.m., drink a cup of instant coffee, catch a bus for work (unless it was Saturday, when he drove his car downtown), go the post office on Main Street for mail at his personal box and catch another bus (unless it's Saturday) for a return to the newsroom at 9:15.

"With a quick, nervous motion," McDowell wrote, "he whips through a pile of out-of-town newspapers, making notes on a scrap of paper of articles, cartoons and photographs that he will clip later in the day for his files."

Then he would go up to his fourth-floor office, lock the door and spend a half-hour filing material. Next, he would repair to the John Marshall Hotel a block away, drink a chocolate malted and buy copies of the *Washington Star* and the *New York Herald-Tribune*. Back at *The Times-Dispatch* at 11 a.m. he would paw over the T-D and the papers he bought. He might go back to the newsroom, read papers again, consult with the editor or gaze out of the

F.D.R. Keeps on Sayin' Nothin'!

"Love Somebody But I Won't Say Who"

There Goes Harry—"He Done His Damndest"

TRUMAN'S PLACE IN HISTORY

©1-18-53

FRED O. SEIBEL

Retreat From "Moscow"

Saturday Feb 14 1948 Valentine Candies

window. If he didn't have an idea by 2:30 p.m., he would take a mild sedative. Usually the idea had come and he'd begin drawing by 3 p.m.

His cartoons took about two hours, although the Lindbergh cartoon in 1927 was begun at 4 p.m. and finished in 45 minutes.

On a normal day, Seibel showed his cartoon to the editor, whose simple nod meant approval. They chatted perhaps for a few minutes over a minor detail or the caption, and Seibel left for the engraving department, where he deposited the cartoon.

And, chronicled McDowell, "30 minutes later he is in a restaurant eating his first, and only, real meal of the day."

Seibel's work was widely recognized. In 1944, the Virginia Museum of Fine Arts displayed many of his cartoons and brought in Arthur Krock, then Washington Bureau chief of the *New York Times*, as speaker for the occasion. *The Times-Dispatch* editorial page noted then that as many as four of Seibel's cartoons had been reprinted in a single issue of the *Times*.

In 1951, Seibel's work was among that in the first editorial cartoon exhibit at the Metropolitan Museum of Fine Art. His work was included in a similar exhibit at Hilton House on Fleet Street in London in 1958. Many who were subjects of his cartoons asked for the originals—including Franklin D. Roosevelt and John L. Lewis. The champion individual collector was Sen. Harry F. Byrd, Sr., whose Washington office had more than 200 on the walls.

The Alderman Library at the University of Virginia has some 6,000 originals, half of which were taken there in 1968 with Seibel's research files. The university also has accouterments of his craft, such as his drawing board, pen knives and globe. It was at the Alderman Library in 1946 that he made one of his rare public appearances. McDowell reported that Seibel said he couldn't make a speech, but commented, "I couldn't make one if I wanted to. Any 10-year-old boy could make a better speech. For the past 20 years I have drawn cartoons, and I hope they speak for themselves. If not, I have wasted a great deal of time."[295]

His last cartoon was published January 25, 1968. It showed an upset Uncle Sam, worried about the Vietnam war and the latest indignity—the seizure of the naval ship Pueblo by North Koreans. Moses Crow stands there, much concerned.

A year later, Seibel was dead at 82. Some recalled a tribute to him and to Moses Crow penned by Robert Golden in *The Times-Dispatch*. It concluded:

> *"When you fulfill your mission and pass on to your reward,*
> *Which should be something pretty, we'll erect in our front yard,*
> *A tablet of enduring stone on which—that all may know—*
> *Shall be engraved:* 'Hic jacet *Fred O. Seibel's Moses Crow.*'"[296]

Briefly in the 1950s, *The Times-Dispatch* had two editorial cartoonists, although the No. 2 man, Hugh Haynie, spent most of his time in the newsroom, touching up photographs and drawing only when Seibel had a day off.

Haynie left the paper in 1951 to enter the Navy, returned in 1952 and was allowed to resign in 1953 by John Colburn, the managing editor, who always watched expenses closely and figured the job could be eliminated.

Seibel, recalled Haynie, had an office "up on the fourth floor back in the plumbing" and would give advice to the younger man—if asked. Haynie said he never argued with editorial writers—"those people were gods"—and he can't recall that any of his cartoons was rejected.[297]

Others, including the author, can.

One day when Seibel had the day off, Haynie turned in a cartoon showing President Eisenhower trying to restrain a tenacious bulldog with the face of Sen. Joseph McCarthy. Virginius Dabney was away, so K.V. Hoffman, the fiercest conservative among the editorial writers, was in charge. He rejected the cartoon.

James Eichner, a reporter in the 1950s before becoming a lawyer, recalled it well 40 years later. Haynie "was mad as hell about it," said Eichner.[298]

Colburn's getting rid of Haynie didn't hurt his career. He went to the *Greensboro* (North Carolina) *Daily News* and then to the *Louisville Courier-Journal.*

The News Leader had been without an editorial cartoonist since the mid-1950s, when a young dropout from the University of North Carolina walked into the editorial office in 1970. "Yet there he was—splay-footed, tie loosened, brush tucked behind his ear, sketch pad under his arm—smiling drolly like a Labrador puppy."

That's the description of Jeff MacNelly by Ross Mackenzie, editorial page editor of *The News Leader*, on the occasion of the artist's winning his first Pulitzer Prize in 1972—at age 24.

By the time he left *The News Leader* in 1981, MacNelly's syndicated cartoons were in 450 papers and his comic strip, "Shoe," was in 650. In 1993, he added another comic strip, "Pluggers."

Perhaps no journalist knows MacNelly better than Mackenzie, who, after the demise of *The News Leader*, now is editor of *The Times-Dispatch's* editorial page, one of the nation's most conservative. MacNelly's work—if it must be labeled—is probably conservative, but he is no ideologue.

Again, Mackenzie: "Jeff is an unassuming genius. Better than practically anyone, he perceives myth in reality, the childish in what is supposed

ARIZONA
DETROIT

GUNS
Butter

to be a world of adults. Each weekday morning he comes to work to distill the effluvia of the day before and hold it up. He possesses no passion to put America down, no desire to hurt. Rather, he seeks to elicit a laugh. Perhaps more than anything else, his cartoons are daily reminders that in this theater of the absurd called life there is no such thing as a single cockroach."

That appeared after MacNelly had won his second Pulitzer.[299] He was still 30. In 1985, he won his third Pulitzer for cartoons syndicated by the *Chicago Tribune* and carried in *The News Leader*.

In 1975, MacNelly was asked to accompany President Gerald Ford on a trip to Europe. He did so, drawing cartoons and reporting in *The News Leader* on his return. "Your initial awe at watching the President move in and out of cars, palaces and castles subsides very quickly," he said. "It is replaced by a mesmerizing astonishment at a much larger spectacle of the press—from the grizzled foreign correspondent scribbling notes in his palm, to the sea of photographers to the TV technician and his 60-pound humming, blinking backpack.

"During an infrequent lull, you find yourself wondering if all the hoopla is really necessary—if it couldn't be done a lot more easily and simply. But before you can complete the thought, there is another bus to catch—another deadline to meet."

The News Leader editorial page was gleeful in 1978, when MacNelly's cartoons submitted for an exhibition in Gabrovo, Bulgaria, were turned down.[300] A letter from the director of the House of Humor and Satire said,

". . . we are afraid your works are in contradiction with thc basic principles of the exhibition which is aimed at understanding and rapprochement of all nations. We believe this traveling exhibition will successfully fulfill this particular task, but some tendencies in the works of artists from one country against other countries cannot contribute to its proper realization. In connection with it, we'll be very glad to have works of yours which will help us to express our good will to all countries included."

The *News Leader* editor said that "the penitent MacNelly can be found in his office, undergoing re-education to purge his guilt."

As if the editorial cartoons and Shoe weren't enough to keep him busy, MacNelly illustrated *A POLITICAL BESTIARY* by former Sen. Eugene J. McCarthy and James J. Kilpatrick, the former editorial page editor of *The News Leader*. It was published in 1978 by McGraw-Hill Book Co.

On June 1, 1981, MacNelly announced he was giving up the daily cartoon business but planned to stay in Richmond.

"I almost punched a woman in New York a few years ago when she said, 'Jeez, it must be horrible to have to work in a place like Richmond.'" he told *The News Leader*.

"I'm just not a big city man," he said, "even though I grew up in the New York area. I've had opportunities to move to bigger cities, and maybe if I had not been syndicated, I might have moved to a big city. But when you're syndicated, you've got a good situation. You can work anywhere.

"Besides, I like Richmond."

His favorite years as a cartoonist, he said, were those of the Carter presidency. "I spent years down in North Carolina drawing gas stations and pickup trucks and rednecks and hound dogs," he said. "That's been my favorite setting. So when President Carter and Brother Billy came along, that probably was my heyday."

Mackenzie said in a column June 1 that MacNelly was "a reluctant assassin." Yet, MacNelly said, "This is a negative business. I find myself in agreement with some of the ideas being thrown around in Washington these days, and that makes it tough to be negative."

In a Newsweek article on cartoonists, accompanied by a cover picture of him, MacNelly said, "Political cartoonists violate every rule of ethical journalism—they misquote, trifle with the truth, make science fiction out of politics and sometimes should be held for personal libel. But when the smoke clears, the political cartoonist has been getting closer to the truth than the guys who write political opinions."[301]

In a statement on *The News Leader* editorial page, MacNelly explained why he wanted to concentrate on his comic strip, "Shoe."

"I would like to devote less time to the birdbrains on the national and international stages, thereby making room for new projects and new ideas."

SECTION G

• Controversy

Your Family Newspaper

THE RICHMOND NEWS LEADER

Blue Streak

117,521

RICHMOND, VA., 23219, MONDAY, JANUARY 10, 1972

10 CENTS

Merhige Calls for Metropolitan School System by Next September

By STEWART JONES

JUDGE ROBERT MERHIGE

See MERHIGE, Page 11

Surgeon General: People Still Smoke

Report Urges Safer Cigarettes

See SAFER, Page 7

Stock Trend Is Firmer After Skid

Wild Throng Welcomes Sheik Mujib

See MUJIB, Page 2

NORMAN RUSSELL ADAMS HOLDS HIS SON KEITH

Dad Calms Son In Trunk 'Prison'

By DEAN LEVI

Today Inside

Humphrey

State

Women

Head Restraints

Sports

The Index

News Bulletins

Ex-'Queen' Capsizes; Fire Spread Very Fast

See FORMER, Page 7

Second Slaying Laid to Suspect

By BILL WASSEN

See SUSPECT, Page 2

Today's Chuckle

North Anna Dam Closed

This mile-wide dam across the North Anna River in Louisa County was closed by the Virginia Electric & Power Co. in ceremonies today. Closing of the dam will create a 9,600-acre lake in about two years when filling is completed. The dam was plugged as part of the development of Vepco's North Anna Power Station, the company's second nuclear facility. The lake will be used for recreation. See story on Page 6.

MASSIVE RESISTANCE

Not since Lee's surrender at Appomattox had sleepy Southside Virginia been so much in the news. But now, in 1951, Prince Edward County's public school system, segregated by race as were other schools in the Old South, was being challenged by the National Association for the Advancement of Colored People.

The Prince Edward case and four others were considered together by the United State Supreme Court. In the editorial offices of Richmond's daily newspapers, opposition to integration was strong—as it was in most of the other dailies run by whites in the South.

Normally, editorials on the subject—the most important to the area in generations—would have been written by the papers' ranking editorialists. Such was not the case at *The Times-Dispatch*. Its editor was Virginius Dabney, an urbane, one-time liberal in his mid-50s, who had sympathized with the plight of blacks but who nevertheless opposed integration.

When the publisher approved a policy of Massive Resistance to integration, *The Times-Dispatch* editorials on that approach were written by Alan S. Donnahoe, vice-president of Richmond Newspapers Inc. At other times, K.V. Hoffman, who wrote a column under the pseudonym of Ross Valentine, flailed away at integrationists.

At *The News Leader*, James J. Kilpatrick, a brilliant reporter who had succeeded the revered Douglas Southall Freeman, as editor several years earlier, was ready to do battle. "Kilpo," who had few peers as a wordsmith, was some 20 years younger than Dabney. A transplanted Missourian, he was as determined a segregationist—by means always short of violence—as any Alabamian or Mississippian. If he was not the father of Massive Resistance, he was its godfather.

On March 8, 1952, *The News Leader* editorial page looked approvingly on a decision by five of six federal judges who found no harm to either race in Prince Edward County's segregated school system.

Kurt V. Hoffman was the most conservative of editorial writers in the Dabney regime. He also wrote a column under pseudonym of Ross Valentine.

Alan S. Donnahoe started out as researcher for Richmond Newspapers Inc. and ended up as president.

The paper agreed with a lower court ruling that the county must improve its Negro schools, but it noted that the appellate court had added, "It is not for us to adjudge the [segregation] policy as right or wrong—that the Commonwealth of Virginia should determine for itself."

That position, said *The News Leader*, recognized "the South's determined fight to leave state policy in the hands of the states. That is precisely where the decisions should be made."

Edward R. Murrow (left) of CBS came to Richmond in 1959 and talked with James J. Kilpatrick, editorial page editor of The News Leader *and one of the leading advocates of massive resistance to racial integration.*

Fifteen months later, in June 1953, when the U.S. Supreme Court decided the entire issue of school segregation should be reargued in its next term, *The News Leader* took heart. "For Virginians," said the editorial page, "there is nothing to be done now except to continue our efforts, as fairly and faithfully as possible, to equalize the white and Negro schools. If the court is as divided as yesterday's announcement would indicate, a vigorous demonstration of good intentions by the South in the next few months might well have a persuasive effect on the court's decision next Winter."

The court showed May 17, 1954, that it was not so persuaded.

During the rest of the decade, no single issue so engaged the editorial departments and news departments of *The Times-Dispatch* and *The News Leader* as did segregation. For reporters and editors in the news departments, it meant covering a ceaseless round of lawsuits, appeals, press conferences, regular and special sessions of the General Assembly and speeches ranging from the bombastic to the temperate.

The editorial pages of the Richmond papers had consistently supported racial segregation in the schools and in most other public places, although Dabney and *The Times-Dispatch* had urged, unsuccessfully, during World War II that enforced racial segregation—or "Jim Crow" practices—be ended on public transportation in Virginia.

But schools were special, the editorialists argued.

When the U.S. Supreme Court in 1954 showed that *The News Leader's* assessment of the justices' feelings 11 months earlier was hopelessly wrong, the editorial pages—for a while—urged calm and asked that the rest of the nation give the South time. That position lasted less than a year. Soon, both papers' editorial pages were routinely condemning the court and, with *The News Leader* directing the assault, urging virtually anything other than violence or secession to thwart the court's ruling.

Meanwhile, reporters went about covering the conflict. In late 1953, *The Times-Dispatch* heard that some of the plaintiffs in the Prince Edward County suit seeking desegregated schools were not really in favor of the course charted by the NAACP.

So, off to Prince Edward went two young general assignment reporters—Alf Goodykoontz and Bill McIlwain. Both would later have distinguished newspaper careers. Goodykoontz became managing editor of *The Times-Dispatch*, executive editor of *The Times-Dispatch* and *The News Leader* and national president of the Society of Professional Journalists. McIlwain moved on to high editing positions with *Newsday* and with papers in Boston, Washington, Toronto, Little Rock and elsewhere.

Goodykoontz and McIlwain interviewed 19 of the 69 families listed as plaintiffs in the suit; those 19 families included 36 of the 118 plaintiffs.

Their story, in the off-lead position of the December 13 *Times-Dispatch*, began: "Negro students, parents and guardians involved in the Prince Edward County school segregation suit are in sharp disagreement on how they hope the United States Supreme Court will rule in the case."

Of those interviewed, "Some of them say they want segregation ended.

"Some of them say they definitely do not.

"Some of them seem to stand in the middle."

The totals, as listed by Goodykoontz and McIlwain, were five families for integration, six opposed and eight somewhere in between.

Dorothy Davis, a key plaintiff whose reputed disavowal of integrated schools had sparked the reporters' trip to Prince Edward, was quoted by them as saying that with a new school for Negroes, "I'd rather have it go on the way it is. . . . I don't think we'd be happy, and I don't think they'd [the whites] be happy." Her mother praised the new school and said of desegregation, "I don't want it. The new school is what we wanted and that's what we got. I don't see why anybody wants to go any further."

The story continued with lengthy quotes from advocates and opponents of integration.

Oliver Hill, a former member of Richmond's city council, the leading black lawyer in the city and a member of the plaintiffs' legal team in Prince Edward, quickly assembled a meeting of black parents and children with the lawyers.

On December 22, *The News Leader* reported that Dorothy Davis, after the meeting, had changed her mind and now favored integrated schools. Hill said that "regardless of what we have read in the newspapers, up to the present time, the attorneys have not been advised that anyone is not satisfied with the course of action we have taken nor has anyone asked to withdraw from the case."

Anticipating a Supreme Court ruling on school segregation, politicians of varying political hues were urging action. Del. John B. Boatwright, a most conservative Democrat, suggested a convention to amend the Virginia constitution in case the high court ordered desegregation. But leaders of the ruling Byrd organization disagreed, and *The Times-Dispatch* on March 5 editorialized: "We can well afford to await the court's decision, and then to act in the light of that decision."

Del. Armistead L. Boothe, a liberal Democrat, wanted a race relations commission appointed by the legislature, and State Sen. Ted Dalton, the Republican loser in the previous year's gubernatorial race, pushed for a study group headed by Colgate W. Darden Jr., president of the University of Virginia and a former governor.

The legislature accepted neither, leaving Boothe, a prominent Episcopal layman, to urge "prayerful individual consideration" of race relations and *The News Leader* editorial page to express its own regrets.

"Our view," said the paper on March 13, "is that if advance study had any influence at all on the [supreme] court, it would be taken as a sign that Virginia is ready to undertake its duties in a calm, sensible frame of mind and that the solution should best be left where it belongs—*in the hands of the State*."

On March 19, 1954, *The Times-Dispatch* editorial page found itself in agreement with Harry Ashmore, a Southerner who later would be a harsh critic of segregationists and who earlier had talked with executives about an editorial job in Richmond. What *The Times-Dispatch* liked was this quote from Ashmore's *The Negro and the Schools*: "If at any point in the past, discrimination had been wiped out by total integration, the effect would have been that some Negroes would have gone to better schools and some whites to worse—but no appreciable economies would have resulted to make additional funds available for improvement of the total system."

On March 28, *The News Leader* editorial page commended Gov. Thomas B. Stanley, who had said schools would open in the fall on a regular [segregated] basis and who had indirectly rebuked the NAACP. "In the course of time—in the course of a quite considerable time," said *The News Leader*, "some tax-supported schools in the South may be operated on an integrated basis, but this will come first in areas of minute Negro population."

The following day, *The Times-Dispatch* editorial page criticized the NAACP for pushing for integration the next September (assuming, of course, that the Supreme Court would outlaw segregation). Similar criticism of the civil rights organization was voiced by the *Atlanta Constitution* and the *Greensboro* (North Carolina) *Daily News*.

The decision came May 17, and *The News Leader's* front page in its final edition had these banner headlines:

School Segregation Ruled Out

Stanley to Call Conference on Decision

The wire service story said: "WASHINGTON, May 17—(AP)—The Supreme Court today declared unanimously that race segregation in the public schools is unconstitutional and so eventually must end."

At the bottom of the page was a separate story quoting Sen. Byrd as saying the decision was "the most serious blow that has been struck against the rights of States in a matter vitally affecting their authority and welfare."

The next morning's *Times-Dispatch*, with eight or more hours to prepare its presentation, had a banner head on the lead story by the Associated Press out of Washington and other front-page stories by James Latimer on Virginia officials' reaction and by the author on Richmond school officials' decision to look to the state for guidance. Inside the paper was a map showing Negro school enrollments, locality by locality. Additional stories dealt with the new role of Negro teachers and reaction to the decision from other localities.

Editorialists on Richmond's dailies had been quite clear in their desire for continued segregation in the schools. Yet, their initial reactions to the

Supreme Court ruling of May 17 were calm, dispassionate and, to some degree, accepting. That would not last. Both papers—especially *The News Leader*—soon supported Massive Resistance to integration, as proposed by the Byrd organization.

In the months and years to come, *The News Leader* passionately led the fight against integration and advocated, in frequent and lengthy editorials, a position of "interposition" of state sovereignty against federal power. It was a modern day version of nullification. The chief advocates were *The News Leader's* editor, Kilpatrick, and William Old, judge of Chesterfield Circuit Court in the Richmond metropolitan area.

The Times-Dispatch, while not as all-out a "resister" as its sister paper, ran numerous editorials pointing to segregation and hypocrisy north of the Mason-Dixon line and condemning Northern liberals who pointed fingers of guilt at the South.

In general, *The News Leader* attacked; *The Times-Dispatch* wrung its hands.

The morning after the decision—May 18—*The Times-Dispatch* said editorially: "We had hoped that the court would uphold the 'separate but equal doctrine,' but since it did not do so, this is a time for calm and unhysterical appraisal of the situation by the officials and people of Virginia and the 16 other states where segregated schools are now required. The serious problems created by this decision can only be solved in such an atmosphere, and over a period of time.'"

The paper said the court would have been "on sounder ground" if it had granted "a specific number of years for compliance." Why, asked the paper, didn't the court suggest steps such as segregation "10 percent eliminated the first year after the decrees became effective and 40 percent more two years later, perhaps, and the remaining 50 percent some years after that."

Concluding its two-column long editorial, the paper said, "So, despite yesterday's ruling by the court, epoch-making though it still is, segregation in the public schools of the South is not about to be eliminated. Final achievement of that objective is years, perhaps many years, in the future.

"What seems desirable today, in the light of the court's finding, is for men and women of good will in both races to keep their heads, to avoid threats and hysteria, and to seek reasonable and sane solutions. It is only thus that the many knotty problems posed by yesterday's truly historic decision can be solved."

The News Leader of May 18 was similarly thoughtful. "This is no time for rebellion," it said. "It is no time for a weak surrender either. It is a time to sit tight, to think, to unite in a proposal that would win the Supreme

Court's approval. It is a time, if you like, for prayer. The profound implications of the court's opinion are well understood in the South, and now that the basic opinion has come—now that the suspense has ended—we can ponder those implications, and consider the best and wisest recommendation to offer to the court next Fall."

In conclusion, the paper said, "We accept the Supreme Court's ruling. We do not accept it willingly, or cheerfully or philosophically. We accept it because we have to, and we accept it in the profound and prayerful hope that the court, when it comes to writing a final decree many months from now, will exercise wisdom and forbearance in drafting a mandate that will preserve good race relations, encourage continued public education, and recognize that the States and localities should be left a wide area for local responsibility consistent with the court's opinion."

Calm was still the word in Richmond and much of the rest of Virginia throughout the spring and early summer of 1954. Gov. Stanley announced he would appoint a commission, probably in the late summer, James Latimer reported in *The Times-Dispatch* May 20, to study "the problem of reconciling Virginia's education system to the Supreme Court's decision ending racial segregation in the public schools."

The News Leader of May 24 noted in a front-page story that Stanley was to meet that day with Oliver Hill and other leading blacks. On the editorial page, all was peace and calm. "The sun has continued to rise in the morning," the paper said; "it still sets in the afternoon. We still have with us the Indochina situation, the McCarthy hearings, and one-run losses by the Virginians [Richmond's entry in baseball's International League]. . . . This is not Fort Sumter but is not Appomattox either." The paper cautioned that a "long and uncertain" road was ahead and that many white Southerners wouldn't send their children to integrated schools. It suggested—perhaps ominously—further exploration of private schools.

On June 7, *The Times-Dispatch* commended to its readers an article in *The New York Times Magazine* by Cabell Phillips, who had studied Jeffersonville, Indiana That city, with a 10 percent black population, took three years to integrate its schools. Phillips argued that "it is wise to make the change gradually, beginning with the lower grades and working up over a three-to-six-year period to the high school level."

Phillips was a former *Times-Dispatch* reporter, which the editorial did not mention.

If the editorial pages in Richmond were calm, readers throughout *The Times-Dispatch* circulation area (roughly a third of the state) were increasingly concerned. There were so many letters to the editor that *The Times-*

Dispatch said it would run only those advocating a new approach to the segregation issue and offering "some fresh or novel analysis or facts." It would continue not to run letters that were violent or abusive or involved personal attacks on others.

On June 20, Thurgood Marshall, chief counsel of the NAACP, told a group of Richmond Negroes that since segregation was on the way out, they "shouldn't walk around with a big stick or with hat in hand."

Five days later, *The Times-Dispatch* reported that Del. Armistead Boothe, rebuffed earlier by Gov. Stanley, was still trying to get Virginia to act. He had sent a 19-question form to members of the legislature asking their ideas on desegregation. About a third replied. Boothe sent the responses to Stanley with the suggestion that the Supreme Court "should be made to understand the intensity of feeling in Virginia and should be shown a constructive way and Virginia way to meet the problem."

Stanley would neither release Boothe's letter nor comment on it. Instead, one day later, he recommended amending the section of the state constitution requiring the legislature to "establish and maintain an efficient system of free public schools in Virginia." The legislature, said Stanley, should have "full rein" to deal with the Supreme Court's ruling on desegregation.

Things began heating up. State Sen. Garland Gray and Rep. William M. Tuck, a former governor, praised Stanley's plan, *The Times-Dispatch* reported, whereas Del. Robert Whitehead and State Sen. Ted Dalton opposed it. "This could be the first step toward doing away with our public school system," said Dalton. "This must never happen in Virginia."

The Times-Dispatch editorial page of June 27 accused Stanley of muddying the waters by talking about a constitutional amendment, when Attorney General J. Lindsay Almond Jr. had said such a move was unnecessary to keep the races segregated.

If public schools were not to admit blacks and whites together, the Catholic schools would. *The News Leader* of July 15 reported that Catholic high schools in Roanoke and Northern Virginia would integrate in the fall. In Richmond, Catholic school officials announced even before the Supreme Court ruling that they would integrate in the fall. Nowhere in the state were there any Catholic high schools solely for blacks.

On August 28, Gov. Stanley fulfilled part of his promise of mid-May. He appointed a 32-member commission on Virginia's answer to the desegregation decree. It was an all-male, all-white, all-legislative commission. Explaining his switch from the promised citizen commission, Stanley said he acted after "further thought and many discussions with citizens, school officials and legislators."

Editorial reactions differed. *The Times-Dispatch* of August 30, reminding readers that it had favored a commission of blacks and whites and including non-legislators, pointed to the 1950 census. It showed 734,211 blacks among the state's 3,318,680 citizens—between a fourth and a fifth of the total.

"It is taken for granted," said the paper, "that Negroes will have an adequate opportunity to express themselves before the commission, along with other Virginians."

The same day's *News Leader* noted that it, too, had favored citizen members of the commission but now agreed with the governor. "Gov. Stanley," it said, "was on the right track . . . when he created a commission to study problems of school segregation and confined its membership to legislators only."

The commission, titled the State Commission on Public Education, met for the first time September 13 and chose State Sen. Gray, a staunch Byrd organization conservative, as chairman. Most of its deliberations were closed, *The News Leader* reported in its lead story. Gov. Stanley told the group that its mission was to find a "legal means" to preserve school segregation in Virginia.

Two weeks later, Chief Justice Earl Warren of the United States Supreme Court kept a long-standing commitment to attend a ceremony at the College of William and Mary, the nation's second oldest institution of higher learning. Ranking Virginia politicians made a point of not attending the event in Williamsburg. *The News Leader* used the visit as the basis for a stern editorial lecture to Warren, who, it said, would have little time for "the Not Very Important People of Virginia."

In content and tone, it spelled out *The News Leader's* stance for the years ahead.

Acknowledging past wrongs in race relations, the editorial said Virginians have concern for "the preservation of a way of life that seems to them the best that can be devised in a biracial society. . . .

"We would say to the Chief Justice: You and your associates have dishonored the Constitution, as we have known and cherished it; you have substituted the vague precepts of "psychology" for the plain mandates of law and precedent; you have trampled upon the clear right of States when it was your duty to preserve them; you would impose tyranny upon the South, a form of tyranny that the Not Very Important People deeply, strongly resent. And they are a proud people, these ordinary men and women; they do not choose to be coerced.

"We would say to the Chief Justice that the South proposes no wrong to the Negro, but the South does not propose to go backward either. We will resist this judgment of the court; we will resist it quietly, honorably, lawfully, but we will resist it with the strength of a tradition that has resisted tyranny before."

On October 27, *The Times-Dispatch* reported on the front page the chartering of an organization that would be at the forefront of resistance to any integration of any school anywhere in Virginia. It was the Defenders of State Sovereignty and Individual Liberties, dominated by Southside Virginians. Its president was Robert Crawford, a former member of the Prince Edward County School Board and a dry cleaner in Farmville.

The Defenders, said the secretary, William B. Cocke, clerk of the Sussex County Circuit Court, "will act with determination and firmness to retain, by all honorable and legal means, segregated schools."

On November 15, the State Commission on Public Education—now informally known as the Gray Commission, for State Sen. Gray—held a public hearing at the Mosque, a large city-owned auditorium with 3,732 seats. Between 10 a.m. and 11:30 p.m., 100 or so people spoke to an audience of about 2,000. *The Times-Dispatch* reported three choices were offered. The first, favored by most white speakers, was to keep segregation—by some method. The second, favored by all black speakers, was integration—either slowly or fast. The third was local option on desegregation or segregation.

Coincidentally, the same day's paper reported in its off-lead story that Virginia had asked the Supreme Court to remand the Prince Edward case to a federal district court for further proceedings and no timetable for desegregation.

Editorially, *The Times-Dispatch* found the hearing well-handled although no new arguments were advanced. "Those who argued. . . for a maximum amount of local discretion with respect to the schools were the ones who appealed most strongly to *The Times-Dispatch*," said the paper.

The News Leader delayed a day putting its thoughts on record, then declared November 17 that "Monday's 13-hour Chautauqua in the Mosque was as profitless a performance as that gaudy opera house has witnessed in many years. The hearing constituted a perfunctory, *pro forma* gesture on the part of Sen. Gray's commission; it produced nothing new, it changed no one's mind. It was as useless as the debates of Congress."

Yet, the paper had not reached its position of defiance. The editorial said the state could endorse full segregation or full integration.

". . . Or we could search for a legal, constitutional solution by which the education of all Virginia children could be continued in a pattern that suits the individual localities most deeply concerned.

"This newspaper does not believe Virginia is ready for anarchy or for surrender either."

On January 20, 1955, *The Times-Dispatch* reported that the Gray Commission "formally declared its goal to be sought in its studies is a lawful way to prevent enforced integration, of white and Negro pupils in Virginia public schools." Gray said after a three-and-one-half-hour closed session that the "overwhelming majority" of Virginians wanted segregated schools.

The commission also named as counsel David J. Mays, a noted Richmond lawyer, constitutional scholar and winner of a Pulitzer Prize for biography.

Now that school segregation had been ruled unconstitutional, other forms of public segregation were to be wiped out by court ruling. Richmond editorialists were not happy with a Fourth U.S. Circuit Court ruling that racial barriers on playgrounds must be lifted.

". . .[A]dequate time must be allowed," said *The Times-Dispatch* of March 16, "for the South to become adjusted to the court decisions which now are coming with accelerated tempo."

The News Leader of the same day said that the Fourth Circuit Court, "one of the strongest and most highly regarded benches in the nation, flubbed a key decision." It was wrong, said the *Leader*, to say the Brown case swept away all public segregation, and the appellate court went further than the Supreme Court in "vitiating the well-established police power of State and local governments." Brown vs. Board of Education was the title of the desegregation case that also involved Prince Edward County, Virginia.

It would be better, said the editorial, to close publicly owned swimming pools. "The people of Virginia in our view," said the paper, "are emphatically unwilling to accept mixed bathing."

Earlier the paper had said the state should sell its parks because it had no business in the "commercial resort business."

On April 13, the editorial page of *The News Leader* displayed charts to show that Negro children did significantly worse than whites on the Iowa Silent Reading Test and the American Council on Education scholastic aptitude test. The paper said it didn't understand why the results were as they were, but "it is the 'how' that should be soberly considered by the high court before it attempts to impose upon the South a violent dissection in the operation of our public schools. It is the 'how' that counts if white children are not to be unfairly dragged down to the intellectual level of the Negro children, or the Negro children are to be ordered to keep up with a level of educational capacity that is demonstrably beyond their immediate reach."

Eight days later, *The News Leader* was back with the same figures, saying it seemed, based on American Council on Education statistics, that in Virginia cities, the lower half of the class would contain three-fourths of the blacks and one-fourth of the whites, while the upper half would contain three-fourths of the whites and one-fourth of the blacks.

"It is entirely possible," the editorial conceded, "that a Negro student could be the most brilliant student in the class, and a white student the slowest of the lot—but these would be unusual exceptions."

On May 31, 1955, the Supreme Court let the other shoe drop—giving local federal courts and local school systems responsibility for ending school segregation "with all deliberate speed." Virginia's attorney general, Lindsay Almond, said, "I feel we got about all we could ask for." He added that it was not for his office to make policy or law; that was the executive office's job.

Spottswood W. Robinson III, a lawyer for the Prince Edward plaintiffs, said the latest opinion along with the original Brown decision, "destroyed all vestiges of racial segregation in public schools. . . .The court has afforded the South a reasonable period within which to make an effective transition to non-segregated education."

The Times-Dispatch's editorial of June 1 said the South had "reason for relative gratification."

The News Leader of the same day had a good bit more to say. Quoting the court as saying if Prince Edward sought more time, it must show that time was "necessary in the public interest and is consistent with good faith compliance at the earliest practicable date. The paper had its own timetable.

"And when is the earliest practicable date? In Prince Edward County, we should place it somewhere around the turn of the next century."

Furthermore, said *The News Leader*, Virginia should repeal laws requiring compulsory attendance and segregated schools, should let localities that wish to integrate do so, permit individual pupil assignments, decentralize schools as much as possible and perhaps pass some legislation that would give fresh stimulus to the operation of private schools. The paper didn't know how that would work but said it was worth trying.

"Is all of this to advocate that Virginia attempt, by lawful means, to get around the law?

"That is exactly what we advocate.

"In May of 1954, that inept fraternity of politicians and professors known as the United States Supreme Court chose to throw away the established law.

". . . When the court proposes that its social revolution be imposed upon the South 'as soon as practicable,' there are those of us who would respond that 'as soon as practicable' means never at all."

If readers had thought *The News Leader* was accepting desegregation, even grudgingly, a year earlier, they knew differently now.

Del. Robert Whitehead, commenting on *The News Leader's* editorial of June 1, said the only reason the paper didn't "advocate that Virginia secede from the Union is because the last attempt at secession was a failure." The paper replied June 8 that it believed in public education but that it was not the be-all and end-all for everyone.

The News Leader, said the editorial, "does not take an 'extremist' position; it favors local desegregation if that's what locals want.

"At no time has this newspaper joined those 'who would close every public school in Virginia irrespective of the decision reached by the local people, rather than have one colored child in school with white children."

Even that position would change as resistance became more massive.

The Defenders of State Sovereignty and Individual Liberties were quickly becoming a bigger player. On June 9, the lead story in *The Times-Dispatch* was James Latimer's, telling of the Defenders' call for an early session of the legislature to deny any public money for any racially integrated schools.

Delivering a nine-point plan to the Gray Commission, the Defenders said, "Unless something be done now, integration might well begin in Virginia, and once begun, now, it, like every other vile pestilence, will spread to the point where it has covered the whole body politic."

Two days later, the Gray Commission urged retaining segregation at least one more year. Gov. Stanley endorsed the plan, told the State Board of Education to follow it and ruled out a special session of the legislature. *The Times-Dispatch* editorial page of June 11 called the plan "a sane and sense-making statement" and commended the governor and the commission for "the calm, reasonable and intelligent position they have taken." *The News Leader* of the same day said editorially that the commission had no specific legislative proposals. Standing pat is fine if it works, said the paper, but "the Federal courts may not be so accommodating as Gov. Stanley hopes."

On June 12, *The Times-Dispatch* carried a front-page story by one of its reporters who had toured Southside Virginia and found, to the surprise of few, that whites there feared social change, while blacks said that "separate but equal" didn't work.

The reporter, L.M. Wright Jr., a young graduate of Wake Forest University, was fascinated by race relations in the South. His stories were so detailed, so frequent and so long that colleagues, part in admiration and part in jest, called him "The Arm." He was also so factual and so fair that when he left *The Times-Dispatch* to become a Nieman Fellow at Harvard University, he received letters of commendation from both the NAACP and the Defenders.

On June 24, *The News Leader*, in an editorial titled "A Weak Reed in the Storm," accused the state administration of "abandoning Prince Edward County as a pawn in the larger game." The state, said the *Leader*, should have provided the county with a tax exemption law, a pupil assignment law or an educational aptitude law—or something—that the county could take back to the federal court as the basis for seeking additional time "in which to strive to keep public education alive."

One June 30, *The News Leader* trotted out a soul mate, W.E. Debnam of Raleigh, whose latest book was *Then My Old Kentucky Home, Good Night*. In it, Debnam wrote, "Integration, no matter how gradually it comes, is still integration and means the destruction of both races. . . . A man is just as dead if he slowly bleeds to death from slashed wrists as if his throat be cut from ear to ear."

The News Leader declared: "We share Mr. Debnam's conviction entirely."

On July 25, that paper's editorial page criticized the *Roanoke Times* for saying a court ruling on desegregating state parks shouldn't slow work on Breaks Interstate Park in Dickenson County. *The News Leader* didn't complain about Mount Vernon and Monticello being open to all, but state parks were commercial state resorts with the same diving floats and meals in the same dining lodge. It didn't think Virginians of either race favored "mixed bathing and close social mingling."

The Times-Dispatch worried in a July 16 editorial titled "The Blitzkrieg Speed of Race Decisions" that desegregation decisions from the courts "are coming too rapidly for the good of both races." The paper traced its own opposition to Jim Crow laws for public transportation and noted there had been none until 1902. But Negro leaders saw a conservative approach didn't work and "they turned to Harlem. The results are obvious to all."

The News Leader's editorial page was concerned not only about Virginia. On August 16, it commended Gov. Luther Hodges of North Carolina for pleading for continued segregated schools by the voluntary acceptance of them by whites and Negroes. Four days later, the paper told Norfolk to forget any idea of "three-way" schools—white, Negro and desegregated. The trouble was, said *The News Leader*, that the Supreme Court had said Negroes couldn't be denied access to a school based on race alone.

On August 22, *The Times-Dispatch* editorial page found a black soul mate—Zora Neale Thurston, the writer—and reprinted a letter she had written to the *Orlando Sentinel* in which she called the Brown decision "insulting rather than honoring my race." *The Times-Dispatch* called Ms. Thurston an "extraordinarily courageous woman."

With the arrival of fall, *The News Leader's* editorial page was becoming more fierce. On October 3, it declared that the Supreme Court's erred in its second decision—giving the states time to adjust to the first (Brown). "First, the court would stab us in the back; a year later it would hit us in the head." The idea, said the paper, was that the South would adjust.

"It is evident now," continued the editorial, "that the court's slick strategy has misfired. Far from calming down, opposition is growing daily more resolute. Far from cooling off, the heat or resentment grows more intense."

A year of grace has enabled the South to set up roadblocks, and, "We begin to take heart."

Concluding, *The News Leader* said, "We can say to the NAACP that it will have to fight a hundred times harder for each inch of ground that it gains; and we can say to the Supreme Court, with more than mere bravado, *the South has just begun to fight.*"

Now, *The News Leader* waded into the position of the Stanley administration, which it found less firm than those of Sen. Byrd, leader of the state's Democratic organization, or former Gov. and now Rep. Tuck. The paper understood Byrd's position to be that any locality that chose desegregation would get no state money for schools.

"Virginians have needed firm, vigorous leadership, and Mr. Stanley has sadly failed to provide it," said the paper on November 2. "Now that the big two in Virginia public life have entered the field, we may yet have some leadership to rally to. Mr. Tuck and Mr. Byrd are the more welcome because they have stayed on the sidelines so long."

The Times-Dispatch that day applauded Sen. Byrd's tentative endorsement of a local option plan proposed by Reps. Tuck and Watkins M. Abbitt. "The localities own the school facilities," said the editorial. "It is reasonable to conclude, therefore, that the 'right to ascertain the will of the qualified voters in each locality' must be 'reserved to the people.'"

The Gray Commission timed the release of its plan for Sunday papers, and *The Times-Dispatch* obliged not only by reporting on it at length as the lead story in the November 13 paper but also by reprinting the entire report on facing, inside pages.

"The official blueprint for reconstructing Virginia school policy so as to avert compulsory integration of white and Negro pupils was unveiled yesterday," reported James Latimer.

There were two key features of the plan. The first called for a special session of the legislature to consider a bill for a referendum on whether a limited constitutional convention should amend Section 141 of the state constitution. That section prohibited using public funds for private schools. The Supreme Court of Virginia had just ruled out such spending even if the benefit were indirect.

Secondly, if the state's constitution were amended so public funds could benefit private schools, the Gray Commission plan would (a) let localities assign students for any reason other than race, (b) provide, through tuition grants, for private schooling of students and (c) amend attendance laws so that no student would be forced to attend an integrated school.

The tuition grants would go to children in localities with no public schools or to those whose parents didn't want them in integrated schools.

Although the plan was obviously designed to ward off all possible integration, it appealed both to moderate whites and to conservative editorialists—such as those in Richmond.

The Times-Dispatch, in an editorial titled "The Gray Commission's Good Report," wondered if the plan—which it said was halfway between never-never integration and pro-integration—would satisfy the Supreme Court. The paper, noting that the report was signed by all 32 members of the commission, was reassured that it did not tamper with the constitutional provision for the General Assembly to "establish and maintain an efficient system of free public schools throughout the state."

The News Leader endorsed the plan but used the occasion also to flail the Supreme Court and put in a plug for withholding tax money for any integrated schools. The effort took three editorials.

"What the Court did in *Brown vs. Board of Education*, said the paper, "was to abolish long-established law and to amend the Constitution by its own lawless and unconstitutional action. And having flouted the law and the Constitution, it has had the arrogance to say to the South: *'We are the law and will compel you to obey.'*

". . . So twisted, the Constitution in the hands of this court has ceased to be a shield against oppression and has become an instrument of tyranny instead."

There was an emotional appeal to defiance, said the paper, but "calm consideration leads inevitably to the conclusion that no state could be permitted to pick and choose the court opinions it would abide by. . . . To urge repudiation of the court's authority, in the end, is to urge secession from the Union."

The editorial added that it would have preferred the Tuck-Abbitt plan be added to the recommendations. That would have said no taxpayer would have to approve money for local, integrated schools. But, overall, the commission's plan was "a good and desirable program and should merit State-wide support."

By November 16, *The Times-Dispatch* was back on integration problems elsewhere. It noted editorially that in New York City, children were in schools that were about 90 percent black or white and that the *New York Times* and other "doctrinaire liberals" favored redrawing attendance lines to promote more integration.

The 21st day of November in 1955 may go down as the day that *The News Leader* embarked on its all-out resistance to any integration. It seemed that Kilpatrick's thinking on the issue had crystallized, for his editorial page began the first day of three days' analyses of constitutional rights and "the law of the land."

The first dealt with the Kentucky-Virginia Resolutions and is believed to be the first editorial mention in the 1950s of "interposition," as proposed by Jefferson and Madison in the second Kentucky Resolution. That amounted to nullification of the Sedition Act, which had by then expired anyhow.

"Yet, said *The News Leader*, "we may well ask ourselves in 1955, confronting a manifestly unconstitutional action *not by the Congress but by the Supreme Court*, whether the principles enunciated so forcefully by Jefferson and Madison may not have great validity today."

One editorial of November 22 was titled "The Right of Interposition" and urged the Gray Commission to explore the "fundamental principles" of Jefferson and Madison. "Virginians of today may yet inquire if these great men, long ago, did not foresee the constitutional crisis before us in 1955 and point a way toward its peaceful solution."

There were three editorials on the matter and a reprint of excerpts from a 1799 committee headed by James Madison in the Virginia House of Delegates.

The next day's *News Leader* carried five editorials on the issue and a reprint of John C. Calhoun's document on interposition. The paper said that on May 17 of the previous year, "on the naked and arrogant declaration of nine men, the Supreme Court itself undertook to . . . amend the Constitution." The paper foresaw a court ruling out state laws on interracial marriage and urged all states to resist "this rape of the Constitution.

". . . Unless interposition is made now, in a desperate effort to halt this process of judicial amendment of the Constitution, the States inevitably will be reduced to non-entities; and the whole structure of our Union will be radically altered."

Meanwhile, *The Times-Dispatch* had assigned a general assignment reporter, Larry Weekley, to go to Washington and look at its already desegregated schools. Weekley's four-part series, beginning January 31, 1956, noted that the process had been "thorough, peaceful and compulsory" and with no violence.

At the same time, the campaign led by *The News Leader's* editorial page and other bitter-end opponents of any integration paid off. On February 2, *The Times-Dispatch* reported there was overwhelming legislative support (36-2 in the Senate; 90-5 in the House) for interposition. To the General Assembly, the Supreme Court had engaged in "illegal encroachment" on states' rights. But Del. Robert Whitehead, in a one-hour, 48-minute speech, declared that the resolution, despite its "sweet-sounding name," meant nullification.

The last of Weekley's reports from Washington in *The Times-Dispatch*, on February 3, stressed white flight and concluded, "Yet, the trend is there. Another 20 years like the past and there will be practically no young white families with children living in the District of Columbia."

An editorial page can go much further than a reporter as observer. *The Times-Dispatch* did so on February 5, citing Weekley's series. The editorial noted the white flight and further alleged curtailed extra-curricular activities, tardiness and personal uncleanliness in the District schools. It saw a Pandora's box in what the South would face in a similar situation: a "multiplicity of difficulties that would be turned loose upon the South if coercive integration became a reality."

On February 10, *The Times-Dispatch* editorial page took pride in local behavior over that further south. Still, it had a warning. The paper tut-tutted the behavior of a crowd at the University of Alabama, where Autherine Lucy, a black student, had been admitted. By comparison, the entry five years earlier of Jean Harris, as a student at the Medical College of Virginia, in Richmond, had been marked by no demonstration.

But, said the paper, "if the federal government attempts to compel the whole South to integrate in the face of overwhelmingly hostile popular sentiment, other similarly indefensible episodes are inevitable."

In the General Assembly, Speaker E. Blackburn Moore, an intimate friend of U.S. Sen. Byrd, had proposed holding the line on total segregation for a year. *The Times-Dispatch* of February 20 found that "dismaying." Joining the *Norfolk Virginian-Pilot* and *Roanoke Times* in opposing that move, *The Times-Dispatch* said Virginians in the northern and western parts of the state had been told they could prevent integration in the Southside and Tidewater areas and go ahead with it in their own areas if they chose, as provided by the Gray Commission and the special session of the legislature in December.

Following that special session, Gov. Stanley signed a bill for a January 9 referendum on whether the state constitution should be amended to permit public funds to be used for private schools as an alternative to integrated schools. The vote was affirmative and on February 21, voters chose delegates to a constitutional convention on March 5. Its purpose was to amend Section 141 of the constitution so as to provide the tuition grants the Gray Commission envisioned.

Although it was moving toward a no-integration-at-all stance, *The News Leader's* editorial page couldn't buy a proposal by Del. Sam Pope of Southampton County to prohibit any Virginia public school athletic team from competing against a team with members of another race. "When the South goes to this extreme in attempting to prevent association between the races," said the paper, "the South does not appear wise and prudent; the South appears silly and picayune. We do not strengthen our case; we weaken it."

Before the month was out, Harry Byrd was on the interposition bandwagon. *The Times-Dispatch* carried an Associated Press story out of Washington February 26 in which the senator said, "If we can organize the Southern states for massive resistance to this order, I think that in time the rest of the country will realize that racial integration is not going to be accepted in the South." He called interposition a "perfectly legal means" in the fight.

That Page One story may have been the first time "massive resistance" was described in print as the course Virginia would follow. In any case, the phrase became THE description of Virginia's posture toward racial integration in the schools.

James Latimer wonders, however, if perhaps he misunderstood Byrd during a conversation several weeks earlier. Byrd was in Richmond to make a speech, and Latimer slipped away from the General Assembly session he was covering to talk briefly with the senator. In a noisy room at the hotel where Byrd was to speak, Latimer understood Byrd to say the state's position should be "passive resistance" and used the phrase in a story in *The Times-Dispatch*.[302]

Then, several weeks later, came the AP story quoting Byrd as recommending "massive resistance." Byrd never corrected Latimer for using "passive" instead of "massive," and the two never discussed the change of phrasing. Latimer wonders if perhaps someone, impressed by Secretary of State John Foster Dulles' advocacy of "massive retaliation" in case of a military move by the Soviet Union, might have suggested that Byrd urge "massive resistance" to integration.

An editorial in *The Times-Dispatch* March 7 commended William Faulkner for his article in *Life* magazine in which he urged the NAACP and its allies to go slow on pushing for "immediate and unconditional integration."

That same day's paper reported on the front page that the state's constitutional convention had unanimously voted to amend the constitution to provide tax money through tuition grants to students in private, non-sectarian schools.

The House of Delegates passed the Pope bill on integration in athletics, to the dismay of *The Times-Dispatch* editorial page of March 9, which noted also that moderates like Dorothy Thompson and Walter Lippmann were coming to understand the South's position on race relations.

The regular 1956 session of the General Assembly ended, and *The Times-Dispatch* editorial page of March 12 observed that as for integration, the legislators' action was "nothing to shout about. The best that can be said is that matters might have been worse."

The paper toted up the actions: (1) Approval of interposition with an amendment that it can't be said to be nullification, (2) defeat of a resolution favoring total segregation for the next school year, a move that would have killed any local option, (3) defeat of a move to let Arlington elect its school board because that could lead to integration in line with Gray Commission recommendations and (4) passage of the Pope bill on athletics, which, said the editorial said, was grist for the Communist propaganda mill.

On March 21, *The Times-Dispatch* editorial page twitted James Wechsler, editor of the *New York Post*, for pulling Murray Kempton, a *Post* writer, from a story on segregation in New York schools that Kempton and Grover C. Hall Jr., editor of the *Montgomery Advertiser*, would do jointly. Wechsler would substitute Ted Poston, a Negro reporter. Hall, who later would become *The News Leader* editorial page editor, declined the switch.

The News Leader was becoming increasingly uneasy with the Gray Commission recommendations and chided the *Roanoke Times* on March 31 for saying Virginians had "overwhelmingly approved" the plan. All that Virginians did, said *The News Leader*, was approve a constitutional convention to permit the state to appropriate money for education of Virginia students in non-sectarian private schools.

On April 3, *The News Leader* acknowledged that some publications outside the South—even *Time* and *Life*—saw some good in the South's position on race relations. But, it added, "when the polite and well-intentioned overtures are acknowledged, moderation is still spelled 'integration' in the North; and moderation still means 'continued segregation' in the South."

Another Supreme Court decision on desegregation—this time on intrastate buses in South Carolina—brought angry denunciations from both Richmond dailies. "The states have reached Armageddon," said *The News Leader* of April 24. "By successive assaults on the Constitution, the Supreme Court has undertaken, in effect, to repeal the 10th Amendment [reserving various activities to the states] and to write into the 14th Amendment [providing rights to Negroes] sweeping new provisions to which the states have never consented.

"The one possible check upon the court, in our view, lies in interposition by the states. They, and they alone, by concerted action, may restore a constitutional balance of powers."

The answer, said the editorial, was for the states to "dedicate themselves to a rewriting of our Constitution in order to repair the damage the court has done."

The next day's *Times-Dispatch* reminded readers again of its anti-Jim Crow editorials of 1943—a position now decreed by the Supreme Court, in "just another in a long series of unwarranted extensions of the federal authority by this tribunal.

"One by one, the rights formerly reserved to the states are being eroded and eaten away by the Supreme Court and also by Congress." Blame the people, too, said *The Times-Dispatch*, for looking increasingly to Washington.

On May 7, *The News Leader* devoted its entire editorial columns to a treatise entitled "Sovereignty and School Boards."

"Not until recent months," it said, "have we begun to think in different terms, not of compliance, but primarily of resistance; not of acknowledging the court's authority but of challenging it in every honorable and constitutional way. The proposal now being advanced [by Judge Old of Chesterfield and former Gov. Tuck] falls in this second line of thinking: its aim is to make it legally impossible for school boards to comply with court orders by making it legally impossible for school boards, as such, to be sued."

"The legal theory behind this approach goes to the fundamentals of American constitutional doctrine," said the editorial. "It holds that the states are sovereign political entities"—in delegating certain powers, they reserve others. "Further, that the power of a sovereign state to fix the conditions under which it (or its creatures) may be sued is an inherent power of sovereignty which has never been surrendered."

The paper praised Judge Old as "the father of interposition" and declared finally, "Our purpose here is only to raise the matter for discussion."

Old was an old Chesterfield politician who yielded to no one in his abhorrence of integration. He was a pleasant, rotund man who looked a bit like a frog. His Zippo cigarette lighter had a Confederate flag on the cover and played "Dixie" when it was opened. His office in the courthouse had a desk that was covered with unopened mail and stacked with segregationist tracts from Arkansas. During a murder trial in December 1960, he glanced at his watch, recessed court for 10 minutes and beckoned two reporters to join him at his car, parked at the courthouse, to listen to the national news and "check on those ladies in New Orleans." The "ladies," according to an Associated Press report, were "fanatical women—screaming insults [who] manhandled a university student" in front of an integrated school because the young man, son of a cleric, "had led recent sit-in demonstrations."

In an editorial on May 17, 1956—two years after the Brown decision—*The News Leader* saw more understanding nationally of the South's position, although the whole region "has been scorned and condemned as a morass of bigotry, ignorance and base prejudice."

The paper added, "Long ago, this newspaper urged that the South prepare to litigate this evil scheme for 50 years.

"We still have 48 years to go."

The opposition was working. The next day's *Times-Dispatch* reported on Page One that Gov. Stanley, after meeting with the Gray Commission's executive committee, hinted he was willing to postpone the commission's recommendations and try other weapons to preserve a completely segregated school system in Virginia.

J. Segar Gravatt, judge of Nottoway County Trial Justice Court and a director of the Defenders of State Sovereignty and Individual Liberties, said flatly that there was no way Virginia could abide by the Brown decision and the state constitution section that compelled the legislature to establish and maintain a free school system throughout the state, because Prince Edward County would close its schools if forced to.

Therefore, said Gravatt, the county could say it would comply only with the constitutional section and litigate endlessly. Like Gravatt, Judge Old met with the commission and said that Virginia should withdraw its consent for school boards to be sued. He also envisioned endless litigation.

The News Leader editorial page, reflecting further on the two years after the Brown case, said on June 1 that "both sides are hoarse and a bit wearied by strenuous exertion, but neither has heard the other one yet." Men of good will in the South, said the paper, think compulsory integration is not a "positive good," but "on the contrary, is a positive evil."

On June 12, *The News Leader* drew on material from the *Washington Post* and printed a list of racial incidents in the public schools there—mostly blacks on whites.

"Some of the more fervent advocates of compulsory race-mixing," said *The News Leader*, "doubtless will find this official report a gratifying document."

On June 22, L.M. Wright Jr. reported on the front page of *The Times-Dispatch* that from seven to 14 members of the 32-member Gray Commission now wanted stronger resistance to possible desegregation envisioned in the original plan. Among those was State Sen. Mills E. Godwin Jr., a future governor.

On July 19, James Latimer reported in *The Times-Dispatch*, "A mighty effort was building up yesterday to convince most Gray Commission members that they should forsake the pupil assignment phase of their school program in favor of the stern policy line of no-integration-anywhere in Virginia."

The logical next step was reported July 23 on the front page of *The News Leader*: "Gov. Stanley said today he will convene the General Assembly in special session on August 27 to prevent any integration in public schools anywhere in Virginia."

In mid-July the snowball was rolling. "Gov. Stanley," reported *The Times-Dispatch* of July 24, "launched his administration yesterday onto the total resistance line of no-integration in any public school as Virginia's answer to the Supreme Court's desegregation decision." Stanley wanted a special session of the General Assembly to (1) withhold funds from any locality that integrated white and black pupils and (2) oppose the Gray Commission plan of pupil assignment that would accept the principle of racial integration.

Both papers' editorial pages bought the program—*The Times-Dispatch* hesitantly, *The News Leader* enthusiastically. *The Times-Dispatch* said Stanley's moves had a "legitimate and proper objective so long as it can be pursued honorably and without nullificationist defiance of the Supreme Court."

But, the paper added, the plan "of course" was contrary to what voters were told the previous winter when they approved 2 to 1 a state constitutional amendment needed to implement the Gray Commission's tuition grant arrangement.

The News Leader's editorial, titled "Mr. Stanley's Sound Position," said that pupil assignment would mean "Virginia's schools would be mixed," furthermore, "'pupil assignment' means 'surrender' and it is useless to say that it would mean just a little surrender.

". . . This thing is seen now a great deal more clearly than it was when Mr. Warren's opinion first came down. And the more clearly the concept of compulsory integration is seen, the more determined the South will be to resist it.

". . . We believe Mr. Stanley is sound as a matter of constitutional principle, and that he bespeaks the wishes of most Virginians in resisting integrated schools—anywhere in Virginia."

The Times-Dispatch still had worries. In an editorial July 27, it noted a split among Gray Commission members on Stanley's move to halt *any* integration in Virginia and pointed to a suggestion by Donald Richberg that the General Assembly take over the schools. Richberg, an early adviser to Franklin D. Roosevelt, had become disillusioned and increasingly conservative and had moved to Charlottesville. He also was a strong segregationist.

Yet, said *The Times-Dispatch*, "let's think through these plans." It recalled cases in which the Supreme Court had held governors in contempt. "These proposals that are being made are so sweeping that we should be extremely careful not to let ourselves in for them without knowing what we are doing," said the paper, which also questioned centralizing all education in Richmond.

The News Leader of the same day acknowledged there was no perfect solution but disassociated itself from what it said were the two extreme positions. "The first is to integrate every school in Virginia as of this September; the second is to secede from the Union. The former is undesirable, the latter is impracticable."

Virginia's aim, said the editorial, is "to prevent integration of our schools as long as possible." It apologized for taking "some months of reflection" to realize that pupil assignment is not the first step, but an acceptance of integration. One device to achieve Virginia's goal, said the paper, was to repeal the compulsory attendance law.

Two weeks later, *The News Leader* had come full circle from its grudging acceptance of *some* integration under the Gray Commission plan and now was, in the words of its editorial of August 6, "Thinking About the Unthinkable."

After looking at other Virginia papers' editorials, *The News Leader* had concluded that abandoning public schools "is not unthinkable." It added:

"To abandon public education in favor of genuinely private education certainly would mean a difficult period of readjustment; it would demand heavy financial sacrifices; it doubtless would have, for a time, a seriously detrimental effect on the Virginia economy. No Southerner who holds an abiding affection for the Negro people can look happily upon the plight of Negro children deprived of public schooling. From many standpoints, the total abandonment of tax-supported education would be disastrous.

"What are the prospective damages on the other side? To permit 'some integration' of schools is to permit total integration. Let us be clear on that point. That race-mixing cannot be held to some politely minimal level already has been demonstrated in Baltimore, where it was hoped Negroes voluntarily would remain in their own schools under a plan of 'some integration.' The first year, some 1,500 colored pupils entered white classrooms; the second year the figure was almost 3,000. Once our schools are race-mixed, the last essential barrier to complete racial amalgamation will have been abandoned. The damage may not be apparent for 20 or 30 years; it may not be serious for 50 years; it may not be complete for a century. But on what we do now depends the society and culture of Virginia. If we fail now to preserve the essential separateness of the races in the South, we invite the inevitable day when the Southern States must dwindle to the melancholy status of another Cuba, a Puerto Rico, a Brazil."

On August 17, *The Times-Dispatch* editorial page turned its gaze northward again—this time to Chicago, where there had been anti-black demonstrations and where Democrats were attending their quadrennial national convention.

"But maybe occurrences such as these, far above the Mason-Dixon line," said the paper, "have tempered the anti-Southern attitudes of many Northern and Western delegates. On August 22, the same day the Republican convention renamed the Eisenhower-Nixon ticket, members of the Gray Commission back in Virginia voted 19 to 12 to support Gov. Stanley and to avoid any integration in the schools by abandoning the pupil assignment plan.

Del. Robert Whitehead, the renegade Democrat, was quoted in *The Times-Dispatch* of August 23 as saying, "The Supreme Court of the United States reversed itself. Next Gov. Stanley reversed himself. Now the Gray Commission has reversed itself. This leaves the situation in a profound state of confusion."

The next day's *News Leader* quoted Stanley as saying he had the support of 95 percent of Northern Virginians. It also quoted Gray on why he now disavowed his own plan. He'd hoped in late 1955 that assigning pupils on bases other than race would be an acceptable solution for Virginia, he said, but developments had made it so that assignments would not prevent integration and would result in school closings "in vast areas of Virginia."

The split by Gray Commission members on the new Stanley plan was mirrored on the State Board of Education. *The Times-Dispatch* of August 30 reported on Page One that four of the seven members opposed

Stanley and favored the original Gray plan, two were undecided and one sided with the governor.

By that time, outsiders were getting in the act. John Kasper, a fiery, radical segregationist, visited Charlottesville, where for a second time a cross was burned in the yard of Sarah Patton Boyle, a most proper lady who was vice president of the Virginia Council on Human Relations.

The News Leader said, "We have enough troubles without Mr. Kasper's unwanted help. His is a queer role and a mighty distasteful one." But one day later, August 31, *The News Leader* took on Autherine Lucy, who, when she tried entering the University of Alabama, had said she wanted to start people thinking. She "sure did," said the editorial.

It denounced her as "a smug, self-satisfied, cotton-mouthed sort of talker, seeking trouble and publicity and finding plenty of both. Under the open sponsorship of the NAACP, she sought to force her way into an institution built, operated and maintained by the people of Alabama for the education of white students. To this institution, the Negroes of Alabama had contributed scarcely a nickel on the dollar. The state maintained and still maintains excellent educational institutions of higher learning for Negro students.

". . . For the first time, a good many outsiders got a glimpse of a trumped-up case of the poor Negro in his new Cadillac, and caught a glimpse not of the downtrodden colored man but of the well-heeled and high-riding NAACP."

Gov. Stanley's new tack brought opposition not only within the Gray Commission and the State Board of Education but also from key Virginia whites long identified with education—among them Colgate W. Darden, Jr. and Dabney S. Lancaster. Darden, president of the University of Virginia, was a former governor and Byrd organization member. Lancaster was a former president of Longwood College and former state superintendent of public instruction.

Darden said the Stanley plan was a "first step" toward damaging or destroying the public school system. Any "single unyielding formula" was "doomed to failure," he said. The Stanley formula for cutting off state funds for any integration struck at the very roots of local government, he added.

The Times-Dispatch spoke up editorially. It ran pro and con comments from papers around the state but commended Darden for his "effective and largely unanswerable attack." Again, it reminded readers that Darden had campaigned for the original Gray plan and referendum that envisioned tuition grants and pupil assignments.

Clearly, Richmond's two dailies were not in accord editorially.

The News Leader wasn't saving all its scorn for Virginians opposed to the Stanley plan. On September 4, it praised Gov. Orval Faubus for calling out the Arkansas National Guard during an integration crisis.

"He should look Judge Ronald Davies squarely in the eye," said *The News Leader*, "and tell him that he, Faubus, is Governor of Arkansas and will carry out his duties as Governor without interference by any judge." Davies, a federal judge, had ordered the Little Rock School Board to "proceed forthwith with racial integration of public schools," and Gov. Faubus called out the National Guard to prevent such action.

". . . The so-called 'rights' awarded seven Negro plaintiffs to attend a white school in violation of the law and Constitution of Arkansas are Johnny-come-lately 'rights,'" said *The News Leader*. "But the right of the people of Arkansas to be protected against violence, riot and domestic intranquility is a right that comes to them from the instant their State came into being."

After a school was blown up in Nashville, *The News Leader* editorial page of September 11 told "the Earl Warrens and Herbert Brownells of this world and all their associates in high places, 'We told you so.'" Brownell was U.S. attorney general.

The violence of September 1957, said *The News Leader*, "is only the beginning.

"Sophistry is lost on the white laborer, machineworker, clerk, farmhand. *His child ain't going to go to school with a Negro*."

The next day Texas' governor, Allan Shivers, received plaudits from *The News Leader* for resisting a federal order and removing three black students from a school for whites. Whether it was nullification or not, said the paper, "what he did was wise, and prudent, and wholly within his powers as Governor of a sovereign State."

Back in Virginia's legislature, members were determined to retaliate against the NAACP, which was pushing desegregation. Various bills were introduced to restrict its actions; one bill would have set up a procedure to get public information on organizations "whose activities may cause interracial tension and unrest."

The Times-Dispatch was upset. "We hold no brief whatever for that association [NAACP], to many of whose objectives we are irrevocably opposed," said an editorial September 21. "But when the lawmaking body of Virginia sets out to penalize an agency with which it disagrees, there is a very real danger that other agencies with which it is in entire agreement will likewise be hampered if not destroyed."

The next day, the 169th anniversary of the signing of the U.S. Constitution, *The Times-Dispatch* assured its readers that the document was indeed great and that its framers "are not to blame for the current unhappy turmoil over racial segregation." It's all the fault of the interpreters, said the editorial.

At 2:11 a.m. Saturday, September 22, the General Assembly wound up its special session that had begun August 27. Sunday's *Times-Dispatch* lead story by Latimer began, "Gov. Stanley was armed yesterday with all the legislation he had asked for—plus some extra weapons he didn't ask for—to wield against the threat of racial integration in Virginia schools."

The legislation, said Latimer, contained possibly "some land mines and booby traps yet unrecognizable as such."

The aim of the legislation, the story continued, was to commit Virginia to "the policy of stern, unyielding resistance" to integration and to make the governor "the offensive spearhead."

New laws would cut off state money for any individual (white) school as soon as one Negro entered and would empower the governor to intervene wherever integration began and to use state sovereignty to checkmate integration. A new, three-member pupil placement board was created to assign students for any reason but race. Also, when state funds were cut off from a school, the governor—on petition from the locality—could take over the school and reopen it as a segregated school in a new state system.

Under that plan, the governor would be taking over the school and reopening it on a segregated basis under his police power, saying it had to be that way to preserve peace and tranquility.

Furthermore, the NAACP and other organizations active in racial matters would be required to register and disclose their membership. Not content with that, the General Assembly set up its own unit to investigate the need for more legislation.

The Times-Dispatch editorial page that day was skeptical, noting that some localities, such as Arlington, might prefer to integrate without state funds. The paper also wondered if putting the governor in charge of schools conflicted with the constitutional mandate for "supervision" by the State Board of Education.

Yet, said the paper, since most Virginians want segregation and open schools, "we should do our utmost to make the Governor's plan work."

The News Leader had its say before *The Times-Dispatch*. About nine hours after the special session adjourned, its editorial page declared, "The legislators went at this terribly difficult problem with all the disorderly zeal of a housewife let loose in a supermarket with a $20 bill. Into the cart went a box of 'fund withdrawal,; two cans of 'pupil placement,' one jar of 'interposition,' and a half-dozen packages of frozen goods intended to put the NAACP on ice."

While the General Assembly was plugging the dike to prevent any seeping integration in Virginia's schools, *The News Leader's* news department dispatched three reporters to the nation's capital to look at integration there. James W. Baker, William B. Foster Jr. and Robert B. McNeil interviewed white and black students and parents, in addition to teachers, administrators, real estate operators, ministers, slum clearance managers, recreation directors and many others involved in the city's changing racial ways. Baker, who looked even younger than he was, dressed casually on the opening day of school, went to Eastern High School and mingled with students.

He, Foster and McNeil turned out stories for nine daily editions. In a tabloid reprint in October, Charles H. Hamilton, managing editor, said their only directive was: "to get the truth about school integration in Washington, and to report it as fully and as objectively as possible."

That they seem to have done. The series won the Virginia Press Association's award for the best series of the year. Radio Station WRNL, owned then by Richmond Newspapers Inc., broadcast interviews with people whom *The News Leader* reporters had taped in Washington. The host for the program: Roger Mudd, a former reporter for the station who had by then moved to reporting in Washington. His own national network days were ahead.

The News Leader reporters reached one basic conclusion: "Whatever the Washington experience may mean, it cannot—on the simple objective grounds of comparability—serve as a model for the South to follow. Even if the experiment were successful, it would be incorrect to infer that it could be transplanted to Richmond, or Atlanta, or New Orleans—much less Prince Edward county in Virginia. We are dealing here with conditions in respect to neighborhoods and total integration that are alien and apart, with only a thin thread of comparability."

They added that almost nowhere did they find "acceptance of indiscriminate racial intermingling as a wholly commonplace thing."

However cautious the reporters were, Alan S. Donnahoe, the newspaper company's director of research and later its president, came to his own conclusions. He had helped arrange for maps, census data and "scientific block-by-block sampling of opinion." Donnahoe's summary appeared on the back page of the 16-page tabloid under the head, "Capital Integration: Dismay, Unrest."

Donnahoe concluded: "(1) Educational standards have been lowered by integration, (2) Teaching difficulties have been increased by integration, (3) This sensitivity carries over to matters of health and hygiene, (4) Social activities have virtually disappeared from massively integrated schools, (5)

Interracial conflict has sometimes involved a degree of violence which is new and shocking to many whites, (6) Two years of integration have brought white and Negro children together in the same school building and in the same classroom, but there the process of intermingling has ended, (7) Outside of the schools themselves, integration has sliced sharply into the neighborhood structure of Washington."

Thus, concluded Donnahoe, "This is the nation's capital today. But this is more than the story of one city alone. Here is the two-year fruition of the great social experiment of the Supreme Court. Here is what the President of the United States hoped would be a model for the nation to follow."

On November 13, *The News Leader* commended the *Atlantic* and the author of an article in the magazine, Herbert Ravenal Sass. He had written, "The crux of the race problem in the South is the nearly universal belief of the Southern white people that only by maintaining a certain degree of separation of the races can the racial integrity of the white South be safeguarded."

That, said *The News Leader*, goes to "the most delicate and least talked about aspect of the whole segregation issue.

". . . What is feared is not racial amalgamation tomorrow or next year or the year after. The apprehension is that 20, 30 or 50 years hence, when a couple of generations will have been exposed to the long intimacy of massively integrated schools, patterns of racial preference will be thoroughly disrupted. Once that happens, the vitality and character of the different races inevitably must be impaired. And the South, where the prospect is most acute, would deteriorate into a region of mixed bloods."

The Times-Dispatch of December 16 commented editorially that "The race problem will be with us for generations to come. . . .

"Somehow, perhaps, with the help of intelligent Negro leaders of good will, Mr. Eisenhower's Justice Department will be made to realize the folly of seeking to impose on the South a way of life for which it is not ready, and for which it may never be."

When U.S. District Court Judge Walter E. Hoffman ordered integration of Newport News public schools, *The News Leader* lashed out at him February 12 for "rubber stamp[ing] the mandate of his fellow Republican, Chief Justice Earl Warren."

"The State of Virginia, exercising her plain rights under the supreme law of the land," said the editorial, "has said that schools shall be segregated. Judge Hoffman, asserting powers unlawfully seized by nine mortal men on a Monday in May, has commanded that the schools not be segregated. This is the head-on collision. In the end, we will all somehow walk away from the wreckage, but neither the schools nor the Commonwealth, nor the Constitution nor the public's respect for the courts, will ever be the same again."

The Times-Dispatch was back taking pot shots at Yankees—this time in Chicago. When, after three years, police were removed from Trumbull Park, a housing project, the paper said, "Congratulations are in order for the city of Chicago, chief metropolis in the state of Abraham Lincoln, the great emancipator."

The paper also noted racial tension in Detroit and commented, "Half a century seems not to have lessened the fury of the pursuing abolitionist mobs in Chicago and Detroit."

The News Leader of March 29 had advice for parents under the desegregation gun in Charlottesville and Arlington: "[B]egin making calm, deliberate plans for operating a private school system, if, in the last resort, this should become necessary."

If schools were closed, said the paper, tax rates would drop and a drive for funds could be mounted. Of course, it acknowledged, classroom space and libraries and books would be needed. "This is a hard time, a sacrificial time," said the paper, "but Virginians can make it less hard, and expose themselves to smaller sacrifice, by prudent, efficient planning now."

In June 12, *The News Leader* began a series of articles by William B. Foster, Jr. and John Connors on Charlottesville's school problems. That city was under a desegregation order for September. Colgate Darden, president of the University of Virginia, again urged a return to the original Gray Commission plan. If there were some integration, that could be handled, said Darden. "The genius of Virginia," he said, "lies in her local governments."

No matter what Darden and other moderates recommended, *The News Leader's* editorial page was unmoved. On June 17, it reviewed its stand on desegregation from the Brown decision of May 1954, when "this newspaper reacted, as many others did, with an instinctive sense of automatic obedience to the Supreme Court commands. Searching for a way to minimize the impact of that decision, we, too, once urged that localities be given highly flexible powers to deal with local problems in order to preserve the greatest possible separation of the races."

It was not until the summer of 1955, continued the editorial, that "the terrible violence the Court had done to the Constitution became clear to us." In June of that year the paper fixed on a policy of massive resistance to integration. "That policy still seems to us, after months of reflection, the best and wisest and boldest course, the course most calculated to benefit the people of Virginia and the law of the land.

"If a public school should be closed, as a consequence of superior Federal force, soon enough the genius of the people would provide an alternative educational opportunity."

After the criticism by Colgate Darden and Ted Dalton, again the GOP gubernatorial nominee, of his plan to continue all-out resistance to integration, Gov. Stanley denied it would lead to school closings. The only closings, *The Times-Dispatch* of July 8 quoted him as saying, would result from "a parent entering his child in a school attended by members of the other race."

On August 1, *The Times-Dispatch* had sharp words for Sens. Paul Douglas and Jacob Javits because their states, Illinois and New York, were undergoing racial conflict.

On August 24, *The Times-Dispatch* had a rare commendation for Arthur Schlesinger Jr., the historian, who had written a foreword in a book by John Bartlow Martin on Southern resistance to integration. Schlesinger wondered if the gradual approach of the Supreme Court under Justice Fred Vinson might not have been wiser than the strategy of the Warren court to meet the issue head-on. He also said that if the Warren court was going at the issue head-on, maybe it should have decreed change at once before opposition solidified.

But *The Times-Dispatch* said Schlesinger was off base in not being able to think of "a white leader in the South who has warned against hate with equal eloquence" of Martin Luther King, Jr. They may not be as eloquent, said the paper, but "hundreds and hundreds of Southern white leaders" are trying to help solve racial problems without violence. "Their efforts are routine; they don't make the headlines in the Northern press."

On August 27, *The News Leader* again predicted that if the South could hold out for 10 years after the Brown decision, it would "win the war." The paper was pleased that the North was understanding better the South's ideas on race, especially with the heavy Negro migration there. The North is learning "something of the problems of bi-racialism." The paper commended *U.S. News and World Report* for its work, compared with *Time* and *Life* magazines, "those great house organs of the NAACP."

The editorial added: "We take comfort in reflecting that with the exception of three cities in North Carolina, the whole of the Old South— the Solid South—next month will go into its fourth school year since the court's decree with schools still completely separate."

Republican Ted Dalton had some advice for Virginians. *The Times-Dispatch* of September 17 quoted him as saying that Judge Albert V. Bryan's order three days earlier for Arlington to integrate was a forerunner of what the rest of Virginia could expect. Local pupil assignment was much better than the Stanley plan, he said, and the Supreme Court was not going to reverse itself.

"Think about it," said Dalton. ". . . Don't be swayed by somebody who can holler the most for white supremacy."

Dalton's prediction seemed accurate on September 30, when *The Times-Dispatch* reported that nine Virginia localities were then in litigation about segregation. Three more cases had been filed in the federal district court in Norfolk.

Nine days earlier, the Supreme Court refused to overturn a lower court decision that the state's pupil placement law was unconstitutional. The act had been in effect less than 10 months and had been enacted by the governor's friends at the special session of the legislature. Originally, the governor didn't ask for it.

Judge Hoffman in the district court had said the law was unconstitutional when considered in the context of other laws passed to prevent integration.

The Times-Dispatch was back at the Yankees on October 8. An editorial, "The North's Crucial Race Problem," criticized New York newspapers for failure to identify as Negroes assailants in fights. It added that it was the policy of authorities and newspapers in "many Northern communities to deny that fracases of this kind are interracial." By contrast, said the editorial, the *Philadelphia Inquirer*, "not noted for its understanding of the South's race problem," laid out the facts, including racial identification in recent attacks, especially blacks on whites.

On October 23, *The Times-Dispatch* commended Alastair Cooke, the transplanted English writer, for his report from Atlanta, where he said most Negroes "suspect the North and its easy offers of 'freedom' as much as they trust their own whites to steer them through the rough surf of the integration storms."

The editorial also liked Cooke's depiction of Northern liberals "who neither protect nor advance a Negro servant or feel any personal responsibility for him, but buy off their conscience easily with a higher wage and blot out the horror of the slums of Harlem with the smug thought that one in a thousand Negroes might go to school in a New York progressive school—a fate one would not wish on the children of one's enemy."

In an unbylined story that led *The Times-Dispatch* on Sunday, November 3, two of three white Virginians were reported to favor school closings in their localities over compulsory integration. The results came from a survey conducted by Alan Donnahoe.

Some of the questions and the percentages of "yes" responses:

Would you strongly object to limited integration: to just a few Negroes in a white school?	*71%*
Do you think Virginia should continue to resist integration by every legal means?	*87%*
If a federal court ordered integration in your school district, would you favor closing the school?	*72%*

The questionnaires were sent out with every 50th paper on October 24. Returns from black readers were so few that their answers were not tabulated.

The paper noted editorially that the survey showed "The vast majority of Virginians are making it clear that they are vehemently opposed to the introduction of mixed schools anywhere in the state."

Lindsay Almond trounced Ted Dalton almost 2 to 1 in the gubernatorial election, and the segregationists were delighted. Sen. Byrd said the vote "will be recognized throughout the South and the nation as showing Virginia's determination to resist integration."

The News Leader was ecstatic. Its editorial of November 6 said the result was a "vote of overwhelming confidence in the position of 'Massive Resistance' taken by Sen. Byrd against the integration of public schools."

In the end, said the paper, "it was public school policy and nothing else, with Mr. Dalton willing to accept some school integration and Mr. Almond willing to accept none at all.

". . . This is the harvest of Little Rock; it is the whirlwind reaped by a Republican administration that chose to sow the winds of social revolution."

On January 8, 1958, *The Times-Dispatch* editorial page had still another swipe at the North's racial problems, this time citing the experience of a black minister who headed the Brooklyn Chapter of the NAACP and who was turned down for lodging at hotels in Pennsylvania, Ohio and Indiana.

"His experience," said *The Times-Dispatch*, "serves to point up the wide gap that exists in the North between profession and performance.

On January 20, a 5-column advertisement on Page 5 of *The Times-Dispatch* was devoted to Virginia's school segregation problem. It was a proposal from Leon Dure, the managing editor who resigned from the paper in 1946 in a dispute with corporate executives over the size of a headline on a front-page story.

Dure opposed both compulsory segregation and compulsory integration. His complicated proposal involved "tax remission scrip" based on per-pupil expenditures that would be given to each parent who wanted to send his child to school outside his district. The state would not have jurisdiction over private schools, and parents and guardians of students there, under Dure's plan, would get excess buildings and equipment and teaching contracts from the localities.

Dure wondered, in the ad, what any court would say about an act of the legislature setting up "efficient" schools and then saying that "efficient" precluded Negroes and whites in the same class?

On February 18, Almond, the new governor, sent the General Assembly a bill to tighten segregation in the schools. It would provide both the school board and the governing body in a locality that so wished to take back from the governor's control an integrated school that he had not "reorganized." The locality then could operate the school with local money. Almond also wanted the right to approve or reject any of those local petitions.

During that session of the legislature, Del. Frank Moncure of Stafford County, a fierce conservative, lost his temper, was rude to a colleague and received sharp criticism himself. *The News Leader* of February 27, however, said, "Some years from now. . . a generation of Virginians will acknowledge the great debt that is owned to the Frank Moncures of our own time."

It saluted "those who have done so much to preserve separate schools in Virginia," such as Byrd, Stanley, Almond, Tuck, Abbitt and "such private citizens as Bob Crawford of the Defenders, such unflinching editors as Barrye Wall of the *Farmville Herald*. . ."

On April 10, *The Times-Dispatch* criticized the *Washington Post* and *Times-Herald* for supporting Negro boycotts in the South but burying on back pages the news of a one-day boycott by Negroes in the District of Columbia who complained that merchants hired too few blacks.

The other paper, said *The Times-Dispatch*, "editorially made a clam sound almost noisy."

Things were tightening. The lead story in *The Times-Dispatch* of April 28 was Allan Jones' report of the governor's ordering six Norfolk schools closed after the school board there assigned 17 Negroes to white schools. The same day's paper reported the 4th U.S. Circuit Court of Appeals affirmed lower court orders for immediate desegregation in Norfolk and Warren County.

On May 4, Jones reported the formation of a 19-member Co-ordinating Committee to Maintain Efficient Education in Virginia. Its aim: to set up private schools in localities threatened with integration. The group, called together by the Defenders' Robert Crawford, elected as chairman Lewis S. Pendleton, Jr. of Richmond. Perhaps, the new group said, students could be educated by closed-circuit television.

The News Leader said May 7 that "no possible harm can come from their deliberations and it is possible that much good will emerge."

On May 23, *The News Leader* advised five localities where Negroes had applied to white schools to begin "binding registration" as soon as possible so that a picture would develop as to which schools the Negroes wanted to enter—and vice versa, since "we assume that some of the more articulate integrationists in Arlington and Charlottesville will want to demonstrate their sincerity by asking that their children be placed in Negro schools." Besides Arlington and Charlottesville, Negroes had applied to white schools in Newport News and Norfolk and Prince Edward County.

Parents should realize, said the editorial, how perhaps the governor would return a school to the locality as an integrated school and cut off state fund for all the high schools in the locality. Maybe Arlington would do so with only local money and tuition grants.

"With deliberate, thoughtful preparation now," said *The News Leader*, "many of these problems can be foreseen and perhaps avoided; a prospect of school closings, certainly a melancholy prospect, may not seem so catastrophic on methodical examination."

Some church groups had become increasingly uneasy about continued segregation, so *The Times-Dispatch* noted the anti-integration stance of the vestry of Christchurch in Middlesex County, in contrast to that of the Episcopal Diocese of Virginia. And it applauded Dr. George S. Reamey, editor of the *Virginia Methodist Advocate*, who opposed attempts to bring white and black "impressionable teen-agers together not only in the classrooms and churches but at socials and parties and at camps and picture shows. . . ."

It was unusual, said *The Times-Dispatch*, "to see a church publication speaking with such candor on this highly controversial subject."

When Martin A. Martin, a black lawyer in Richmond, chided *The News Leader* for failing to stress that the Brown decision was unanimous, the editorial page on July 15 replied that in 1899 a unanimous Supreme Court upheld the separate-but-equal concept.

"Abandon hope? Give up the battle? Not yet, Brother Martin, not yet. Why, the South has been fighting this opinion for just barely four years. It isn't even breakfast time yet. After a while, when the sun gets up, we'll settle down to some real Massive Resistance."

On July 30, *The News Leader* felt it necessary to explain "Why the Fight Goes On." It did so by devoting the entire editorial column to why two Richmond schools—Westhampton and Nathaniel Bacon—should be closed because six Negroes want to attend classes with 1,000 whites.

Virginia is fighting, said *The News Leader*, (1) to preserve a constitutional position that ought never to be voluntarily surrendered, (2) "to preserve the ethnic and social structure of the South against forces that would destroy it, (3) to preserve the greatest possible educational opportunities for the greatest number of children, white and Negro alike.

". . . [M]eeting these aims demands a great deal of the people of Virginia. We are asked to rise above those interests which are personal, concrete and immediate, and to dedicate ourselves instead to goals that, to a degree, are abstract and remote—like the Constitution of the United States and the structure of the American republic."

The Times-Dispatch of July 31 expressed "distinct reservations" about some of the actions in the past of Gov. Orval Faubus of Arkansas, but it said his renomination for a third term as governor showed "overwhelming opposition of the people of Arkansas to integration of the public schools with federal bayonets, such as took place last year in Little Rock."

On August 5, *The Times-Dispatch's* lead story by Frank Walin dealt with another federal court decision, this one by Judge Sterling A. Hutcheson of the district court in Richmond, whose timetable was light years away from his brothers on the federal bench elsewhere.

"Believing that some assurance of stability of conditions in the immediate future may be beneficial to the people of [Prince Edward] County in their efforts to meet the changed conditions," he said, "I fix 10 years following the 1955 decision in the Brown case as the time for such compliance." That decision called for "all deliberate speed" in ending racial segregation in schools.

In other words, the county had seven more years to integrate, and editorialists at Richmond's dailies were jubilant.

"An excellent decision," said *The Times-Dispatch*, noting that the judge had cited Solon, the Greek lawyer, as having given Athenians 10 years to accept his code of laws.

The News Leader called the ruling the "second superlative opinion from this distinguished jurist in less than two years." The other was a dissent in an NAACP case. The latest opinion was marked, said the editorial, by "calm reasoning, temperance and a clear understanding of the functions of a court of law."

The paper added that the judge considered that "under the best conditions, moral and social reform requires great time; and when society attempts to enforce reforms by the compulsions of law or by military force, a resentful and embittered people will simply rebel."

As for the precise time the judge gave the county, *The News Leader* said, "In our view, that date was entirely too soon."

The Times-Dispatch of August 12 said that if schools in Warren and Arlington were closed, "let us hope that this drastic action will be sufficient to convince the nation of Virginia's determination to operate its own system of public schools in accordance with its long recognized constitutional rights."

On August 30, a day after the Norfolk School Board, at the direction of U.S. District Court Judge Walter E. Hoffman, assigned 17 Negroes to a white school, *The News Leader* wondered where was the Pupil Placement Board. The paper said the school board had no right to assign anyone and that the Pupil Placement Board of 1958 was different from the Pupil Placement Board of 1956, which Hoffman dismissed as unconstitutionally formed.

The news columns of that day's paper quoted Sen. Byrd at his annual apple orchard gathering of the faithful as urging no surrender in the fight for segregation. "We shall fight for our position with dignity but with every lawful means at our command," he said, adding, "I stand firmly and four-square with the governor."

Arlington and Norfolk delayed opening their schools, and on September 4, *The News Leader* reported that Gov. Almond was sending state troopers to school superintendents in Norfolk and Charlottesville and Prince Edward and Arlington Counties advising them to admit no Negroes to white schools. He said that only the Pupil Placement Board could assign pupils and that no federal court had the right to order assignments.

On September 5, *The Times-Dispatch* editorial page turned its gaze to Russia and the Far East, where, it said, racial discrimination was worse than in the South.

Gov. Almond said September 9 that unless an appellate court stayed a desegregation order, he would order Warren County's high school closed. Two days later, Chief Judge Simon Sobeloff of the Fourth Circuit Court denied the stay.

It was a month of major news stories day after day. *The Times-Dispatch* of September 12, for instance, reported all of these items on Page One: (1) Warren County, under court order to admit 22 Negroes, says it will close its only high school on Monday, (2) Charlottesville postpones further any school openings, (3) Judge Hutcheson refuses to restrain Richmond's school board from barring six Negro children from white schools, (4) Gov. Almond, at a press conference, hints time isn't yet here to close Warren County's high school, (5) Little Rock's desegregation is argued before the Supreme Court and (6) President Eisenhower says the islands of Quemoy and Matsu will not be given up to the Chinese Communists.

The same day's *News Leader* had a banner headline, "Little Rock Denied Delay in Integration." Other stories included Eisenhower's appeal to

Americans to "avoid defiance of the court's order" in that matter, Warren County's officials' visit to the governor and that county's preparation to suspend classes next Monday—thus becoming Virginia's first school system shut down under Massive Resistance.

There was so much news on the school scene that *The Times-Dispatch* of September 13 had a "Segregation at a Glance" box on the front page, referring readers to stories elsewhere. The governor took control of Warren County High School and closed it. But segregation at all costs was losing support in Norfolk, where the school board asked Judge Hoffman to dissolve a state court injunction prohibiting it from assigning students, because it planned to admit 17 Negroes to six white schools.

The News Leader's story on Page One out of Front Royal on September 15 was by George Gill, a young reporter who was to become managing editor and later publisher of the *Louisville Courier-Journal*. Gill's lead that day read, "All was quiet today as the automatic opening bell rang through the empty halls at Warren County High School—the first school to be closed under Virginia's Massive Resistance laws."

The school grounds were empty but for reporters and a few teachers. "No Negro pupils appeared," Gill said. Town officials had painted over some "stay out" signs at the school that were aimed at Negroes.

Editorially, it was "A Time to Begin to Fight," said *The News Leader* that day. "Now the opportunity is at hand," said the paper, "to demonstrate to a skeptical country that our people mean what they have said so often and so clearly. Faced at last with a bitter choice between race-mixing and a school's closing, we will close the school and make other arrangements."

The next day's editorial of *The News Leader* noted Richmond's desegregation case was pending and recommended plans for private schools. "A year is too short a time to set up truly efficient private schools, but a year is all we have left," it said.

The September 18 *Times-Dispatch* reported that Judge Sobeloff refused to stay an order for Charlottesville to admit 12 Negroes to two white schools, thus setting the stage for closings there. And in Petersburg, Gov. Almond had advice for President Eisenhower. He didn't preach secession, said the governor, so the president shouldn't preach sedition against Virginia to its residents.

The News Leader that day carried a special feature by its associate editor, John A. Hamilton, son of the paper's managing editor and a future editorial writer for *The New York Times*. Hamilton was described in *The News Leader* as writing "from a long and intimate background in Northern Valley public affairs."

His article declared, "Warren County will never voluntarily integrate its schools. It will search first for a system of private schools. Integration, if it comes at all, will come only after a fruitless search; it will be a painful surrender of proud parents who feel that they must put the education of their children above their own beliefs in States' Rights."

The tide was running ever more strongly against delayed integration. *The News Leader* of September 19 bannered James Baker's story that Judge Hoffman denied a stay of his order and refused to give Norfolk a year's delay in desegregating. The outcome of a second story in that paper would have more impact on Virginia than Judge Hoffman's ruling. The story said that Chief Justice John W. Eggleston of the Virginia Supreme Court was glad to expedite a ruling on a test case of the state's tuition grant program, which had been brought by Attorney General Albertis S. Harrison Jr. and Gov. Almond.

The News Leader was still leading the charge for Massive Resistance. Its September 19 editorial titled "Surrender?" said it appeared that nine schools with 14,000 pupils would close. Nevertheless, it said, "This newspaper is not convinced that Virginia's cause is lost. And if here and there in the state, a few timid men are urging that the commonwealth strike her colors, we are not urging so pusillanimous a course.

"Quit now? After these few shots? What nonsense! This is the good moment in a fight, when the waiting has ended, and the forces are at last engaged."

The same day's editorial page also asked, "Have Southern Negroes given sufficient thought to the probable future of their own schools? They may wish to do so.

"It is not to be imagined that the white people of the South will submit indefinitely to a preposterous situation in which Negro children are in school, largely at the whites' expense, while white children are idled or inconvenienced. In the course of time, if the NAACP persists in pushing Virginia more and more toward private schools, Negro public education is bound to suffer. It cannot be otherwise."

So far nine white schools have closed, the editorial said, and Negro schools have "suffered not at all. That happy state of affairs, we submit, will not last forever."

The Times-Dispatch let fly at the NAACP on its editorial page September 20, because the organization's leader in West Virginia had said it was "disgraceful" that so few blacks were applying to white schools.

"The militant, belligerent attitude of the NAACP," said the paper, ". . . is the most effective refutation we have seen if Negroes are given the 'right' to enter white public schools, hardly any of them will do so."

On September 22, *The News Leader* struck out at those who were upset that Norfolk schools might close under desegregation orders. It sniped at the "integrationist *Virginian-Pilot*," which *The News Leader* said would "unleash a flood of tears and recriminations," and a handful of "a few immature students and liberal teachers will make statements that will be magnified far beyond their importance."

Warren County and Charlottesville will hold, and so will Norfolk, *The News Leader* predicted. *"Virginia has just begun to fight;* and we will fight the harder in the year ahead because of the example of these past two weeks."

On September 29, the Supreme Court agreed unanimously that "evasive schemes for segregation, which attempted ingeniously or ingenuously," were illegal. It was dealing with the plan of Little Rock, Arkansas, to lease public schools to private groups.

The next day, Gov. Almond vowed to continue fighting integration but said the Supreme Court decision was "designed to reduce the states to the status of mere puppets." James Latimer said Almond's criticism of the court involved the "strongest terms he has ever used."

Norfolk was rebelling against Massive Resistance. *The News Leader* of October 1 reported that the city council there resolved to require Almond to open on an integrated basis all six schools closed in that city. The governor did talk with officials from Norfolk, and from Charlottesville, *The Times-Dispatch* of October 3 reported, but he delayed any moves to reopen the schools.

On October 6, William Foster's front-page story in *The News Leader* said, "A race got under way in state and federal courts in Virginia today to determine which will be the first to pass on the validity of key statutes in the state's Massive Resistance program."

Virginia's supreme court was asked to determine the validity of tuition grants and the school closing law "that brings them into play." In federal court, counsel for Negro children sought "further relief," saying their right to attend desegregated schools was thwarted by the closings.

The Times-Dispatch of October 9 reported that Judge John Paul of the U.S. District Court had ruled that teachers from Warren County and Charlottesville could not be paid in public funds to teach in private, segregated schools.

That same day *The Times-Dispatch* editorial page took solace in two articles. One, in the *Chicago Sun-Times*, was by a black reporter who told of discrimination in Chicago. And James Baldwin had written in the *Atlantic* that "not all white people [in the South] are 'mean' and that the North need not be immune to their troubles."

Correct or not, a report in the *Atlantic* began giving Almond trouble. The magazine said the governor hoped to see the Virginia Supreme Court overturn the state's Massive Resistance laws, and that was why the test case was brought there instead of the U.S. Supreme Court. The procedure, said the magazine, was part of Almond's plan to run for the U.S. Senate.

Almond, of course, denied the report and was quoted on the front page of *The News Leader* of November 3 as saying, "Virginia is so well represented in the Senate that I have never given the slightest thought in that direction. I do not entertain any such ambition." Virginia's senators were Harry Byrd and A. Willis Robertson, also a staunch conservative but less talkative on segregation than Byrd. Robertson was the father of Pat Robertson, the television evangelist.

The News Leader of November 6 reflected on public schools in the District of Columbia, where, with 74 percent Negro enrollment overall, there were five all-white schools, 20 all-Negro schools and 129 that were more than 50 percent Negro. Thus, said *The News Leader's* editorial page, the District had "a system of segregated schools all over again." Whites continue to flee to the suburbs, said the editorial, and they are the fortunate ones. In rural counties of the South, "there is no such thing as escape to the suburbs."

The dam against Massive Resistance was crumbling, and the editors of the Richmond newspapers acknowledged it without saying it in so many words. A *Times-Dispatch* editorial on November 12 said, "We must be prepared to retreat at some points, in order to attack at others" and called for "prompt appointment" of a legislative study commission to chart a new course in desegregation. *The News Leader's* Kilpatrick gave a speech that called for new tactics, including some local option and long-range planning for permanently operated private schools financed in part by tuition grants.

Those statements prompted questions at a press conference November 12, at which Almond was quoted on the front page of *The News Leader* as saying he would appoint such a legislative commission to draft policy recommendations in case massive resistance were struck down.

That same day's *News Leader* delineated Kilpatrick's position. Entitled "To Win This War," it traced four years' history and praised the state's resistance to integration.

"What we must ask ourselves now, candidly and searchingly, said the editorial, "is whether our best hope of winning lies in the laws we have now, or whether we should seek new tactics that offer a more hopeful prospect.

"This newspaper has concluded, in the light of recent events, that new defenses are urgently needed. If Virginia is to avoid defeat—if we are to be spared the awful tragedy of violence and race hatred that would result from integrated public schools *to which there was no workable alternative*—then we must prepare ourselves for speedy abandonment of a legal position that cannot be held much longer.

". . . In a matter of weeks, Virginia's defensive laws of 1956 almost certainly will be rendered void, and when these laws are torpedoed, Virginia's tuition grant program will disappear with them."

The paper still believed a tuition grant program not geared to the integration controversy could work. Only that way can the state have segregation and education, said the editorial. There was a need for "some plan of freedom of choice." The best way to thwart advocates of social integration, said *The News Leader*, is "a policy of studied contempt by the state for the Supreme Court, coupled with private resistance by private individuals."

The next day's *News Leader* editorial titled "Toward Private Schools" raised questions about Gov. Almond, then supported him. It wondered why Almond chose to "abandon any thought of deliberately contemptuous defiance" of federal authorities by accepting service of process in suits in federal court. Perhaps, continued the paper, "Mr. Almond the Governor is in his heart of hearts Judge Almond the lawyer. Whatever his reasons, Lindsay Almond is our Governor; we support him."

The News Leader's answer to the current crisis: statewide tuition grants to any parent who wants for any reason unrelated to segregation or integration to send his child to a private school. That could lead to "the destruction of the public free school system," but "such a prospect no longer holds great terrors." Norfolk, Front Royal and Charlottesville were doing fine, said the paper.

The lead story in *The News Leader* of November 13 was the suggestion by Rep. Watkins Abbitt that localities forced to close their white schools because of integration should also close their schools for blacks.

Whatever the Norfolk School Board sought, the voters in that city declared 3 to 2 in a straw poll against release of six schools from state control—in other words, don't reopen the schools. The results, reported in *The Times-Dispatch* of November 19, brought an editorial reminder in the paper the next day that the vote was "another impressive piece of evidence of the profound opposition in the South to compulsory mixed education." Norfolk, declared the editorial is "a cosmopolitan Southern city."

Whatever impressions were abroad two weeks earlier that Kilpatrick and *The News Leader* had had a change of heart, the paper of November 25 carried an editorial, "Tell It in Herald Square," intended to dissuade anyone of such assumptions.

"This newspaper has but one aim in mind in this school integration field," said the editorial. "We believe that aim is shared by the overwhelming majority of the people of this State. It is to continue resisting the usurpations of the Supreme Court of the United States by every effective means that can be devised."

The editorial explained that a Supreme Court ruling on Little Rock and recent elections precluded judicial or political relief. All the paper sought was "new defenses."

"Across this broad land, from St. Louis to Chicago, and from Washington to New York and Boston, a veritable chorus of hallelujahs has arisen. Virginia at last has seen the light. Even *The Richmond News Leader* has acknowledged the 20th Century. A new era of brotherhood dawns. The editor of this paper is being called a statesman, and that sort of thing is very hard to take.

". . . It is a pity, in a way, to disillusion the *Times*, the *Herald-Tribune*, and the *Washington Post*, for they have been remarkably noble these past few weeks. There is more joy in heaven for the one sinner who repents than for the ninety-nine who are just, but this time their heavenly joy is vexingly premature. Nobody has quit resisting down here. Nobody is about to quit."

The next day's *Times-Dispatch* had editorial praise for a letter to President Eisenhower from one Carleton Putnam, a "retired businessman and able historian," about the South's race problem. The letter had been published in *The Times-Dispatch* October 16, and now the *Birmingham* (Alabama) *Post-Herald* had distributed 18,000 reprints. Hoping not to be outdone, *The Times-Dispatch*, which carried the letter first, distributed about 3,800 reprints. "The problem, as we see it, said the editorial page of *The Times-Dispatch*, "is to get the letter before the people of the North and West." It urged contributions to a Birmingham lawyer who would distribute copies. Putnam was described as founder of Chicago & Southern Airlines and a graduate of Princeton and Columbia Universities.

Putnam accused the Supreme Court and the North, in general, of arrogance in forcing upon the South a change in its way of life. He contrasted London or Paris with "the pure-blooded African in his native habitat as he exists when left on his own resources."

Putnam concluded that the Supreme Court had "set back the cause of the Negro in the South by a generation.

"He may force his way into white schools, but he will not force his way into white hearts nor earn the respect he seeks. What evolution was slowly and wisely achieving, revolution has now arrested, and the trail of bitterness will lead far."

On December 8, in an editorial titled "Lindsay Almond, Realist," *The News Leader* commended the governor: "Every time he looks at the truth of this school situation, he sees nothing but ugly facts." The paper commended him for saying, ". . .We do not have the power to overwhelm the government. . .which does not have the authority but does have the power."

Summing up the year, *The News Leader's* editorial page of December 31, concluded, "Yet is quite conceivable that 1958 also will be remembered, more pleasantly, as 'the year that private schools began.' For the year's most significant story, in the long run, may prove to be not the closing of public schools, but the operation of private alternatives."

Perhaps, said the paper, "nobody will win this war. But the South most certainly is not going to lose it. Ten years from now, when other parts of the country are torn by interracial violence, chaotic school conditions, and the social evils of miscegenation, the South will still be doing business serenely as before: Separate but equal."

On January 14, 1959, U.S. Judge Albert Bryan ordered desegregation of Alexandria's schools by February 2.

Five days later, Massive Resistance was dead—by action of both state and federal courts. By a 5-2 vote, the Virginia Supreme Court invalidated the state's school closing law because it violated the state constitution's provision for local control of local schools. The court also said that the governor had no right to set up a new school system for students displaced by federal court orders for desegregation.

Thus, wrote William Foster in *The News Leader*, the court said it rejected Virginia's contention that the legislature could "deal with the public free school system in any matter it may deem fit, unfettered by any requirements of, or limitations in, the Constitution of Virginia."

That same front page said that a three-judge federal court in Norfolk also had struck down the school-closing legislation. Since the statutes "effectively require a continuance of racial discrimination, they are patently unconstitutional," the court said.

Gov. Almond's proclamation of September 27, 1958, closing schools, the federal court said, was "predicated upon an unconstitutional statute and hence is void." Thus, said the court, the Norfolk School Board had restored to it the rights that "existed prior to the enactment of the unconstitutional statutes." That suit had been brought by Norfolk parents against the school board and superintendent, the governor and the attorney general.

The News Leader that day found room for the entire text of the Virginia Supreme Court's majority and minority opinions.

The Times-Dispatch of January 20, with more time to prepare, carried on its front page a six-column, two-line headline on the Virginia Supreme Court opinion, a two-column headline on the federal court opinion and a feature on the number of children in the schools that had been closed.

James Latimer's lead story said the state court based its opinion "mainly on finding that the Constitution still requires the General Assembly to maintain efficient public schools throughout the state."

On Page Two of the same day's *Times-Dispatch* was a report of an address to the Richmond Area Council on Human Relations by James McBride Dabbs, president of the Southern Regional Council, who said segregation had been doomed since its beginning—mainly because of industrialization.

The Times-Dispatch that day devoted most of its first seven pages to the developments in desegregation. The text of the state court's majority and minority opinions were printed, along with separate stories on the situations in Charlottesville, Warren County and Arlington, the reaction of Virginians in Congress and a half-page on highlights of the school segregation situation since 1951.

The editorial writers were far from acknowledging defeat. *The Times-Dispatch* of January 20 urged Virginians to retain their perspective even though the word across the nation would be that "Massive Resistance has collapsed—that Virginia has capitulated.

"This is, of course, nonsense. The simple fact, disagreeable as it may be to the NAACP and its liberal cohorts, is that this tangible abuse of federal power has not lessened Virginia's will to resist. We have lost the first battle, but the war has just begun."

The paper acknowledged that there might be some integration. "If so, it is a minimum evil which simply must be accepted as such."

Virginia must "alter the form but not the substance" of resistance to integration, said the editorial.

The News Leader's editorial page that day was headed,

The Vise Closes

"In one sentence," said *The News Leader*, "Virginia's Massive Resistance statutes have been wiped out as cleanly as if someone had taken a wet sponge to a blackboard. The slate is clean now, and for our own part, we have no particular regrets. These laws were intended to interpose the power of the state between federal courts and local school officials; the laws were intended, in Madison's famous phrase, 'to arrest the progress of the evil,' and this they have done. Let them rest in peace.

". . . As a beginning, let us abandon any talk of surrender. *This war is not over!*"

The News Leader advised killing the constitutional provision for the General Assembly to maintain a free and efficient system of public schools throughout the state. Remember, too, the editorial continued, the Virginia Supreme Court upheld tuition grants as such if they were not tied to segregation.

"Ten or 20 years from now," it said, "when Virginia is still resisting, it will be plain enough who is winning the war as a whole."

The editorial pages of *The Times-Dispatch* and *The News Leader* were no more unbending than Gov. Almond. The lead story by Latimer in *The Times-Dispatch* of January 21 read: "Gov. Almond pledged himself last night to an unyielding fight against racial integration of Virginia's public schools—and hinted the key to his battle plan would have something to do with state tax revenues."

". . . In tone and impact," said Latimer, "the Governor's prepared address was a stern, militant call for rededication to the policy of Massive Resistance, though he didn't use that phrase."

William Foster's Page One story in that day's *News Leader* also pointed out the vagueness of Almond's plan. The governor had said, "I propose to restore the tax revenues of this commonwealth to the control of the people." Sen. Byrd liked what he heard and said the speech would strengthen the resistance to integration.

The News Leader, however, wanted more. A January 23 editorial said Almond spoke in parables. "It is time now," said the paper, "to discuss some realities in plain language."

On January 27, *The News Leader* reported that Charlottesville's city council was unanimously in favor of "a minimum of integration" rather than closed schools. And the paper said Almond was to ask the General Assembly for a tuition grant bill that would provide $250 per pupil per year.

Three days later, *The News Leader* editorial page followed with a blistering attack on Oliver Hill, the Richmond area's leading black lawyer, for saying black-white relations could be restored "once the white people decide to work constructively on the problems, real and fancied, related to the elimination of racial segregation."

The paper said, "The white people of the South have been working constructively upon segregation problems for the past several generations, and they have had mighty little help from the Negro people.

"Patiently, the white citizens have borne the social burdens of Negro crime, Negro illiteracy, Negro disease. . . It is overwhelmingly white tax money, not Negro tax money, that has financed Negro education. They were white voters who put Mr. Hill on [City] Council; it seemed then a constructive thing to do.

". . . Next week, integration comes to a few of the white schools of Virginia. What, we ask ourselves, will Mr. Hill have won, in terms of his own race and its future, at what price, at what price?"

A *Times-Dispatch* editorial of January 31, titled "United We Stand," said Massive Resistance wasn't a failure since it had held for four years. There was no reason for division just because a few Negroes were going to white schools.

"Our need today," said the paper, "is to regroup and rededicate our forces to the long struggle that lies ahead. We need, more than ever before, to stand together, united, in this historic effort."

The paper praised Almond for accepting reality and avoiding "mere theatrics of resistance, which would accomplish nothing except the loss of dignity for the state as a whole."

On February 2, the first day of any racial integration in Virginia's public schools, *The News Leader* said editorially, "Virginia will continue to resist a racial movement that seems to her people unwise, ill-timed and violently executed. The battle that may appear to some men today to be ending is seen by us as a war that is barely beginning. To those who could impose social change by force, we would say that such an aim is impossible of achievement. And to those who sanction constitutional change by judicial usurpation, we would sound a warning of disaster ahead."

The four-column headline on the lead story in *The Times-Dispatch* of February 3 read:

Segregation Era Ends
In State Public Schools

And under it in smaller type, this:

21 Negroes Enroll Quietly
At Norfolk and Arlington

"Calmly and quietly," said *The Times-Dispatch*, "Virginia yesterday accepted the end decreed by federal courts of its long era of racially segregated public schools." In separate stories, Al Wagner of *The Times-Dispatch* and Ed Young of the Associated Press reported from Norfolk and Allan Jones reported from Arlington. A separate story told of the General Assembly's recessing, to return March 31. Gov. Almond said he'd name a commission of about 40 people to try to check segregation.

"Virginia Shows the World," trumpeted *The Times-Dispatch's* editorial page that day. It praised the state for its "reluctant acquiescence" to integration and added that the best course for Almond and the General Assembly was "orderly containment of the amount of integration in the schools of the commonwealth."

On February 4, Almond named State Sen. Mosby G. Perrow of Lynchburg to head a 40-member legislative commission to seek "a legal anti-integration formula for the state's future public school policy." Nineteen members had been on the Gray Commission.

State Sen. Mills E. Godwin Jr., a leading Southside segregationist and later a two-time governor—once as a Democrat, again as a Republican—warned February 16 that the NAACP was not satisfied with token integration. "The time has come," he said, "for Virginia and her leaders to stand fast, resist with courage and assert her constitutional rights."

The News Leader of February 18 said it understood "what an agonizing experience this complex and lonely man [Almond] has gone through," although he was wrong "in letting his hopes dominate his reason over a critical four-month period." He was wrong, too, said the editorial, to have spoken to the Virginia Education Association "with such flaming confidence" in November, and it wondered about his speech of January 20, "tactically all wrong." That was his fiery call for continued all-out resistance to integration.

Still, said *The News Leader*, relegating Almond to a lower level of statesmanship, "he did all he could do—not all that Bill Tuck, or Harry Byrd of Wat Abbitt might have done, but all that he, Lindsay Almond, was capable of doing. This is no measure of failure. It is a measure of mankind."

As the months wore on, the trends continued. The Virginia Supreme Court reaffirmed March 11 that the Virginia Constitution required the legislature to maintain public schools—with or without segregation—throughout the state. *The Times-Dispatch* editorial page favored amending the constitutional section rather than repealing it.

The Perrow Commission appointed by Almond proposed a policy of tuition grants and the substitution of local option for Massive Resistance as ways to cope with desegregation orders. Its report split the Byrd organization. Perrow, a portly lawyer who seemed unnatural without a cigar in his mouth, was a longtime organization conservative. His political activity went back to his days at Washington and Lee University, when he led the campaign for student body president for Lewis F. Powell Jr., later a U.S. Supreme Court justice.

But Perrow was determined that massive school closings would be catastrophic for Virginia. In the special session of the General Assembly that was called to consider his commission's report, he led the fight. In a bitter struggle with the old guard, the Perrow forces won 20-19 in the Senate, and Virginia's experiment with Massive Resistance was over.

One continuing trend was *The Times-Dispatch* editorial page's finding racial problems elsewhere. On March 23, it brought attention to an article in *Commonwealth* magazine in which the supervisor of housing for the Philadelphia Commission on Human Relations said the Negro faces "a grave racial quandary."

The Times-Dispatch commented, "The solution to this riddle of human relationships cannot be hurried. Impatient judicial and legislative attempts to hasten it will only complicate the problem."

And *The News Leader* editorial page was back to analyzing Gov. Almond. On June 12, it went back to the governor's speech of January 20 ("I will not yield.") and his speech of January 28 ("The time has arrived to take a new, thorough and long look at the situation which confronts us.").

The editorialist said no one knew what happened to Almond in those days, but it had figured out that there's Almond the lawyer and Almond the politician. "His every professional instinct," said *The News Leader*, "is to obey established law; his every political belief, so far as integrated schools are concerned, cries out against this."

But, said the paper, it wouldn't desert the governor, for he had guided the new Perrow plan through the legislature.

"He is more to be pitied than censured," said the editorial, which also accused him of dividing the state. "We beg the Governor to return more militantly to the wars."

On September 10, James Baker reported for *The News Leader* from Prince Edward County, where nearly 1,500 white children were going to private schools set up to thwart desegregation. There were no arrangements for Negro children, and all public education was abandoned. In Washington, the Associated Press quoted Arthur Flemming, secretary of health, education and welfare, as saying the situation was "the most serious development to date" in the school integration controversy.

The News Leader editorial page that day was plugging for books for a library at Prince Edward Academy, attended by whites only. Those at the academy were counting on 7,200 books, or more than 21 per pupil. The editorial was accompanied by a page-wide picture of the library.

The bitter-end segregationists were unreconciled to events. *The News*

Leader of November 19 reported in a story by William P. Cheshire, that the Defenders of State Sovereignty and Individual Liberties had opened fire on Gov. Almond. At a meeting in Victoria, in Southside Virginia, the Defenders blasted Almond, Lt. Gov. A.E.S. Stephens and Attorney General Albertis S. Harrison, Jr. One speaker, John W. Carter, said, "Virginians will never forget how these men broke and ran in the face of the enemy."

Virginia could not escape new developments in race relations. On Saturday, February 20, 1960, the front page of *The News Leader* carried a story that began, "About 150 Negro students from Virginia Union University, armed with pens, books and papers, brought a spreading sitdown movement to the lunch counters of two downtown variety stores today." Of those seen at Woolworth's and Murphy's, one was reading Faust and another, *Man and His Biological World*, reporter James Hanscom wrote.

Between the publication of *The News Leader* story and the end of the day, the Richmond sit-ins spread. Two stores, Sears and Grant Department Stores, closed their lunch counters before any demonstrators arrived. Throughout the South, sit-ins increased.

The Times-Dispatch story by Thomas W. Howard the next morning began, "Six Richmond stores closed their lunch counters yesterday after a day-long series of sit-down demonstrations by about 20 Negro college students."

Most were from VUU and there were no incidents of physical conflict, Howard wrote. "They whiled away the hours sitting at the closed counters by reading, studying textbooks they brought and talking among themselves." There were a few white counter-demonstrators and police generally stayed in the background.

On the following Monday's editorial page in *The News Leader*, Kilpatrick reflected at length on the developments. "Many a Virginian," he wrote, "must have felt a tinge of wry regret at the state of things as they are, in reading of Saturday's 'sitdowns' by Negro students in Richmond stores. Here were the colored students in coats, white shirts, ties and one of them was reading Goethe and one was taking notes from a biology text. And here, on the sidewalk, was a gang of white boys come to heckle, a ragtail rabble, slack-jawed, black-jacketed, grinning fit to kill, and some of them, God save the mark, were waving the proud and honored flag of the Southern States in the last war fought by gentlemen. *Eheu*. It gives one pause."

Nevertheless, the editorial went on, "whatever grievances they may have on the grounds of custom, the students are assuming a constitutional position that cannot possibly be defended. They are mistaken in believing they have some 'constitutional' right to be served at Woolworth's, or

Murphy's, or Grant's or the Soup Bar [at one of the two leading department stores]; they have no such right at all."

The rights, said *The News Leader*, belong to "the restaurateur, the innkeeper, the store owner." The Negro students, it went on, have the rights of free speech and petition, but not the right to "willful trespass upon private property."

On March 21, *The News Leader* conceded editorially, "By and large, the Negro leadership has been shrewd and effective. By relying upon the processes of law, the resurgent Negroes have won support from law-abiding people across the nation; if their deliberate speed has antagonized many Southerners, at least the pace has moved the Negroes' cause steadily toward the goals they are seeking.

". . . The South was becoming more tranquil," said the editorial, as moderates of both races began rebuilding bridges, and the "integration of a few schools in Southwest Virginia scarcely even made the front page of many Virginia papers."

But, "All this is vanishing now. In place of a policy predicated upon obedience to the law, this new Negro leadership has substituted a policy of frozen violation of law. Willful trespass has replaced patient compliance; arrogant invasions have taken the place of peaceful petitions."

Both papers praised former President Truman for his denunciation of the sit-ins. *The News Leader*, on February 26, said Truman was correct in telling the NAACP that leaders of the sit-ins "are doing the wrong thing and are losing friends instead of making them." The next day's *Times-Dispatch* not only praised Truman but also denounced the press in New York and Washington for giving his remarks so little coverage.

On April 5, *The Times-Dispatch* said that because of whites who preferred segregation but who wanted to be fair, "freedom of choice" had replaced Massive Resistance in the schools. But sit-downs at lunch counters "have already cost the Negroes the support of many moderate segregationists."

Two days later, the front page of *The Times-Dispatch* quoted the NAACP as saying four drug stores on Church Hill, in the East End of the city, already had desegregated their lunch counters.

The Times-Dispatch editorial page of May 4 added that although the Communist Party had only about 3,000 members in the United States, they were trying to exploit tensions caused by the lunch counter sit-ins.

Whatever their position on segregated schools, the Richmond newspapers' ideas on segregated public libraries were something else. Richmond's own public library was desegregated in 1947. Twenty miles from Richmond,

Petersburg still had not desegregated its library in 1960, and *The News Leader* of March 16 headlined its editorial "Petersburg Can't Win."

"Sooner or later," it said, "the Petersburg Library will have to be freely opened to white and Negro patrons alike, or the Library will have to be abandoned altogether." Convictions of students from nearby Virginia State College [on charges of trespassing], said the paper, were "not worth a lead nickel. The first appellate court with sense enough to read the plain English language will set the students free. All that will have been accomplished will have been the making of a few collegiate martyrs."

Three months later, *The Times-Dispatch* chimed in, making sure that it didn't appear to be weakening. "It was only because of the overriding power of the United States Supreme Court," said an editorial June 13, "that we reluctantly accepted a limited degree of integration in certain Virginia schools. We expect to resist massive integration of our schools with all legal and proper means. We also oppose the mixing of races in restaurants, hotels, swimming pools and so on."

But libraries, the editorial continued, "are in a different category, and any attempt to deny Negroes the use of those which are tax-supported, is doomed to failure.

"The kingdom of books should be freely available to everyone."

By mid-1960, the State Pupil Placement Board had voluntarily assigned black students to white schools in Arlington. It did so "voluntarily" because federal courts had ruled that the old pupil assignment plan, although constitutional in form, was administered unconstitutionally. In three and one-half years, assigning 605,000 students, it had never voluntarily put a black in a white school.

Thus, said a *Times-Dispatch* editorial July 27, if the new pupil placement board doesn't automatically reject each Negro applicant to a white school, it may prevent "the massive integration to which a majority of Virginians are strongly opposed."

The Times-Dispatch of August 9 noted editorially that Arnold Toynbee, the historian, had written in *The New York Times Magazine* that Mexico and Brazil had paved the way for good race relations, adding that "what is already an accomplished fact in Mexico today will come to pass tomorrow in the Old South of the United States."

So, the paper compared Toynbee and Allen Nevins, a history professor at Columbia University, to "those naive liberals, whether clergy or lay, who have been pooh-poohing the idea that integration would bring ultimate racial amalgamation, and have been accusing apprehensive Southerners of 'seeing things under the bed.'"

By the time the Pupil Placement Board had assigned two blacks to Chandler Middle School in Richmond—the first integration in the state capital—and 12 more to white schools in Fairfax and Roanoke, *The News Leader* took a ho-hum approach.

"Very well," said an editorial August 17. "Let the facts be accepted as disagreeable facts must always be accepted, with a view toward making the best of a regrettable situation. It would be unthinkable for Richmonders to manifest their distaste in [some] sort of public display; at the same time, nothing in the rule book requires that we burst into joyful song.

"The two pupils will be at Chandler when school opens next month; so will nearly 700 white children. The city's social order will not collapse overnight; the educational level will not be affected perceptibly; the sun will rise in the morning; So two of the city's 20,000 Negro pupils have been integrated. We don't like it but we don't propose to have hysterics either. What else is news?"

By the end of August, seven more stores had desegregated their eating facilities—but not Miller & Rhoads, Thalhimers and People's Service Drug Stores for their upper and mezzanine levels. On August 31, *The News Leader* carried a "Reflections on the Sit-Ins" editorial.

"There is undoubtedly some sort of 'moral right,'" said the paper, "that vests in a Negro customer who is encouraged to buy a suit of clothes but denied the privilege of buying a sandwich." Stores' decision to desegregate lunch counters was the result of economic coercion, but merchants acted "in the end on their own volition," said the paper. "No man's freedom has been usurped by any force of civil law.

". . . We have said a hundred times that the South is not static, as its detractors insist. The South changes; it changes socially, economically, culturally, politically, as it should and must change. Today, in Richmond, we have a change to accept. If it proves an unwise change, both the merchants and the body of white consumers retain the right and the power to compel a reconsideration later on."

On April 13, 1960, *The News Leader* reported on Page One that Danville was desegregating its library but was moving out its tables and chairs. Its chief librarian, Frances Robertson, was quoted as saying, "We'll be open just to circulate books." A *News Leader* editorial the next day said that a $2.50 annual registration fee at the library "is more regrettable than silly; it probably will succeed in keeping as many poor whites as poor Negroes from making use of the library. Removal of tables and chairs is more silly than regrettable. How is one to study, take notes, browse? Have members of Danville's City Council, doing research on a term paper, ever read a book standing up? Have they ever read a book?"

On November 17, *The News Leader* reported on its front page that 54 Negroes were attending four predominantly white institutions of higher learning in the state: 20 at Medical College of Virginia, 24 at University of Virginia, six at Richmond Professional Institute (later to merge with MCV into Virginia Commonwealth University) and four at Virginia Polytechnic Institute. Also there were 10 Negroes at Eastern Mennonite College, two at Bridgewater College and one at Union Theological Seminary. Eight or 10 whites were reported at Hampton Institute.

In early 1961, Benjamin Muse, a longtime political observer who wrote a column in the Washington Post about Virginia politics, wrote a 185-page book, *Virginia's Massive Resistance*. James Latimer, writing in *The Times-Dispatch* of April 20, quoted Muse as saying the state's political leaders "were actually more extreme in their opposition to school desegregation than the people of the state as a whole."

The whole tone of the book was too much for *The News Leader*, whose editorial page of May 15 said that Muse had "no memory of the human bewilderment, the passions, the long-held and hard-surrendered habits of those people who filled the stage of this history."

On May 21, *The Times-Dispatch* reflected on the seven years since the Brown vs. Board of Education decision of the U.S. Supreme Court. "Resistance, especially in the Deep South, is as adamant as ever," it said. "But more and more people in the 'border states' seem to be reconciling themselves to the prospect that the 'separate-but-equal' doctrine is on the way out.

". . . The Negro has always had a rational respect for the forces of nature; racial consciousness and instinct to preserve cultural identity come pretty close to being a natural force."

Two days later the paper condemned Alabama for not giving adequate protection to "freedom riders" in the state, thereby leading to mob activity. The example to follow, said *The Times-Dispatch*, was Virginia's, where the riders' rally at Virginia Union University was a flop and in Fredericksburg, where "nobody paid them any heed." In Farmville, the editorial continued, more than 1,000 people attended an NAACP rally at the courthouse, where Sen. Byrd was denounced—and all was peaceful.

Byrd himself deplored the violence in Alabama but, as reported in a front page story by Guy Friddell in *The News Leader* on May 23, said, "[I]t must be realized that it was deliberately provoked by a mixed group of outsiders who went to Alabama presumably to inflame the people there for propaganda benefits."

A *News Leader* editorial the same day blasted the "freedom riders" as "spurious martyrs" and said both they and their white assailants were enemies of their respective races and their country.

On June 6, *The News Leader* took heart from action by Federal Judge Frank M. Johnson in Alabama, who directed an injunction at both the "freedom riders" and the Montgomery police. The editorial quoted Johnson as saying the travelers were not engaged in "bona fide interstate trips" and knew "such publicized trips will foment violence." Public opinion in Alabama, said *The News Leader*, was "sickened by the actions of a trashy white minority."

The Times-Dispatch of June 7 had praise again for former President Truman's criticism of the "freedom riders." It liked Truman's advice to Northerners that "they ought to stay at home and tend to their own business and work through the people who are interested [in the Negroes' welfare] in an orderly, legal manner."

By another year, *The News Leader* had taken a benign approach to the issue that had transfixed it since 1954. The editorial, "Eight Years After," concluded that Thurgood Marshall, of the NAACP, had been wrong in predicting full integration in five years.

"Marshall missed his guess," said the editorial. "Many of us on the other side did, too. The revolution in race relations that began in the public schools has advanced much further than we would have predicted eight years ago. And looking back on this amazing period of transitions, one recalls surprisingly few moments of high-pitched tension. . . .

"Prodigious currents of new thought, of new attitudes, have flooded over the South; old institutions have been washed away, new channels have been cut. But it is a tribute to the abiding good will of the people of both races that the changed landscape has been accepted, by and large, so philosophically."

By late summer of 1963, the last vestiges of public segregation were over in Richmond because of court decisions or practical acceptance of integration by whites. This included movie houses, restaurants, and Parker Field, where the Triple-A baseball team played.

Elsewhere, things hadn't changed. Ross Weeks, Jr., reported May 14 in a front-page story in *The News Leader*, "Not much has changed in Prince Edward County in 10 years, except leaders say, the ardent segregationists are possibly more ardent now."

Whites are proud, Weeks said, that the county has had its way; although public schools are closed, there is no integration. "And for Negro leaders, the irony of the 1954 U.S. Supreme Court desegregation decision is that it has given them nothing."

Fifteen years later, a young *Times-Dispatch* reporter, Eston Melton, charted statistics on poverty, income, felons in prison, housing discrimination and shortage of elected officials in a massive story for *The Times-Dispatch.*

The three-column headline that Sunday, September 24, 1978, read:

Prospects Are Still Bleak

For Most Blacks in State

The lead read: "More than a decade after the major civil rights legislation of the 1960s, almost 25 years after the landmark U.S. Supreme Court ruling against school segregation and 115 years after the Emancipation Proclamation set their forebears free, life for most black Virginians is bleak."

REGRETS

"*I was an ardent segregationist once. I long ago put all that racist ugliness behind me."*—James J. Kilpatrick *in his nationally syndicated column, September 15, 1987.*

After attacking the state's Democratic leadership for backing down on local option for school desegregation, "This was the last time that I was able to assail the machine leadership for its manhandling of the school situation.

". . . I had managed to go along with the policy of [massive] resistance, so long as it was legal and so long as I was not involved in writing such editorials as had graced the columns of The News Leader.*"*—Virginius Dabney, pp. 232-236, *Across the Years.*

When those who wrote about the Massive Resistance era for the Richmond newspapers reflect on their own coverage, they express pride if they were in the news departments and varying degrees of regret if they determined editorial policy.

Dabney, who was editor of *The Times-Dispatch*, is the saddest case. Not an integrationist, he resigned from the Southern Regional Council when it endorsed integration.[303] He nevertheless favored local option for school districts but oversaw an editorial page that espoused resistance. Kilpatrick, who led the resistance charge for *The News Leader*, says his paper's—and the state's—stance helped to buy time.

Publisher D. Tennant Bryan conceded that perhaps *The News Leader* supported Massive Resistance and interposition a bit too strongly. Yet in a second interview nine days later, he said, "But that's looking back 25 years." Still, he said, "I didn't think so at the time."[304]

In an interview with Gregory Gilligan of *The Times-Dispatch* on the occasion of his stepping down as Media General chairman on July 1, 1990,

Bryan said, "Looking back, it was silly but it seemed like a good idea at the time. It made a lot of people think and that was good."

Bryan, Kilpatrick, the late John Dana Wise, vice president/general manager, and Alan Donnahoe, vice president on the rise in the Richmond Newspapers hierarchy, were the chief advocates of Massive Resistance, said Dabney. Each of the several *Times-Dispatch* editorials endorsing that stance was written by Donnahoe, Dabney added.[305]

Donnahoe, who retired after years as research director, executive vice president, president and chief executive officer, sees those days a bit differently.

"I don't recall that I was totally devoted to this Massive Resistance doctrine," he said. But, he added, "we were committed to it. . . . We had to play out the cards we had at the time."[306]

As for interposition, "Jack Kilpatrick was the one who developed the thing." Donnahoe is not so willing as Kilpatrick to say *mea culpa*. "From this standpoint," he said, "it's easy to say the whole thing was absurd. From that vantage point, back in those days, it didn't look so serious. . . . Even if it were an absurd position, it might have served the purpose in easing Virginia into this new situation, which it did with really very little turmoil."

Charles McDowell, a *Times-Dispatch* reporter who was based in Richmond at the time, thinks that James Latimer of his paper and reporters for other papers covering the school crisis performed magnificently.

"It would never have occurred to Jim Latimer any more than that he was going to wake up and have some terrible disease," said McDowell. . . that he would do anything but go down there [to the legislature] and report exactly what it was about and what was happening.

". . . It was the best period I ever saw a newspaper perform in. I just credit those senior reporters."[307]

McDowell, who has trouble with what he calls "mean-minded" editorials today, says the same people who encourage that also "encouraged the news department to be uninfluenced by any of that, to go its own way.

"I've watched both Bryans say the news department is clear, it's free. I've never felt any restriction. So the very same people that can be so vigorous in doing things I disagree with on the editorial page are just as vigorous in protecting my freedom."

Jerry Finch, who joined *The News Leader* in 1955 and was its managing editor for its last 20 years, ranks the paper's coverage of desegregation with its best performances. "The school integration crisis to me was the major thing we did when I was city editor," says Finch. "In fact, that still stands out in my memory as good reporting, being very careful to avoid reporting rumors."[308]

Finch was assistant city editor during the Massive Resistance era, but in his comments about desegregation, he said, "I'm talking about the whole schmear, really from the Prince Edward school closing to the Merhige decision and the Supreme Court ruling 4 to 4 that turned down consolidation. (U.S. District Court Judge Robert R. Merhige Jr. ordered cross-town busing for Richmond and later ordered the city school system consolidated with those of neighboring counties. The U.S. 4th Circuit Court of Appeals overturned the consolidation order and the Supreme Court split on the matter, thus upholding the circuit.)

Allan Jones, who covered the school desegregation story at the State Capitol and on the road, said he "never, never, never" had a story killed for policy reasons.[309] Once during the period that schools were closed in several places, he returned to Richmond late in the week to do a story for the Sunday *Times-Dispatch*, and he ran into Dabney in the men's room.

Dabney said, Jones recalled, "Isn't it terrible about all those closed schools?" Jones, sure that *The Times-Dispatch* hadn't carried an editorial for more than a year on closed schools, simply replied that the state's leaders should do something.

George Gill, who spent three years with *The News Leader* before going to the *Louisville Courier-Journal*—where he became publisher—vows that he "spent nearly a year in Front Royal," the first Virginia community to have its schools closed. He also spent a lot of time in federal courts in Richmond and Charlottesville.

"*The News Leader* was fun and spritely and kind of brash," said Gill.[310]

One of Gill's contemporaries at *The News Leader* was John Lee, who became business editor before leaving for *The New York Times,* where he rose to assistant managing editor. Lee didn't cover the desegregation front, but he said Charles H. Hamilton, the managing editor, had a hangup on the term "freedom riders." He wanted them called something like "so-called freedom riders."[311]

Hamilton "wasn't very interested in accelerating integration in public life in Virginia," said Lee. Any news department operative might ask, however, whether he should be accelerating anything other than news stories.

Latimer, *The Times-Dispatch's* senior reporter and its most admired among colleagues, often drew the best assignments even away from the Capitol, which he covered regularly. Early in the Prince Edward County case, he was sent there on a story. "Then it became obvious they needed somebody full time on the thing, and, of course, [eventually] everybody had a piece of the story," he said.[312]

Latimer always was careful to keep his opinions out of the news columns and even out of private conversations. He and Dabney had great mutual respect, and Dabney often would show Latimer—and other specialists on the news staff, for that matter—copies of proposed editorials and ask for a check of the facts. Latimer strove to "avoid expressing any disagreement on opinion matters," but in recalling those days, "I've thought, well, maybe I should have set down some things, and I thought that we, uh, were too late. . . "

Keeping news and editorial separate was an article of faith at both Richmond papers. Yet, says Latimer, when the editorial pages were espousing Massive Resistance, "we tried not to be influenced by it, except that there were times, I think, that all of us decided we ought to try to correct the record" in case the editorialists had misstated or omitted important facts.[313]

L.M. Wright Jr. was with *The Times-Dispatch* less than five years—including nine months at Harvard as a Nieman Fellow—before he left in 1958 for the *Charlotte Observer*, but he was identified with the desegregation issue as much as, if not more than, any other reporter in Richmond.

In the fall of 1953, several months after joining *The Times-Dispatch* fresh out of Wake Forest College, Wright was sitting on "clunk row," the desks of general assignment reporters, when City Editor F.J. McDermott handed him a copy of a brief that the Commonwealth of Virginia had filed that day with the U.S. Supreme Court. There were to be oral arguments in December.

"Whoever normally handled the story was out and I apparently was the only live soul in sight. It was about 6 p.m., and, although I had read casually about the case, I had absolutely no background and had never written a piece on the subject," he said.[314]

"I plowed through the morgue to catch up, read the brief and started writing. They told me to quit at the end of about a column and a half because it was press time. I was off the next two days (the story led the front page the next morning), and when I came back to work, Mr. Mac called me over and handed me the galley proofs of the story on which Mr. Colburn [John Colburn, the managing editor] had written a note saying arrange to cover this. I knew you didn't ask Mac a lot of questions about assignments, but I did risk, 'Do you mean in Washington?' The answer was yes. Those three stories from the Supreme Court won first prize for spot news reporting in the Virginia Press Association that year."

Wright not only was good; he also was lucky. He recalls that the Sunday editor, Clarke Bustard, asked him to do a Sunday story on the Supreme Court. He agreed but delayed because of a General Assembly session and finally delivered the story in April. It was a series of profiles of the justices.

Because Bustard had other stories scheduled, Wright's didn't appear until May 16, 1954, the day before the desegregation decision.

"We looked like prophets," said Wright, "by absolute accident and sheer procrastination."

Wright had a field day with the desegregation story. "I never felt any fourth [executive] floor pressure on segregation or any other story," he said. "If there was any, it was exercised in a way that was not apparent to me."[315]

One day in the heat of battle, Wright received letters from the NAACP and its opponent, the Defenders of State Sovereignty and Individual Liberties. One was addressed "Dear Friend," and the other began, "Dear Colleague."

Wright had strong feelings about segregation. "But I never felt it was difficult to write about either side in a manner that I thought. . . was objective and accurate. Thurgood Marshall, Spotswood Robinson and Oliver Hill were open about their intentions, and they were good lawyers. J. Lindsay Almond, the attorney general and later governor, also was a good lawyer who knew he had a losing case.

"He never said so in public at that time, but his private conversations made it very clear that to him the outcome was settled, and all he was doing was bargaining for time. The Defenders were not necessarily people I knew personally, but they were very much like a lot of people I knew very well in North Carolina, because they were my cousins and my uncles. Consequently, I thought I understood how they felt and sought to write about their views objectively and accurately (even though I did not agree) because I thought it was important for people to know what motivated them."

Latimer agrees that Almond "and all of the other good lawyers in and out of the legislature" knew that Massive Resistance was "a house of cards and would come tumbling down in your constitutional cases, and that they had to go through with it."

Latimer acknowledges, too, that "we probably, in a way, got too familiar and accepted things sort of off the record in all of that."[316]

Wright concedes he was touched emotionally when he heard 300 black people stand and sing "We Shall Overcome" during an NAACP rally one Sunday afternoon at the Rev. Wyatt Tee Walker's church in Petersburg. "I had never really understood until that afternoon that it was a hymn," said Wright.

Also, it was that incident, he said, that "made it clear to me who, in the end, would win that struggle."[317]

Over at *The News Leader*, most of the editorials on desegregation were written by Kilpatrick. For about a year, Guy Friddell worked under

Kilpatrick before returning to the news department. One of his last editorials was soon after the Brown decision and Friddell suggested that Virginia appoint a study commission. "I think I suggested [former Governor] Darden to head it," he said.[318]

Although he went back to the news department, Friddell said, "I never had a conflict with Jack." He left *The News Leader* in 1963 for the *Norfolk Virginian-Pilot*, where he directed the editorial page for 12 years.

Louis Rubin, Jr., a leading scholar on Southern literature, a retired professor at the University of North Carolina and the founder of Algonquin Press, wrote editorials for *The News Leader* for about a year and a half in the mid-1950s.

As a graduate student at Johns Hopkins, "I developed a romantic view of the South," he said. "Once I got back and got to the legislature and saw jackasses like [Del.] John Boatwright attacking blacks" and watching blacks viewing the proceedings from the balcony, "the romantic view of the South began eroding swiftly."[319]

Rubin recalled that in the fall of 1955, Kilpatrick wanted to go on vacation; Rubin, the newcomer, would do all the editorials. But Kilpatrick had already done all the editorials on the Gray Commission report on desegregation before he'd left. When Rubin had moved to Richmond in January, 1956, he said, Kilpatrick had repudiated the Gray Commission recommendations and supported Massive Resistance.

Rubin said he wrote one editorial that supported Kilpatrick's new position, but it didn't run. "In two weeks, I was ashamed of it," he said.

"Kilpo and *The News Leader* did a lot of harm," Rubin said.[320]

Rubin also said that John Dana Wise, regarded by the news departments as the arch Tory on the fourth floor, was "a hell of a lot easier to deal with" than Tennant Bryan. He found Wise "more reasonable" on lots of matters than Bryan. One day, Rubin dutifully carried the editorial page up to the fourth floor for inspection. The Supreme Court had invalidated some law, Rubin said, and Kilpatrick had given the court editorial hell. Wise's reply was, "I'm disappointed in this; it's time to integrate some schools."

Although Kilpatrick recanted on Massive Resistance, he still feels the effort was worthwhile, that it thwarted violence. Within a short time after the desegregation ruling, he said, "letters to the editor really began to take on a bloodthirsty tone. The telephone was ringing day and night, by white people saying, 'If a nigger gets in the park, I'll kill him' and 'let niggers get into our schools, and I'm not going to stay there overnight.' That feeling was deep there in Richmond at that time. It was bloody. It was terrible. And it was an effort to control—maybe suppress is a better word—trying to suppress some of those ugly, racist aspects, that we drifted into the interposition thing."[321]

Kilpatrick says that Collins Denny, a prominent Richmond lawyer, counseled him on things in general and suggested that some of the racist anger could be "raised to a constitutional level—states' rights.

". . . So we got into the interposition business—fought, bled and died over that damned thing. And the best lawyers around came up to Tennant's office and said, 'This is nonsense.'"

Kilpatrick recalls that Denny and Robert Y. Button Jr., who was to become attorney general from 1962 to 1970, were advising him.

"And my recollection is pretty clear that both Collins Denny and Bob Button said, 'This would be a diversion, and it might be useful for a while, but then again, it was not going to work. The states, even if they all got together, were not going to be able to fight the whole United States government.

"One of them. . . asked me if I were ready to lead the South into another secession. And I said, 'No, I was not ready to go back to secession.' But it was a grand and glorious campaign while it lasted, and, as an editorial effort, I still look back on it with some pride.

"My turning point came [with] the desegregation of the Thalhimers [department store] lunch counter. I wrote an editorial about it. That was kind of the watershed point, I guess—the turning of the tide."

The editorial contrasted the well-dressed black students from Virginia Union University with "these red-neck yahoos."

Kilpatrick is convinced even the interposition move was worth the effort and helped Virginia buy time "while the other states were wondering what madness Virginia would come up with next."

News Leader editorials frequently differed from those in Norfolk and Roanoke during the mid-50s, but Kilpatrick thinks that Virginia papers, "generally, behaved pretty responsibly through this thing, through this whole period."

His main commendations, however, go to H.I. Willett, Richmond's school superintendent, and to Lewis F. Powell Jr., J. Harvie Wilkinson Jr. and Thomas C. Boushall, all members of the Richmond establishment who served on the Richmond or state school boards.

In 1962, The Crowell Collier Press published Kilpatrick's book, *The Southern Case for School Segregation*. It was eight years after the Brown decision and three years since *The News Leader* had abandoned Massive Resistance. Early on, he wrote, ". . . The South, in general, feels no sharp sense of sin at its 'treatment of the Negro.' Wrongs are everywhere. . .The

South itself has been wronged—cruelly and maliciously wronged, by men in high places whose hypocrisy is exceeded only by their ignorance, men whose trade is to damn the bigotry of the South by day and to sleep in lily-white Westchester by night."[322]

As to history, ". . . By the accepted judgment of 10,000 years [never] has the Negro race, as a race, *ever* been the cultural or intellectual equal of the white race, as a race."[323]

He did have some harsh words for the white South: "If the South had devoted one tenth of the effort toward keeping schools equal that it devoted to keeping them segregated, *Brown vs. Board of Education* would not have created so dramatic a crisis."[324]

Admitting defeat on legal segregation, Kilpatrick advised Southern states to "go through their codes with an art gum, erasing the word 'Negro' wherever it appears. Statutory defenses against segregation, apart from any remaining value they may have in obtaining the law's delays, are useless."[325]

As for the future, " I believe the South will maintain what I have termed essential segregation of the races for years to come. This means very nearly total segregation in education, where the intimate, personal, and prolonged association of white and Negro boys and girls, in public schools, in massive numbers, as social equals, is more than community attitudes will accept."[326]

Across the hall at *The Times-Dispatch*, Virginius Dabney had been fretting for years over the papers' support of Massive Resistance. When his superiors decided in the fall of 1958 to change their position, he felt a new lease on life.

"I was very happy about it because I didn't believe in Massive Resistance anyhow," he said. "It was one of my unhappy periods when Jack Kilpatrick was leading cheers for it, and I just didn't write anything about it because I just didn't believe in it."[327]

In his autobiography, Dabney said, "Most of the time we simply acquiesced in it silently, without making overt gestures in its behalf." As for interposition, *The Times-Dispatch* approved it "as a gesture, with the express proviso that it must not call for any form of nullification." He was happy that Bryan and Donnahoe didn't want to go further than that.[328]

But didn't he express his disagreement with the corporate advocates of Massive Resistance? "Well, I didn't bring it up," he said, "because they made it so clear about what they wanted. They didn't want any dissent at all. I was asked to write an article by Life [magazine] on the attitude of Virginians towards this Massive Resistance. I was in the middle of writing it and Tennant heard about it and asked me to let him see it, which I did. He was pleasantly surprised that it wasn't disagreeing with what he thought, because what I was writing about was what the people of Virginia thought."[329]

Since the article said Virginians—white Virginians, that is—weren't ready for integration, Bryan and Donnahoe "both approved the article, but he thought it was very important that I not get off the reservation and leave."

Dabney said he wrote editorials "on a variety of subjects" that his superiors didn't agree with, but "I refrained at times from expressing my editorial opinion on a few other matters in deference to their wishes. The whole situation made me unhappy over a period of years, and I seriously considered resigning and going to some other paper."[330] But finding the proper opening at a paper with whose opinions he was in sympathy was something else. He stayed.

When the decision was made to give up on Massive Resistance, Dabney, Kilpatrick, Bryan, Donnahoe and K.V. Hoffman (*The Times-Dispatch's* editorial writer who had championed the policy), drove in Bryan's car to Berryville, to inform U.S. Sen. Harry F. Byrd of the decision.

"Byrd was not happy at all," Dabney said. "He said the people of Virginia will not agree with the opposition, but he didn't make a big fight because he saw we were determined to go ahead. Young Harry [State Sen. Harry F. Byrd Jr.] was there; he said practically nothing."[331]

Had the papers decided not to support Gov. Almond's new freedom-of-choice stance, Dabney said, he would have "felt compelled to resign as editor. . . . Fortunately, the paper's management decided on a policy that I could accept."[332]

The strong difference of opinion between Dabney and Bryan, two FFV's each of whom would head the Virginia Historical Society, upset both of them. "I think probably the worst problem we ever had here was when Kilpatrick was for interposition and was bitterly opposed to form of integration and V. Dabney took a much more moderate stand on the thing," said Bryan. "It was pretty hard to justify being publisher of both papers at that time and having them so much in opposition to one another's philosophy."[333]

Dabney said that except for that period, his relationship with Bryan had always been good. "Since then, fine," he said, "particularly now and when he got out from under Jack Wise, he behaved entirely differently."[334]

BUSING

Not since the ill-fated campaign of the 1950s to resist racial integration in the public schools did a local or regional issue galvanize the Richmond dailies' editorial pages as did school busing in 1970.

That summer, Judge Robert R. Merhige Jr. of the U.S. District Court in Richmond ordered the Richmond Public Schools to replace a "freedom-of-choice" plan with one he thought would pass constitutional muster. The school board then brought forth a plan that involved considerable "busing" of students from one area to another to achieve more racial balance.

The plan approved late that summer was, in truth, not a "busing" plan; the city had no school buses. Merhige restricted it for the coming academic year to middle schools and high schools. It was up to parents to see that their children got to the assigned schools by public transit or car pools.

Editorial writers at *The News Leader* and *The Times-Dispatch* went into the journalistic equivalent of basketball's full court press.

An early blast at James E. Allen, federal commissioner of education in the Nixon administration, was tame stuff. *The News Leader* of May 26 said he'd earned the nickname of "Mr. Busing" as head of New York State's Department of Education and that his appointment in Washington "was welcomed with the same enthusiasm that would have been accorded the appointment of Jesse Jackson to the same job."

On July 22, *The News Leader* devoted two entire pages to busing. There were three editorials, and the balance of that left-hand page was taken up with statements from a variety of sources intended to show opinion shifting away from busing. The opposite, right-hand page contained a remarkable "Open Letter to the Supreme Court of the United States" arguing against busing.

The lead editorial asked for signatures on its open letter but warned those who signed not to "expect it to accomplish any miracles." Nevertheless, said the editorial, "the Supreme Court ought to know that the people of the Richmond area support liberty—for all races—and oppose force."

On August 19, a front-page picture in *The News Leader* showed two circulation department employees with bundles of copies of *The News Leader's* open letter. It said there were 29,122 copies with 37,438 signatures protesting "the use of forced busing for the purpose of desegregating Richmond Public Schools."

The appeal to the nation's highest court got nowhere, and the Merhige plan went into effect later that month. What did *The News Leader* hope to accomplish with its "open letter?"

Ross Mackenzie, then editor of the paper, said that it was "basically a safety valve, a release valve. In other words, there was such emotion on the issue that it was our sense, 'Give the people a vehicle for feeling like they're doing something to bear their wrath.' And it was wrath."[335]

He wasn't suggesting violence might occur, said Mackenzie, "but sometimes on local issues—well, on any issue—people get real upset. . ." You let people feel, he said, "'Boy, we're going to really do something about this issue.' That was the primary reason."

Mackenzie was then asked: "I mean, you didn't have any real thought, knowing the way the legal system works, that this would influence the court?"

"No," he said.

When the Supreme Court decided unanimously in 1971 that busing was a legal tool for desegregation in Florida, *The News Leader* said on April 21: "It is the midnight of reason."

It compared the situation in the South to that after Appomattox. "In 1954, the Supreme Court ruled that the South cannot legally compel separation of the races in the schools; now the court rules that the States must compel integration of the races in the schools. The neighborhood school is unconstitutional, and so is freedom of choice."

On March 31, 1972, *The News Leader* devoted most of its editorial space to what it called "The Holton Shuffle." The paper had endorsed Linwood Holton for governor of Virginia, but his decision not to endorse a constitutional anti-busing amendment was too much for *The News Leader*. "At bottom," said the paper, "the Governor—and sadly, Lieutenant Governor [Henry] Howell—support compulsory busing and the compulsory consolidation of school districts for the purpose of achieving what they consider to be a satisfactory racial mix. And this in a State in which the vast majority of the people still regard 'compulsion' as a repugnant word."

Three years later, busing was still a desegregation tool, but *The News Leader* editorial page found some solace. It noted on June 5, 1975 that James Coleman, the educator whose report a decade earlier had endorsed busing, now had second thoughts. "On the basis of a study he had conducted in 1,200 school districts," the paper said, "Coleman now believes that governmental institutions are wrong when they try to force sociological solutions on unwilling individuals."

Although *The Times-Dispatch* was less vociferous in its editorials than its afternoon counterpart, it left no doubt where it stood. "Massive cross-city busing," it said August 6, 1970, "is sheer lunacy." That day it commended Virginia's senators, Harry F. Byrd Jr. and William B. Spong Jr. for efforts to persuade the federal government to oppose busing for racial balance. "It is unfortunate," said the paper, "that Gov. Linwood Holton has chosen to follow a more passive course."

By April 3, 1972, *The Times-Dispatch* was showing its displeasure with Gov. Holton, whom it accused of siding with Sen. Hubert H. Humphrey's "supple philosophy" on busing. By May 9, *The Times-Dispatch* was hopping on "the blind moderates" in the South who, the paper said, cannot understand that "a racially tolerant person can oppose massive, compulsory busing."

"The failure of Southern moderates like [North Carolina Gov. Terry] Sanford, Gov. Reubin Askew of Florida and Gov. Linwood Holton of Virginia to appear concerned about the agony that busing has caused distresses many citizens. And in the anxiety, many turn to George Wallace in Alabama, who, in our opinion, is not the ideal leader of the antibusing movement."

Mackenzie was an unlikely advocate of opposition to busing in the capital of the old Confederacy. He was a Midwesterner who had gone to Yale, edited the *Yale Daily News* and studied for a master's degree in political philosophy at the University of Chicago.

But he had worked two summers for William F. Buckley Jr. at *National Review* and, at Chicago, had become a disciple of Leo Strauss, "a tiny little Prussian Jew who had escaped from Hitler." What impressed Mackenzie was Strauss' philosophy: "Look. We've gotten away from how man ought to behave. Let's get back to that."[336]

When he was ready to leave Chicago, Mackenzie called his old boss, Buckley, who had volunteered to help him get a job. Mackenzie's first choice was the *Wall Street Journal*. The *Journal* wasn't hiring then and Mackenzie was planning to marry and wanted a job soon. Because of his admiration for Kilpatrick, editor of *The News Leader*, that paper was next on his list.

He considered Kilpatrick "a fine prose stylist," and "I wanted someone to say, 'Hey; this is lousy, and this is why."

Mackenzie joined *The News Leader* in September 1965. He had to learn something of the area so he began covering Chesterfield County as a reporter and writing some editorials, "and giving them to Kilpo, and he would fiddle with them, and that was great and they were running."

After a year, he began covering medicine and mental health. His opposition at *The Times-Dispatch* was Beverly Orndorff. "He'd been there forever," said Mackenzie. "He's great now, and he was pretty good then. . . . It was very good for me, and I hope it was good for the paper. But I couldn't match Bev."

Mackenzie took over *The News Leader's* editorial direction in August 1969, a year and seven months after Grover Hall's departure.

Mackenzie is proud of the old *News Leader's* vociferous conservatism. He said he learned from Kilpatrick "never permit the reader, in the end, not to know where you stand."

Readers of Mackenzie's editorials have no trouble knowing.

But Mackenzie is angry that some of his critics feel the paper is anti-black. Even though *The News Leader* abandoned Massive Resistance before Mackenzie arrived, "we still get hung with Massive Resistance tags," he said.

"We have done some pieces and written some long editor's notes saying, 'Massive Resistance was not something that was done in this regime. It was an *ancien regime*, and not something the current editor could embrace.' You know, Massive Resistance would have been a little tough for me to write. The other thing that we repudiated shortly after I took over was George Wallace. Grover was tending toward Wallace." Hall went to work for Wallace after leaving *The News Leader*.

Mackenzie's harshest critics have condemned him as racist in letters to the editor of, first, *The News Leader* and, later, *The Times-Dispatch*. Yet, he favored a proposed slave museum in Virginia and supported Gov. L. Douglas Wilder in banning the display of the Confederate flag on plans of the Virginia Air National Guard.

That latter position won *The Times-Dispatch* editorial page a rare accolade (along with the *Richmond Free Press*, a weekly aimed at blacks) in Wilder's farewell address to the General Assembly January 12, 1994.

The following morning, in a column that covered the top half of the opposite-editorial page, Mackenzie reflected on an interview two days earlier with Wilder. Virginians "have consistently gotten him wrong," said Mackenzie. "I did, too, for a while." He described the departing governor as "clearly an individual of clarity and depth."

Near the end of his tribute, Mackenzie said, "And so departs this man of acid elegance who defied prediction, this man on few schedules. Along the way he read the people well, embraced his principles, learned much—and got better. As other states could emulate Virginia's example under his tutelage, so other Democrats—notably the double-standardists in the Democratic Party here and nationally—might usefully tread the path he has trod."

VIETNAM

The consistent, unyielding conservatism of the Richmond newspapers' editorial pages after World War II was epitomized by their steady support of America's involvement in Vietnam.

Cynics could have argued the papers were looking after one of their own: Frederick Nolting, a Richmond native who was American ambassador to Saigon in the early 1960s and a brother of Buford Nolting, for many years a *Times-Dispatch* copy editor.

Yet, even many liberal papers such as *The New York Times* and the *Washington Post* supported South Vietnam's military resistance to communism and, for a protracted period, America's involvement. A skeleton force of U.S. advisers was in Vietnam during the Eisenhower administration. President Kennedy stepped up American involvement and Lyndon Johnson dramatically increased the number of American servicemen there—up to 500,000.

The Times-Dispatch and *The News Leader*—traditionally internationalist and anti-Communist—never urged American withdrawal from Vietnam and never missed a chance to slam those who did. On *The News Leader*, virtually all the editorials on the subject were by Ross Mackenzie. On *The Times-Dispatch*, various people wrote on about the war until Robert Holland, a former education reporter who'd left the paper briefly to handled public relations at Washington and Lee University joined the editorial department. He was assigned foreign relations—including Vietnam.

As early as July 17, 1963, with John F. Kennedy still in the White House, *The News Leader* was after Ngo Dinh Diem, the leader of South Vietnam. But the paper's criticism was aimed at liberals such as Sen. Mike Mansfield of Montana and Supreme Court Justice William O. Douglas, who, it said, "paraded [Diem] around Washington as the perfect compromise between communism and colonialism."

The News Leader accused Diem of destroying "all centers of power and strength in Vietnamese society" including "landowners, businessmen, Chinese merchants and religious brotherhoods."

The paper said the United States had no choice now but to back Diem. "But the liberals started us out on this absurd policy. They gave us this puppet. They had better find the right combination of strings."

Two months later, *The News Leader* approved the idea of Asians fighting Asians—to rebut any charge of American imperialism—and noted that Nationalist Chinese military leaders were hinting they might offer help. It quoted one as saying, "If they send our divisions to Vietnam, I think we shall seal off that border very quickly."

"All right," said *The News Leader*. "Let's give it a try."[337]

Two editorials in three days following the Gulf of Tonkin engagement in 1964 epitomized *The News Leader's* position on the Vietnam conflict. They appeared after the clash of North Vietnamese and American naval vessels but before it was known how the United States had been probing North Vietnamese waters.

In the first editorial, *The News Leader* urged Congress to give Lyndon Johnson overwhelming support immediately. "There will be time enough later," the paper said, "after our jets have destroyed enemy installations, to observe that in circumstances such as these, extremism in the defense of liberty is no vice."[338]

Two days later, the paper quoted with approval Adlai Stevenson, American ambassador to the United Nations, as saying the attack on U.S. ships was "part of a larger pattern with a larger purpose."[339]

Indeed it was, said *The News Leader*. "The Communists mean quite simply to impose their ideology upon the world. That is the larger purpose." The editorial listed a series of Communist moves across the world over several years and said, "Each of these events fits into the Red tapestry."

So, it added, "The arrogant little torpedo boats were part of the incessant probing, probing, probing that seeks constantly for weakness in the will of the West."

The News Leader support of the war included denunciation of those who differed. Shortly after Martin Luther King Jr. called for negotiations aimed at a neutral Vietnam, the paper let fly.

"It is notable," said an editorial, "that these protestations from the Liberal-Left were not voiced until the United States policy in Viet Nam changed. Until the U.S. began hitting Viet Cong targets and bombing northern Viet Nam military installations, there were no outcries for ending the bloodshed in South Viet Nam, no requests for 'negotiated settlement.' Now that the

United States has taken action that might lead to a victory, the voices demanding a settlement sound throughout liberaldom."[340]

Four months later, *The News Leader* scoffed at the "domestic Liberal Establishment," as epitomized by *The New York Times* and Walter Lippmann, for endorsing U.S. involvement on the ground in South Viet Nam but decrying air strikes in the North. Instead, they wanted American forces to "dig in" along the coast, hold several "unconquerable" beachheads and wait for negotiations.

"The concept, as presented by the liberal press," said *The News Leader*, "often sounds palatable. It is, in essence, no more than new bait on their old line."[341]

By 1968, opposition to America's role in the war was growing, but not in Richmond's editorial pages. *The Times-Dispatch*, while less bellicose than *The News Leader*, said the major objectives of the United States, which would be difficult to obtain, were "to protect the independence of South Vietnam and to prove to North Vietnam and others that aggression does not pay."[342]

The paper endorsed an analysis for the Republican National Committee by foreign policy experts that criticized the Johnson administration for a "flexible response" to aggression and a policy of "gradualism." The experts were headed by two GOP former defense secretaries: Thomas S. Gates, Jr. and Neil H. McElroy.

Like *The News Leader*, *The Times-Dispatch* took delight in sniping at liberals who had come to criticize America's role in the war. An editorial lambasted Sen. Robert F. Kennedy for saying on *Meet the Press* that America should "negotiate with the National Liberation Front and the Viet Cong are going to play some role in the political process of South Vietnam in the future."[343]

That came from the same man, the paper noted, who said in 1962, "U.S. troops will stay in Vietnam until Communist aggression is defeated."

The Times-Dispatch also wondered about the Rev. William Sloane Coffin of Yale and Dr. Benjamin Spock, accused of counseling draft evasion, and anti-war statements of more than 500 editors of college papers or student government presidents.

"It would hardly be surprising," said the paper, "if Hanoi's negotiators in Paris believe that there will be ever-mounting U.S. opposition to the war in Vietnam." That could lead to prolongation of the negotiations, "in the confident belief that the longer they talk, the more hopelessly divided this country will become."[344]

Actions of the most radical protestors were denounced by *The News Leader* in an editorial titled "Hairy Creeps and the Church." Going back to the Middle Ages when churches were "legitimate and inviolable sanctuaries," the paper noted federal marshals recently had dragged some protestors from churches.

"Once churches give up on God in favor of social action," said *The News Leader*, "they also must give up their claims to the special favors properly due holy places. They give up, in short, all claims to public reverence and esteem."[345]

Although *The News Leader* held no brief for Lyndon Johnson in general, it usually supported his policy on Vietnam. But in the heat of the presidential race, it thought it detected a deal whereby the United States would halt all bombing in North Vietnam, and the North Vietnamese would give "some private—or perhaps even public—indication that they'll withdraw a man or two from the South, whereupon the Johnson Administration and the American left will collapse into paroxysms of joy that their policy of accommodation has worked."[346]

The editorialist reasoned that Hubert Humphrey ("the pie-face from Minnesota") wasn't doing as well as Richard Nixon ("the five-o'clock-shadow from New York") and the Communists obviously wanted Humphrey to win.

If the United States capitulated to what *The News Leader* saw, it would have "only one result in Vietnam: More American deaths and, finally, defeat for the Free World. And for that defeat, even if Richard Nixon wins the election, the Free World will have Lyndon Johnson to thank."

As negotiations dragged on in Paris, *The Times-Dispatch* became increasingly impatient. It noted that President Nixon had promised "an appropriate response" if North Vietnam continued shelling South Vietnamese cities. If the response were renewed American bombing in the North, *The Times-Dispatch* found the response "would be endorsed by most Americans."[347]

Fifteen days later *The Times-Dispatch* flailed George McGovern of South Dakota for his "demagogic speech" on the Senate floor that placed most of the blame for the situation at the time in Vietnam on the United States, not North Vietnam.

The Times-Dispatch approved the way President Nixon was handling the war. It said, "His proposal for a phased withdrawal of all non-South Vietnamese forces from South Vietnam is eminently reasonable, and an enemy led by reasonable men would accept it." On June 10, the paper said the Communists described withdrawal of 25,000 American troops as "only a grain of sand thrown in an ocean," but, the paper said, "Mr. Nixon has made a wise move. He has done more than merely talk peace; he has taken an actual step toward de-escalation, though not so large a step as to seriously endanger our forces in Vietnam."[348]

Both Richmond papers, fed up with protests over American policy in Vietnam, suggested counter-rallies. *The Times-Dispatch* said that Americans, whatever their feelings about the war, could join in a "massive demonstration against Hanoi's inhumane treatment of U.S. prisoners of war."[349]

The News Leader suggested a "Confidence in American Day" or a "Back the President Day" or "dare we even whisper it?—why not a Victory in Vietnam Day?"

"Are there no Americans," asked the editorial, "who will demonstrate to register their dissent from the platitudes, placebos, and panaceas of the hard-left nihilists?"[350]

The Times-Dispatch welcomed a column in the *Washington Post* by David Broder, one of the most highly respected journalists in the nation's capital. Broder, noting the continued sniping at President Nixon despite his winding down of American involvement, wrote, "Men have learned to break a President, and, like any discovery that imparts power to its possessors, the mere availability of this knowledge guarantees that it will be used."[351]

On November 3, President Nixon said in a speech on Vietnam that the United States would "not hesitate to take strong and effective measures" to thwart North Vietnamese actions against Americans. "America is fortunate," said *The Times-Dispatch*, "to have in the White House a man who stoutly resists the counsel of those who would send this nation down to humiliating and disastrous defeat."[352]

When air strike against North Vietnam resumed late in 1970, *The News Leader* rebuked critics of the action—especially Sen. McGovern, "who is more suited for the funnies than for the Senate."

"The President is a good man, and tough," said the editorial. "And he deserves the gratitude of this confused nation for smacking the Communists, and thereby implicitly telling his critics where they can go."[353]

SECTION H

• Corporate

RADIO

Richmond's daily papers were in the radio business for roughly 34 years, and for three of those years Stations WRTD and WRNL represented the separately owned *Richmond Times-Dispatch* and *Richmond News Leader*.

WRTD, which went on the air June 27, 1937, got the jump on its competitor, whose debut was November 14 of that year. But the Bryan family's purchase of *The Times-Dispatch* in 1940 wiped out WRTD "after three years, two months and four days of uninterrupted broadcasting," *The Times-Dispatch* reported.

In a news story heavy on promotion, *The Times-Dispatch* said three weeks before WRTD began broadcasting, "Radio engineers will tell you that the perfect type of antenna is a rod suspended vertically in space and they have come very near that perfection in building the broadcasting equipment on Belle Isle for WRTD, Richmond's new station owned by *The Times-Dispatch*."

The 331-foot antenna on the island in the James River served a station with 100 watts of power and carrying NBC's Blue Network.

The paper reported "perfect" reception of its test broadcasting at 1500 kilocycles. Its formal dedication two months later featured the mayor, the city school superintendent, clergy, musicians and representatives of civic clubs. WRTD also would carry a series of programs, "Colored Richmond on the Air," a half-hour variety show featuring Negroes, *The Times-Dispatch* said.

WRNL, a 500-watt station, also reported "excellent reception throughout a wide area" on its first day of broadcasting at 880 kilocycles. Those paying tribute included the mayor, the president of the Ministerial Union of Richmond and the presidents of the University of Richmond and the Medical College of Virginia.

For three years, WRNL had no network affiliation. It joined NBC in 1940 and switched three years later to the new ABC network.

From 1940 until it was sold in 1971 to Rust Communications Group Inc., WRNL had an advantage over other Richmond stations in that it could get carbon copies of stories developed by reporters for both daily papers. So could the Associated Press, although local radio stations that were AP members were not supposed to get *News Leader* and *Times-Dispatch* stories.

One of the WRNL staff members who came across Fourth Street to pick up "dupes" from the news rooms of the papers was a young Washington and Lee University graduate who had been an intern at *The News Leader* one summer but had not been kept on as a staff reporter.

He was Roger Mudd, who had his own local radio program on WRNL in the 1950s and won acclaim by tape-recording interviews with local judges for a WRNL series. From there it was on to the commercial networks and the Public Broadcasting System.

Richmond Newspapers Inc. tried unsuccessfully to get into television also. But in 1955 the Federal Communications Commission awarded a license for the new Channel 12 to Richmond Television, whose main owner was Larus & Brother Co., which owned Radio Station WRVA. In turning down the newspapers' bid, the FCC said it wanted greater diversification in ownership of communications outlets. RNI's owners also included people who owned papers in Norfolk and Petersburg and others who controlled the Tribune Publishing Co. in Tampa and radio and TV stations in Tampa and Norfolk.

But RNI's parent corporation, Media General, did get into TV in a big way. At present, it owns television stations in Charleston, Tampa and Jacksonville and its Fairfax Cable operation in 1994 generated 112 million dollars in revenue, more than a fifth of the Media General's total revenue of 626 million.

SOUTHSIDE VIRGINIAN

As president of Richmond Newspapers Inc. and later of Media General, Alan S. Donnahoe embarked on several ventures beyond publishing *The Times-Dispatch* and *The News Leader*.

One of the boldest was creation of a free weekly paper to be distributed to residents of 15 counties in Southside Virginia, plus the cities of Petersburg, Hopewell and Colonial Heights.

The new paper was the Southside Virginian, immediately dubbed the "Southside Virgin" by reporters on the Richmond dailies. The paper was distributed each Wednesday with regular editions of *The Times-Dispatch* and *The News Leader* and, thus, had a built-in circulation of more than 40,000.

A news story February 5, 1967 in *The Times-Dispatch* said the Southside Virginian would be the fifth largest paper in the state. Donnahoe was quoted as saying the paper was perhaps unique, in that readers in a region of a certain size would have their own newspaper, devoted to their entire area, as logical supplement to the broad news coverage of metropolitan dailies.

In a way, it was a forerunner to today's "zoned" editions in metropolitan areas.

John E. Leard, managing editor of *The Times-Dispatch*, was listed as publisher of the weekly. James P. Berry, a 11-year veteran with *The Times-Dispatch* who had headed three state bureaus, was editor. James L. Dillon, assistant advertising manager of Richmond Newspapers, was general manager, and Guy Cumby, a longtime member of the advertising department of Richmond Newspapers, was advertising director.

Leard said the new paper "will try to give its readers intensive coverage of their own area with regional and local news and pictures with emphasis on people." There was a news staff of eight, with one reporter assigned strictly to sports and another fulltime to women's news.

The paper lasted three years. In a column titled "End of an Experiment" on March 26, 1970, Leard wrote, "The experiment ends with disappointment that The Southside Virginian has proved only helpful rather than essential to its area."

It had received encouragement, he said, from readers and advertisers, "but it has not made the impact measurable from reader and shopper response that is necessary for survival of a publication of this kind."

Donnahoe said, "I thought it was a good venture."[354]

Berry agreed, although he thought that I. Newman Leadbetter, circulation director of Richmond Newspapers, overreached when he tried to push the paper into many more counties of Southside Virginia.[355] Leard said insufficient analysis had been done on an expanded market. He also said that union pressure for the Southside Virginian to be a new press run instead of a continuation of a *News Leader* press run made publishing more expensive than it should have been.[356]

A less successful venture was the *Amex Journal*, which began in January 1982 and lasted a year. The 24-page monthly publication dealt solely with the American Stock Exchange and its members and went to 30,000 corporate executives. At the end, Larry Gould, its publisher, said, "It was not as successful as we'd hoped it would be."

One of Donnhoe's boldest innovations was the *Media General Financial Daily*, which he heralded at its start in August 1971 as "the most comprehensive, accurate, up-to-the-minute financial publication in history."

The full-size paper had 68 pages four days a week and 72 pages in its weekend edition. Fifty pages were devoted to tables and charts of the various financial exchanges. That was one reason that only six production employees were needed for the Financial Daily. Another reason was that Donnahoe, an electronics and computer buff, had seen to it that the paper could be produced with equipment that included a computerized cathode ray tube typesetting unit that composed a full page automatically in about a minute.

For a short time, several thousand copies were flown daily to New York.

Four months after it began, the *Financial Daily* was no more. In its stead was the *Financial Weekly*. Donnahoe said the only way to determine if there were a market for a daily paper with as much information as the *Financial Daily* had was to try.

"Now, after more than four months of publication," he said, "we believe that the demand in the immediately foreseeable future is not enough to justify continued publication on a daily basis, although we have attracted tremendous critical acclaim and a significant number of daily subscribers."

The *Financial Weekly* lasted until the end of February 1990. Its largest circulation, after heavy promotion, was about 10,000.[357] Most observers attributed its death to the increasing availability of information through a variety of computers. The combined circulation of the *Financial Weekly* and a monthly tabloid, *IndustriScope*, also published by Media General Financial Services, was about 3,000, or about what the *Financial Daily* had at its peak.

The Southside Virginian

Thursday, March 26, 1970

Southside's Largest Newspaper

A forward look

Southside in the 70's

By Staff Writers

LARRY JAMES

Greensville youth IFYE delegate

Petersburg's future keyed to annexation

By H. Hugh Moore
Staff Writer

ANNEXATION SUIT TO BE HEARD AT PRINCE GEORGE
City Seeks Territory From Two Adjoining Areas

The Southside Virginian: Its Final Issue

With this issue, The Southside Virginian halts publication.

Started three years ago as an experiment in regional journalism, the weekly has focused attention on the east Southside area, its people, its progress, and its problems. It has served as a medium for regional news and advertising messages to an area drawn constantly closer by improved highways.

But like so many other undertakings these days, the publication faces substantial costs without offsetting revenues.

The management, news and advertising staffs are grateful for the support readers and advertisers have given The Southside Virginian. We count on your continued support of and interest in our parent newspapers for which Southside Virginia is an area of prime importance. The Virginian's staff looks forward to continuing to serve you of Southside Virginia through their columns.

For this purpose the present office at 20 East Tabb St. (Phone 732-7870) will remain in operation as a news bureau of the Richmond Times-Dispatch.

(Related Editorial and "Sidelights" Column on Page 4.)

Cine-Winner

An open sewer?

Color Bailey's Creek 'black'

By Monte Bagall
Staff Writer

VIRGINIA BUSINESS

Four years before the end of the *Financial Weekly*, Media General had embarked on another publication—*Virginia Business*, a monthly magazine targeted for executives across the state.

With its first issue in February 1986, the magazine announced that it was being mailed to "more than 30,000 people on a complimentary basis. The paid subscription rate is $30 per year."

Into its tenth year, its subscription list was 37,500, James A. Bacon, editor and associate publisher, said.[358] It had been as high as 40,000, he said, but the editors decided to trim the list.

Eliminating subscribers is not as strange as it sounds when the copies are sent on a "controlled circulation basis," meaning there's no cost to subscribe. The magazine makes money by advertising; it can tell advertisers that the readers are indeed a high-powered group of executive throughout Virginia.

Virginia Business also has 3,000 to 4,000 paid subscribers, but they aren't counted in the 37,500 total, Bacon said.

"We've gone through major changes from the start," Bacon said. At first, there were four staff writers—Jeff Schapiro, Estelle Jackson, Carl Rhodes and Lisa Antonelli. In 1991, Bacon said, there was a staff shakeup—no more full-time writers. Schapiro and Jackson already had gone to *The Times-Dispatch.* Rhodes remained as managing editor. Antonelli was Lisa Antonelli Bacon, wife of the editor.

Some writers had been hired in the interim, but they were let go. Remaining as editors were Bacon and Rhodes plus a senior editor and an associate editor. Articles were done by free-lancers.

The magazine had gone through a recession and a libel suit over a story about savings and loan associations. And, "We hadn't made a profit," Bacon said.[359] Expenses had to be cut.

What is called traditional business journalism—profiles of executives, financial market stories and the like—make up only 15 to 20 percent of today's articles, Bacon said. Now the magazine concentrates on "advertising-driven" articles, special projects and helping small business.

The result, according to Media General's 1994 annual report, was a 15 percent increase in revenue as expenses were generally flat.

NEWARK ACQUISITION

Three years after stock of Richmond Newspapers Inc. began trading publicly in 1966, the holding company of Media General Inc. was formed. RNI became a wholly owned subsidiary and its stock was exchanged on a one-for-one basis for Media General stock. Principal officers of Richmond Newspapers assumed the same jobs in Media General.

Before 1969 ended, the new corporation had increased its ownership of The Tribune Company, which published the daily papers in Tampa, Florida, from 56 percent to 84 percent and had bought the Piedmont Publishing Company of Winston-Salem, North Carolina. Piedmont, which published the *Winston-Salem Journal*, a morning paper, and the *Twin City Sentinel*, an afternoon paper, had been owned for more than 30 years by Gordon Gray.

Having accomplished that, Alan S. Donnahoe, Media General president, set out on the next major acquisition—the *Newark News* and Garden State Paper Company. The announcement by Media General in January 1970 said the purchase of the two companies plus Fidelity Engraving Company would be effected by an exchange of stock worth about $50 million.

Donnahoe said in an interview, however, that the newspaper was bought for $17 million and Garden State Paper for $17 million from the same owner, "Dick Scudder," or the Scudder family, which had owned the *Newark News* for three generations. They were different transactions, Donnahoe said.[360]

Everything looked rosy at the time. The afternoon *Newark News* was the largest paper in New Jersey. It had a daily circulation of 267,289 and a Sunday circulation of 423,331. The 87-year-old paper served the 13 largest metropolitan area in the nation. Garden State Paper had newsprint mills in Garfield, New Jersey and Pomona, California.

But labor trouble erupted in Newark. Donnahoe says that the American Newspaper Guild struck "immediately."[361] The strike didn't begin until May 26, 1971, two and one-half months after the Guild was certified as bargaining agent for news department employees but only six days after the official sale of the Scudder properties to Media General.

Douglas Eldridge, chairman of the guild's unit at the *News*, said that Bruce Mair, president of the paper, wanted to eliminate 50 of the 200 editorial staff members within six months. Mair said he wanted only to be able to solicit voluntary resignations for two months, when severance pay would be made, and to continue seeking resignations for another four months. Then he would decide, after those six months, if further layoffs were needed. He conceded that his plan would let the *News* reduce the staff by 50 employees.

George Kentera, who had been brought in from the Washington bureau to become managing editor of the *News* in 1967, apparently agreed with Eldridge's interpretation of what Mair wanted. Kentera resigned rather than order 50 people on the editorial staff be fired, on a seniority basis.[362]

Eldridge said, "I was amazed when we won, the Guild caught on like wildfire. Mair was so heavy-handed that the most docile, conservative group of middle-aged newspapermen in the country joined a union. They were a scared bunch of people."[363]

John McLaughlin of the *Trenton Times* called the strike "One of the most spectacularly ill-advised moves in the history of American labor."[364]

Although the Guild voted in mid-November to end its strike, after accepting the company's offer of higher wages, the paper was idled almost 11 months. Two months before the union vote, the *Newark News* sold its Sunday paper to the *Newark Star-Ledger*, thereby necessitating new agreements between the *News* and all the craft unions.

That occurred in mid-February of 1972, but the first post-strike paper was printed April 10, almost 11 days after the strike began.

The sale of the Sunday paper to the *Star-Ledger* was the only way the *News* could keep publishing a daily paper, said Bruce Mair. "Sale of the Sunday paper," Mair said, "and printing of the daily in the *Star-Ledger* plant should lead to material reduction in the capital outlay required for startup purposes. On this basis, we would hope that the *News* can resume daily publication on a sound and continuing basis."[365]

Donnahoe said, "We made a deal with old S.I. Newhouse and, in effect, sold him our Sunday paper. For that, he paid us enough money to reimburse us for what we paid for the *News* and for all our losses during the strike."[366]

When printing of the *News* resumed, the press run was 220,000, or about 47,000 under the daily circulation when Media General bought the paper.

Less than five months later, the *News* folded and more than 500 people were out of jobs. Mair said the problems were "solely financial." Circulation had dropped, thus causing advertisers to cancel ads because too few people were reading them. Mair said losses were growing so rapidly that the paper would have lost $8 million a year. An Associated Press story August 30 said the paper reportedly lost $179,219 in 1970, the year Media General bought it, and another $463,993 in the four months before the strike.

Both Mair and Donnahoe laid heavy blame for troubles at the paper on the unions. When the Sunday paper was sold, Mair talked of "the long and crippling strike by the Newspaper Guild." Unit costs as a result of prior wage settlements were also cited.

Donnahoe said unit costs in Newark were four times those in Richmond. He said there was "unbelievable" featherbedding and that the city editor in Newark, for example, would tell reporters that although they weren't getting a salary increase, they should turn in expense reports, which Donnahoe said were unrealistic.[367]

The Newspaper Guild, Donnahoe said, saw Media General as "someone with deep pockets" and, therefore, aimed for a wage scale equal to that in New York.

Many of Donnahoe's comments about the *Newark News* that Media General bought are backed up by Richard Reeves in an article in the *Columbia Journalism Review* in 1972. He said the paper was "mismanaged, or unmanaged, on a mind-boggling scale by the third generation of the Scudder family before they sold the paper and associated properties." He also said that circulation and advertising figures were "almost certainly inflated," that there were sweetheart contracts with some unions and that reporters' salaries were augmented by phony expense accounts.[368]

Reeves added that Media General couldn't find $500,000 in "circulation receivables" listed as assets of the *Newark News*, nor could they find "$100,000 worth of newsprint listed as inventory."

Was there were any truth to reports that Media General bought the *News* so that it could get Garden State Paper and then close the *News*?

"That's crazy guild propaganda," said Donnahoe. "Of course, absolutely," the new owners intended to publish the paper. The city of Newark, Donnahoe conceded, was a "disaster area," but "the Newark metropolitan area is in the top 10 in the United States in terms of relative income. It's a very wealthy area."

As far as Donnahoe is concerned, "If it hadn't been for that stupid strike," and if the unions had been reasonable in helping to bring down costs, "that paper could have succeeded in no uncertain terms."[369]

TANNER ACQUISITION

In his 18 years as chief executive of Media General, Alan Donnahoe oversaw its expansion into a news media conglomerate. Assets grew from $14 million to $510 million and annual revenue from $18 million $531 million.

That occurred not only through consistent growth of existing units but also by acquisition of a host of firms. One of the most unusual—and most embarrassing in the long run—was the William B. Tanner Co. of Memphis, Tennessee. The company sold radio and television time to advertisers and also produced commercials and jingles.

Donnahoe said that Lehman Brothers, the New York investment firm, brought it to the attention of Media General, one of whose directors was Paul Manheim, a partner in the investment firm.[370] A brief item in *The Times-Dispatch* on May 22, 1982, said Media General was "holding discussions involving the possible acquisition" of Tanner.

By early July, it was a done deal. The price was $36 million in cash plus more money based on earnings in the next 10 years. But slightly more than one year later—August 11, 1983—about 25 FBI agents seized the eight-story Tanner headquarters, forbade its employees to make telephone calls or leave the building and confiscated a mountain of records.

Allegations of former employees, including a one-time controller, were that Tanner kept two sets of books, that the company made routine payoffs in cash, automobiles, trips and women and that there was a "hidden inventory" of advertising time that Tanner acquired through barter with radio stations.

Initially, Donnahoe complained of the manner of the investigation. "If they had wanted to see the records," he was quoted as saying immediately after the raid, "we would've gladly shown them." Four days later, he issued a statement saying Media General had its own investigation going.

"We have found nothing to substantiate any of the material allegations by these informants," he said. "Indeed, on the contrary, some of the allegations appear to be altogether absurd, and others may stem from a combination of ignorance and malice."

But in an interview with Thomas R. Morris in *The Times-Dispatch* of August 21, Donnahoe acknowledged, "We are not in a position to say the allegations are false."

He added: "If these things took place, then we're the principal victim." Morris noted that in the three and one-half days since the raid, Media General stock had fallen 14 percent—from $61.63 to $53.13. The American Stock Exchange halted trading in the stock for two and one-half of those days.

On January 30, 1985, after a 17-month FBI investigation, Tanner pleaded guilty to four counts of mail fraud and income tax violations. Four months later, in a plea bargain in U.S. District Court in Memphis, he was sentenced to four years in prison. The name of his firm had been changed to Media General Broadcast Services and staffed with new executives.

Media General meanwhile sued Tanner for $190 million, alleging he lied about his company before selling it. The case was settled with agreement that terms would not be divulged.

Did Media General do an adequate job of investigating the Memphis firm? Donnahoe thinks it did. In an interview with the author November 5, 1989, he said Tanner had thought about going public and a prospectus had been prepared. Touche Ross & Co. had audited the books for eight years and found nothing wrong, he said.

"The simple fact is," said Donnahoe, "there is no way that anybody could have found out about this unless they were inside the company."

"The background of that company was very impressive. . .It was a leader in its industry," he said. Tanner was "an absolutely fantastic salesman; there's no question about that," said Donnahoe. Tanner's trouble was that "he wasn't content with a good thing. He'd get a client and decide he ought to do some nice things for him. . . a form of commercial bribery. I don't think Mr. Tanner considered it commercial bribery. He was just being nice to his friends."

Whatever the company was like, Tanner himself was not the type who would appeal to the aristocratic Tennant Bryan. Tanner liked flashy clothes and big Cadillacs. *Fortune* magazine, stressing his flamboyance, dubbed him the "Sultan of Swap."

Bryan and Donnahoe mention the investment firm of Wheat, First Securities as bringing the Tanner company to Media General's attention.

Reflecting on the purchase, Bryan said, "I had a feeling, obviously not very strong because I could have stopped it if I felt that strongly about it. I had a feeling about Tanner, about Bill Tanner in Memphis. I never did like that bastard."[371]

SUGARMAN'S BID

In February 1987, Burt Sugarman, producer of television game shows and chairman of a company that made cement, began buying Media General stock. A year later, on "Leap Year Day," he publicly offered to buy out the company for about $1.8 billion.

"He came pretty darn close," D. Tennant Bryan, patriarch of the family that had controlled the Richmond papers and their predecessors for 100 years, reflected.[372]

Sugarman seemed an unlikely news media baron. He had no experience in news, and the division of Media General that seemed to interest him most was the company's highly profitable cable television operation in Fairfax County, one of Virginia's most affluent areas.

Three days before a meeting of Media General stockholders, who were to choose from two slates of three directors each, Sugarman offered to end his move for three seats on the board and sell his 10.1 percent of the company's publicly traded stock for a 43 percent interest in a new company that would control the cable TV operation.

James S. Evans, then president of Media General, saw the offer as "greenmail of the most egregious sort."

The offer also came three weeks after a federal judge ruled against Sugarman in his most likely bid to take control of the company. Sugarman wanted both classes of stock to be treated as one in voting on his takeover attempt.

When stock in Richmond Newspapers Inc. was first traded publicly, in 1966, and when Media General, the holding company, was chartered in 1969, the Bryans were determined who would call the shots.

Media General's charter provided for two classes of stock—A and B. The latter could be considered to stand for Bryan, for the family controlled it. Class B stock, not traded publicly, elected seven of the 10 Media General directors and, thereby, controlled the company. Holders of Class A stock, publicly traded on the American Stock Exchange, elected three directors.

On April 27, 1988, U.S. District Court Judge Richard Williams sided with Media General, which argued that the company's charter and Virginia law called for a two-thirds vote of each class of stock to approve what Sugarman sought.

Sugarman's lawyer, Edward Brodsky of New York, argued that Sugarman's aim to acquire the company was an "acquisition" and necessitated a vote by all shareholders as a single class. That was because, he said, a charter provision came into play since Sugarman owned more than 10 percent of Media General stock, and his plan involved paying money to Media General, which, in turn, would distribute it to shareholders—or in the words of Wall Street, "a reverse triangular merger."

"In no sense of the word," said R. Harvey Chappell, Media General's lawyer, "could this be an acquisition by Media General. It just isn't so."

The judge agreed.

By the time of the annual meeting, Sugarman had raised his offer for Media General stock to $70 a share, when it was trading at only $49 or $50. In mid-February, when he made his first purchase, the stock closed at $49.87. Then it began plunging, down as far as $35 by mid-June. It got back as high as $44.25 on October 18, but the next day the market crashed and Media General was down by $13.63 in two days to $30.63 on October 20.

By early 1988, the market and Media General were looking better. On March 1, the day after Sugarman bid $61.50 a share, Media General rose to $50.37, its highest level, and closed at $49. But in the eight trading days before the annual meeting, the stock was down to $42.50. A chart accompanying a story by Steve Row and Randy Hallman in *The News Leader* on the day of the annual meeting traced the rise and fall of the stock. The paper noted that the precipitous drop in those eight days reflected the feelings of analysts that Sugarman wouldn't get his way.

The annual meeting was as much entertainment as business, so it seemed appropriate for it to be in the theater of the Virginia Museum of Fine Arts. It had to be away from the usual site, the company headquarters, because of the interest not only of stockholders and the financial community but also of the nation's press. The *Los Angeles Times*, the *Wall Street Journal*, *USA Today* and *Business Week* were among the 22 news organizations represented.

The News Leader and *The Times-Dispatch* each had two reporters covering the meeting. Countless others neglected their normal routine to attend. Besides Row and Hallman, there were Thomas R. Morris and Ray McAllister of *The Times-Dispatch.*

Morris was the only reporter who had had a face-to-face interview with Sugarman during the battle for proxies. Morris figured that Sugarman had followed *The Times-Dispatch* coverage, liked it and felt other publications would be biased. In any case, when Morris learned Sugarman was coming to Richmond, he scheduled an interview for April 1 and, at its conclusion, escorted Sugarman into Managing Editor Marvin Garrette's office for an introduction.[373]

At the museum theater, virtually all of the 550 seats were taken. An elaborate procedure as to who could speak how long at what times was established, but not all the time was needed. No one wanted to question the six nominees for the three Class A directors. The meeting lasted an hour and 45 minutes.

Clearly the star of the day was Tennant Bryan. At 81, the board chairman was, as McAllister wrote, "still a charmer—witty and unfailingly polite." When he introduced management's slate of nominees, he got through the Class B list, ending with "uh, me."

Thunderous applause broke out and lasted 25 seconds. Bryan clearly had expected nothing like it. Old-time employees who had fought with management at contract negotiation time were on their feet. "Let me explain," Bryan finally was able to say. "That was not the object."

Each side had its say. When Sugarman finished his presentation, he started down the same steps at the front of the stage that he had used to get to the microphone. Bryan directed him to some steps to the right that were easier to navigate. "Just promise you won't send me out of the building," Sugarman said. The audience liked it.

At the end of the meeting, Sugarman moved across the stage to shake hands with Bryan. Photographer Amir Pishdad caught the greeting in a picture that was on the front page of the next morning's *Times-Dispatch.*

Reporters wanted to know what was said. McAllister said the questions went like this:

What did Sugarman say?

Sugarman: "You'll have to ask Mr. Bryan."

What did Sugarman say?

Bryan: "He just said he was glad he met me. Very polite."

What did Bryan say?

Bryan: "That it was very polite of him."

The final tally on the vote came a week later, although Media General was confident it had won by the time the meeting ended.

Officially it was about 13.56 million votes, or 55.8 per cent, for the Media General nominees, and 10.6 million votes, or 43.7 per cent, for Sugarman's nominess.

Burt Sugarman (left), D. Tennant Bryan at meeting where stockholders turned back takeover attempt.

SECTION I
• Advertising and Production

Top: Al Petzold, longtime printer, sets type.
Middle: Pressmen putting metal plates (one for each page of the paper) on presses.
Bottom: Mail room personnel sort bundles of papers for placement on delivery trucks.

ADVERTISING

News people and ad people at Richmond Newspapers could work in the same building for 30 years, ride the same elevators with nothing more than a perfunctory "good morning" and still not know one another's names.

Although from a social or educational standpoint, those groups might be in the same general class, reporters generally felt closer to printers or stereotypers in the days preceding "cold type."

The reason is that reporters and most newsroom editors suspect that somehow people in the advertising department, given the chance, would try to help their customers or make them look good in the news columns. Although on any respectable newspaper, such collusion is non-existent, the concern remains.

It is almost as if there were "news police," like military police, declaring certain areas off limits. If an advertising department employee enters the newsroom, it is likely to be a ranking member of the department going to see the managing editor about some late shift in ads on page diagrams that have already been sent to the news department.

Aversion to socializing with people in the advertising or circulation departments does not mean reporters and editors are not concerned about the paper's finances. With a thrift plan that enables veteran reporters to retire with more than a quarter-million dollars in their accounts, there are budding capitalists throughout newsrooms.

An axiom of the newspaper business is that circulation pays for only paper and ink. That 50 cents that a customer plunks down now for a copy of his weekday paper (and the penny or 5 cents that his ancestors paid for a copy) covers the cost of only newsprint and the ink that is applied thereto.

In other words, the presses, the computers, the typewriters of earlier days, delivery vehicles, the wages and the health benefits are paid mainly by advertising.

So, when Richmond's two major department stores—both more than 100 years old—closed not only their downtown operations but also their suburban branches in the early 1990s, it hurt *The Times-Dispatch* and *The News Leader* financially. Miller & Rhoads closed at the start of 1990; Thalhimers, early in 1992.

Add to that a nagging recession and the merging of the two papers on June 1, 1992, and the result is less advertising.

Media General, parent of the newspaper, does not break down its profits and losses by city (Richmond, Tampa or Winston-Salem). But it does detail advertising lineage by city. In 1994, *The Times-Dispatch's* total advertising inches amounted to 2,219,353, just a hair more than the previous year's total of 2,218,937. Still, that was a far cry from the 3,083,198 inches of 1991, the last full year *The News Leader* was included.

The peak lineage was 3,387,532 in 1990, and even 20 years earlier the total was above 3,000,000.

But a drop in lineage doesn't necessarily translate into a drop in advertising revenue. Ad revenue in Richmond rose to $84,496,000 in 1994 from $81,752,000 a year earlier. The answer, of course, was higher rates, which the company hesitates to make public.

Albert T. August III, president of Richmond Newspapers, said rates increase each year; the rise in 1994 was only 3 to 4 per cent, but that was deemed insufficient, so rates jumped 8 per cent in 1995.[374]

Compared with a generation ago, today's Richmond Newspapers Inc., has not only one less paper but also fewer unions. The 1971 strike meant the end of the printers' representation by the International Typographical Union, the most potent of the unions. Earlier, the reporters had voted out the American Newspaper Guild in favor of a local union—the Richmond Newspapers Professional Association. The company still bargains with unions for pressmen, drivers and photo-engravers.

Wages, salaries and benefits make up the major outlay of virtually any corporation, and wages of *Times-Dispatch* reporters and editors have risen steadily.

After excluding about 40 people—mostly editors but a few administrative assistants and confidential secretaries, the association today bargains for 189 employees. As of April 1995, almost two-thirds of them (120) were in senior categories—or earning several thousand dollars a year above the $41,545 for reporters with more than four years' experience.

A Senior III employee began drawing at least $51,120 as of April 5, 1994.

Remuneration at the top levels of Media General, of course, is something else. Publisher Stewart Bryan had total compensation of $816,290 in 1994. The four other highest paid executives drew from $177,657 to $448,960.

E.H. Collins, city circulation manager for The News Leader, *checks out one of first papers printed on new presses in 1950.*

PRODUCTION

Producing a daily newspaper has always been hectic, but the job today is done without many of the tools of yesteryear. Linotype machines are museum pieces; stereotypers, who created the metal plates that went on presses, are in the same league as blacksmiths; even typewriters are an anachronism.

Today's *Times-Dispatch*, like other daily newspapers, is still produced by human beings—but human beings with computers.

The reporter works at a video display terminal and sends his story through various editors, the last of whom pushes a button that instructs another machine to set the story in type.

That machine sets up to 10,000 words a minute on film. It is waxed, cut and made sticky on the bottom side. A makeup editor, following a diagram from the newsroom, oversees film containing stories and photographs being pasted on a page.

When a page is completed, a full-page negative is transmitted by a fiber optics line to the production plant eleven miles north of Richmond in Hanover County. One page can be sent every five minutes. From the negative, a printing plate for the press is made. A plate can be produced each five minutes.

Robots, which *The Times-Dispatch* calls Automatic Guided Vehicles, move the 50-inch, 2,700-pound rolls of newsprint to the presses. The rolls have been brought into the production building by three rail cars.

Each of the three Mitsubishi presses is 155 feet long, 12 feet wide and 55 feet high. One press can print up to 75,000 copies an hour of an 80-page paper with 16 page of full color and another 16 of spot color.

A bit of promotion for Richmond Newspapers' new production center in Hanover County with the merger of The News Leader *into* The Times-Dispatch *in 1992.*

THE FUTURE

Almost four years after Stewart Bryan announced the pending merger of *The Times-Dispatch* and *The News Leader*, he again chronicled the changing face of news in America.

Although there was uncertainty about future forms of communication, he said, Media General was in good shape to "be a full and significant participation among them," he said.

He foresaw "the near elimination of time and space as constraints to business." There will be a change in what he called "appointment journalism"—"the morning paper, the 6 o'clock news and an occasional trip to the public library."

This, he said, was "the world of cyberspace, super-computers and information on demand.

The new corporate mission statement of Media General probably would not include the words "newspapers or television."

Rather, he envisioned something like this:

> *"Media General's mission is to be the leading provider of information, especially local and regional information, in markets served, through an unmatched ability to collect information and disseminate it via traditional and non-traditional programs and platforms."*[375]

Stewart Bryan

EPILOGUE

The Times-Dispatch traces its ancestry to 1850, and there's been a male Bryan in control since 1886. Stewart Bryan, representing the fourth generation, is his 88-year-old father's only son. He is 56 and without a male heir.

What, asked an interviewer, does that mean for the future of *The Times-Dispatch*?

"I don't know the answer to that," he said. "If I knew, I'd tell you."[376]

NOTES

SECTION A • Publishers

JOSEPH BRYAN

1. W. David Lewis, "Joseph Bryan and the Virginia Connection in the Industrial Development of Northern Alabama," *The Virginia Magazine of History and Biography*, Vol. 98, No. 4, October 1990. pp. 621-622.
2. *Ibid*, p. 626.
3. *Ibid*, p. 632.
4. *Ibid*, p. 637.
5. John Stewart Bryan, *Joseph Bryan—His Times, His Family, His Friends*, p. 77.
6. *Ibid*, p. 104.
7. Lewis, *op. cit.* p. 621.
8. *Ibid.*
9. Bryan, *op. cit.*, p. 210.
10. James M. Lindgren, "First and Foremost a Virginian. Joseph Bryan and the New South Economy," *The Virginia Magazine of History and Biography*, Vol. 96, No. 2, April 1988, p. 161.
11. *Ibid*, pp. 158-159.
12. Bryan, *op. cit.*. p. 218.
13. *Ibid*, p. 250. Jay J. Levit, a Richmond lawyer specializing in labor relations, said "fair and open" apparently was the union's way of acknowledging that the company wouldn't require workers to join the union but wouldn't discriminate against union members.
14. This must simply be an error. On pp. 249-250, John Stewart Bryan writes, "The Times was but a poor sheet in comparison with The Dispatch. As the glamor of a paper that did nothing but lose money soon palled on Major Ginter, he gave that Trojan horse in 1887 to Joseph Bryan."
15. Bryan, *op. cit.*, pp. 251-252.
16. Lindgren, *op. cit.*, p. 158.
17. Bryan, *op. cit.*, p.254.
18. Lindgren, *op. cit.*, p. 164.
19. *Ibid.*
20. *Ibid*, p. 166.
21. *Ibid*, p. 169.
22. Bryan, *op. cit.*, p. 251.
23. *Ibid*, p. 200.

JOHN STEWART BRYAN

24. *The News Leader*, Oct. 17, 1944.
25. *The Times-Dispatch*, Oct. 17, 1944.
26. *The News Leader*, Sept. 22, 1936.
27. Associated Press article in *Richmond Times-Dispatch*, April 25, 1935.

D. TENNANT BRYAN

28. Interview with author, Oct. 17, 1989.
29. Interview with author, Oct. 26, 1989.

30. Interview with author, Oct. 17, 1989.
31. Interview with Lisa Shaffer on WRIC-TV, Channel 8, Richmond, in 1992 when papers merged.
32. Interview with author, Oct. 26, 1989.
33. *Ibid.*
34. *Ibid.*

J. STEWART BRYAN III

35. Interview with author, Aug. 13,1991.
36. Interview with author, July 14, 1992.
37. *Ibid.*
38. *Ibid.*
39. *Ibid.*

SECTION B • Origins

THE DISPATCH

40. Virginius Dabney, *Pistols and Pointed Pens*, pp. 61-63.
41. Lester J. Cappon, *Virginia Newspapers 1821-1935*, p. 169; Dabney, *op. cit.*, p.64.
42. Dabney, *op. cit.* pp. 65-66.
43. Cappon, *op. cit.*, p.169.
44. *Ibid*, p. 169.
45. *Ibid*, p. 23
46. *Ibid*, p. 31.
47. Dabney, *op. cit.*, p. 69-73.
48. *Ibid*, pp. 73-76.
49. *Ibid*, p. 75.

THE TIMES

50. Virginius Dabney, *op. cit.*, p. 160.
51. Interview with author, Oct. 26, 1989.
52. Unpublished article by James Latimer.

THE LEADER

53. Cappon, *op. cit.*, p. 179.

THE NEWS

54. Interview with author, Oct. 26, 1989.
55. Editorial in *The News Leader*, Nov. 11, 1930.
56. *The Times-Dispatch*, Dec. 1. 1959.

THE OTHERS

57. Virginius Dabney, *op. cit.*, p. 18.
58. *Ibid*, p. 14.
59. *Ibid*, p. 16.
60. *Ibid*, p. 126.
61. *Ibid*, p. 38.
62. Virginius Dabney, *The Dry Messiah*, p. 67.
63. *Ibid*, p. 76.
64. *Ibid*, p. 60.
65. *Ibid*, p. 61.
66. *Ibid*, p. 63.
67. *Ibid*, p. 66.
68. *Ibid*, p. 102.
69. *Ibid*, p. 105.
70. *Ibid*, pp. 69-70.

THE LAST MERGER

71. Thomas W. Howard, interview with author, Dec. 31, 1993.
72. Telephone interview with author, Jan. 18, 1995.
73. *Ibid.*
74. Telephone interview with author, March 15, 1995.
75. Interview with author, March 14, 1995.
76. Media General research department, May 1994.
77. Telephone interview with Allen Walton, circulation director, Feb. 16, 1995.

SECTION C • Page One Stories

CAVE-IN

78. Louis D. Rubin, Jr. "Railway 's Tunnel Collapse" in *Times-Dispatch*, May 8, 1949. Reprinted in Maurice Duke's and Daniel P. Jordan's *A Richmond Reader 1733-1983*.

SNOW, 1940

79. Interview with author, April 17, 1991.

WORLD WAR II

80. Although the incident occurred before he joined *The Times-Dispatch*, Charles McDowell told the story in detail at a retirement party for the author in January 1989.

THALHIMER

81. Interview with author, May 24, 1991.
82. Interview with author, April 17, 1991.
83. Interview with author, Oct. 26, 1989.

ASSAULT

84. Telephone interview with author, Feb. 2, 1993.

POLITICS, LOCAL

85. Interview with author, April 17, 1991.

PROBING THE POLICE

86. Interview with author, March 15,1990.
87. *Ibid.*

THE KENNEDY ASSASSINATION

88. Interview with author, Jan. 30, 1991.
89. Interview with author, Feb. 12, 1992.
90. Interview with author, March 21, 1989.
91. Interview with author, June 12-13, 1991.
92. *Ibid.*
93. Interview with author, Feb. 12, 1992.
94. Interview with author, Jan. 30, 1991.

THE I.T.U. STRIKE

95. Interview with author, April 12, 1994.
96. Interview with author, April 19, 1994.
97. Interview with author, Nov. 5, 1990.
98. Interview with author, April 6, 1994.
99. Interview with author, April 19, 1994.
100. Interview with author, Nov. 5, 1990.
101. Interview with author, April 12, 1994.102. Interview with author, Nov. 5, 1990.
103. Interview with author, April 6, 1994.

KEPONE

104. Interview with Howard, Dec. 31,1993.
105. *Ibid.*
106 *The Times-Dispatch*, July 17, 1976.

STERILIZATION

107. Interview with author, Dec. 31, 1993.

ONE CASE WON

108. All information in this chapter is taken from *Times-Dispatch* accounts of Feb. 17, 1980 and July 3, 1980.

ANOTHER CASE, LOST

109. Telephone conversation with Dr. Robert Marchant of Richmond Public Schools, Feb. 27, 1995.
110. Interview with author, Nov. 29, 1989.
111. Interview with author, March 21, 1989.
112. Interview with author, Aug. 31, 1993.
113. Interview with author, Nov. 29, 1989.

ESCAPE FROM DEATH ROW

114. Interview with author, Nov. 10, 1992.
115. Interview with author, Nov. 10, 1992.

THE DALKON SHIELD

116. Telephone interview with Roscoe Puckett, former public relations director for A.H. Robins, Nov. 26, 1994.
117. Interview with author, Oct. 5, 1990.
118. *Ibid.*
119. Interview with author, July 14, 1992.

SECTION D • The News Staff

THE NEWSROOMS

120. Informal interview with author, May 3, 1991.

121. Larry Gould interview with author, Feb. 12, 1992.

122. Robert P. Hilldrup interview with author, Jan. 30, 1991.

123. Telephone interview with George Gill, Nov. 26, 1991.

124. Interview with author, July 23, 1991.

125. Recalled at Oct. 22, 1991, at meeting of vestry of St. Paul's Episcopal Church, Richmond, at which author introduced bishop.

MARK ETHRIDGE

126. Telephone interview with Norman Rowe, Jan. 25, 1995.

127. John T. Kneebone, *Southern Liberal Journalists and the Issue of Race 1920-1944*, p. 198.

128. *Op. cit.*, p. 229.

JUD EVANS

129. Interview with author, June 6, 1994.

130. Interview with author, July 19, 1991.

BOB GOLDEN

131. Interview with author, June 4, 1994.

CHARLES McDOWELL

132. Interview with author, Feb. 12, 1991.

133. *Ibid.*

134. Charles McDowell, *One Thing After Another*, pp. 165-167.

135. Interview with author, Feb. 12, 1991.

JAMES LATIMER

136. Interview with author, April 17, 1991.

GUY FRIDDELL

137. Interview with author, April 15, 1991.

138. Interview with author, Jan. 23, 1990.

139. Interview with author, March 21, 1989.

140. Interview with author, April 15, 1991.

141. Interview with author, Nov. 21, 1991.

142. *Ibid.*

143. *Ibid.*

144. *Ibid.*

145. *Ibid.*

146. Charles McDowell, *op. cit.*, pp. 157-158.

147. Interview with author, Nov. 21, 1991.

CHARLES W. (MIKE) HOUSTON

148. *The News Leader*, July 13, 1938.

149. Interview with author, April 15, 1991.

150. *The Times-Dispatch* obituary, Sept. 2, 1975.

151. *The News Leader*, Sept. 2, 1975.

152. Interview with author, April 15, 1991.

ROY FLANNAGAN

153. Interview with author, Aug. 23, 1991.

154. Interview with author, April 17, 1991.

ROBERT B. MUNFORD, JR.

155. Interview with author, Oct. 15, 1990.

BEVERLY ORNDORFF

156. Telephone interview with author, Nov. 2, 1993.

157. Interview with author, Nov. 2, 1993.

158. Interview with author, Nov. 5, 1990.

FRANK J. McDERMOTT

159. Interview with author, July 19, 1991.

CHARLES H. HAMILTON

160. Telephone interview with author, Nov. 26, 1991.

161. Interview with author, Jan. 30, 1991.

162. Telephone interview with author, Feb. 12, 1992.

163. Interview with author, Jan. 30, 1991.

164. Interview with author, Nov. 12, 1991.

165. Interview with author, Feb. 12, 1992.

166. Telephone interview with author, Nov. 29, 1991.

167. Interview with author, Aug. 23, 1991.

168. Interview with author, March 15, 1990.

169. *Ibid.*

170. Interview with author, July 23, 1991.
171. Interview with author, Nov. 30, 1989.
172. Interview with author, Nov. 5, 1990.
173. Interview with author, Nov. 30, 1989.

JOHN H. COLBURN

174. Interview with author, May 24, 1991.
175. Interview with author, April 14, 1992.

ALF GOODYKOONTZ

176. Interview with author, June 10, 1991.
177. *Ibid.*
178. *Ibid.*
179. *Ibid.*
180. *Ibid.*
181. *Ibid.*
182. *The Times-Dispatch*, Dec. 26, 1993.

THE COLOR BARRIER

183. Interview with author, June 30, 1994.
184. Interview with author, July 20, 1992.
185. *Ibid.*
186. *Ibid.*
187. Interview with author, April 12, 1991.
188. Interview wity author, Jan. 11,1995.

SECTION E • Sports, Entertainment, Photo

SPORTS

189. Interview with author, Oct. 16, 1990.
190. Interview with author, Aug. 1, 1990.
191. Interview with author, Feb. 27, 1991.
192. Interview with author, Aug. 1,1991.
193. Telephone interview with author, Oct. 7, 1993.
194. Interview with author, Feb. 27, 1991.
195. Interview with author, Oct. 16, 1990.
196. Interview with author, Aug. 1, 1991.
197. Telephone interview with author, July 29, 1991.
198. Interview with author, Aug. 1, 1991.
199. Telephone interview with author, July 29, 1991.
200. Interview with author, Oct. 15, 1990.
201. *Ibid.*

THIS IS ENTERTAINMENT

202. Richmond Newspapers advertisement, April 9, 1961.

PHOTO

203. Interview with Brill, July 20, 1991.
204. Chauncey Durden column, *The Times-Dispatch*, Sept. 28, 1952.
205. *Ibid.*
206. Telephone interview with James Latimer, Feb. 4, 1995.

SECTION F • Editorial

VIRGINIUS DABNEY

207. Interview with author, Oct. 5, 1989.
208. Virginius Dabney, *Across the Years*, p. 100.
209. *Ibid*, p. 105.
210. Interview with author, Oct. 5, 1989.
211. *Ibid.*
212. Interview with author, Oct. 5, 1989.
213. *Ibid.*
214. Dabney, *op.cit.*, p. 106.
215. Interview with author, Oct. 5, 1989.
216. Interview with author, Oct. 5, 1989; Dabney, *op. cit.*, pp. 108-109.
217. Dabney, *op. cit.*, p.118.
218. John T. Kneebone, *Southern Liberal Journalists and the Issue of Race, 1920-1944*, p. 60.
219. Dabney, *op. cit.*, 120.
220. *Ibid.*
221. Kneebone, *op. cit.*, p. 11.
222. Dabney, *op. cit.*, p. 123.
223. Interview with author, Oct. 5, 1989.
224. *Ibid.*
225. Kneebone, *op. cit.*, p. 177.
226. Dabney, *op. cit.*, pp. 128-132.
227. Interview with author, Nov. 28, 1989.
228. Dabney, *op. cit.*, p. 133.

229. *Ibid.*
230. Kneebone, *op. cit.*, p. 184.
231. Dabney, *op. cit.*, p. 138.
232. Virginius Dabney, *Liberalism in the South*, pp. 408-409/
233. *Ibid*, p. 428.
234. Virginius Dabney, *Below the Potomac*, pp. 215-216.
235. *Ibid*, p. 224.
236. Maurice Duke and Daniel P. Jordan, *A Richmond Reader 1733-1983.*, pp.381-397.
237. Kneebone, *op. cit.*, pp. 227-228.
238. *Ibid*, pp. 208-219.
239. Dabney, *Across the Years*, p. 148.
240. Kneebone, *op. cit.*, p. 155.
241. *Ibid*, pp. 166-167.
242. Dabney, *Across the Years*, pp. 165-166.
243. *Ibid.*
244. Interview with author, Oct. 5, 1989.
245. *Ibid.*
246. *Ibid.*
247. *Ibid.*
248. *Ibid.*

OVERTON JONES AND ED GRIMSLEY

249. Interview with author, May 16, 1990.
250. Interview with author, Jan. 16, 1991.
251. *Ibid.*
252. *Ibid.*
253. Interview with author, May 16, 1990.
254. *Ibid.*
255. *The News Leader*, April 15, 1969.

DOUGLAS S. FREEMAN

256. *Time*, Oct. 28, 1948.
257. Mary Tyler Cheek, "Reflections," *Virginia Magazine of History and Biography*, Vol. 94, No. 1, January 1986.
258. *Time, op. cit.*
259. Charles H. Hamilton, *Reader's Digest*, July 1960.
260. *Time, op. cit.*
261. *Ibid.*
262. *The News Leader*, June 15, 1953.
263. *Time, op. cit.*
264. *Ibid.*
265. Mary Tyler Cheek, *op. cit.*
266. *Ibid.*
267. Telephone interview with Mary Tyler McClenahan, Aug. 28, 1995.
268. *The News Leader*, obituary, June 15, 1953.
269. Mary Tyler Cheek, *op. cit.*
270. Interview with author, Nov. 30, 1989.
271. Interview with author, Jan. 23, 1990.
272. Interview with author, Oct. 25, 1989.
273. J. Bryan, III, *The Sword Over the Mantel*, pp. 23-25.
274. Interview with author, Oct. 26, 1989.

JAMES J. KILPATRICK

275. Interview with author, Nov. 30, 1989.
276. Interview with author, Aug. 23, 1991.
277. *The Times-Dispatch*, Dec. 25, 1988.
278. Interview with author, Aug. 23, 1991.
279. *The Times-Dispatch*, Dec. 24, 1952.
280. Harry S. Ashmore, *Hearts and Minds*, pp. 114-115.
281. Universal Press Syndicate, 1987.
282. Interview with author, Aug. 23, 1991.
283. *The News Leader*, Nov. 13, 1958.
284. Interview with author, Aug. 13, 1991.
285. Interview with author, Feb. 9, 1993.
286. Interview with author, Aug. 23, 1991.
287. Interview with author, Nov. 21, 1991.
288. Telephone interview with author, Oct. 25, 1991.
289. Interview with author, Aug. 23, 1991.
290. Interview with author, Aug. 2, 1994.
291. Interview with author, Aug. 23, 1991.

GROVER HALL, JR.

292. Interview with author, Feb. 9, 1993.

CARTOONISTS

293. *The Times-Dispatch*, obituary, Feb. 20, 1969.
294. *The Times-Dispatch*, June 24, 1956.
295. *Ibid.*
296. *The Times-Dispatch*, Sept. 28, 1935.
297. Telephone interview with author, July 2, 1991.
298. Conversation with author, March 29, 1993.
299. *The News Leader*, June 17, 1978.
300. *The News Leader*, Sept. 15, 1978.
301. *Newsweek*, Oct. 13, 1980.

SECTION G • Controversy

MASSIVE RESISTANCE

302. Interview with author, Jan. 11, 1995.

REGRETS

303. Interview with author, Oct. 5, 1989.
304. Interview with author, Oct. 17, 1989.
305. Interview with author, Oct. 5, 1989.
306. Interview with author, Nov. 5, 1990.
307. Interview with author, Feb. 12, 1991.
308. Interview with author, April 15, 1991.
309. Interview with author, Aug. 24, 1992.
310. Telephone interview with author, Nov. 26, 1991.
311. Telephone interview with author, Feb. 12. 1992.
312. Interview with author, April 17, 1991.
313. *Ibid.*
314. Letter to author, Dec. 30, 1992.
315. *Ibid.*
316. Interview with author, April 17, 1991.
317. Letter to author, Dec. 30, 1992.
318. Interview with author, Nov. 11, 1991.
319. Telephone interview with author, Oct. 25, 1991.
320. *Ibid.*
321. Interview with author, Aug. 23, 1991.
322. James J. Kilpatrick, *The Southern Case for School Segregation*, p. 21.
323. *Ibid*, p. 26.
324. *Ibid*, p. 35.
325. *Ibid*, p. 184.
326. *Ibid*, p. 192.
327. Interview with author, Oct. 5, 1989.
328. Virginius Dabney, *Across the Years*, pp. 232-236.
329. Interview with author, Oct. 5, 1989.
330. Dabney, *op. cit.*, p. 235.
331. Interview with author, Oct. 5, 1989.
332. Dabney, *op. cit.*, pp. 232-236.
333. Interview with author, Oct. 26, 1989.
334. Interview with author, Oct. 5, 1989.

BUSING

335. Interview with author, Aug. 12, 1991.
336. *Ibid.*

VIETNAM

337. *The News Leader*, Sept. 12, 1963.
338. *The News Leader*, Aug. 5, 1964.
339. *The News Leader*, Aug. 7, 1964.
340. *The News Leader*, March 5, 1965.
341. *The News Leader*, July 26, 1965.
342. *The Times-Dispatch*, April 21, 1968.
343. *The Times-Dispatch*, April 30, 1968.
344. *The Times-Dispatch*, May 25, 1968.
345. *The News Leader*, June 12, 1968.
346. *The News Leader*, Oct. 16, 1968.
347. *The Times-Dispatch*, March 6, 1969.
348. *The Times-Dispatch*, May 15, 1969.
349. *The Times-Dispatch*, Oct. 12, 1969.
350. *The News Leader*, Oct. 23, 1969.
351. *The Times-Dispatch*, Oct. 15, 1969.
352. *The Times-Dispatch*, Nov. 4, 1969.
353. *The News Leader*, Nov. 23, 1970.

SECTION H • Corporate

SOUTHSIDE VIRGINIAN

354. Interview with author, Oct. 5, 1990.
355. Telephone interview with author, March 11, 1995.
356. Telephone interview with author, March 13, 1995.
357. Telephone interview with Larry Gould, March 13, 1995.

VIRGINIA BUSINESS

358. Telephone interview with author, May 15, 1995.
359. *Ibid.*

NEWARK ACQUISITION

360. Interview with author, Nov. 5, 1990.
361. *Ibid.*
362. Richard Reeves, "Newark's fall giant: euthanasia or murder?" *Columbia Journalism Review*, Vol. XI, No. 4, November/December 1972, p. 54.
363. *Ibid.*
364. *Ibid*, p. 51.
365. Associated Press story in *The Times-Dispatch*, Sept. 15, 1971.
366. Interview with author, Nov. 5, 1990.
367. *Ibid.*
368. Reeves, *op. cit.*, p. 31.
369. Interview with author, Nov. 5, 1990.

TANNER ACQUISITION

370. Interview with author, Nov. 5, 1990.
371. Interview with author, Oct. 26, 1989.

SUGARMAN'S BID

372. Interview with author, Oct. 26, 1989.
373. Interview with author, Oct. 5, 1990.

SECTION I • Advertising and Production

ADVERTISING

374. Telephone interview with author, April 3, 1995.

THE FUTURE

375. Address to annual meeting of stockholders, May 19, 1995.

EPILOGUE

376. Telephone interview with author, May 4, 1995.

BIBLIOGRAPHY

Books

Ashmore, Harry S. *Hearts and Minds*. McGraw-Hill Book Co. New York. 1982.

Berger, Meyer. *The Story of The New York Times*. Simon & Schuster. New York. 1951.

Bryan, J. III. *The Sword Over the Mantel—The Civil War and I*. McGraw-Hill Book Co. New York, Toronto, London. 1960.

Bryan, John Stewart. *Joseph Bryan—His Times. His Family. His Friends*. Privately printed by Whittet & Shepperson. Richmond, Va. 1935.

Cappon, Lester J. *Virginia Newspapers 1821-1935*. D. Appleton-Century Co., Inc. New York, London. 1936

Dabney, Virginius. *Pistols and Pointed Pens*. Algonquin Books of Chapel Hill. 1987.

Dabney, Virginius. *Liberalism in the South*. University of North Carolina Press. Chapel Hill. 1932.

Dabney, Virginius. *Below the Potomac*. D. Appleton-Century. New York, London. 1942.

Dabney, Virginius. *Across the Years*. Doubleday & Co., Inc. Garden City, N.Y. 1978.

Dabney, Virginius. *Dry Messiah: The Life of Bishop Cannon*. Alfred A. Knopf. New York. 1949.

Duke, Maurice and Jordan, Daniel P. *A Richmond Reader 1733-1983*. The University of North Carolina Press. Chapel Hill, London. 1983.

Kilpatrick, James J. *The Southern Case for School Segregation*. The Crowell-Collier Press. New York. 1962.

Kneebone, John T. *Southern Liberal Journalists and the Issue of Race, 1920-1944*. The University of North Carolina Press. Chapel Hill, London. 1985.

McDowell, Charles Jr. *One Thing After the Other*. The Dietz Press Inc. Richmond, Va. 1960.

Magazines

Columbia Journalism Review. "Newark's fallen giant: euthanasia or murder?" Richard Reeves. Vol. XI, No. 4. November/December 1972.

Newsweek. October 13, 1980.

The Reader's Digest. "The Most Unforgettable Character I Ever Met." Charles Henry Hamilton. July 1960.

Time. October 18, 1948.

The Virginia Magazine of History and Biography. "First and Foremost a

Virginian. Joseph Bryan and the New South Economy." James M. Lindgren. Vol. 96, No. 2. April 1988.

The Virginia Magazine of History and Biography. "Joseph Bryan and the Virginia Connection in the Industrial Development of Northern Alabama." W. David Lewis. Vol. 98. No. 4. October 1990.

The Virginia Magazine of History and Biography. "Reflections." Mary Tyler Cheek. Vol. 94. No. 1. January 1986.

Newspapers

The Richmond Dispatch

The Richmond Leader

The Richmond News

The Richmond News Leader

The Richmond Times

The Richmond Times-Dispatch

INDEX